The New Global
Oil Market Order
And How To Trade It

Simon Watkins

First Published in 2023 by Simon Watkins
Copyright © Simon Watkins 2023
Simon Watkins has asserted his right under the Copyright, Designs and
Patents Act 1988 to be identified as the author of this work.
A CIP catalogue record for this book is available from the British Library.

This book is dedicated to my son, James Harper-Watkins

Contents

Part One: Core Elements Of The New Global Oil Market Order

The Pre-COVID Order

Prior to the first major outbreak of COVID-19 across the globe in early 2020, the global oil market order was perhaps the clearest it had been since before October 1973.

Before The 1973 Oil Crisis

Up to that month in 1973, the clear global oil market order had centred on the broad and deep relationship between the world's leading superpower of the time, the US (see *'Key Players In The Global Oil Market: The US'* section), and its leading oil power at that point, Saudi Arabia (see *'Key Players In The Global Oil Market: Saudi Arabia'* section).

The foundation stone of this relationship had been the deal struck at a meeting on 14 February 1945 between the then-US President, Franklin D Roosevelt, and the then-Saudi King, Abdulaziz bin Abdul Rahman Al Saud.

The deal, which ran smoothly until October 1973, was this: the US would receive all of the oil supplies it needed for as long as Saudi Arabia had oil in place and, in return for this, the US would guarantee the security both of the ruling House of Saud and, by extension, of Saudi Arabia.

This meant that the US and those other Western countries that were reliant on oil to drive their continued economic expansion could obtain it very cheaply through several formal and informal networks centred around their international oil companies (IOCs).

The most significant of these networks was known as the 'Seven Sisters' and these Western IOCs were able to control oil exploration, development, transport and pricing for decades up to October 1973.

The 'Seven' were the Anglo-Persian Oil Company (which changed its name in 1935 to the Anglo-Iranian Oil Company, and is now BP), Royal Dutch Shell (Shell), three iterations of Standard Oil (Standard Oil of

California, Standard Oil of New Jersey, and Standard Oil Company of New York), Gulf Oil, and Texaco.

Give or take the odd hiccough, most notably the 1953 UK Secret Intelligence Service/US Central Intelligence Agency coup in Iran (codenamed 'Operation Boot' or 'Operation Ajax', respectively), these companies controlled at least 85% of the world's petroleum reserves, having often paid the host countries a minimal percentage of the resulting sales profits in return. For example, Iran's pre-1951 share of profits from its indigenous oil sector was just 16%. This extremely low figure was the key reason why Iran's parliament voted in March 1951 to nationalise the country's oil sector, cancel Anglo-Iranian Oil Company's oil concession, and expropriate its assets.

This, in turn, was the principal reason for the 1953 coup by the UK and US, in which the highly popular Iranian Prime Minister, Mohammad Mosaddegh, was removed from power and imprisoned. He was then replaced by the new government of General Fazlollah Zahedi, which allowed the UK/US-backed Shah, Mohammad Reza Pahlavi, to increase his hold over the country and restore matters to their previous order.

The monetary return for Saudi Arabia from its indigenous oil sector was even worse. The US's Standard Oil made a one-off payment to the country of USD275,000 in April 1933 – equivalent to around USD6 million in 2023 – to secure the exclusive rights to drill across the entire Kingdom.

The share of profits assigned to Saudi Arabia varied at the discretion of the principal oil fields' operator involved. From the first major discovery in 1936, this was California-Arabian Standard Oil (a wholly-owned subsidiary of Standard Oil of California). The name then changed in 1944 to Arabian American Oil Co (Aramco). In 1950, Saudi Arabia's King Abdulaziz threatened to nationalise his country's oil facilities, which led to a 50/50 profit share split between the operator and the country.

The influence of the Seven Sisters declined slightly in the first instance after the formation in 1960 of the Organization of the Petroleum Exporting Countries (OPEC, see *Key Players In The Global Oil Market: OPEC* section). With initial membership comprising Iran, Iraq, Kuwait, Saudi Arabia and Venezuela, OPEC was founded with the intention to 'co-ordinate and unify the petroleum policies' of all its member states.

The formation of OPEC can be seen as part of the broader rise of the Pan-Arabism ideology in the 1950s and 1960s. This ideology has seen several subsequent notable resurgences since that period, and the 1973 Oil Crisis can be seen as one notable example of these ideas in action.

The systematic undermining of this ideology in order to circumvent the devastating real-economy impacts that it can have on oil-dependent developed economies, particularly in the West, has been a central plank of US foreign policy since then (see the *'Post-1973 Crisis Implementation Of The Kissinger Doctrine'* sub-section below).

1973 Oil Crisis (The First Oil Price War)

The clear order of the global oil market up to 1973, founded on the core agreement made between the US and Saudi Arabia in 1945, came to an end in October of that year. This was when OPEC members plus Egypt, Syria and Tunisia, began an embargo on oil exports to the US, the UK, Japan, Canada and the Netherlands.

This embargo was in response to the US's supplying of arms to Israel in the Yom Kippur War that it was fighting against a coalition of Arab states led by Egypt and Syria. As global supplies of oil fell, the price of oil increased dramatically, exacerbated by incremental cuts to oil production by OPEC members over the period.

The 1973 Oil Crisis Shifted Power Between Oil Consumers And Producers

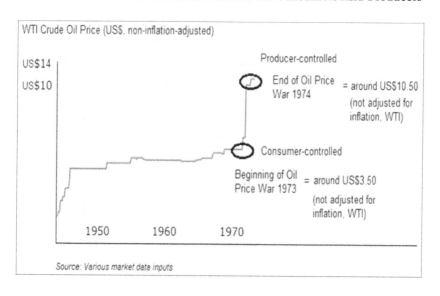

By the end of the embargo in March 1974, the price of oil had risen from around USD3 per barrel (pb) to nearly USD11 pb before settling down for a while, but then it trended higher again. This, in turn, stoked the fire of a global economic slowdown, especially felt in the West.

Some have branded the embargo a failure, as it did not result in Israel giving back all the territory that it had gained in the Yom Kippur War. However, in a broader sense, a wider war had been won by Saudi, OPEC and other Arab states in shifting the balance of power in the global oil market from the big consumers of oil (mainly in the West at that time) to the big producers of oil (mainly in the Middle East at that point).

This shift was accurately summed up by the slick, clever and urbane then-Saudi Minister of Oil and Mineral Reserves, Sheikh Ahmed Zaki Yamani, who was widely credited with formulating the embargo strategy. He highlighted that the extremely negative effects on the global economy of the oil embargo marked a fundamental shift in the world balance of power between the developing nations that produced oil and the developed industrial nations that consumed it.

Post-1973 Crisis Implementation Of The Kissinger Doctrine

This shift in power had also been well-noted in the US, particularly by Henry Kissinger, the highly influential US geopolitical strategist who served as National Security Advisor from January 1969 to November 1975 and as Secretary of State from September 1973 to January 1977.

At that point in the 1970s, the US lacked the crude oil production capability that made its economy immune from the damaging effects of such future oil embargoes by Saudi Arabia, OPEC and the other big oil-producing countries.

Economic power was the basis of all US power across the globe, as it remains today, so it was evident to Kissinger – and to the senior politicians he advised – that a strategy be devised urgently that would make it less likely that such embargoes would happen again.

The strategy he used was a variant of the 'triangular diplomacy' that he advocated in formulating the dealings of the US with the two other major powers of the time, Russia and China. This strategy was, in turn, a variant of the simple 'divide and rule' principle that undermines opponents over time by playing one side off against the other, leveraging whatever fault lines ran through target areas at either a community, national or international level. These fault lines could be economic, political, or religious, or any combination thereof.

A core element of this triangular diplomacy was the use of 'constructive ambiguity' in the language used in dealing with the countries involved. In practical terms, this meant the US appearing to be on the side of various elements of the Arab world but in reality seeking to exploit their existing weaknesses to set one against another.

In the 1970s, there was one key issue that dominated the thinking of all major Arab countries in the Middle East and which was one of the key interests of the broader Pan-Arabism that had gained impetus in the 1950s and 1960s. This issue was the future of the Palestinian people, and there were sufficient differences in the approach to it of several Arab states for the US to exploit.

Broadly speaking, within the Arab world, there were two sides on how the question of the Palestinian Diaspora should be settled. On the one hand, there were the hawks, a particularly notable example of which was the President of Syria, Hafez al-Assad, who believed that the Palestinian Diaspora should be able to return to a recognised independent self-governing Palestine as quickly as possible.

On the other hand, there were the doves, who were open to a more gradual and evolutionary approach to the situation. To this group, after long-running negotiations with the US, belonged the then-President of Egypt, Anwar Sadat.

This more dovish approach by the President of Egypt was all the more fractious in the Arab world because one of the original proponents of the Pan-Arab ideological resurgence in the 1950s – which included a hawkish approach on the Palestine question - was Egypt's President from 1954 to 1970, Gamal Nasser. Syria's President al-Assad regarded himself as Nasser's ideological successor.

Utilising these fault lines in the approach of the Arab world on the Palestine issue, the US was the key sponsor behind Sadat's controversial visit to Israel in 1977 and the subsequent signing in 1979 of the Egypt-Israel Peace Treaty. This was guaranteed to cause seismic disturbances across the Arab world, which it did, and these divisions were then kept alive by the subsequent assassination of Sadat in 1981.

2014-2016 Oil Price War – Initial Saudi Success

By continuing to play one side off against another in such a way, the US and its allies were able to avoid another major rupture in the global oil market order for over 40 years, until the beginning of the Second Oil Price War in 2014, which ran until 2016.

In the run-up to 2014, a major problem had emerged for Saudi Arabia that it could not ignore forever. Crude oil exports still accounted for well over 80% of its economy at that point. Its political influence in the world was based on its position as a leading oil producer and, as the largest oil producer in OPEC, its position as *de facto* leader of that organisation.

For decades, the top three oil producers in the world had been, in alphabetical order only, Russia, Saudi Arabia and the US, with the top spot varying over that period. Crucially, though, for much of that period, the US's influence in the global oil market had been much less than its production might have implied, as it had banned most crude oil exports to other countries in 1975 in the aftermath of the problems created for it by the 1973 Oil Crisis. This ban was lifted in 2015 in reaction to the then-ongoing 2014-2016 Oil Price War.

For Saudi Arabia in 2014, though, its economic and political influence in the world was under enormous threat from the rise of the US shale energy industry. For the ruling family of Saudi Arabia, the Al Sauds, the threat was existential, as their enduring rule in the country was founded on ongoing prosperity in the Kingdom and this prosperity was founded on its oil revenues.

The US shale energy sector truly began to make its presence felt in the gas world in around 2006 and in the oil world in about 2010. From a modest start, US shale oil production increased from an average of slightly less than 0.2 million bpd in 2011 to just over 0.8 million bpd in 2012, and then by nearly 1 million bpd in 2013, and then by another 1.2 million bpd in 2014, to 8.7 million bpd in total, according to Energy Information Administration (EIA) figures.

Not only did these figures represent the largest such volume increase since record-keeping began in 1900 but also by 2013 it meant that the US had overtaken Saudi Arabia and Russia as the world's largest producer of crude oil. Worse still for Saudi Arabia at that point was that both the US and Russia were producing far more gas as well than was the Kingdom.

The Rise Of The US Shale Energy Sector Was A Danger For Saudi Arabia

Estimated U.S., Russia, and Saudi Arabia petroleum and natural gas production

Source: U.S. Energy Information Administration
Note: Petroleum production includes crude oil, natural gas liquids, condensates, refinery processing gain, and other liquids including biofuels. Barrels per day oil equivalent were calculated using a conversion factor of 1 barrel oil equivalent = 5.55 million British thermal units (Btu)

The only encouraging factor for the Saudis at that point in this dramatic expansion of oil production in the US was that, according to virtually all industry estimates, the cost at which each barrel of US shale could be produced (the 'lifting cost', in industry parlance) was around USD70 per barrel of West Texas Intermediate (WTI) crude oil, the US benchmark oil grade.

Given the historical USD5-10 per barrel discount of WTI to the higher-quality Brent crude oil benchmark grade, this meant a lifting cost for US shale in Brent terms of USD75-80 per barrel. By stark – and positive for the Saudis – contrast, the average lifting cost for Saudi oil (and Iranian and Iraqi oil, incidentally) was USD1-2 per barrel only.

This apparently high lifting cost and the relatively nascent point of development of the US shale oil sector, and Saudi Arabia's success in the 1973 Oil Crisis (which can be regarded as the First Oil Price War), meant that the Kingdom was extremely confident of another success when it launched the Second Oil Price War in the middle of 2014.

The strategy that Saudi Arabia decided to use was based on the widespread belief at the time that US shale oil producers had a breakeven price point of USD70 pb of WTI. Therefore, the Saudis reasoned, if the price of oil was pushed below that level for long enough - by it and its fellow OPEC members dramatically increasing production while demand in the global market was predicted to remain around the same level for some time - then many of the new US shale oil producers would go bankrupt. Any others would have to cease production at such uneconomic price levels and shelve future investment plans aimed at boosting their production even more.

Saudi Arabia And OPEC Increased Oil Production To Drive Prices Down

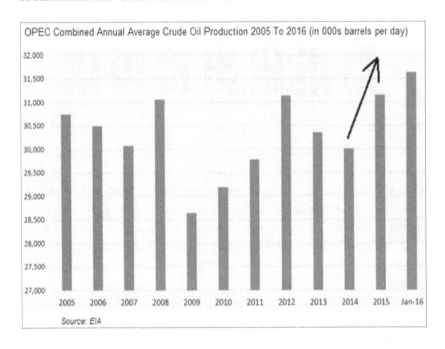

So confident was Saudi Arabia of the success of its strategy that shortly after the onset of the Second Oil Price War, senior figures in its government and oil ministry it held a series of private meetings in New York to tell them in detail about the strategy it was to use and how well it would go.

At these meetings, the Saudis revealed that, far from looking to keep prices high – as had also been the usual inclination of OPEC for many years in order to boost the prosperity of member states – it was willing to tolerate 'much lower' Brent prices 'of between USD80-90 per barrel for a period of one to two years' or 'even lower prices if necessary'.

According to several sources at the New York meeting, the Saudis made it clear that it had two key aims in allowing prices to be pushed much lower than the rough average of USD111 pb of Brent in 2011 and 2012, and the rough average of USD108 pb of Brent in 2013.

The first – and most important – objective was to destroy, or at least significantly damage for as long as possible, the US's developing shale oil industry. The second was to re-impose a degree of supply discipline on other OPEC members.

This policy marked a significant divergence from the acceptable range of prices per barrel of crude oil previously stated by the then-Saudi Oil Minister Ali al-Naimi as being 'USD100, USD110, USD95 [per barrel].' As it transpired, the strategy pushed the WTI oil price near to USD30 pb.

Saudi Thought US Shale Oil Players Had A USD70 Pb Breakeven Price

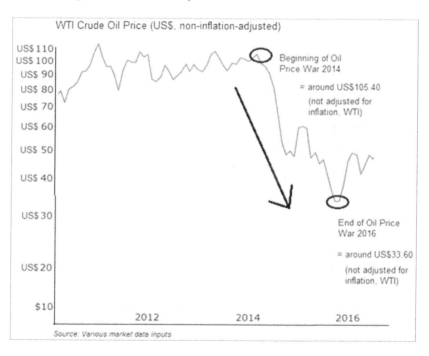

Looking at the second objective first, there were always – and remain – a few OPEC member states which, for various country-specific reasons, breach Saudi-led OPEC oil production guidance. However, overall this had little effect on the wider trajectory of the 2014-2016 Oil Price War.

In terms of the first objective, the initial signs augured well for a Saudi victory. The US oil rig count in January/February 2015 saw its biggest period-on-period fall since 1991, and the gas rig count fell substantially at that time as well.

According to industry figures as at the end of the first quarter of 2015, around one third of the 800 oil and gas projects (worth USD500 billion and totalling nearly 60 billion barrels of oil equivalent) scheduled for final investment decisions (FID) in that year were 'unconventional' and were subject to possible postponement or cancellation.

Early Data Suggested The Saudi Strategy Might Stop Shale In Its Tracks

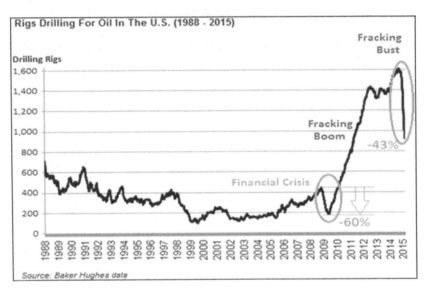

Notable retrenchments at that time included French energy giant, then-Total, postponing the FID on the Joslyn project in Alberta, Canada (estimated cost USD11 billion). Additionally, according to company reports, Shell's liquefied natural gas (LNG) project in British Columbia required oil at USD80 pb of Brent to break even. Shell's chief financial officer at that time, Henry Simon, indicated in October 2014 that it was 'less likely' to go ahead with unconventional projects in West Canada if oil fell below that USD80 pb level.

Even in the US-centric Gulf of Mexico, one of the most attractive conventional oil production areas in the world, planned projects were facing considerable challenges. A case in point was BP putting on hold a decision on its 'Mad Dog Phase 2' deep water project in the Gulf after its development costs ballooned to USD20 billion against a falling global oil price structure. In sum, any offshore project with a development cost above USD30 pb for Brent was likely to be put on hold at that point.

2014-2016 Oil Price War – US Shale Turnaround

However, although 2015 saw oil output from the US shale producers typically decline by around 50%, forcing them to cut investment to approximately USD60 billion over the year (compared to the USD100 billion or so spent in 2014), this adjustment was sufficient to steady shale oil production after that.

Allied to this were remarkable productivity gains, most notably in the Permian basin that spans western Texas and south-eastern New Mexico – where each rig by 2015 produced more than 400 bpd, compared to only 100 bpd in 2012. A similar pattern manifested itself in the Bakken region of North Dakota.

Productivity Dramatically Improved In US Shale, From The Permian...

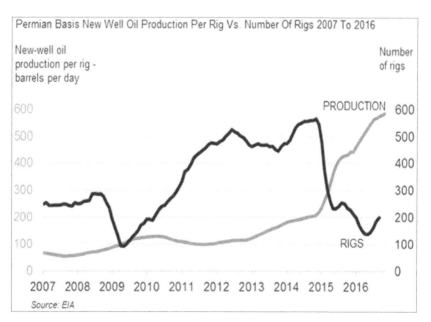

Permian Basis New Well Oil Production Per Rig Vs. Number Of Rigs 2007 To 2016

Source: EIA

...To Bakken And Beyond

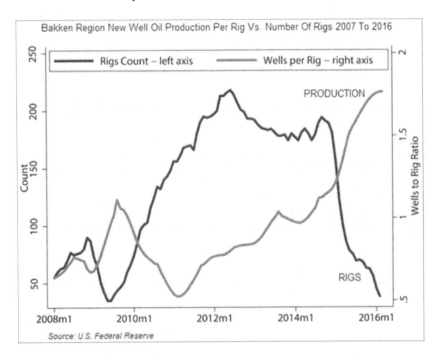

Bakken Region New Well Oil Production Per Rig Vs. Number Of Rigs 2007 To 2016

Source: U.S. Federal Reserve

Moreover, compared to the steep fall in horizontal rigs (two thirds of which were discontinued from November 2014) US shale-oil production only fell modestly, from a peak 5.1 million bpd to around 4.8 million bpd by the end of the first quarter of 2016.

From this point in 2015, not only did productivity in the US shale oil sector dramatically improve but also, in line with this, the breakeven price per barrel of US shale oil fell spectacularly.

More specifically, over the 2014-2016 period of the Second Oil Price War, the US shale oil sector went from an industry that was widely perceived as being unable to profit unless the WTI price was above USD70 pb (meaning a Brent price per barrel of between USD75-80 or so, based on historical average price differentials between the two grades) to one that could – at that time – broadly survive and profit at WTI prices above around USD35 pb.

They managed to achieve this mainly through the advancement of technology that enabled them to drill longer laterals, manage the fracking stages closer and maintain the fracks with higher, finer sand to allow for increased recovery for the wells drilled, in conjunction with faster drill times. They gained further cost benefits from multi-pad drilling and well spacing theory and practice.

For some time the only factors holding back further improvements in output and pricing were infrastructure constraints, but even those improved as the war progressed. At the same time, the quality of the US shale product made it a natural competitor for all other light, sweet grades, which included some of the Saudi's major export grades.

WTI Was An Immediate Natural Competitor To Many OPEC Grades

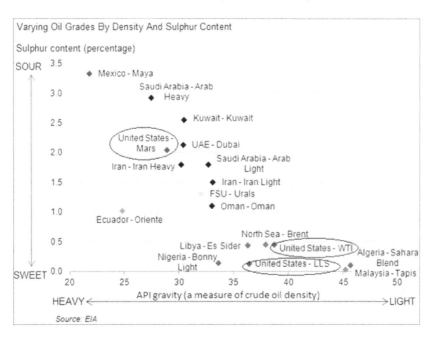

Over the period of the 2014-2016 Oil Price War, the US shale oil sector had two key operational advantages over its conventional oil sector adversaries. First, conventional fields incur much higher fixed costs than shale fields whether they are closed or open. Second, conventional fields cannot bounce back as quickly as shale operations as and when required.

For example, Saudi Arabia's flagship oil and gas company, Saudi Aramco – originally, of course, and not forgotten by either the US or Saudi Arabia, the ARabian AMerican oil COmpany – cannot close down any of its major fields as and when needed. Additionally, it still has to pay all of the fixed costs attached to maintaining those fields' integrity (staff, systems, payments to contractors and so on) whether they are open or closed.

In addition, over and above the sheer bureaucracy involved in making decisions in such state or neo-state institutions (all of the Middle East's major oil companies belong in this bracket), bringing a conventional oil field back online takes more planning than it does for a US shale oil field.

Some of the best US shale oil operations during the period of the 2014-2016 Oil Price War, and to this day, can bring their oil fields back online in as little as a week, from a standing start, although the refinery-related lead time is slightly longer.

In this context, shale oil end-buyers (most notably refineries) will buy the majority of their crude supplies 30-45 days out from when they actually want them delivered. So what happens in practice is that refineries will start to increase their run rates (the rate at which they utilise crude oil supplies) and will start buying. After that, crude oil buyers will begin to buy the oil from the shale producers to fill this demand, and then the producers will turn the supply back on.

There are some risks for all oil operations from a shut-in (a temporary shutdown) – such as water encroachment in the reservoir, well bore or surface facility damage, plus other possible rusting, corrosion and deterioration – and these all have to be tested for. However, the vast majority of US shale wells can come back to full production capacity within a week of the order being given.

In fact, contrary to what many people think, the reservoir damage of the vast majority of US shale oil wells is fairly minimal. In a significant proportion of cases, when a well has been shut-in, pressure rebuilds and when it is brought back online it often performs slightly better for a while before settling back into the previous operational parameters.

Similarly negative for the Saudis at the time was that their view that the US shale oil sector would see a mass exodus of the newly-skilled shale drilling personnel was proven completely wrong. In reality, after the initial shock to the US shale oil sector in 2014, staffing levels at all of the major US shale operations were maintained and in many cases expanded.

Similarly, Saudi expectations that the US shale oil sector's access to finance would suffer a catastrophic hit also proved ill-founded. Most of the shale operations at that time were small businesses. This made them structurally extremely well able to manage drilling operations on a week-to-week basis and also enabled them to benefit from vast rolling financial programmes initiated by US banks and financial institutions that recognised the positive opportunity of getting in early at the birth of a new, game-changing, high-profits industry.

2014-2016 Oil Price War – Saudi's Disastrous Loss

Over the course of 2014 to 2016, then, Saudi Arabia suffered such catastrophic effects on its economy that it had no choice but to end the war. Saudi Arabia's neo-economic conflict with the US had also destroyed much of the economic power of its fellow OPEC members. The war had also critically undermined the reputation of OPEC in the global oil market and Saudi Arabia's position as its *de facto* leader.

As of August 2014, before the Second Oil Price War began in earnest, Saudi Arabia had record-high foreign assets reserves of USD737 billion. This war-chest allowed it considerable room for manoeuvre in sustaining its economically crucial Saudi riyal (SAR)/US dollar (USD)-currency peg and covering the huge budget deficits that would be caused from the oil price fall caused by overproduction.

Saudi Lost Over One Third Of Its Precious FX Reserves

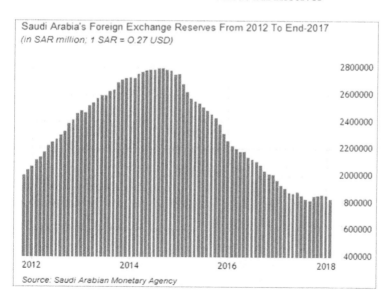

Saudi Arabia moved from a budget surplus before the full onset of the Second Oil Price War to a then-record high deficit in 2015 of USD98 billion. It also spent at least USD250 billion of its precious foreign exchange reserves over that period that even senior Saudis said was lost forever, and so it has proven.

So bad was Saudi Arabia's economic and political situation back towards the end of the Second Oil Price War in 2016 that the country's deputy economic minister, Mohamed Al Tuwaijri, stated unequivocally (and unprecedentedly for a senior Saudi) in October 2016 that: 'If we [Saudi Arabia] don't take any reform measures, and if the global economy stays the same, then we're doomed to bankruptcy in three to four years.'

Saudi Arabia Moved From Healthy Budget Surpluses Into Huge Deficits

Saudi Arabia Government Budget 2010 To 2018 (% Surplus Or Deficit)

Source: Saudi Arabian Monetary Agency

Appalling though the economic consequences of the 2014-2016 Oil Price War were for Saudi Arabia, the damage to its political standing and reputation was at least as bad. Aside from the damage to its own economy, Saudi Arabia had cost the OPEC member states collectively at least USD450 billion in revenues since it embarked on its US shale oil sector-destruction strategy in 2014, according to International Energy Agency (IEA) estimates.

In essence, Saudi had destroyed for years to come the economies of the very OPEC membership upon which it depended in large part for its projection of geopolitical power and with this the faith that they had in the judgment of Saudi Arabia as their leader.

Saudi's 'Leadership' Destroyed Fellow OPEC Members' Finances

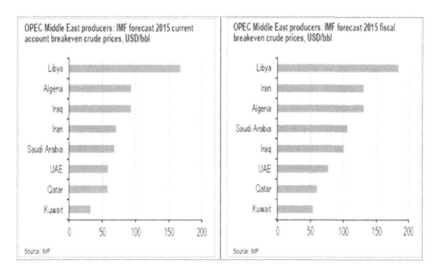

OPEC Member States' Budgets After 2016 Faced A Massive Challenge

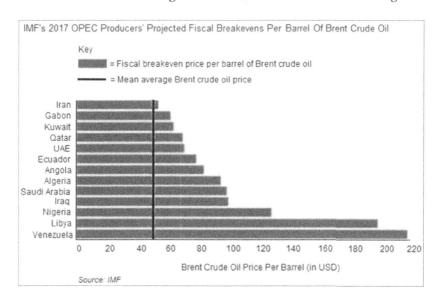

Perhaps even more dangerous for Saudi Arabia's long-term future – and for the future of the Al Saud ruling family – was that the Kingdom had also destroyed the basic trust with the US that had been established in the 1945 agreement.

According to many highly-placed sources in Washington, as far as the US was concerned, the cornerstone 1945 agreement from then on meant nothing. It was precisely at the point that the US decided that it would do everything in its power to keep its shale oil sector going, with the ultimate aim of gradually reducing and then completely ending its dependence on Saudi Arabia for any energy requirements.

Given the degree of economic and political damage wrought on itself and its fellow OPEC members - and the reality that the US shale sector had mutated into an apparently indomitable force - Saudi Arabia in the third quarter of 2016 halted its overproduction of oil (designed to push prices down) and completely reversed the strategy (to push prices back up again).

In September 2016, Saudi Arabia and its fellow OPEC members dramatically cut their oil production in an attempt to produce a sustained increase in oil prices through which they could begin to restore their broken government budgets.

2014-2016 Oil Price War – US In Prime Position

During the entire course of the Second Oil Price War that ran from June 2014 to February 2016, total oil production (conventional plus shale) in the US dropped by only 0.7 million bpd, from about 9.4 million bpd to about 8.7 million bpd, and even that was not for long.

By the second half of 2017, total US production was back up to 9.1 million bpd, roughly up to where it was a year before the price war had been started by Saudi Arabia. Moreover, the shale production element of that number was still around half of the total, a result that fell way short of the Saudis' objective at the beginning of the war.

In effect, all that Saudi Arabia had achieved in its oil price war was to weaken its own position – economically and politically – whilst forcing the US shale sector to re-organise into a much more economical and high-producing sector. Once Saudi Arabia surrendered, and then reversed its oil overproduction into underproduction to push up prices to save its economy from further damage, the US shale producers found themselves flush with cash from the profits of the resultant higher prices.

Utilising this cash pile, they immediately boosted their drilling budgets ten times faster than the rest of the world to harvest fields that registered large profits even at USD40 to USD50 pb. Indeed, at that point, North American shale drillers made plans to lift their 2017 outlays by 32%, to USD84 billion, compared with just 3% for international projects, according to industry reports at the time.

US Shale Went From Strength To Strength After 2016

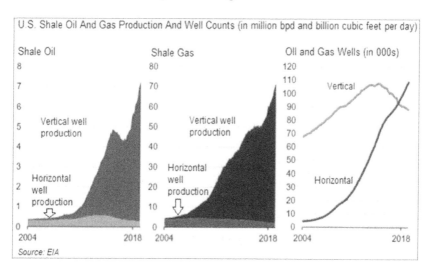

This prompted OPEC itself to revise up its estimate of oil supply growth from shale producers by 600,000 bpd in 2017, just a few months after the end of the oil price war. As a whole, in the same report, OPEC also revised up its estimate of oil supply growth from all oil producers outside the OPEC group during 2017 to 950,000 bpd, from a previous forecast of 580,000 bpd.

Factoring this into the global supply/demand balance at that point made very grim reading for Saudi Arabia, and OPEC, Their 'production cut' had still left oil stocks in industrialised nations at 276 million barrels above the five-year average, according to the EIA.

The EIA also estimated that US crude production would surpass the 10 million bpd mark by late 2018 – which it did, and more – breaching the record high set in 1970, with the shale boom propelling non-OPEC output up by some 1.3 million bpd in 2018. This completely nullified any OPEC cut and effectively filled up almost all the expected growth in demand.

These profits, accrued from the abrupt Saudi production reversal, also allowed many of the best US shale producers to take out hedging positions for any fall in the oil price resulting from future Saudi and OPEC overproduction for as long as two years or more.

2014-2016 Oil Price War – China Makes An Offer

From the first year of the 2014-2016 Oil Price War, Saudi Arabia's government budget went into deficit, to double digit levels of GDP in the first full year of the war and faced the prospect that it would stay that way for many years. In fact, the Kingdom's government budget did remain in deficit every year from 2014 up to the end of 2021.

At the same time as this was happening, then-Prince Mohammed bin Salman (MbS) was not the natural successor to King Salman. Prior to June 2017 when the succession was changed in MbS's favour, the heir-designate to King Salman was Prince Muhammad bin Nayef (MbN). Nonetheless, MbS had ambition to position himself to take over the role from MbN should the opportunity present itself.

Precisely how he came to achieve his aim is analysed in depth later in this section but suffice it to say here that back in the immediate aftermath of the 2014-2016 Oil Price War, when Saudi Arabia faced the bleak economic consequences of its actions, MbS had an idea that he thought would allow him to take the heir-apparent position quickly.

It was his belief, floated publicly in the second half of 2016, that if Saudi Arabia listed 5% of the shares of its flagship hydrocarbons company, Saudi Aramco, on international stock markets then such a flotation would raise at least USD100 billion for the Kingdom in much-needed funds.

This figure of USD100 billion would also mean a valuation for Saudi Aramco of USD2 trillion, making it by far the most valuable company listed anywhere in the world ever, and so restoring some of Saudi Arabia's damaged reputation in the process. MbS also thought that a listing of Saudi Aramco in multiple major financial centres around the world, including the two most prestigious stock exchanges – the New York Stock Exchange

(NYSE), and the London Stock Exchange (LSE) – would project Saudi Arabia's presence as an international player in financial markets as a whole and not just in the oil sector.

MbS Sold The Aramco IPO Idea As A Cure-All For Saudi's Troubles

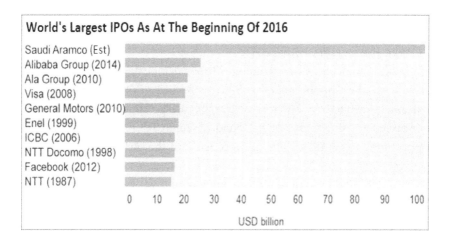

MbS's idea of such a stock flotation for Saudi Aramco was approved by King Salman and MbS brought in advisers to set the initial public offering (IPO) of Saudi Aramco into its early stages.

Almost immediately as this process began, questions began to emerge from international investors targeted by MbS's advisers to be big buyers of Saudi Aramco stock in the IPO. These doubts and questions are also analysed in depth in the *'Key Players In The Global Oil Market: Saudi Arabia'* section and they are still relevant to this day. The upshot of these doubts and questions was that no serious international investor wanted anything to do with the Saudi Aramco IPO either in terms of buying its shares or allowing the company to be listed on their prestigious stock markets.

This put MbS into an extremely dangerous position personally, given that he was the original champion of the idea, which effectively meant that his reputation was staked on the Saudi Aramco share offering being successful according to each of the criteria that he had mentioned in his pitching of the idea to the senior Saudis, including King Salman.

The detailed parameters that MbS had laid out, by which the success of the IPO could be measured, were that: at least 5% of shares would be offered; at least USD100 billion would be raised; at least a valuation of

USD2 trillion would be placed on the company as a whole; and the company would be listed on at least two major international stock exchanges, in addition to the procedural local listing on the Saudi Tadawul.

Ramping up the significance of failure personally for him even more was that this idea of a successful IPO of Saudi Aramco – also carrying with it the restoration of Saudi Arabia's finances and international reputation – had been a key reason behind his finally usurping MbN as heir-designate ('Crown Prince') on 21 June 2017.

Many senior Saudis, including MbN's supporters, were extremely hostile to the appointment of MbS as Crown Prince and were also extremely keen to have him removed at the earliest opportunity. Any failure connected to MbS's idea of the Saudi Aramco IPO would be a perfect opportunity to get rid of him, in every sense of the phrase, and MbS knew this very well.

Crucially, at this point of ultimate vulnerability for MbS, China appeared to him with a solution to all his problems. It was a gesture that probably saved MbS's ascension to power in Saudi Arabia and perhaps his life as well, and he has never forgotten it. It was also the reason for the marked shift in the geopolitical allegiance of Saudi Arabia from then away from the US sphere of influence and into that of China and Russia, although the shift to Russia occurred slightly earlier, as discussed shortly.

China's offer was that it would buy the entire 5% stake in Saudi Aramco through a private placement to a China state-controlled entity (or several, if required) for the entire amount needed – that is, USD100 billion. This would allow MbS to state that his idea had achieved nearly everything he had said it would: the entire 5% stake had been sold; it had raised USD100 billion (that could be used to plug a part of the hole in the government budget); and the entire company had been valued at USD2 trillion.

The only downside to this near-perfect solution for MbS was that there would be no truly international element to the IPO, as he had promised. However, he would be in a position to argue to the senior Saudis that this lack of exposure on international stock markets was perhaps due to prejudice in the West against Saudi Arabia and/or its business practices.

The key reason why MbS did not take China's offer was that, at that point back in 2016 and later when China made the same offer again, King Salman and other senior Saudis were not ready to decisively alienate the US and to do away with the political and military security that it afforded them.

At this time, a new era of relations between Saudi Arabia's nemesis, Iran, and the West had just been brought into view, in the shape of the Joint Comprehensive Plan of Action (JCPOA, colloquially 'the nuclear deal') created on 14 July 2015 and implemented on 16 January 2016. The Saudis were aware of China's longstanding broad and deep relationship with Iran, as analysed in depth in the *'Key Players In The Global Oil Market: China'* section and preferred to rely on the US for assurances of its security against its regional rival at that stage of the then-new JCPOA era.

For China, there was no downside to the offer made to MbS, either at the time or since. If the deal had gone ahead, then China would have ended up with the core component of Saudi Arabia's oil and gas sector, with a very significant say over its future, which was worth considerably more than USD100 billion. China would also have been able to expedite Saudi Arabia's geopolitical shift away from Washington and towards Beijing.

Even without the deal going ahead, though, the mere fact that China made the crucial offer to MbS personally, at the time when he needed it most, was sufficient for it to gain all of these advantages, albeit at a slightly slower pace than it would have done otherwise.

A key part of this early increased cooperation between Saudi Arabia and China was in the usage of China's renminbi (RMB) currency. 'Renminbi' is the official currency name, while 'yuan' is a unit of that currency (as with 'sterling' and 'pound' in the UK). China has long regarded the position of its renminbi in the global league table of currencies as a reflection of its own geopolitical and economic importance on the world stage.

An early indication of China's ambition for its currency came at the G20 summit in London in April 2010, when Zhou Xiaochuan, then-governor of the People's Bank of China (PBOC), flagged the notion that the Chinese wanted a new global reserve currency to replace the US dollar at some point. He added that the RMB's inclusion in the IMF's Special Drawing Rights (SDR) reserve asset mix would be a key stepping-stone in this context, and this occurred in October 2016.

In August 2017, then, shortly after Saudi Arabia had been defeated in the 2014-2016 Oil Price War, the then-Saudi Vice Minister of Economy and Planning, Mohammed al-Tuwaijri, told a Saudi-China conference in Jeddah that: 'We will be very willing to consider funding in renminbi and other Chinese products.'

Even more tellingly he said: 'China is by far one of the top markets' to diversify [the funding basis of Saudi Arabia] ... [and that] We will also access other technical markets in terms of unique funding opportunities, private placements, panda bonds [Chinese RMB-denominated bond from a non-Chinese issuer, sold in China] and others.'

Given that the vast majority of Saudi government borrowing (including large bond and syndicated loan facilities) in the previous years was denominated in US dollars, a switch away from US dollar funding was seen by some senior Saudis as a means to allow Saudi Arabia more flexibility in its overall financing structure, albeit after an initial financial dislocation connected to its currency peg to the US currency.

Al-Tuwaijri's comments came during the visit of high-ranking politicians and financiers from China to Saudi Arabia in August 2017, which featured a meeting between King Salman and Chinese Vice Premier, Zhang Gaoli, in Jeddah. During the visit, Saudi Arabia first mentioned seriously that it would consider funding itself partly in renminbi, raising the possibility of closer financial ties between the two countries.

Also at the meetings it was decided that Saudi Arabia and China would establish a USD20 billion investment fund on a 50:50 basis. According to comments at the time from then-Saudi Energy Minister, Khalid al-Falih, this fund would invest in sectors such as infrastructure, energy, mining and materials, among other areas.

The Jeddah meetings in August 2017 followed a landmark visit to China by Saudi Arabia's King Salman in March of that year. During the visit around USD65 billion of business deals were signed in sectors including oil refining, petrochemicals, light manufacturing and electronics.

Since the end of the 2014-2016 Oil Price War, China continued to gradually expand its relationship with MbS and Saudi Arabia in all of these key areas. Moreover, after China became the largest annual gross crude oil importer in the world in 2017, it became even more aware that it was subject to the vagaries of US foreign policy as exercised through the pricing of the key global oil and gas benchmarks principally in US dollars.

This view of the US dollar as a weapon had been reinforced to China and others by the US-led sanctions that had been placed on Iran prior to the signing of the JCPOA on 14 July 2015. China's view on this issue and its moves to address it, including its use of Saudi Arabia and other Arab and Middle Eastern states in this regard, are analysed in depth in the *'Key Players In The Global Oil Market: China'* section.

2014-2016 Oil Price War – Russia Enters The Fray

In theory, the 2016 cut to crude oil production that marked the surrender of Saudi Arabia and its OPEC brothers in the Second Oil Price War – the first cut since 2008 – was to involve the reduction of OPEC's oil production by 1.3 million bpd, from 33.8 million bpd to 32.5 million bpd. This figure compared to total global oil production at the time of around 92 million bpd.

Even before the final figure for the cut was announced, though, the basic credibility of the deal was undermined by the fact that in the month or so ahead of the intended cut, key OPEC members – including Saudi Arabia – pushed their production to record-high levels. Therefore, in effect, the scheduled 2016 cuts were only cutting back to the usual levels before any idea of a production cut deal had been officially mooted.

The other core problem with the intended 2016 production cut deal was that Saudi Arabia's loss of credibility in failing to crush the then-nascent US shale oil sector – and the resultant massive financial difficulties it had created for its fellow OPEC members – meant that its leadership position in OPEC had been critically undermined. It was still the cartel's biggest oil producer certainly, but its judgement was no longer trusted either by fellow OPEC members or by the global oil market as a whole.

Both of these factors meant that OPEC members regarded the upcoming 2016 OPEC production cut (intended to push oil prices higher, just after the end of the Second Oil Price War that had aimed at doing the exact opposite) as extremely fluid in its interpretation.

Additionally negative in terms of compliance with the intended cut by OPEC members was that they had no idea of how long the new supposed cut would last, or indeed if it would turn into another OPEC production hike as part of a new Saudi Arabia-led oil price war.

In any event, all OPEC members desperately needed money to prop up their decimated government budgets. Consequently, it was their collective view, especially felt by those hardest hit by the previous two years of selling their oil at levels under their budget breakeven oil price, that they would not abide by the production quotas assigned them in the upcoming production cut agreement. These OPEC members were content to leave Saudi Arabia itself to shoulder much of the economic burden of reduced oil revenues from the production cut deal as they neither trusted it nor feared it anymore.

Adding to this new-found pervasive distrust by OPEC members of Saudi Arabia were rumours, which were well-founded it transpired, that Saudi itself was cheating on the new oil production cut deal that it had instigated. There was considerable evidence that Saudi was utilising its own strategic oil stockpile to sell up to 350,000 bpd into the spot market via investment banks in 'dark inventory'.

Cognisant of this, perhaps, OPEC member Venezuela reportedly reached a deal, also with China, to safeguard its own interests. This deal involved China investing USD25 billion into equipment and engineering for the Venezuelan oil sector that would lift its oil production by at least 55% over that period, bringing it up to just over 3.4 million bpd.

In addition, the late-2016 OPEC oil production cut deal did not include Iran, which aimed to increase its crude oil output to 6 million bpd as soon as possible. It also did not include Nigeria and Libya. Nigeria was nearing production of 1.8 million bpd at the time and planning to increase exports to at least 2 million bpd by the end of that year. Libya was targeting production of 1 million bpd, again by the end of that year, up from an average of 650,000 bpd in the first quarter of the year.

Another terrible irony of Saudi Arabia's ill-fated attempt to destroy the US shale oil industry over 2014-2016 was that the more the Saudis were able to hold up the oil price through cutting back on production, the more the US shale oil producers were able to fill those gaps to meet demand for barrels, and barrels at lower prices.

The initial phase of the late-2016 Saudi Arabia-led production cut also allowed the US shale producers even more leeway in hedging their future oil production to lock in profits for 2017, 2018, 2019 - and even as far out in some cases as 10 years - at highly beneficial prices. This made increased future supply from them, even at oil prices well below those required by the Saudis in their budget breakeven calculations, a certainty.

In sum, then, if the 2016 OPEC cut was 'successful' in pushing up prices by reducing crude oil supplies then US shale producers would make even more money and if it 'failed' then US shale producers would be the only producers capable of surviving the downturn in prices at that point. It was a case of 'Heads You Win, Tails I Lose' for Saudi Arabia versus the US shale oil producers.

Given Saudi Arabia's self-induced lack of credibility in the global oil markets and the widespread cheating in the early stages of the late-2016 OPEC production cut, it was obvious even to the Saudis that a new element was needed to catalyse a significant sustained increase in oil prices that would enable OPEC members to gradually repair their budgets.

That element was Russia, a long-time rival with the US and Saudi Arabia for the top crude oil producer in the world, but by that point at the end of 2016 firmly occupying the number one spot.

At the end of 2016, then, and fully cognisant of the enormous economic and geopolitical possibilities that were available to it by becoming a core participant in the crude oil supply/demand/pricing matrix, Russia agreed to support the OPEC production cut deal in what was to be called from then on 'OPEC+'. However, Russia approached its new role in OPEC+ in its own uniquely self-serving and ruthless fashion, analysed in depth in the 'Key Players In The Global Oil Market: Russia' section.

2016-2020 Post-War Era - US Dominance Under Trump

As touched on above, one of the most enduring effects of the 2014-2016 Oil Price War was that the US had lost all of the trust in Saudi Arabia that had been in place from the foundation stone 1945 deal between the then-US President, Franklin D Roosevelt, and the Saudi King at the time, Abdulaziz. As one senior White House official commented off-the-record at the end of 2016: 'We're not going to put up with any more crap from the Saudis.'

Shortly after this comment was made, Donald Trump became the US's new president. The period of his presidency that began on 20 January 2017 coincided with this pre-existing shift in the US's view of the global oil market that heralded a broad-based change in US foreign policy towards many of its allies and enemies alike.

President Trump added an element of unpredictability to the practical application of this new US view of the world, which, twinned with the US's top global superpower status, proved extremely successful in several foreign policy areas, particularly those related to the oil sector.

In practical operational terms what this new US outlook meant was that Washington was prepared to keep the Al Sauds in power in Saudi Arabia, but only on the condition that they did nothing to disrupt either the economic growth of the US or the commercial growth of its shale oil or gas sectors.

It can reasonably be said, then, that the original 1945 core agreement between the US and Saudi Arabia was effectively modified after the end of the Second Oil Price War in 2016 – and especially after Trump took over as president at the beginning of 2017 - along the lines of: 'The US will guarantee the security both of the ruling House of Saud and of Saudi Arabia for as long as it receives all of the oil supplies it needs whilst Saudi Arabia has oil in place *and for as long as Saudi Arabia does nothing to prevent the US's shale oil sector or its economy from continuing to grow and prosper*'.

2016-2020 Post-War Era – Trump Oil Price Range

In economic and political terms for the US and its presidents, there is a specific range of oil prices that fall into 'acceptable territory', given the country's status both as an oil and gas exporter and importer (it does both because of different grades and/or forms requirements).

The top side of the crude oil price range is around USD75-80 per barrel of Brent, and the bottom side of the range is around USD40-45 per barrel of Brent. Both of these ranges are determined by two factors - one economic and the other political.

The economic factor that determines the topside of the oil price range is a function of the longstanding estimates that every USD10 per barrel change in the price of crude oil results in a 25-30 cent change in the price of a gallon of gasoline ('petrol' in the UK) and for every 1 cent that the average price per gallon of gasoline rises, more than USD1 billion per year in consumer spending is lost. In basic terms, therefore, every increase in the price of gasoline directly reduces consumer spending on other things, which in turn reduces US economic growth.

In this context it is crucial to know that historically around 70% of the price of gasoline is derived from the global oil price and, as a rule of thumb over decades, a WTI oil price per barrel of about USD100.00 has equated to a US gasoline price per gallon of around USD3.00.

Gasoline Prices Are Crucial For US Presidential Re-election Chances

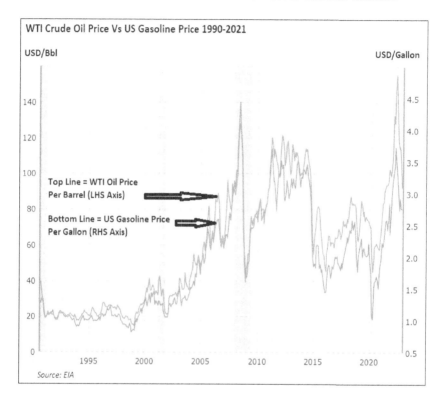

Historically as well, a gasoline price of under USD2 per gallon of gasoline has been most advantageous for US economic growth, and USD2 per gallon has historically equated to a WTI oil price of around USD70 per barrel. As WTI has historically traded at a discount of between USD5-10 per barrel to the global Brent oil benchmark, this USD70 per barrel of WTI price broadly equates to around USD75-80 per barrel of Brent.

The political factor that determines the topside of the oil price range is founded in the cold, hard reality of re-election chances for sitting US presidents in various economic scenarios.

According to statistics from the US's National Bureau of Economic Research (NBER), since the end of World War I in 2018, the sitting US president has won re-election 11 times out of 11 if the US economy was not in recession within two years of an upcoming election.

However, sitting US presidents who went into a re-election campaign with the economy in recession won only one time out of seven. Even this only win is debatable, as the winner - Calvin Coolidge in 1924 – had not strictly speaking won the previous election (and thus could not be 're-elected'), but rather had acceded to the presidency automatically on the death in office of Warren G Harding.

In any event, the statistics make grim reading for incumbent US presidents and every single one of them and their key advisers know this statistic and the economic ones relating to the price of oil and gasoline. As Bob McNally, the former energy adviser to former President George W. Bush put it: 'Few things terrify an American president more than a spike in fuel [gasoline] prices.'

The bottom side of the of the crude oil price range – around USD40-45 per barrel of Brent - is also determined by one economic and one political factor.

The economic factor is a function of the breakeven price of US shale oil producers. As analysed earlier, by the end of the Second Oil Price War in 2016, the vast majority of US shale oil producers could breakeven at between USD35-40 per barrel of WTI, which, given the USD5 per barrel or so premium of Brent to WTI at that time, equated to around USD40-45 per barrel of Brent.

The political factor connected to this again relates to the re-election chances of a sitting president or to the electoral chances of whichever of the US's two main parties are in power at the time. Specifically, neither wish to be the ones to preside over mass bankruptcies in the country's shale oil – or shale gas – sector, with the significant direct and indirect unemployment that these would create.

A key additional concern is that the shale oil sector is the crucial economic and geopolitical importance of the US shale oil and gas sector for the country at home and abroad.

At home, the sector has made the US economy much less reliant on foreign oil – and gas – than it was even 10 years ago. Consequently, the core US economy is much more able now to withstand shocks in supply from outside its borders than it has been before.

Trump's Oil Price Range

Allied to this is that the US has less genuine need to become involved in as many theatres of political, military, or economic operations in foreign countries as it did before in order to secure sufficient energy supplies to drive its continued economic growth.

It is apposite to reiterate at this point that Saudi Arabia's budget breakeven oil price after the end of the 2014-2016 Oil Price War was around USD84 per barrel of Brent. Some of Saudi Arabia's fellow OPEC members had even higher budget breakeven prices.

However, one country that did enjoy a comparatively very low budget breakeven oil price – aside from US shale oil producers – was Russia. It had a longstanding budget breakeven oil price of well below USD40 per barrel of Brent.

Given all of these factors, then, it was only to be expected that when Saudi Arabia (with the help of US Cold War nemesis Russia) was pushing oil prices up over the USD80 per barrel of Brent level in the second half of 2018, President Trump sent a clear warning to Riyadh to stop doing this.

Specifically, in a speech before the UN General Assembly, Trump said: 'OPEC and OPEC nations are, as usual, ripping off the rest of the world, and I don't like it. Nobody should like it.'

He added: 'We defend many of these nations for nothing, and then they take advantage of us by giving us high oil prices. Not good. We want them to stop raising prices. We want them to start lowering prices and they must contribute substantially to military protection from now on.'

Russia Could Also Withstand Lower Oil Prices Better Than Saudi Arabia

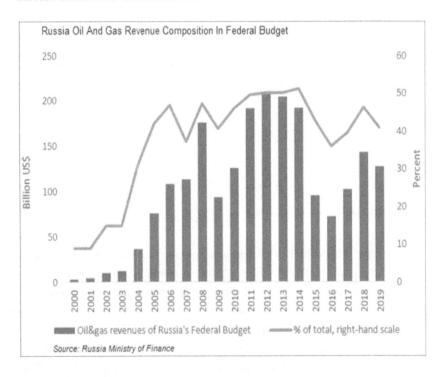

This was Trump's first demonstration of how he wanted oil prices to range during his tenure as president and he sought to use as leverage over the Saudis the foundation stone of the core 1945 agreement between the two countries and its amendment after the end of the 2014-2016 Oil Price War.

That is, not only did Trump link continued US protection for the Saudi Royal Family and Saudi Arabia to the country continuing to send the US all the oil it needed, but he also added in the extra post-War conditionality that the oil should be at prices that allowed the '*US economy to continue to grow and prosper*'.

As the Saudi Arabian- and Russian-led OPEC+ oil production cut agreement continued to push oil prices up, to slightly over the 'Trump Cap', Trump made the same warning again, even more clearly at a rally in Southaven, Mississippi, in October 2018. He said: 'And I love the king, King Salman, but I said, "King we're protecting you. You might not be there for two weeks without us. You have to pay for your military, you have to pay."'

Following Trump's direct and clear warnings to Saudi Arabia's Royal Family in the third quarter of 2018 of the catastrophic consequences if the Kingdom continued to keep oil prices higher than the USD80 pb Brent cap in the Trump price range, Saudi Arabia increased production and oil prices came down again.

The Kingdom, though, was well aware that from that point in 2018 it was back to the no-win situation that it had faced in the immediate aftermath of the 2014-2016 Oil Price War. More specifically: the Saudi Royal Family faced the prospect of multiple threats to its continued reign if the country continued to push oil prices above the level that Saudi Arabia needed to stop it going bankrupt, as the US would withdraw its protection of them.

But, with oil prices below the level at which the US wanted them, Saudi Arabia would never properly recover financially from the effects of the Oil Price War that it started in 2014, and for which the US had never – and would never – forgive it.

Worse still, was that at the oil price levels that the US demanded, the US shale oil producers would continue to make huge profits. They would also be able to lock in massive long-term hedges against any future falls in oil prices below their breakeven price of around USD40 per barrel of Brent. The situation was virtually the same for Russian oil companies.

The ultimate endgame of this Trump Oil Price Range would be that the US would be completely self-sufficient in all the oil it needed from either its own resources or from those of highly trusted allies, and it would be able to completely cut Saudi Arabia out of its top allies' grouping and to leave it on its own, should it wish to do so. This, of course, was precisely what the US wanted, and had wanted to do since the 1973 Oil Crisis.

In short, after the end of the 2014-2016 Oil Price War and after the Trump warnings in the third quarter of 2018, the Saudis could see no metaphorical light at the end of the tunnel and if they could it was just the headlights of a huge oncoming high-speed train.

Russia, for its part, could also only win in this scenario. With a budget breakeven oil price as low or lower than that of many of the US shale oil producers, it was perfectly happy to see oil prices in the Trump Oil Price Range as well. Higher prices than the US wanted were also fine, but they were not critical to the economic future of Russia.

There was one other crucial reason why Russia was happy with the situation as it was unravelling: it was obvious to Moscow that something had to give between the US and Saudi Arabia. It would benefit Russia if one or other of those countries was damaged, both in its capacity as a top oil and gas producer and as a leading geopolitical power as well.

The Peri-COVID Order

It is critical at this point to remember that at the beginning of 2020, when the full reality of Saudi Arabia's terrible economic and political position following the 2014-2016 was truly starting to bite, news about a new respiratory disease that had started in China was not especially concerning to most people.

Calm Before The Storm

For many decades, news had periodically emerged from some part or other of Asia of one influenza ('flu')-like disease after another and nothing of particular consequence had happened anywhere else in the world.

The 1997 outbreak in Asia of H5N1 Bird Flu had, for example, caused 455 deaths from 861 cases in 18 countries (a mortality rate of 52.8%), and the 2013 H7N9 Bird Flu outbreak had caused 616 deaths out of 1,568 cases (a mortality rate of 39.3%). In a similar vein, a major outbreak of Severe Acute Respiratory Syndrome (SARS) had first been reported in Asia in February 2003. It too had been caused by a coronavirus - the SARS-associated coronavirus (SARS-CoV) – and had spread to 29 countries.

However, ultimately that outbreak had not gained traction anywhere outside Asia and had been contained just a few months after that February report, having infected 8,096 people and caused 774 deaths.

It was against this backdrop, then, that the first reports of a new 'Asian flu-like disease' were received by the global public. The very first of these reports came on 31 December 2019, when the Wuhan Municipal Health Commission, in China, stated the discovery of a small cluster of cases of 'pneumonia' in Wuhan, Hubei Province. A new coronavirus was identified as being the cause.

The World Health Organization (WHO) then reported the same information via social media on 4 January 2020. On 10 January 2020, the WHO then issued a package of technical guidance online with advice to all countries on how to detect, test and manage potential cases, based on what was known about the virus at the time.

This guidance was based on experience with the SARS and Middle East Respiratory Syndrome (MERS) diseases. Sporadic outbreaks of the MERS virus had occurred without major incident since 2012, in 24 countries, causing around 2,500 infections and about 900 deaths to that point.

It is true that by mid-February 2020, COVID-19 – as the new virus was being called - had spread far beyond its initial outbreak radius around central Wuhan, with cases having been reported in over 20 countries. However, it is equally true that at that point the virus had supposedly caused only around 900 deaths out of about 41,000 reported cases, or a mortality rate of about 2%.

Although it is always advisable to build in some sort of leeway into any figures that come from China – be they GDP growth or export numbers or imports of Iranian oil – in empirical terms each of the numerical elements connected to the COVID-19 outbreak were small compared to other similar outbreaks at that point.

Aside from the diseases mentioned earlier, figures reported from the US's Centers for Disease Control and Prevention (CDC) showed that the 2009 H1N1 flu outbreak that also began in Asia resulted in around 274,304 hospitalisations and 12,469 deaths in the US alone. According to a CDC report in 2012, the total number of deaths from the 2009 H1N1 was at least 284,500. As it stood in February 2020, for those in the US, the mortality rate from the regular flu-like illnesses and related pneumonia in that country was over three times higher – at around 7% – than from the COVID-19 virus.

In Early March 2020, COVID-19 Looked 'Manageable'

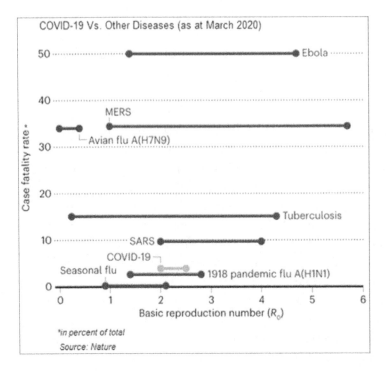

It was only on 11 March 2020 when the WHO, concerned about rising infection rates and the severity of the virus, made the assessment that COVID-19 could be characterised as a pandemic.

2020 Oil Price War – Saudi's COVID-19 Gambit

To Crown Prince Mohammed bin Salman, then, the COVID-19 outbreak back in February/March 2020 may have been a positive factor in deciding whether to launch a new oil price war to halt the increasing marginalisation of Saudi Arabia as a global oil power. This at the same time has led to the ongoing erosion of the political power of the Al Saud ruling family in Saudi Arabia and abroad.

Given the likelihood of some level of demand reduction in the global oil market as a consequence of COVID-19, it may well have seemed to MbS and his advisers that crashing oil prices to levels below the breakeven price of the US shale oil producers – under USD40 per barrel of Brent (around USD35 per barrel of WTI) – could be achieved at that point with a lot less overproduction on Saudi Arabia's part.

This would mean less barrels having to be sold at prices under the Kingdom's own USD84 pb of Brent budget breakeven price. In short, with COVID-19 in circulation, it would cost the Saudi Arabian economy less money to crash global oil prices and to bankrupt US shale oil producers.

It should also be remembered that at around the same time – late February/early March 2020 – MbS was also facing one of the most serious crises to his authority to that point. The first of these – analysed in depth in the 'Key Players In The Global Oil Market: Saudi Arabia' section – had followed his appointment as Crown Prince on 21 June 2017. MbS had usurped the heir-designate at the time, Muhammad bin Nayef and many senior Saudis had made their opposition to the change of lineage clear.

Salman's response had been to order a round-up on 4 November 2017 of around 400 of the most senior of these Saudis who were then imprisoned and allegedly tortured, albeit in the unlikely setting of the Ritz-Carlton in Riyadh. They were released when they felt more supportive of MbS's accession to the Crown Prince role and had collectively handed over around USD800 billion to Salman's operatives.

In a very similar vein, in early 2020 Salman was again facing increasing criticism from senior Saudis over the ongoing appalling financial consequences of the 2014-2016 Oil Price War. This criticism had been compounded by several other factors, including the disastrous IPO of Aramco at the end of 2019 that had lumbered Saudi with more debts in the form of massive dividend payments guaranteed to those who had bought shares in the offering. This is examined in depth in the 'Key Players In The Global Oil Market: Saudi Arabia' section.

Added to this was concern over the increasing role that China and Russia were playing in in Saudi Arabia's oil and financial policies, the widespread condemnation surrounding the murder of Saudi journalist Jamal Khashoggi in 2018 that even the CIA concluded had been personally ordered by MbS, and the treatment of several of Saudi Arabia's neighbours, also on his orders.

These included the continued Saudi war in Yemen, the Saudi-led blockade of Qatar beginning in 2017, and the alleged enforced resignation in 2017 at Saudi hands of Lebanon's President, Michel Aoun. Again, all of these incidents, and others in a similar vein, are examined in depth in the *'Key Players In The Global Oil Market: Saudi Arabia'* section.

Given this increasing groundswell of criticism against his new-found authority as Crown Prince, MbS decided again to order a round-up of those he believed were key figures for those who opposed him, and this began in earnest on 6 March 2020. Among those rounded up was Prince Ahmed bin Abdulaziz, a younger brother of King Salman, and Prince Muhammad bin Nayef himself - the King's nephew and the former crown prince.

It should be remembered that before the surprise appointment of Salman as crown prince in June 2017, Muhammad bin Nayef (MbN) had occupied the heir-designate position and Prince Ahmed had been one of three members of the Allegiance Council (the senior royal organisation that endorses the line of succession) to oppose MbS's appointment.

Prince Ahmed was seen by Salman both in 2017 and in 2020 as being a key threat to his authority, and a key supporter of bin Nayef, as the Prince remained King Salman's only surviving full brother. The Prince had also criticised Salman's ever-more-brutal tactics in the war in Yemen, posing the question in a video: 'What does this [the war in Yemen] have to do with the Saud? Those responsible are the King and his Crown Prince.'

Given the increasing opposition against MbS domestically and internationally, and the fact that Saudi Arabia's oil-fuelled economic and political power in the world was inexorably being drained away from it by the US shale oil sector, Salman needed to show the opposing senior Saudis, the Saudi people, and the US that he was still a force to be reckoned with.

The final catalyst for his decision to launch another oil price war, effectively against US shale oil producers, using the same strategy that had failed do dismally before, came on the same day as Salman ordered the 2020 round-up of his principal domestic opponents – 6 March 2020.

Whilst Prince Ahmed and MbN, and their supporters, were being 're-educated' somewhere in Saudi Arabia, Russia publicly rejected Saudi Arabia's calls at the 5 March OPEC Summit to cut oil production by an additional 1.5 million bpd through the second quarter of 2020. This would have brough the total production cut since the OPEC+ production cut deal at the end of 2016 up to 3.6 million bpd.

This cut had been an important part of Saudi Arabia's strategy from when it had lost the 2014-2016 Oil Price War to bring oil prices back up to levels at which it could begin to repair the damage it had done to its economy. To recap, at this point Saudi Arabia still had a budget breakeven oil price of around USD84 per barrel of Brent.

What happened next is open for debate. The Saudis said that Russia rejected the idea of the cut outright and refused to support it within the context of OPEC+. The Russians said that they did not reject the idea of the cut outright, but rather thought it should be considered over time in order that the full effects of the then-nascent COVID-19 pandemic and other oil-specific factors could be more accurately assessed.

In any event, on 8 March 2020, Saudi Arabia announced unexpected price discounts of USD6-8 pb of its key oil grades to customers in Europe, Asia, and the US - the first shots in the Third Oil Price War.

2020 (Third) Oil Price War – Two Storms Collide

Whatever Russia did or did not say to Saudi Arabia behind the closed doors of the 5 March OPEC Summit, the reality always was that Russia had joined OPEC in the OPEC+ grouping back in 2016 precisely so that it could undermine either the Saudis, or the Americans, or preferably both.

One might reasonably posit that when Salman signalled that Saudi Arabia was once again going to produce oil to the maximum to crash oil prices in a full-scale oil price war, Russian President Vladimir Putin fell off whichever horse he was riding bare-chested somewhere in Siberia in front of well-placed publicity photographers because he was laughing so much.

There is a phrase in Russian intelligence circles for clueless people who are ruthlessly used in covert operations without their knowledge, which is 'a useful idiot,' and it is hard to think of any idiot more useful in this context to the Russians than MbS.

Not only had Salman again launched another oil price war in less than five years, which the US would see as another attack by the Saudis against its crucial shale oil sector, but he also intended to use the same strategy and tactics that had so spectacularly failed in the previous oil price war as well.

Not just this, though; fate had placed another spoke in the wheels of MbS's plan, which was that almost immediately after he had signalled the start of the Third Oil Price War on 8 March 2020, COVID-19 escalated dramatically around the world – much more than anyone, including Salman, had expected.

On 11 March 2020, as highlighted earlier, only three days after Salman had started the new oil price war, the World Health Organization made the assessment that – based on rising infection rates and the severity of the virus - COVID-19 could be characterised as a pandemic.

For Russia, Crown Prince Mohammed bin Salman's 2020 Oil Price War was a wondrous gift and he was the useful idiot who just kept on giving.

The Third Oil Price War Instigated By The Saudis

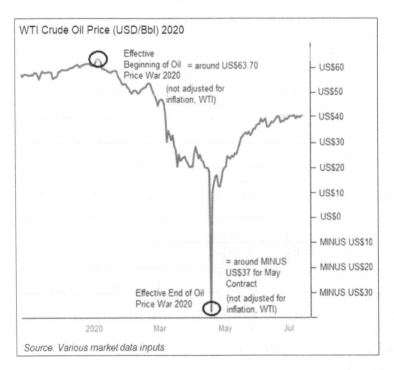

In purely basic oil economics terms, as highlighted earlier, Russia had a budget breakeven price of USD40 per barrel of Brent at the time and the Saudi's was USD84. Moreover, Russia could produce over 11 million bpd of oil without figuratively breaking sweat, whereas Saudi's average from 1973 to that point was just over 8 million bpd (see the full analysis of this in the *'Key Players In The Global Oil Market: Saudi Arabia'* section).

Russia's major oil producer, Rosneft, had been begging President Putin to allow it to produce and sell more oil since the OPEC+ arrangement was first agreed in December 2016 as it had abundant capacity. It could also make good profits at much lower levels than it was allowed to under Russia's OPEC+ production quotas.

Saudi's major oil producer, Aramco, however, only suffered value-destruction in a lower-price, higher-volume scenario. Investors who had bought shares in the Aramco IPO would also see the value of those shares subject to significant destruction and any such future offerings in Aramco would be negatively affected.

In sum, if required, Russia could cope with oil prices as low as USD25 per barrel from a budget and foreign asset reserves perspective for up to 10 years, whereas Saudi could manage two years at most and with considerable economic pain attached.

A key reason why Russia could survive for much longer than the Saudis was, ironically, thanks to MbS himself who had been instrumental in expanding OPEC to make room for Russia in the OPEC+ grouping. Underlining this – and the fact that the Russians do have a very impish sense of humour – was effusive praise from Russia's Energy Minister, Alexander Novak, of the OPEC+ grouping in the run-up to the 2020 Oil Price War. He said: 'OPEC+ has earned Russia 10 trillion roubles [USD140 billion at that point].'

Presumably just to highlight the irony of this further, Russia's Finance Ministry then chipped in that the accumulated funds from the previous OPEC+ agreements would help Russia to support the rouble and would also help Russia to cope with oil prices as low as USD25 per barrel for up to the aforementioned 10-year period.

The metaphorical icing on the cake, though, was Novak saying that: 'We may reach new agreements [with OPEC] if needed.' In practical terms this meant that if, in fact, it took longer than originally thought by Russia for Saudi Arabia to go bankrupt and it started to have any negative impact on Russia, then Moscow would just click its fingers together and Riyadh would come running to sign a new OPEC+ output cap deal.

Overall, for Russia, whose core foreign policy strategy under President Putin had always been to create chaos and then to project Russian solutions, and therefore power, into that chaos, Saudi Arabia's oil price war could not have been better.

On the one hand, if oil settled back at around the USD40 pb of Brent level when Chinese demand came back in scale after the negative effects of the COVID-19 outbreak then Russia's budget would be fine and its oil companies could produce as much oil as they wanted.

Russia Was Building Its Influence Across The Shia Crescent Of Power

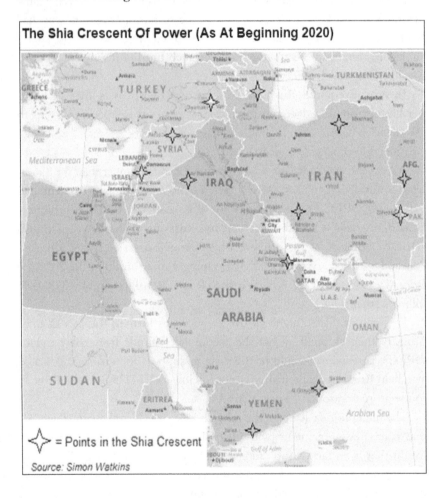

The Shia Crescent Of Power (As At Beginning 2020)

✦ = Points in the Shia Crescent

Source: Simon Watkins

Even if it did not trade back above those levels for a while then Russia would still benefit from the fact that twice in less than 10 years Saudi had declared economic war on its only important ally in the world at that time – the US. This would put the US at a long-term disadvantage to Russia, and its key ally China, in the region for years to come.

A US-ostracised Saudi Arabia would also be highly receptive to new 'cooperation' deals suggested by either Moscow or Beijing, it seemed to Russia (and also to China).

Already in a controlling position in all key countries in the Shia crescent of power in the Middle East – Lebanon, Syria, Iraq, Iran and Yemen (via Iran) – Russia was continuing to work on those countries on the edges of the crescent in which it already directly or indirectly had a foothold.

These included Azerbaijan (75% Shia and an FSU state) and Turkey (25% Shia and furious at not being accepted fully into the European Union). Others also remained longer-term targets, including Bahrain (75% Shia) and Pakistan (up to 25% Shia and a home to sworn-US enemies Al Qaeda and the Taliban).

2020 Oil Price War – US Shale Cannot Fail

The US had already lost its trust in Saudi Arabia when Riyadh had launched the 2014-2016 Oil Price War, breaking the fundamental agreement that had been reached between the two countries in 1945, as Washington saw it.

The US had remained unconvinced by the Saudis' subsequent political back-pedalling in the years after 2016 aimed at trying to assure Washington that the Kingdom was still its key ally in the Middle East and that it would work with the US in future in the best interests of the two countries.

Washington, for its part, did not believe any of this and was working privately on the strategy of keeping Saudi Arabia broadly on side – as a regional bulwark against Iran's growing power in the Middle East – until such time as the US was producing so much oil that it no longer needed any of the Saudis' oil or until Saudi Arabia could be replaced as a source of oil imports for the US with another country.

Washington still hoped in that this other country could be Iraq, which has the potential to easily outstrip Saudi Arabia as the Middle East's top crude oil producer, as analysed in depth in the *'Key Players In The Global Oil Market: Iraq'* section. The US believed that over time it might be possible to break the political, economic and military hold that Iran had long maintained over its neighbour through its powerful proxies in those areas.

The specific policy actions threatened and taken by the US against Saudi Arabia at this time are detailed in the *'Key Players In The Global Oil Market:*

The US' section later in this book. However, the US's attitude broadly can be summed up in the idea that 'shale cannot be allowed to fail'.

When the US shale industry began in earnest in 2006 with natural gas and in 2010 with crude oil, it offered the US the long-awaited opportunity to finally shrug off any shackles to Saudi that remained by dint of the Kingdom's oil power. Within a relatively short time, the US had become the number one oil producer in the world, pushing Saudi frequently into third place behind Russia, and producing an average of around 13 million bpd, with around 60-70% of that coming from the shale oil sector.

Saudi Arabia Had Residual Use To The US As A Bulwark Against Iran

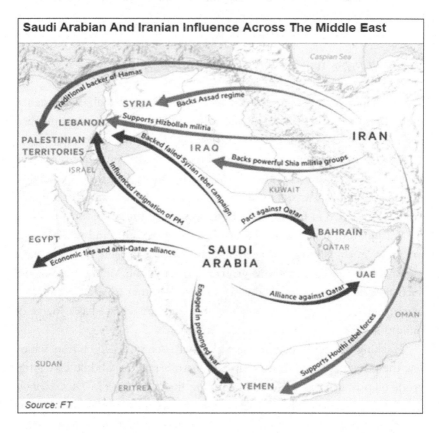

One of the many advantages of this relative independence from Saudi Arabia in the oil sphere was that it allowed the US a new-found ability to sanction major oil producing nations that fell afoul of it for one reason or another – most notably Iran, Venezuela and Russia – without fear of the repercussions for its own energy security. Another major advantage to the US was, conversely, that it could reward geopolitically advantageous cooperation by other countries with huge contracts, mainly in the oil and gas sectors but in others too, regardless of Saudi Arabia's views on the country involved. Both of these factors together meant that both geopolitically and economically, the US was significantly better off being less reliant on Saudi Arabia for its energy imports.

For these enormously important reasons alone, it should have been blatantly obvious to the Saudis that the US would never capitulate on its shale-centric power or even allow it to be materially damaged. This ethos was clearly stated early in the 2020 Oil Price War by President Trump when he said: 'I will do whatever I have to do [...] to protect tens of thousands of energy workers and our great companies.' Consequently, Trump stated that shorter-term plans to impose tariffs on Saudi Arabia's oil exports into the US were 'certainly a tool in the toolbox.'

From a practical volumes' viewpoint, putting tariffs on Saudi oil rather than Russian oil at that point would have made sense from two key perspectives. First, at that time the US imported around 95% more oil from Saudi than it did from Russia, so sanctioning Russian oil would have had little effect on the US's supply glut that was overhanging its already-stretched domestic storage facilities. Second, Russia was in much better economic shape than Saudi Arabia back then to handle any shocks to its oil revenues, with a budget breakeven oil price of USD40 pb of Brent rather than Saudi's USD84 pb point.

On the downside, Saudi at that time provided one of the few large-scale sources of sour crude (including the benchmark Arab Heavy) that were available to the US, which was essential to its production of diesel, and to which purpose WTI is less suited. Much of the US's Gulf Coast refinery system at that point was geared towards using sourer crude, having invested heavily in coking systems and other infrastructure to better handle heavier crudes from the Middle East in recent decades.

The other major historical sources of this for the US were not capable of filling the gap. There were still US sanctions at that point on oil imports from Venezuela, Mexican oil flows were unreliable, and Canada's pipeline capacity to the US was not able to handle any more exports south until progress was made on the long-delayed Keystone pipeline.

At the same time as these policies were being considered, though, the US shale oil sector was capably withstanding the lower price environment, as it had done after the first year of the 2014-2016 Oil Price War. It was true that the sector cut more than USD50 billion from its planned spending in 2020, that the number of operating rigs fell by around 40% in March and early April of that year, and that output fell by nearly 1 million bpd over the same period as well. It was equally true, however, that the US shale oil sector continued to benefit from the core resilience that had been established in the 2014-2016 Oil Price War.

All of the enormous efficiency and technical improvements remained in place: the ability to drill longer laterals, to manage the fracking stages closer and to maintain the fracks with higher, finer, sand to allow for increased recovery for the wells drilled, in conjunction with faster drill times and so on. Additionally positive was that the US shale oil producers had gained further cost benefits from multi-pad drilling and well spacing theory and practice.

As it was in 2020, the best US shale operations could shut down almost immediately if the price fell to below uneconomic levels and then re-start within a week, although the refinery-related lead time was slightly longer. Moreover, the price levels that were economic for them to start up again had fallen into the USD25-30 pb of WTI range, provided that these prices looked sustainable for at least six months.

The often-stated fears at the time that the specialised crews needed for the shale oil sector would simply vanish forever were also evidently ridiculous, as highlighted by one very senior shale oil sector executive at the time: 'The idea that these crews will just stay away from a sector that pays much bigger money than they can get elsewhere to go and re-train as coders or something is just not true and didn't play out last time either.'

In sum, the only real question was whether Wall Street and the other financial sources that had funded the US shale oil boom would continue to foot the bill. Given the critical domestic political and broader geopolitical reasons already mentioned, considerable government pressure was brought to bear on them to ensure that they kept their financing in place.

Consequently, the pullback in the US shale oil sector during March and April 2020 can be reasonably seen as just a standard phase of the Business Cycle. The first phase was marked by the rush for volume and the second phase marked by some demand for capital repayment from Wall Street in a generally lower price environment after 2016. The third phase, the onset of which was hastened by the 2020 Oil Price War, had been characterised by a move to more mergers and acquisitions activity, particularly by the acquisition of smaller shale operations by bigger firms.

US Shale Oil Just Going Through The Usual Business Cycle

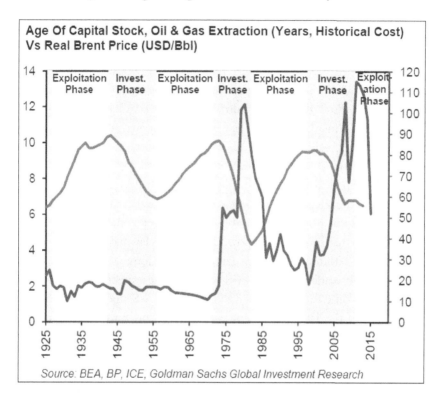

Age Of Capital Stock, Oil & Gas Extraction (Years, Historical Cost) Vs Real Brent Price (USD/Bbl)

Source: BEA, BP, ICE, Goldman Sachs Global Investment Research

A significant proportion of these deals in the immediate aftermath of the War featured a heavy equity-funded element, given that the value of the stocks of the bigger oil firms started to rebound at the same time as those of the smaller firms were still at relatively low valuations.

For the big firms – such as Exxon, Chevron, BP, Shell and then-Total – having a good-sized shale oil (and/or gas) operation looked an excellent fit in the overall business model. It sat well in the short-cycle perspective so that when prices were rising they could ramp up production quickly to take advantage of that and when they were falling they could just cut capital expenditure quickly and trim back production.

2020 Oil Price War – Game Over For The Saudis

Having warned Saudi Arabia repeatedly that the US would not tolerate any sustained threat to its shale oil sector (and, by extension, to its economy and its domestic political landscape) – in speeches and tweets and in the increasingly close-run legislative passage of the 'NOPEC Bill' (analysed in depth in the *'Key Players In The Global Oil Market: The US'* section) – Washington had seen and heard enough from the Saudis by the beginning of April 2020.

US President Donald Trump had made previous warnings about withdrawing all US military support for the Al Sauds, and by extension to Saudi Arabia, directly to King Salman. The last one had been that: 'He [Saudi King Salman] would not last in power for two weeks without the backing of the US military'.

However, on 2 April, according to a very senior source in the White House, Trump clearly and specifically told Crown Prince Mohammed bin Salman over the telephone that unless OPEC started cutting oil production – so allowing oil prices to rise (above the danger zone for US shale oil producers) – that he would be powerless to stop lawmakers from passing legislation to withdraw US troops from the Kingdom.

It was also made very clear by Trump that he expected from then on that the next time the Saudis tried to destroy the US shale sector it would be the end of the 1945 agreement entirely, with no further warning, and that the US military would be withdrawn immediately. According to the same source, corroborated by others in similar positions, Salman agreed to gradually cut oil production to bring prices back up.

However, before the full effects of these cuts could feed through into the global oil system, towards the end of April 2020 the futures prices for WTI to be delivered in May fell into negative territory for the first time in history. The stunning headline figure – minus USD37.63 per barrel – was a technical product of the fact that there was simply a lot more oil still flowing around the US system than could be removed by demand plus storage. This meant that refineries and traders were effectively paying not to have to take physical delivery of the WTI oil blend.

The figure also, though, carried with it a danger for the US that supply could be cut back so much (as demand from China was returning at that point) that oil prices quickly spiked the other way.

Consequently, it was further made clear by Trump to MbS that this cut in oil production to push prices back up again was not to be overdone either. Specifically, MbS was told that production should begin to level out again when oil prices were back up around USD70-75 per barrel of Brent.

In sum, Trump demanded, and received, a commitment from Saudi Arabia to absolutely abide by the *de facto* Trump Oil Price Range of USD40-80 per barrel of Brent.

The US's Patience Ran Out When WTI Futures Prices Went Negative

From that point the Saudis were faced again with the situation that they would have to sit back and allow oil to trade in a band that did not allow the Kingdom to recover from its 2014-2016 and 2020 Oil Price War follies for decades. At the same time, the band would allow the US shale oil industry to expand its own supplies and contracts to an eventual point when the US could cease its support for the Al Sauds anyway.

By the time the 2020 Oil Price War ended, Saudi Arabia had a budget breakeven price of well over USD90 per barrel of Brent oil and was looking at budget deficits running into the mid-2030s at least. It was a lose-lose position that Saudi Arabia had engineered itself into, from which it could not pump and export its way out. In short, the ruling Al Saud family found itself caught in a death spiral of its own making.

In the context of the Saudis' dwindling financial and economic safety net, March 2020 saw the Kingdom's central bank deplete its net foreign assets at the fastest rate since at least 2000.

Saudi's Squandered Fortune

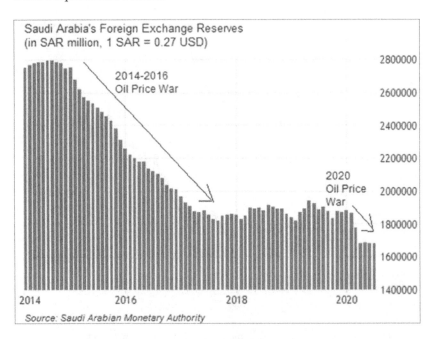

Source: Saudi Arabian Monetary Authority

In that month alone, according to the Saudis' own figures, the Kingdom's foreign reserves fell by just over SAR100 billion (USD27 billion). That was a full 5% decrease from just the previous month, with the total reserves figure then standing at around USD450 billion, the lowest level since 2011.

This figure left only USD150 billion of 'fighting reserves' that could be used on anything else that the Saudis might need it for, once the USD300 billion required to keep the SAR/USD-peg intact was subtracted. This peg had acted as the foundation stone for the Saudi economy since June 1986.

One of the endgames that was clearly in view at that time was the removal of Crown Prince Mohammed bin Salman from the key position of power and longer-term the end of the Al Sauds as the ruling family of the country.

Shorter-term, the prospect was that there would be various grim economic and financial milestones along the way for Saudi Arabia, such as the continued value destruction of Saudi Aramco, the collapse of the SAR/USD3.75 currency peg and the corollary meltdown of the Saudi economy within months of that.

The other alternative – which MbS gravitated to from that point – was to increasingly shift his country toward the sphere of influence of China and Russia, and away from that dominated by the US. All of the key developments in this regard are analysed in depth in the relevant *'Key Players In The Global Oil Market'* sections on Saudi Arabia, China, and Russia, respectively.

China Rebounds Quicker Than Expected In 2020

On the other side of the demand-supply equation, under the 'zero-COVID' policy of maximum control over and suppression of the virus, personally backed by President Xi Jinping, China rebounded from its COVID-19 outbreaks in 2020 much quicker than expected. It remained robust in its economic activity for many months afterwards, despite the heavy waves of infection and re-infection that repeatedly devastated many other economies that year and into 2021.

For those readers new to the oil sector, it is apposite to note the impact on the global oil market that a fully functioning China had, and still has, on oil pricing through its enormous demand for energy. This demand for energy was, and remains, the result of a massive disparity between, on the one hand, China's enormous economy-driven oil and gas needs and, on the other hand, its minimal level of domestic oil and gas reserves.

As a result of this imbalance, China almost alone created the 2000-2014 commodities 'supercycle', characterised by consistently rising price trends for all commodities that are used in a booming manufacturing and infrastructure building environment.

As late as 2017, China's high rate of economic growth allowed it to overtake the US as the largest annual gross crude oil importer in the world, having become the world's largest net importer of total petroleum and other liquid fuels in 2013.

China Rebounded Just As Others Felt The Full Impact Of COVID-19

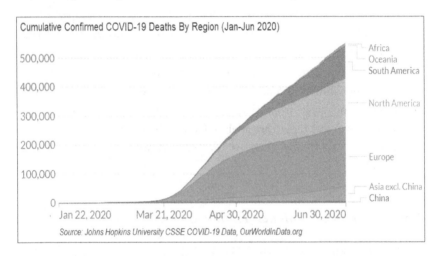

Cumulative Confirmed COVID-19 Deaths By Region (Jan-Jun 2020)

Source: Johns Hopkins University CSSE COVID-19 Data, OurWorldInData.org

More specifically on China's economy, from 1992 to 1998, the country's annual economic growth rate was basically between 10 to 15 percent; from 1998 to 2004 between 8 to 10 percent; from 2004 to 2010 between 10 to 15 percent again; from 2010 to 2016 between 6 to 10 percent, and from 2016 to 2022 between 5 to 7 percent.

For much of the period from 1992 to the middle 2010s, a large element of this growth was founded on energy-intensive economic drivers, particularly manufacturing and the corollary build out of infrastructure attached to the sector, such as factories, housing for workers, road, railways and so on. Even after some of China's growth began to switch into the less energy-intensive service sectors, the country's investment in energy-intensive infrastructure build-out remained very high.

In sharp contrast, as analysed in depth in the *'Key Players In The Global Oil Market: China'* section, the China National Offshore Oil Corporation (CNOOC) – the country's largest producer of offshore crude oil and natural gas – had been trying for years to boost its crude oil reserves, without much net effect on the country's indigenous energy supply/demand balance.

As at the beginning of 2020, the disparity between China's energy requirements to keep its economic growth on schedule and the amount of its own oil and gas reserves that it could use for this remained acute. However, China's schedule was to overtake the US as the world's largest economy by nominal GDP by 2030 at the latest – despite already being the world's largest economy by purchasing power parity, the largest manufacturing economy and the largest trading nation at that stage.

Given this ambition, to which all major political figures in China were, and remain, thoroughly committed, the country began to rebound economically in the second quarter of 2020 at a pace that was truly startling.

China's Rebound Surprised Everyone

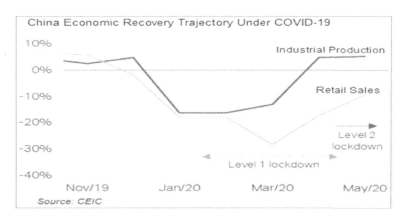

By just the second week of April 2020, the lockdown of Wuhan – the Chinese city in which the global COVID-19 pandemic began – was eased. This occurred only three to four weeks after COVID-19 had begun to notably surface elsewhere in the world.

In fact, by the same point in April 2020 when the lockdown of Wuhan was eased, elsewhere around half of the world's population was under some form of lockdown, with more than 3.9 billion people in more than 90 countries or territories having been asked or ordered to stay at home by their governments.

Although as an export-led economy China would still face some trouble in the following weeks and maybe months, moves were immediately afoot to mitigate these downside risks to its economy. Even before the easing of the lockdown in Wuhan, China's industrial sector had been back operating at levels above the pre-COVID-19 rates for over two weeks.

Broadly, despite the slowdown in domestic activity indicators for the two months to February 2020, March saw an extraordinary turnaround, especially in the core manufacturing sector of China's economy.

China's Exports Bounced Back Fast

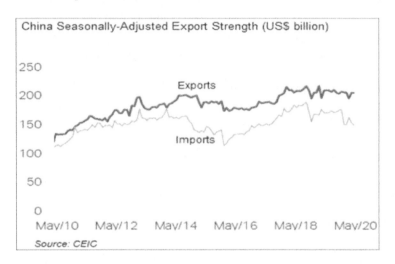

According to data released by China's National Bureau of Statistics at the beginning of April 2020, the official manufacturing purchasing managers index (PMI) – a survey of sentiment among factory owners in the world's second largest economy – was 52.0 in March. Not only was this a huge leap from the all-time low reading of 35.7 in February but also a reading of above 50 shows that a country's manufacturing sector is growing.

At the same time, China's non-manufacturing PMI – a gauge of sentiment in the services and construction sectors – also jumped, from the all-time low 29.6 in February 2020 to a growth-indicating 52.3 in March.

For the global oil sector this resurgence at that time meant two things. The first was that a key demand element in the supply/demand pricing matrix was in the process of returning. The second was that China would take the opportunity afforded it by other leading global economies facing the peak of the COVID-19 outbreak to make long-term strategic deals with key oil suppliers at extremely advantageous terms to itself.

These economic readings also translated into a broader confidence amongst China's population, as seen in the fact that the renminbi-denominated China A-share index rose in the last week of March from just over 2,600 to just below 2,800.

Confidence In China was Echoed In The Performance Of The SSE

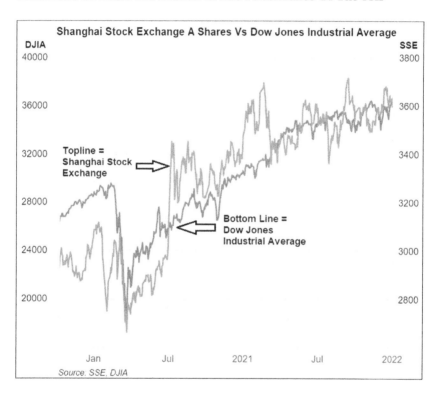

It then continued to rise in the coming weeks, to outstrip the performance of other global stock market benchmarks, including the US's Dow Jones Industrial Average.

For Saudi Arabia all of this had meant that it was caught in the worst position it could be, as of March/April 2020. On the one hand, the early part of its Third Oil Price War had coincided with the point at which oil pricing had been highly negatively affected by China's present lack of demand and by the prospect of extreme demand destruction in other major oil consuming countries. This had led to a much more dramatic crash in prices than Saudi Arabia had expected, including pushing the price of WTI in the one-month futures market to negative levels, which had infuriated the US.

On the other hand, though, just after the damage had been done with the US, the prospect of an imminent return of Chinese demand to the global oil market had meant that the Saudis were not even likely to be able to keep prices towards the low end of the historical scale to at least maintain some pressure on the US shale producers.

If Chinese demand had not appeared back in full view at that point in March/April then the Saudis could at least have tried to assuage the US by decreasing production again, albeit knowing all the time that much of the positive pricing effect of this on oil would be lost in the face of still-declining global demand.

China Prospered As Others Foundered

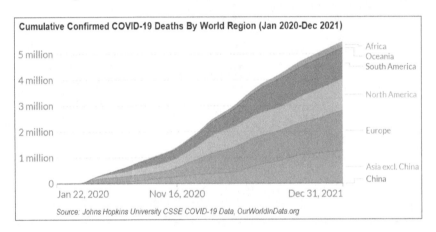

Source: Johns Hopkins University CSSE COVID-19 Data, OurWorldInData.org

The US Regroups And Refocuses Inwards

As China continued to go from strength to strength in its economic rebound in 2020, the US – along with all other major developed countries of the West and many others – continued to see COVID-19 infections and deaths increase dramatically.

In response, broadly speaking - but with the notable exception of scientific collaboration in producing a vaccine – countries focused in on themselves and on their efforts to do what they could to minimise the effects of the pandemic on their own populations.

These efforts were partly logistical ones founded on medical advice, most evidently the introduction of societal lockdowns to flatten the curve of infections to ease pressure on domestic health resources. They were also partly financial, most obviously the effective resumption of full quantitative easing measures, to mitigate the financial pressure on individuals and businesses arising from the effects of the virus.

The understandably more insular approach by countries in the midst of the then-rampant COVID-19 pandemic coincided in the US with a move that had been gathering momentum since before the end of the Iraq War in 2011. This was for the country to be more circumspect in its foreign policy, particularly when it came to taking significant military action abroad.

This view was also shared by the US's major allies in the NATO security alliance, including the UK, France, and Germany. It reflected a broad-based loss of trust in the political apparatus of those countries by their people as a result of the evidence that the pretext for the war to depose Saddam Hussein – that he had weapons of mass destruction and was prepared to quickly deploy them against the West - had been a lie.

In the US, this distrust among many segments of the population had been sown in the events leading up to, surrounding and marking the end of the Vietnam War.

It is apposite to note at this point that this groundswell of discontent across large swathes of the US population was increasingly seized on and played on by Donald Trump in his campaign to become president. It is also apposite to note that this more insular idea of the US was twinned with the negative financial consequences of becoming involved in such foreign conflicts and formed the two-pronged foundation of Trump's highly successful 'Make America Great Again' 2016 presidential campaign.

Coming in the midst of the COVID-19 pandemic - and so swiftly after the March/April 2020 Oil Price War launched against the US by its supposed long-standing Middle Eastern ally, Saudi Arabia, plus OPEC (which had held the US to ransom in the 1973 Oil Crisis) - it is little wonder that Trump's 'Endless Wars' commencement address to the United States Military Academy at West Point on 13 June 2020 found such resonance.

Aside from being a masterclass in speech writing, regardless of individual political views, the commencement address clearly laid out that for Trump and his many supporters the days of the US being the 'policeman of the world' were over.

To be more specific, he said: 'We are restoring the fundamental principles, that the job of the American soldier is not to rebuild foreign nations but defend and defend strongly our nation from foreign enemies. We are ending the era of endless wars. In its place is a renewed, clear-eyed focus on defending America's vital interests. It is not the duty of US troops to solve ancient conflicts in faraway lands that many people have never even heard of. We are not the policemen of the world.'

A few months prior to making this speech, Trump's team in the White House had laid the groundwork for future discussions that would see the US withdraw some or all of its military presence from several countries. These included most notably Syria (in 2019) – including protracted internal White House discussions about withdrawing from the strategically vital Al-Tanf exclusion zone that was the tri-border junction of Syria, Jordan, and Iraq - Afghanistan (2021), and Iraq (2021). In 2018, the US had pre-empted its imminent rolling disengagement from the Middle East by its unilateral withdrawal from the JCPOA ('nuclear deal') with Iran, as analysed in depth in the *'Key Players In The Global Oil Market: Iran'* section.

Aside from the additional impetus to become more inward-looking that had resulted from the spread of the COVID-19 pandemic, and the added political impetus that had come from the latest OPEC oil price war against it, the US was more insulated against pushback from the countries it was leaving by dint of its rising energy independence.

As analysed earlier, from the 1973 Oil Crisis the US had been determined reduce its dependence on other countries for its energy, particularly on countries from the Middle East. Initially, through the Kissinger Doctrine, this had been achieved through diplomatic manipulation. Later, this was augmented by the fast-rising oil and gas production that came from the US's shale oil and gas producers.

By early 2020, then, the US had become a net exporter of petroleum. It is important to note here that petroleum and crude oil are not interchangeable words in global oil market terms. Several hydrocarbons producers around the world use them interchangeably, most notably Saudi Arabia in its fantastical 'oil production' estimates that will be analysed in depth in the *'Key Players In The Global Oil Market: Saudi Arabia'* section. However, these words are not the same and cannot be used as such. Basically, 'crude oil' is just crude oil, but petroleum includes crude oil, refined petroleum products, and other liquids (including gas condensates).

The US becoming a net exporter of petroleum in 2020 was extremely significant. As highlighted by the EIA, after generally increasing every year from 1954 through to 2005, US gross and net total petroleum imports peaked in 2005. Since 2005, increases in domestic petroleum production and increases in petroleum exports helped to reduce annual total petroleum net imports. In 2020 and 2021, annual total petroleum net imports went negative for the first time since at least 1949.

The US Had New-Found Petroleum Independence In 2020

U.S. petroleum consumption, production, imports, exports, and net imports, 1950-2021

million barrels per day

2020
- consumption: 18.19 million barrels per day
- production: 18.42 million barrels per day
- imports: 7.86 million barrels per day
- exports: 8.50 million barrels per day
- net imports: -0.64 million barrels per day

Source: EIA

The EIA also highlighted that US petroleum imports rose sharply in the 1970s, especially from OPEC members, so that by 1977 OPEC nations were the source of 70% of US total petroleum imports and the source of 85% of its crude oil imports.

Since 1977, though, the percentage shares of US imports of total petroleum and of crude oil from OPEC generally declined. By 2021, OPEC's share of US total petroleum imports was about 11% and its share of US crude oil imports was around 13%. Saudi Arabia, the largest OPEC petroleum exporter to the US, was the source by then of just 5% of its total petroleum imports and 6% of its crude oil imports.

China Exploits US's Disengagement From The Middle East

The US's then (as now) up-and-coming superpower rival, China, knew at least three key things about President Donald Trump even before he became president in January 2017.

The first was that he wanted the US to pull back from as many foreign commitments as possible in order to focus all US resources on the US. At one stage, according to US National Security Advisor, John Bolton, Trump was even seriously considering withdrawing the US from NATO.

The second was that there was no dividing line in his thinking between political/security considerations and business ones. An early case in point of this was the almost complete reversal of initially hard-hitting US sanctions imposed on Chinese telecommunications company, ZTE, for committing major and repeated violations of the US's sanctions on Iran and North Korea. After a private telephone call to President Xi - in which it later transpired that Xi told Trump that he would 'owe [Trump] a favour' if he reduced the sanctions against ZTE – Trump did exactly what Xi had asked for – trading security considerations for commercial ones.

The third was that he was highly unpredictable in the scope and scale of his reactions, but that this behaviour was founded in his unwillingness to be personally seen to lose in any public confrontation with another party. The US-China Trade War began in July 2018 because Trump, like many at the time and since then, believed that China was artificially manipulating its mechanisms of trade (especially through the USD/RMB exchange rate) to give China a huge trading advantage over the US.

However, based on the other factors that it knew about Trump, China knew that he was concerned with only the optics of this war and not with the substance of how those negotiations were progressing. Therefore, Beijing tailored all of its so-called concessions to being items that in practice were meaningless, but which would allow Trump to make victory-sounding tweets as he wished.

Attesting to Trump's focus on the optics only of the Trade War was an often-repeated comment by the then-President: 'Every time there's a little bad [Trade War] news the [stock] market would go down incredibly...Every time there was a little bit of good news the market would go up incredibly... And yet, other news that was also very big, the market just didn't really care.'

The practical ramifications for China of these three elements in Trump's presidency was that it could do whatever it wanted in foreign lands provided that it did not threaten Trump's winning view of himself. Both sides of this dynamic are analysed in depth in the 'Key Players In The Global Oil Market' 'China' and 'The US' sections.

Aside from the aforementioned manipulation of negotiations during the Trade War to maximise the optics for Trump but to offer little of substance in return, China was able to extend its influence dramatically in the oil and gas fields of the Middle East provided that it did so in low-key manner.

China's hold on Iran had already been cemented with its broad and deep 'Iran-China 25-Year Comprehensive Cooperation Agreement' first revealed anywhere in the world in my 3 September 2019 article for Petroleum Economist. The full details of this are to be found in the 'Key Players In The Global Oil Market: Iran' section.

Suffice it to say here that the deal - to which was later added specific wide-ranging military and technological programmes that are also covered in depth in that section - made Iran effectively a client state of China in many key respects. It also gave China a significant hold over Iraq, given the enormous influence that Iran wielded over its neighbour in terms of its political, economic and military proxies in those areas. All of this is covered in the 'Key Players In The Global Oil Market: Iraq' section. However, at this point it is important to note three key aspects associated with China's stealthy increase in its influence across Iran and Iraq.

The first is that up until it became clear that Trump had personally decided to dramatically ramp up the pressure on China during the Trade War – when the US imposed 25% tariffs on a further USD16 billion of Chinese goods on 23 August 2018 – Beijing had taken a relatively overt approach to its activities in both Iran and Iraq. This approach then changed to a more covert methodology.

In the case of China's overt approach at first, over the years to 2018 some of the country's best-known oil and gas companies signed major exploration and development deals for several oil and gas fields, big and small, in the two neighbouring countries (these deals are analysed in depth in the 'Key Players In The Global Oil Market: Iran' and the 'Key Players In The Global Oil Market: Iraq' sections).

After Trump signalled in 2018 that he was taking the Trade War with China very seriously indeed – which also followed shortly after the unliteral withdrawal of the US from the JCPOA with Iran and the reimposition of severe sanctions on it and any country that traded with it – China became much more covert in its development of the oil and gas riches of both neighbouring countries.

The most-used covert method of continuing its activities in the two countries was to avoid being seen to make the sort of high-profile exploration and development contracts that were widely reported in the oil industry media and often beyond that. Instead, China would utilise little-known companies and these would apply for, and invariably be granted, 'contract-only' work for some anodyne-sounding work programme.

Notable early examples of this switch in strategy of China in Iran relate to China's pledge in the 25-Year Agreement mentioned earlier to increase crude oil production from Iran's massive West Karoun oil fields cluster.

At that time, Iran's West Karoun fields – which include the huge oil reservoirs of South and North Azadegan, South and North Yaran, and Yadavaran, among other lesser-known sites – were together producing only around 355,000 bpd of oil, based on a recovery rate across the West Karoun oil region of just 4.5-5.5%.

Iran's Foreign Minister, Mohammad Zarif, and his China counterpart, Wang Yi, decided back in the lead-up to the August 2019 Agreement that Chinese companies would increase the 355,000-bpd output from West Karoun by another 145,000 bpd in the first phase (to 500,000 bpd) and then by another 500,000 bpd (to 1 million bpd).

Soon after this, two peculiar types of low-key announcements started to appear regarding new developments in Iran (and Iran-sponsored Iraq as well). The first of these involved extremely high-cost projects announced in Iran – bewildering given the fact that it was technically bankrupt – and the second cited new 'contract-only' involvement by various firms, all of which were Chinese.

Two early typical examples of this new form of announcement concerned developments in the supergiant West Karoun fields region. The bigger one of the two was that Iran's Petroleum Ministry had awarded a USD1.3 billion development deal to more than double oil production at the South Azadegan oilfield. The second of the two announcements signed in the same month was of a USD300 million development contract for the Yaran oil site in the West Karoun fields.

The full truth of the situation was that various Chinese companies had been awarded 11 'contract-only' projects in various operational areas of Iran's South Azadegan oil field development, including contracts for drilling-only, field maintenance-only, engineering-only, construction-only and technology-only, and so on. These added up to what was, in effect, a full exploration and development programme for the huge oilfield.

Iran's Huge Oil And Gas Resources

A further indication of what was really going on with South Azadegan was that the supposed Iranian lead partner in South Azadegan – Petropars – was also the partner at that point to the China National Petroleum Corporation (CNPC) in the stalled flagship Phase 11 project of the supergiant South Pars non-associated natural gas field, as analysed in depth elsewhere in this section. In reality, it did not make any difference what name was on the publicly available contract, China was just going ahead with what had already been agreed.

The same switch in strategy was used in Iraq as well. A case in point was when China oil giants, CNPC and the China National Offshore Oil Corporation (CNOOC) were reportedly 'considering acquiring' ExxonMobil's 32.7% stake in Iraq's supergiant West Qurna 1 oil field.

These reports completely missed the point that China was already dominant at the site, not only through the 32.7% stake held by PetroChina but also through the gradual acquisition of a range of huge 'contract-only' awards made to Chinese companies for work on the field. These included the USD121 million engineering contract to the China Petroleum Engineering & Construction Corp (CPECC) to upgrade the facilities that were used to extract gas during crude oil production.

Exactly the same 'contract-only' model was used in Iraq's massive Majnoon oil field. Here, two major new 'drilling-only' contracts were signed: one with China's Hilong Oil Service & Engineering Company to drill 80 wells at a cost of USD54 million, and the other with the Iraq Drilling Company to drill 43 wells at a cost of USD255 million.

In reality, it was China that was in charge of both, having given the funds required to the Iraq Drilling Company as a 'fee' for its own participation. Again, this all amounted to an exploration and development programme across the enormous oil field.

It is also extremely apposite to note in this context that Iran and Iraq share many of their major oil reservoirs and that many of the two countries' oilfields are just two parts of these same oil reservoirs.

For example, Iran's Azadegan oil reservoir (split into North and South fields) is exactly the same reservoir upon which sits Iraq's Majnoon oilfield. The same feature applies to Azar (on the Iran side)/Badra (on the Iraq side), Yadavaran (Iran)/Sinbad (Iraq), Naft Shahr (Iran)/Naft Khana (Iraq), Dehloran (Iran)/Abu Ghurab (Iraq), West Paydar (Iran)/Fakka/Fauqa (Iraq), and Arvand (Iran)/South Abu Ghurab (Iraq), plus many others.

The second key aspect associated with China's covert increase in its influence across Iran and Iraq was that it was done in tandem with Russia. After the two big events in the Middle East oil business in 2018 – the unilateral withdrawal of the US from the JCPOA with Iran, and the initial agreements towards what would become the 25-year Iran-China deal – plus the added pressure on China that came from Trump's gradual focus on the

Trade War, the previous loose co-operation between Chinese and Russian efforts in the Middle Eastern oil producing states was firmed up.

Iraq's Massive Oil And Gas Reservoirs, Some Shared With Iran

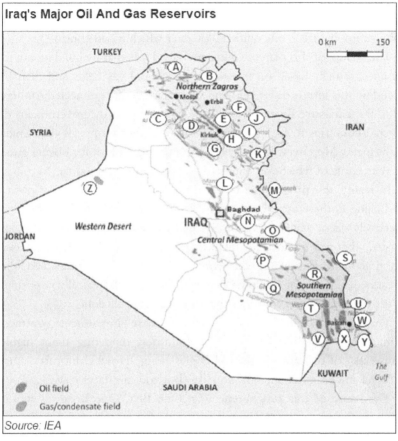

[Chart Key: A = Tawke, B = Shaikan, C (1) = Najma, C (2) = Al Qayyarah, D = Bai Hassan, E = Kirkuk, F = Taq, G = Jambur, H = Khormor, I = ChemChemal, J = Miran, K = Sarqala, L = Mansuriyah, M = Naft Khaneh, N = East Baghdad, O = Badra, P = Ahdab, Q = Gharaf, R = Halfaya, S = Missan Group, T = West Qurna, U = Majnoon, V = Rumaila, W = Nahr Umr, X = Zubair, Y = Siba, Z = Akkas]

For China there were two priorities in this region. The first was to secure as much of the big oil and gas reservoirs in the big Middle Eastern producing countries as it could, in order to drive its economic growth to a level at which its economy was bigger than the US's.

The second was to concomitantly build out its land and sea infrastructure around these sites so that it could move goods quicker (and, therefore, cheaper) to its targeted export destinations, which would further bolster its position as the world's top trading nation too. A crucial adjunct of this latter point was that by building out its land and sea infrastructure in such a way, China could also build out its political power across these regions into, in effect, one unified bloc over which it had control.

The beauty of this plan as China envisaged it is that by building out its presence, initially based on investment in oil and gas fields and then by extending this into broader land and sea infrastructure connected to these fields, these massive financial flows would pre-dispose the governments of targeted countries to look favourably on any other proposals that China might make. Moreover, China could present this build-out as being good for the people of whichever country it was targeting at the time.

In reality, this programme would mean the steady accretion of power for Beijing in these targeted countries to the point at which they became effectively client states of China. If the targeted countries at any point resisted what was planned for them then China would be able to exercise the draconian clauses in the contracts that had accompanied the investments. This would allow Beijing to seize the strategically important parts of those targeted countries that it had wanted all along.

These clauses are central to all of these investment contracts promulgated by China in its target countries, rendering them highly reminiscent of the ethos in the old Eagles' song, 'Hotel California' – that is: 'You can check out any time you like/But you can never leave'.

The name of this programme was 'One Belt, One Road' as it was originally called until the Chinese decided that it sounded a little too colonialist for its public relations campaigns. After all, it was obvious to anyone who looked into it that the 'One Belt' and 'One Road' in question were China's. Therefore, China changed the name of the programme to 'Belt and Road Initiative', which sounds a lot more inclusive, and Beijing did much to ensure that as many media organisations as possible from then on used this new term.

These OBOR deals have been seen in various countries along China's OBOR route, which itself is derived from the old land and maritime 'Silk Road' routes through which China sought to expand its trade and political influence in centuries gone by. One notable recent example of Beijing's modus operandi in this context was Sri Lanka. Here, Beijing began its push by extending unlimited loans to beleaguered former President, Mahinda Rajapaksa, for his Hambantota Port Development Project.

This project – as the Chinese well knew - stood little chance of succeeding as a port and when it failed to generate any significant business and Rajapaksa was voted out of office, the new government was unable to meet the loan repayment demands.

China's 'One Belt, One Road' Multi-Generational Power-Grab Programme

One Belt One Road (And Previous Silk Road) Routes

Source: The Economist Group

At that point, the new Sri Lankan government had little choice but to hand over the port to China (plus 15,000 other acres of surrounding land) for a period of at least 99 years in restitution.

Hambantota may have been useless as a standard port from the money-making perspective, but for China it was of enormous strategic significance, overlooking South Asia's major sea lanes, and allowing it in the future to establish a dual-use (commercial and military) facility for its naval assets.

Exactly the same methodology has been applied elsewhere in the Middle East, from Iran and Iraq to Oman and Saudi Arabia, including many countries in between. These are analysed in depth in the relevant major sections later or in the *'Key Players In The Global Oil Market: China'* section.

For Russia at that time there were also two priorities in the Middle East. The first of these was that although it did not need other countries' oil and gas to power its economic growth, it did want to control as much of their oil and gas flows as possible, in order to increase its power over its own energy customer countries. One such prime target was Europe, over which Russia had developed an extraordinary hold by dint of its gas and oil exports to the region (this is examined in depth in the *'Key Players In The Global Oil Market: Russia'* section).

With Europe dependent on Russia for around 40% of its gas imports, plus another sizeable proportion of its oil imports, Russia was able to leverage this into real political influence across key countries in the region, especially Germany, the effective leader of the European Union (EU) and a key member of NATO. Given this, the possibilities for Russia to cause serious breaches in Europe's cornerstone security relationship with the US – in the shape of the NATO alliance and beyond – were abundant.

Russia did not want this power over Europe to be diminished by the region being able to obtain gas and oil in sizeable quantities from any other major suppliers, and most of these were located in the Middle East.

Before heavy sanctions were reimposed after May 2018 by the US on Iran and any country that traded with it, there had been several major gas and oil projects lined up by European companies in Iran. Even after the US reimposed heavy sanctions, there were many manoeuvres by European governments and companies to circumvent the sanctions and to go ahead with these projects (these are examined in depth in the *'Key Players In The Global Oil Market: Iran'* section).

This was a clear and present danger to Russia's power over Europe, so Russia was extremely determined to engage in deals in the same countries that Europe was looking to for new gas and oil deals, and thereby to have control over where those flows went. Specifically, Russia wanted to prevent them from going into Europe.

Consequently, with much of Europe's focus in the Middle East having fallen on Iran after the signing of the JCPOA on 14 July 2015, Russia moved to secure control over as much of Iran's gas and oil flows as it could, as quickly as possible. Given Iran's influence over neighbouring oil-rich Iraq, Russia could also extend its influence there into the bargain.

Iran, specifically, has an estimated 157 billion barrels of proven crude oil reserves, nearly 10% of the world's total and 13% of those held by OPEC. As great as its oil reserves are, its gas reserves are even greater, with the Islamic Republic having estimated proven natural gas reserves of 1,193 trillion cubic feet (Tcf), second only to Russia, 17% of the world's total and more than one-third of OPEC's.

Russia, aside from holding the world's largest natural gas reserves at 1,688 Tcf, has at least 80 billion barrels of proved oil reserves and has been a top three producer of crude oil for many years. It is easily able to produce at least 10.5 million bpd of petroleum and other liquid fuels.

The full details on the deals done by Russia in Iran are analysed in the '*Key Players In The Global Oil Market: Iran*' section, but the upshot of all of Russia's manoeuvrings was that initial agreements were signed by Russia's Gazprom Neft, the oil-producing subsidiary of state gas giant Gazprom, for feasibility studies for the Changouleh and Cheshmeh-Khosh oilfields; by Zarubezhneft for the Aban and Paydar Gharb fields; and by Tatneft for the Dehloran field. These were on top of the previous memorandum of understanding (MoU) signed by Lukoil and the National Iranian Oil Company for studies of the Ab Teymour and Mansouri oil fields.

This flurry of activity resulted in Russian firms being assigned seven field studies, the most of any country to that point. These deals were only a part of a very wide-ranging 22-point MoU signed by Iran's then-Deputy Petroleum Minister, Amir-Hossein Zamaninia, and Russia's Deputy Energy Minister, Kirill Molodtsov, at the time. This included the transfer of gas, petrochemical swap operations, research on the supply and marketing of petrochemical products, the manufacture of oil equipment together with local Iranian engineering firms, and technology transfer in the refinery sector.

As an adjunct of this, Russia also planned to dramatically expand its operations in neighbouring Iraq, given the sharing of several of the world's major oil reservoirs between Iran and Iraq, as mentioned above. Gazprom Neft announced in late 2020 that it planned to launch a fourth well at the Sarqala field in the Kurdistan region of Iraq (KRI) in the first half of 2021, to begin with.

In addition, Gazprom Neft's deputy general director for exploration and production, Vadim Yakovlev, said: 'We remain interested in exploring new options for development in the region.' Gazprom Neft also held an

80% stake in the neighbouring Shakal block, with the remainder held by the semi-autonomous region of Kurdistan in northern Iraq.

Iran And Iraq Were Still Full Of Potential

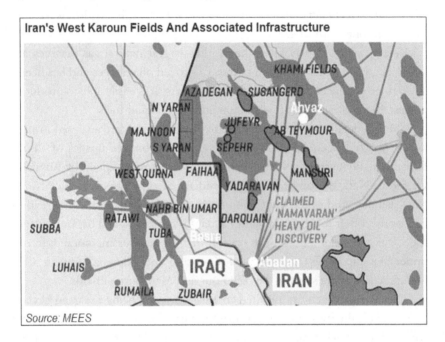

Iran's West Karoun Fields And Associated Infrastructure

Source: MEES

Another key aspect associated with China's stealthy increase in its influence across Iran and Iraq was that it and Russia used the same sort of 'triangular diplomacy' strategy suffused with 'constructive ambiguity' language tactics that Henry Kissinger had made the basis of US strategy in the Middle East since the 1973 Oil Crisis.

In the case of Iran, both China and Russia used the threat of Saudi Arabia, and for Saudi Arabia they used the threat of Iran, with further details in the relevant major sections on these countries later in this book.

For Iraq, there were already very strong fault lines that could be exploited by China and Russia, although as Russia was so much further ahead in its on-the-ground presence in Iraq than China, Beijing agreed that Moscow should continue to take the lead there at that point.

Specifically, the fault line across Iraq – which had also been exploited by the US in its fight against Islamic State from 2014 to early 2018 – was to do with the Kurdish population in the north of the country.

Crucially in this context, it was not just Iraq that had a sizeable population of Kurdish people (around 18%). Iran, Turkey and Syria each had very sizeable Kurdish populations of their own: about 15%, 18% and 16% respectively. Additionally crucial was that the Kurdish people had long been promised a recognised independent state of their own. The most recent assurance at that point had come from US and its key allies, including the UK and France, just after ISIS (Islamic State of Iraq and Syria) had driven Iraqi security forces out of several key cities during the Anbar campaign of 2014.

Wishing to galvanise the Iraqis and its Middle Eastern supporters to meaningfully deal with the problem themselves, and to avoid a recurrence of the images of dead Western troops on television that had precipitated the US withdrawal from the Vietnam War, the Western allies had used the fearsome Kurdish Peshmerga forces to provide 'boots on the ground presence' in the fight against ISIS. In return, the Kurds had received a heavy 'nod and a wink' assurance from the West that they would gain their independent Kurdistan after the fight against ISIS had been won.

Given the likelihood that the granting of a separate Kurdistan state in what had been northern Iraq would lead to similar calls from the large Kurdish populations in Iran, Turkey and Syria, the assurances that had been given to the northern Iraq Kurds were quickly renegued upon once the threat from ISIS had been largely dealt with.

A hangover from these assurances was that the Kurdish people in northern Iraq had been granted a referendum on independence, although the vote had been carefully worded so as not to be legally binding. The referendum, which took place on 25 September 2017 saw 93% of the Kurds in Iraq's northern Kurdish region vote for independence.

The reaction to the vote from Iraq, Iran, and Turkey was draconian, as analysed in the *'Key Players In The Global Oil Market: Iraq'* section and was aimed at stopping any such move to independence in Iraq and in other countries with large Kurdish populations in its tracks, which it did.

However, the opportunity to exploit this massive fault line was not lost on Russia, which offered to sweeten the bitter pill of the Kurdish people in Iraq in not gaining independence from Baghdad by giving them huge funding for various projects to be led by Russian state oil giant, Rosneft. This financing would also help the northern Iraq Kurds in dealing with Baghdad over the perennially thorny issue of disbursements of budget payments from Baghdad to Erbil, the capital of the semi-autonomous region of Kurdistan, in exchange for oil from the region.

Russia's financing for the Kurds in northern Iraq, as disbursed to the government of the region (the KRG) meant that the Kremlin's corporate oil proxy, Rosneft, effectively took over the ownership of Kurdistan's oil sector in 2017 through three principal means.

First, Russia provided the KRG with USD1.5 billion in financing through forward oil sales payable in the next three to five years. Second, it took an 80% working interest in five potentially major oil blocks in the region together with corollary investment and technical and equipment assistance. And third, it established 60% ownership of the vital KRG pipeline through a commitment to invest USD1.8 billion to increase its capacity to one million barrels per day.

At that point, Moscow considered itself well-placed to leverage this presence into a similarly powerful position in the south of the country, in particular by striking new oil and gas field exploration and development deals with Baghdad. This was tangential to Russia's role in intermediating in the dispute between Kurdistan and the Federal Government of Iraq in Baghdad on the budget disbursements-for-oil deal.

Having gained enormous influence in the very centre of the Middle East – Iran and Iraq – in a very short time while the US had focused in on itself, China and Russia quickly began to use these countries as leverage to extend their influence elsewhere across the region, particularly in the other big oil player in the area, Saudi Arabia. This is analysed in full in the 'Key Players In The Global Oil Market: Saudi Arabia' section.

Trump Tries To Regain Ground With 'Normalisation' Deals

Whilst China and Russia had been busy expanding their influence into Middle Eastern countries most receptive to their combined mix of economic and military incentives, Iran continued to increase its uranium enrichment capabilities.

This process had picked up pace in Iran since the US's 2018 withdrawal from the JCPOA and is analysed in depth in the 'Key Players In The Global Oil Market: Iran' section. However, the salient point here was that Washington's key ally in the Middle East, Israel, had become increasingly sure that Iran was no longer 'years' away from being able to create a nuclear weapon but rather just 'weeks' away – around three weeks away, in fact.

The US And Israel Knew Iran's Growing Nuclear Threat

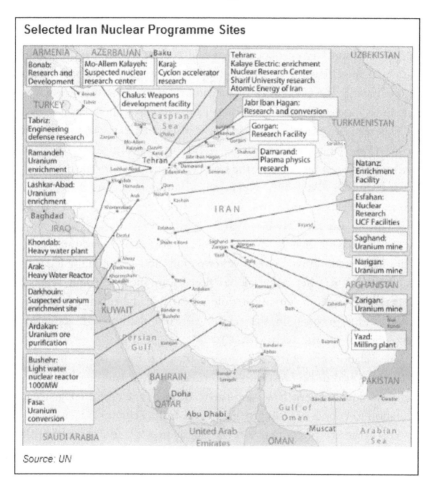

Selected Iran Nuclear Programme Sites

Source: UN

In several conversations with Trump it was made very clear by Israel that if the US did not do something to halt this progress – and, if nothing else, the JCPOA had at least allowed the US a means to try to do this – then Israel would take matters into its own hands. Israel had already undertaken several covert missions – under the level that denoted outright war – to delay Iran's progress towards being nuclear weapon ready.

The US knew that any escalation by Israel against Iran, over and above what it had been doing, could well be a catalyst for a broadening and deepening of the conflict across the entire Middle East, which could eventually draw China and Russia into the conflict, in direct opposition to the US. This was a conflict scenario in war planning on all sides that almost inevitably led to global nuclear war.

Those around Trump knew what had been happening in the Middle East since the US withdrawal from the JCPOA in 2018 in particular and to counterbalance the US's loss influence in key countries in the region – and to help to appease Israel as well - they had come up with a plan.

This plan became clear on 13 August 2020 when it was announced that Israel and the United Arab Emirates (UAE) would normalise relations in a deal that had been brokered by the US. This coincided with the then-Israeli Prime Minister Benjamin Netanyahu's announcement that he was suspending plans to annex more areas of the West Bank that Israel had seized during the 1967 Six Day War.

Intelligence alliances in the Middle East are often even more fluid in their interpretation than in many other regions and although the UAE had dealt with all of the major global powers in the preceding years, its overriding concern from the middle of 2018 had been Iran's growing power and aggression in the region as exercised through its Islamic Revolutionary Guard Corps (IRGC).

The relationship normalisation deal that the UAE signed in August 2020, then, had in one respect just formalised what had been happening for some time between Israel and the UAE in the field of intelligence co-operation to counteract this growing threat from Tehran.

This structure of cooperation was augmented by another relationship normalisation deal in the Middle East between Israel and Bahrain on 11 September 2020, and two further deals in Africa, with Morocco in December 2020 and with Sudan in January 2021.

The US hope had been that Saudi Arabia – Iran's longstanding rival in the region – might publicly signal its support for the relationship normalisation deals initiative and eventually make such a deal itself after MbS succeeded to the throne. This fitted in with the widely held view that the Crown Prince was far more sympathetic to the agreement than his father, King Salman.

An indication that such a deal with Saudi Arabia might take place came when Saudi's Foreign Minister, Prince Faisal bin Farhan, cautiously welcomed the Israel-UAE agreement, saying: 'It could be viewed as positive.' It is also apposite to note that back in 2002 it had been the Saudis who had launched the 'Crown Prince Abdullah Peace Plan' at the Beirut Arab summit, offering Israel full recognition in exchange for a return to its pre-1967 borders.

However, at that time the outlook for a second term for President Trump looked uncertain and caution prevailed in Saudi Arabia over aligning itself too strongly to the ethos of the new relationship normalisation deals.

In part, this was to have been expected as Saudi's clerical establishment retains a very powerful role in the Kingdom: each Saudi king is also the custodian of the two holy mosques, and Saudi Arabia was the founder of the Organization of the Islamic Conference (OIC). Additionally, King Salman had told the OIC as recently as 2019 that the Palestinian cause remained a core issue and that the kingdom, 'refuses any measures that touch the historical and legal position of East Jerusalem.'

The UAE's Key Roles In The US's New Middle East Order

Aside from the plans to use the UAE's capabilities as an intelligence conduit for Israel and the US, Washington also saw other advantages in having the UAE tied into the broad relationship normalisation deals framework that it intended to build out in the region.

One of these was the plethora of ports and storage facilities spread across the UAE's seven constituent emirates of Abu Dhabi, Ajman, Dubai, Fujairah, Ras Al Khaimah, Sharjah, and Umm Al Quwain.

Fujairah in particular was recognised as having an extremely strategically advantageous position to deal with any potential oil supply disruptions that might come from the increasingly aggressive Iran after the withdrawal of the US from the JCPOA in 2018.

Located both outside the Persian Gulf and a healthy 160 kilometres from the Strait of Hormuz, Fujairah was also seen as unaligned to any possibly pro-Iranian country, such as Oman, which at that time was considering plans to cooperate with Tehran's planned build-out of a world-scale liquefied natural gas (LNG) sector.

Fujairah's Strategic Position Away From The Strait Of Hormuz

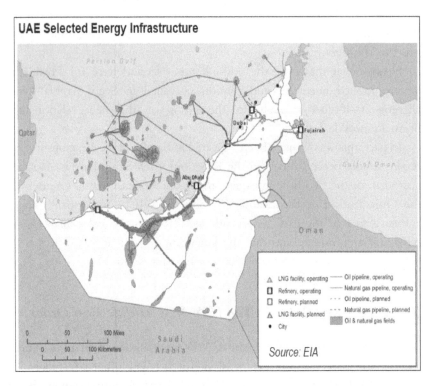

UAE Selected Energy Infrastructure

Source: EIA

Various stages of Fujairah's expansion plans were subject to delays prior to the onset of the major downturn in global oil prices in 2020, due to lower forward oil prices making hydrocarbons storage a less attractive option. However, each element of the project to make Fujairah the pre-eminent Middle Eastern storage hub – termed 'Black Pearl' – gradually came into line.

The pace of this process notably picked up after the 380-kilometre Abu Dhabi Crude Oil Pipeline from the Habshan onshore field in Abu Dhabi to Fujairah city became operational in June 2012. This pipeline would be capable of transporting 1.8 million bpd of oil and allowing for the smooth movement of UAE crude into the global market.

At that time, Fujairah also expedited the rolling out of a wide range of the corollary services required in a global storage hub. These included facilities for the loading and discharge of partially laden very large crude carriers (VLCCs) for crude oil and refined products, the blending of crude oil, fuel oil and clean products, the storage and supply of bunker fuel, and inter- and intra-tank cargo transfer.

Within a relatively short time, the Fujairah port's jetties had the capacity to accommodate both small barge vessels – 3,000 deadweight tonnage (DWT) - and the larger VLCCs (up to 300,000 DWT). In 2015, Vopak Horizon Fujairah also announced that it was building five crude oil storage tanks with total capacity of 478,000 cubic metres at the port and intended to increase that number.

Another part of the positive backdrop for the continued expansion of the Fujairah hub was expected to be the trade flows coming out of the Dubai Multi-Commodities Centre, with more storage capacity allowing traders greater flexibility in their deals, and a very supportive financial infrastructure created by the Fujairah authorities. This proved to the case and Fujairah was also seen as likely to benefit from the continued rise in volumes traded over the Abu Dhabi-based ICE Futures Abu Dhabi (IFAD) platform. The IFAD focused on the trading of futures contracts for the light, sweet Murban crude oil that constituted around half of the UAE's total near-4 million bpd crude oil production before the outbreak of the COVID-19 pandemic in 2020.

The importance of finding alternative transit routes for global oil increased again as the finalisation of Iran's own game-changing crude oil storage, transport and delivery mechanism - the Jask Oil Terminal and the 42-inch Guriyeh-Jask pipeline - drew nearer. These developments are analysed in depth in the *'Key Players In The Global Oil Market: Iran'* section.

The significance of the new Iranian crude oil export terminal could barely be overstated. It was built to enable Iran to transport huge quantities of oil and petrochemicals from its major oil fields via Guriyeh in the Shoaybiyeh-ye Gharbi Rural District of Khuzestan Province, 1,100 kilometres to Jask port in Hormozgan province, which is perfectly strategically placed on the Gulf of Oman.

At the same time, the Guriyeh-Jask pipeline would allow Tehran the option of disrupting all other oil supplies that travelled through the Strait of Hormuz - around 35% of the world's total. In this context, the extreme narrowness of the Strait of Hormuz means that oil tankers have to travel very slowly through it, so pushing up the transit costs and delaying revenue streams. It also means that it is relatively easy to disrupt the flow of oil through it, as the tankers carrying the oil can be attacked either by other ships in the Strait or from the shoreline.

It was precisely due to such an incident, the 2011/12 Strait of Hormuz Dispute, that the once fanciful notion of Fujairah becoming one of the world's great oil storage and trading hubs - alongside the Far East's Singapore hub, Europe's ARA (Amsterdam-Rotterdam-Antwerp), and the US's Cushing - gained real momentum. This Dispute began in December 2011 when Iran threatened to cut off oil supply through the Strait should economic sanctions limit, or halt, Iranian oil exports, and it included a 10-day military exercise in international waters near the chokepoint.

Another advantage for the US in having the UAE embedded in its relationship normalisation deals alliance was that the country had sizeable oil and gas reserves in its own right. These could be utilised to compensate in part for the loss of supplies from countries in the region that were shifting into the China-Russia sphere of influence.

ADNOC Output To Be Supercharged By Normalisation Deal

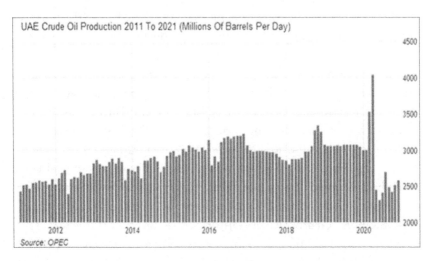

At around the same time as the relationship normalisation deal with the UAE was announced, the Abu Dhabi National Oil Co (ADNOC) – announced massive new oil discoveries, a huge new investment programme, and received the go-ahead to award major oil and gas exploration blocks.

These developments looked set to enable the company to reach and then surpass its new 5 million bpd oil output target. This, in turn, was central to a new corridor of cooperation being developed from the US (and Israel), through the UAE (and Kuwait, Bahrain and, in part, Saudi Arabia) to India, as a regional counterbalance to China's growing sphere of influence.

According to the UAE's Supreme Petroleum Council (SPC) at that time, 22 billion stock tank barrels (STB) of recoverable unconventional onshore oil resources had been discovered by ADNOC, plus another 2 billion STB in recoverable conventional oil reserves. These new discoveries would mean that the UAE's recoverable conventional oil reserves would rise to 107 billion STB, on a level with the best US shale oil plays. The UAE's oil output was set for a boost, even beyond this, with the SPC approving AED448 billion (USD122 billion) of new investments by ADNOC over the next five years from that point.

In order to generate the funding for this volume expansion, the US was confident that the UAE would strike deals that would heavily involve US and US-allied firms. This would have been in line with the USD10 billion+ that ADNOC had earlier secured from a consortium of international investors by selling a 49% stake in its gas pipelines a year after striking a similar transaction for its oil pipelines. ADNOC had also secured a USD5 billion+ deal a year earlier with a similarly constituted group of heavy-hitting US financial companies, including BlackRock and KKR.

ADNOC had also announced, in tandem with the aforementioned new discoveries and investments, that it had received the required permissions from the SPC to proceed with the awarding of five potentially big oil and gas blocks as part of its second competitive bidding round that was launched in May 2019. The five blocks – Offshore Block 3, Offshore Block 4, Offshore Block 5, Onshore Block 5 and Onshore Block 2 (which had two separate licensing awards available – one for conventional, the other for unconventional) covered an area of around 34,000 square kilometres.

The first round of these concession awards that ended in March 2019 had featured a consortium led by Italy's ENI and Thailand's PTT Exploration and Production Public Co. for Offshore Block 1 and Offshore Block 2. Onshore Block 1 was awarded to India's Bharat Petroleum Corp.

and the Indian Oil Corp., Onshore Block 3 was awarded to the US's Occidental Petroleum, and Onshore Block 4 was awarded to Japan's INPEX Corp.

The US Saw The UAE-India Alliance As Key To Its Counter-China Policy

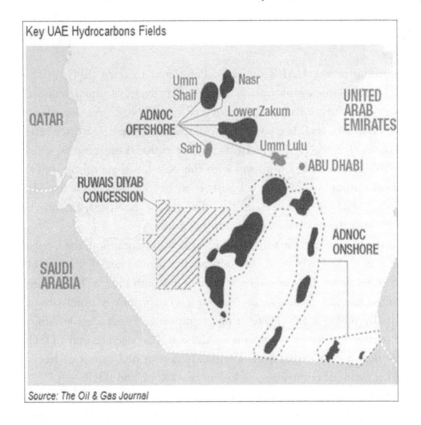

Key UAE Hydrocarbons Fields

Source: The Oil & Gas Journal

ADNOC's chief executive officer, Sultan al-Jaber, stressed at the time that he looked forward to exploring partnerships with even more Indian companies across the energy giant's hydrocarbon value chain.

Alongside all of this, and seemingly in line with removing any undue obstacles to ADNOC achieving its 5 million bpd crude oil production target by 2030, Abu Dhabi's ruler, Sheikh Khalifa bin Zayed Al Nahyan, issued a decree late in 2020 to re-organise the SPC. The organisation was to be transformed into a more oil- and economy-friendly Supreme Council for Financial and Economic Affairs, chaired by Abu Dhabi Crown Prince Mohamed bin Zayed, who was formerly the vice-chairman of the SPC.

Crucially as far as new oil projects and corollary financing were concerned, according to the notes accompanying the decree: 'The law also stipulates that the Supreme Petroleum Council's regulatory powers will be merged with those of the new council and its members will continue to exercise their role as ADNOC's board members until a new board of directors is appointed.'

It added that: 'The council's methodology allows the boards of concerned authorities the corporate autonomy to develop their strategies to be approved by the council, and the independence to develop, approve and implement their annual plans.'

In short, the US believed that the new version of the SPC would make quicker, bolder and more financially-savvy decisions than the previous version. This augured well for several crude oil production-boosting initiatives that were key to ADNOC's ambitious crude oil production plans. It was, in turn, a key to the US's plans to create a viable counterpoint to aggressive Chinese and Russian expansion in the Middle East.

India's Vital Role As A Rival To China In The US Plan

A clash between military units of the two great Asian powers – China and India – on 15 June 2020 in the disputed territory of the Galwan Valley in the Himalayas reflected a much greater change in the core relationship between the two countries than the relatively small number of casualties might have implied. It marked a new 'push back' strategy from India against China's policy of seeking to increase its economic and military alliances from Asia through the Middle East and into Southern Europe, in line with its multi-layered multi-generational OBOR project.

Until China dramatically upped the tempo of this OBOR-related policy – at around the same time as the US signalled its own lack of interest in continuing its large-scale activities in the Middle East (through its withdrawal from the JCPOA and its withdrawal from much of Syria) – India had stuck to a policy of trying to contain China. With the announcement in August 2020 of the US-brokered Israel-UAE relationship normalisation deal it appeared that a new corridor of cooperation was being developed from the US (and Israel), through the UAE (and Kuwait, Bahrain and in part Saudi Arabia) through to India.

Given that much of China's turbo-driven expansion into the Middle East was predicated in the first instance on the energy sector, the starting point for the build-out of the US-Israel-UAE-India corridor also appeared to focus on that same sector. This made additional sense as the oil industry more than most other industries involves activities that countries wish to conduct quietly. These include the movement of money, ships, equipment, technology and personnel of any type – including intelligence and military operatives - who can pass as high-level oil technicians, security people, or other roles connected broadly to the energy industry.

India And China Rivalry Was Set To Increase

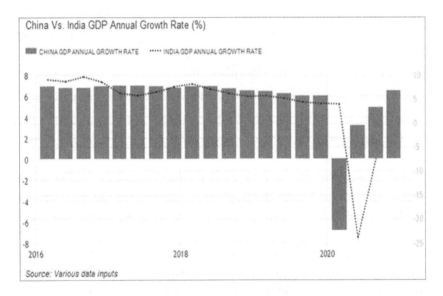

China Vs. India GDP Annual Growth Rate (%)

Source: Various data inputs

In this context, shortly after the announcement on 13 August 2020 of the US-Israel-UAE relationship normalisation deal, it was also stated that the three countries agreed to cooperate in the fields of oil and gas and 'related technologies'. This term - as China and Russia know from their activities in Iran, Iraq and Syria - could mean absolutely anything at all.

In the Abu Dhabi National Oil Co, the US thought it had an ideal corporate proxy to advance such broader policy and power projection all the way up to China's border through increased co-operation with India. At that time, ADNOC – the UAE's biggest energy producer and OPEC's third-largest oil producer – was pumping around 4 million bpd of crude oil and was aiming to increase this output by at least another 1 million bpd by 2030 at the latest. It was also looking to increase its gas output as well.

With this initiative moving forward and given the US endgame in securing India as a direct counterbalance to China in Asia, the last piece of the puzzle appeared to be moving into place in 2020/2021. ADNOC's chief executive officer, Sultan al-Jaber, stated that he looked forward to exploring partnerships with even more Indian companies across the energy giant's hydrocarbon value chain. He added that he wanted this to include expanding the commercial scale and scope of India's vitally-important strategic petroleum reserves (SPR) partnership, in line with ADNOC being the only overseas company allowed at that stage to hold and store the country's SPR.

India's government at that stage approved a proposal that would allow ADNOC to export oil from the SPR if there was no domestic demand for it. In the first instance this would be done from the Mangalore strategic storage facility, with the other major SPR pool being at Padur. This decision marked a major shift in the policy of India in the handling of these vital energy reserves, with the country having previously banned all oil exports from the SPR storage facilities.

A further sign of this relationship between the UAE and India moving up a gear was the likelihood of ADNOC being 'top of the list' of foreign companies that would be considered for the purchase of a substantial stake in the high-profile privatisation of major Indian refiner, Bharat Petroleum. Russian state corporate proxy, Rosneft, had expressed an interest in buying the Indian government's 53.29% in the company as recently as the middle of 2020 - following a visit to New Delhi by Rosneft's chief executive officer, Igor Sechin – but these overtures were side-lined by India.

Given the then-low oil price environment and low demand for a range of refined products, it might have been thought that buying a refining-centric operation would not appeal to many companies. However, as far as the UAE was concerned, it would have fitted well not just into the broader geopolitical manoeuvring that was going on but also – commercially – into the slew of deals being planned with Indian companies in the UAE.

This was underlined by al-Jabber at the end of 2020 when he said: 'Today, Indian companies represent some of Abu Dhabi's key concession and exploration partners… [and…] As we continue to work together, I see significant new opportunities for enhanced partnerships, particularly across our downstream portfolio.' He added: 'We have launched an ambitious plan to expand our chemicals, petrochemicals, derivatives and industrial base in Abu Dhabi and I look forward to exploring partnerships with even more Indian companies across our hydrocarbon value chain.'

This longer-term view accorded with the outlook given at around the same time by India's minister of petroleum and natural gas, Dharmendra Pradhan, who stated that India's demand for refined products was expected to rise dramatically, requiring a 40% increase in its refining capacity to 350 million tonnes a year, or 7 million bpd, by 2030. Part of the policy to accommodate this increase was the plan to build a 1.2 million bpd refinery and petrochemical plant on India's west coast through a joint venture comprised of Indian state refiners and ADNOC.

The final push for this series of announcements indicating an even deeper relationship developing between the UAE and India might have come from the unscheduled visit in September 2020 of India's defence minister, Rajnath Singh, to Iran where he met his Iranian counterpart, Brigadier General Amir Hatami. This visit in large part focused on India trying to establish exactly what the true scope of the 25-year deal between China and Iran was and, more immediately for Indian security and financing, how it would impact on the long-running development of Iran's Chabahar Port.

The beginning of 2018 had seen Iran's then-premier, Hassan Rouhani, and his Indian counterpart, Narendra Modi, sign an agreement that gave operational control of the Shahid Beheshti Port (one of the two port segments of the key Chabahar Port development project, the other being Shahid Kalantri) to India for an initial period of 18 months. This marked a major operational advance on the strategically crucial development that would allow Iran easier access to its top priority markets of Asia, and India to finally make substantive progress on its 'Neighbourhood First' policy as an alternative to China's 'One Belt, One Road' initiative.

Also crucial for India was that Chabahar Port was the most obvious transit alternative to the China-built and operated Gwadar Port in Pakistan, just 75 kilometres away, which was the key departure point in the China-Pakistan Economic Corridor. However, no reassurances were made by Hatami to Singh that the Chabahar Port project would continue to be regarded as primarily an India-led development and the intimation was that China would be taking the lead role from that point.

India's role as the US counterpoint to China in the Asia-Pacific region, led by its economic development and the corollary development of its demand for oil and gas, was further underlined by data released in the first quarter of 2021 by the IEA. This showed that India would make up the biggest share of energy demand growth - at 25% - over the next two decades, as it overtook the European Union as the world's third-biggest energy consumer by 2030.

India Was Concerned What Iran's Deal With China Might Mean For It

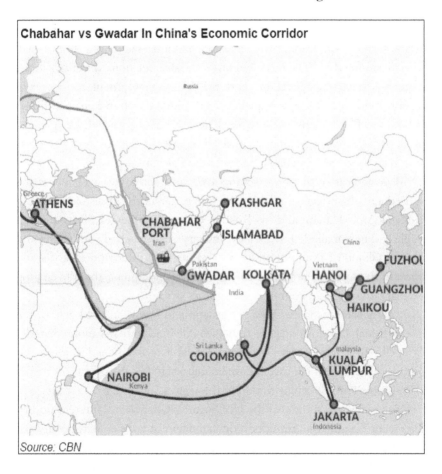

India's energy consumption was expected to nearly double as the nation's GDP expanded to an estimated USD8.6 trillion by 2040 under its national policy scenario. This was underpinned by a rate of GDP growth that added the equivalent of another Japan to the world economy by 2040, according to the IEA.

Iran's Reaction To The Relationship Normalisation Deals

Given the obvious opportunities for increased intelligence-gathering and economic and political disruption within Iran's borders stemming from the Israel-UAE deal in particular, Iran was extremely hostile to it.

Iranian Parliament Speaker's then-Special Aide for International Affairs, Amir-Abdollahian, made a very public show shortly after the announcement of meeting with Palestine's Ambassador to Tehran, Salah Zavavi, stating that: 'The UAE's act to normalise relations with the Zionist regime is a strategic mistake, and the UAE government must accept responsibility for all its consequences.' He added that Iran remained firmly behind the Palestinians. Meanwhile, Palestine's Zavavi asked the speakers of all parliaments of Islamic countries to condemn the action of the UAE and to support the inalienable rights of the Palestinian people.

More indicative of future actions over and above just words was the subsequent high-level meeting of Iran's Defence Minister Brigadier General Amir Hatami and his Russian counterpart Sergey Shoygu. Even publicly, Hatami alluded to the new military deals reached with China and Russia, talking of the joint strategic, regional and international goals and interests between Tehran and Moscow, and underlining the 'developing mutual defence co-operation' between the two sides.

Hatami then castigated the US's attempts to invoke a 'snapback' of full international sanctions against Iran through the United Nations Security Council. 'In recent years, Iran and Russia have launched a joint and purposeful effort to counter the unilateralism and bullying policies of the US and the Trump administration in the region,' he noted.

'The realistic response of the UN Security Council and the rejection of the recent US anti-Iran resolution on extension of arms embargoes against Iran, once again brought a major defeat for the US and its regional allies and proved the global opposition to unilateralism,' he underlined.

With this new US-sponsored Israel-UAE relationship normalisation deal then in place, the IRGC (with the blessing of Supreme Leader Ali Khamenei) was fully set to allow the presence of Chinese and Russia naval assets in and around Iran's key ports at Chabahar, Bandar-e-Bushehr and Bandar Abbas.

This was in line with the military element of the 25-Year Comprehensive Cooperation Agreement between China and Iran. Such provisions were also part of the rolling 10-year agreement between Iran and Russia at the time. The military elements of both of the Iran-China and the Iran-Russia deals are analysed in full in the *'Key Players In The Global Oil Market: Iran'* section.

China's Responds By Expanding Its Presence In Iraq

At the end of 2020/beginning of 2021, shortly after the second relationship normalisation deal with a Middle Eastern country, Bahrain, had been signed, China decided to use the same strategy in southern Iraq that Russia had used in the northern Kurdistan region.

The Russians had used an initial massive flow of financing, through a huge prepayment deal for oil, as the first step in effectively taking control of the Kurdistan Region of Iraq's oil industry. Mirroring this, China's Zhenhua Oil signed a USD2 billion five–year prepayment oil supply deal with the Federal Government of Iraq (FGI) in Baghdad.

This development was extremely troubling for Washington for three key reasons. First, was that the deal was straight out of the playbook that Russia had used to gain control over Iraq's semi-autonomous northern region of Kurdistan in 2017, as analysed above.

Second, it was clear that the degree of strategic cooperation between China and Russia in the Middle East had continued to increase. The 2017 agreement between Russia's Rosneft and the government of Kurdistan meant that Moscow was able to cause such disruption in the budget payments-for-oil deal between Kurdistan and Baghdad that the resultant financial crunch for the FGI pre-disposed Baghdad to look beneficially at the China proposal in the first place.

This increased cooperation appeared to imply an endgame for China and Russia that envisaged them carving up the Middle East after the withdrawal in large part of the longstanding military, economic, and political presence across several of its countries by the US.

The third reason that China's new drive in the Middle East was troubling for the US at that point was that it meant that China was directly testing the then-incoming President Joe Biden's ability to separate trade considerations from security considerations – as Trump frequently traded the latter off for the former – to see what the new US president's reaction would be. This was particularly apposite in the newest prepayment deal for the FGI in Baghdad, as Zhenhua Oil was well-known as an arm of China's huge defence contractor Norinco.

Looking in more depth at the Russian Kurdistan deal as a comparison point for the new China-FGI deal - and as a leverage point through which the deal was in a position to be struck - from the moment that Russia had gained control in Kurdistan it began to create problems for the FGI in southern Iraq, particularly focused on the budget disbursements for oil deal, as alluded to above.

China Saw Iraq's Huge Potential

Iraq Oil Resources By Region And Supergiant Field (in Billion Barrels)					
	Proven reserves, end-2017	Ultimately recoverable resources	Cumulative production, end-2017	Remaining recoverable resources	Remaining % of URR
Southern Mesopotamian	113	164	25	139	85%
West Qurna	47	55	3	53	95%
Rumaila	17	35	16	19	55%
Majnoon	13	15	1	15	96%
Zubair	7	11	3	8	70%
Central Mesopotamian	13	19	0	18	98%
East Baghdad	9	10	0	10	98%
Northern Zagros Fold Belt	23	62	19	42	69%
Kirkuk	7	25	16	8	34%
Western Desert	0	1	0	1	100%
Total Iraq	149	246	45	201	82%

Note: Proven reserves are approximately broken down by basin, based on information provided by the Iraqi Ministry of Oil, supplemented with company presentations. Figures include crude oil and natural gas liquids. URR = ultimately recoverable resources

Source: IEA

Having taken over control of the Kirkuk oil fields from Kurdish forces in October 2017, following rioting after Baghdad failed to recognise the 'yes' vote on independence referendum in September 2017, the Federal Government of Iraq found itself dependent on the regional government of the Kurdish region, as the Kurds possessed the only operational export pipeline (to Turkey's port of Ceyhan) for oil into southern Europe out of Iraq.

This, in turn, had been a recurrent major contributing factor in Baghdad's subsequent financial troubles, which were again approaching a potentially catastrophic point in August 2020 when the then-new Prime Minister, Mustafa al-Kadhimi, had to visit Washington to ask for funding.

Given the financial chaos that Russia created for Baghdad by using its own 2017 oil prepayments deal with the KRG and the political schism it had created between Baghdad and Washington, al-Kadhimi's only realistic route forward was either Russia or China.

As Russia was already politically occupied in northern Iraq, and China already had a 25-year multi-generational deal with Iraq's key sponsor – Iran – it was China that clearly felt best positioned at the end of 2020/beginning of 2021 to attempt to sequestrate southern Iraq.

This was helped in China's case by the fact that, unlike Russia, Beijing already had a long history of getting around pesky US sanctions on any country. The previous most notable occasion that it had dramatically gone its own way was in 2012 when the US tried to sanction the massive state-owned oil trading firm Zhuhai Zhenrong Corp.

It was a company that had been founded by the man who had started oil trading between Beijing and Tehran in 1995 as a means by which Iran could pay for arms supplied by China for use in the Iran-Iraq war. Consequently, it was not particularly susceptible from warnings or sanctions from the US and the company flatly refused to toe the US line on China's dealings in southern Iraq as well. IOC Sinopec, Asia's biggest oil refiner, also took no notice of repeated warnings from the US, having little or no exposure to it.

This highlighted a key factor at play in China, and not in Russia, which was the relative lack of exposure of China's firms to the US financial infrastructure (particularly to the US dollar). China also benefited in this context from the ease with which its companies could create new special purpose vehicles to handle ring-fenced areas of their businesses to operate normally, despite US sanctions.

Although the deal agreed at the end of 2020/beginning of 2021 between Baghdad and Zhenhua Oil – according to the original letter sent out by Iraq's State Organization for Marketing of Oil (SOMO) – stated that the initial upfront payment would be for one year's worth of oil, the prepayment period for 4 million barrels a month was for five years in total.

This suited China well, not just in terms of securing energy supplies for that long but also more importantly for securing even more political influence with Iran's neighbour - a key stepping-stone in its One Belt, One Road programme. It also tested how resolutely incoming US President Biden would stick to his initial China plan, as analysed in depth in the *'Key Players In The Global Oil Market: The US'* section.

US's President Biden Positively Surprises On China

Surprisingly to those who had found it difficult to imagine Joe Biden in the leading role of president rather than in the supporting one of vice president that he had held for eight years previously, the new incumbent of the White House at the beginning of January 2021 made a positive start on several issues.

The most pressing of these at that time was China, and Biden made his new administration's position clear to Beijing at the June 2021 G7 Summit in the UK. At the meeting, Biden received the backing of the world's seven largest advanced economies (comprised of the US, the UK, Germany, France, Italy, Canada and Japan) to set up an alternative to China's OBOR initiative as part of a broad pushback against Beijing's increasing influence around the globe. This initiative was in line with Biden's correctly grouping China together with Russia in the context of both the Middle East and Asia during his presidential election campaign and stating that he regarded China as a 'serious competitor' to the US and Russia as an 'opponent'.

The broad approach of the Biden team to China in his early presidency approximated the highly trade-centric policies of predecessor Donald Trump to ensure that Beijing continued to move in the direction of an equitable trade policy with the US, not the imbalanced one that had endured for so long.

However, a key difference between the two men's approaches – especially as it pertained to the growing security questions surrounding China's activities in the Middle East – was that Biden would not 'give up security considerations for trade' as Trump frequently did, according to Trump's former National Security Adviser John Bolton.

For China's leadership – much like that of Iran – the idea of a Biden presidency had long been anticipated as offering a much easier ride than that of former President Trump. China had decided to do very little except the bare minimum to keep Trump from increasing sanctions in the final few months of his presidency for the very same reason that Iran stayed in the JCPOA – that is, hoping that Trump would lose and a softer Democrat would become president.

China was very aware that Trump was extremely concerned with the optics of the US-China Trade War and not with the substance of how those negotiations were progressing. Therefore, Beijing tailored all of its so-called concessions to being the sort of things that in practice were meaningless, but which would allow Trump to make various victory-sounding tweets.

Biden's China Inheritance From Trump

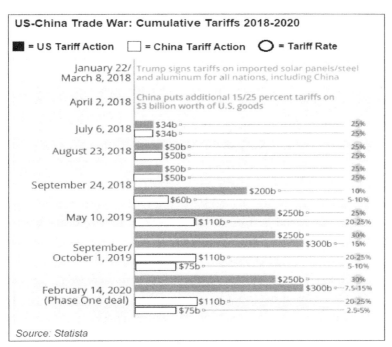

All the way through Trump's presidency, though, China benefited both from Trump's almost schoolgirl-type crush on China President Xi Jinping (along with a similar infatuation with other strongmen leaders, including Russia President Vladimir Putin and Turkey's Recep Erdogan) and from

Trump's erroneous conflation of two completely distinct sets of policies: security and trade, which was virtually unheard-of for US presidents.

An early notable case in point had been the almost complete reversal of hard-hitting US sanctions imposed on Chinese telecommunications company ZTE for committing major and repeated violations of the US's sanctions on Iran and on North Korea, as briefly mentioned earlier.

According to Bolton, after a private telephone call to President Xi – in which it later transpired that Xi told Trump that he would 'owe [Trump] a favour' if he reduced the sanctions against ZTE – Trump did exactly what Xi had asked for: selling security considerations for trade. Trump tweeted: 'President Xi of China and I are working together to give massive Chinese phone company, ZTE, a way to get back into business, fast. Too many jobs in China lost. Commerce Department has been instructed to get it done!' As Bolton wrote: 'Since when had we started to worry about jobs in China?'

Exactly the same methodology of personally flattering Trump and then offering him some vague commitment on China's part to buy more of some product or another from the US was again used by Xi to hold off Trump from imposing quick, full and irreversible sanctions on another Chinese intelligence operation working under the guise of a telecoms corporation, Huawei.

The new Biden government also focused on trade considerations but did so having made clear to China that there was no similar opportunity for Beijing to parlay such vague commercial considerations on China's part into concrete security rollbacks on the US's part. More importantly, the Biden team also made it clear that addressing the trade imbalance between the US and China would be front and centre of all Biden's dealings with China and that security considerations and other foreign policy decisions would be dealt with separately, with no crossover between the issues.

More specifically, at the outset of Biden's first term there were three key items related to China at the top of the agenda. First, US companies would no longer be allowed to sign any contracts with Chinese companies that included any element of sharing technology. For decades, the Chinese had insisted that any US company that wanted to do business with China must share its technology with its Chinese partner, including the likes of General Electric, Westinghouse and Ford, among many others.

This had allowed China to systematically reverse engineer everything that was shared and then to re-sell China-made versions back to the US and the rest of the world at much lower prices, given the much lower unit cost of labour in China than in the US. The practice had been one of the keys to the creation of such huge trade surpluses for China and deficits for everyone else.

The second major item on Biden's agenda at that point was to seek to redress that imbalance, with his team looking to introduce a new metric for China that would create a 'long-term steady-state equilibrium in trade', as there had been with Japan when it had operated basically the same economic model in the 1960s and 1970s.

A Long Way To Go On Redressing The Trade Imbalance

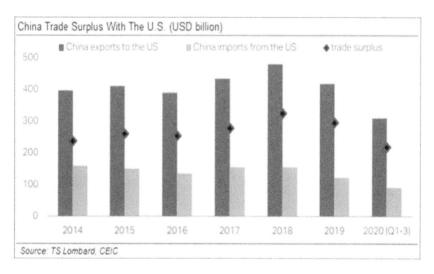

This new approach was to be focused on correcting the long-term bilateral structural trade imbalance that had existed between the US and China for decades. This imbalance it was thought could only be the product of all the following factors to varying degrees – Chinese export dumping, ongoing manipulation to keep the Chinese renminbi currency undervalued and the construction of implicit import barriers by China.

Instead, the Biden team was looking to impose a strict percentage ratio between the five-year rolling mean average of the US-China goods trade number (a deficit for the US) to the US's GDP number. For 2019, for example, the figures were a US-China goods trade deficit of USD345 billion, and a US GDP of USD21.43 trillion, so the percentage ratio was around 1.6%. Whatever exact metric was taken, the five-year rolling mean average would be looking for a reduction in that percentage ratio of at least half within the first term of the Biden presidency.

It was also thought at that time by the Biden team that this policy could be sold as being beneficial to China from various perspectives. The policy in practice would in one part mean that China would have to allow the renminbi greater flexibility because a market-determined fundamental effective exchange rate (FEER) would ensure the correction of the trade imbalance between the two economies over time.

China's Carefully Managed Competitive Advantage

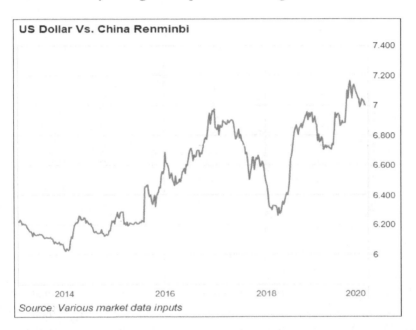

By putting into place such a metric for trade and GDP there would also finally be, by implication, a similar metric come into play for the movement of the USDRMB FEER. This over time would allow China to reduce its inflationary pressures from imported goods, benefit Chinese investment abroad (as it would facilitate greater transfer pricing to be done) and would also take the strain off the already then-pressured shadow banking system.

From the US side, all of this would strictly be compartmentalised away from matters of national security – so there would be no concessions, for example, on Huawei – and also away from foreign policy, the discussions over which would not be traded off for commerce as they were occasionally under Trump. This compartmentalisation of trade away from the potential for 'trade-offs' with other policy areas would also mean that the presidency of Joe Biden would not consider softening its stance on Iran in exchange for China offering to reduce its increasingly powerful grip over the country.

The Biden Team's First Take On The China Trade War

Former President Trump had used a mix of tariffs and sanctions against China, particularly when it came to technology issues. Both sides had committed to stop raising tariffs with the signing of the Phase 1 Trade Deal on 15 January 2020 and from that point Trump had relied on sanctions to address economic grievances against China.

The switch from using tariffs (which require only clearance from the US Executive to implement) to using sanctions (which require much more convoluted and time-consuming procedures to implement) meant a slower response time from the US to counteract Chinese manoeuvres.

There had been much talk that Biden might nullify the Phase 1 agreement entirely. However, when he took office there was speculation that he might decide that such a move would allow him to pressure China into making further concessions on issues that concerned the US. Indeed, Biden said before he formally took office that: 'My goal would be to pursue trade policies that produce progress on China's abusive practices — that's stealing intellectual property, dumping products, illegal subsidies to corporations [as well as forced tech transfers from US to PRC companies].'

The consensus was that China's commitment to buy an additional USD52.4 billion in US energy products in 2020/21 as part of the Phase 1 trade deal between the two countries was impossible to achieve. However, some commentators believed that it was eminently achievable, given the massive political change that had been taking place in China without most people noticing it.

Specifically, this new Chinese power structure began to emerge when Xi Jinping took over as General Secretary of the Communist Party in China in November 2012 and later as President of the People's Republic of China in March 2013. From then, the leadership of China had increasingly stressed the virtues of self-reliance and had also attempted to develop relationships with global partners to make up for the decline in the constructive elements of its relationship with the US and its allies.

This shift in thinking was initially manifested early after 2013 in a broadening and deepening of the Communist Party's role across all key areas of economic management in China, including a directive designed to enhance the political supervision of its state-owned enterprises (SOEs).

Accounting for 26% of China's total imports, the SOE's could from that point expect to see their role increased in line with the 'centralisation' ethos of the Chinese Communist Party, as encapsulated in Xi Jinping's statement that: 'Government, military, civilian, and academic, east, west, south, north, and centre, the [Communist] Party leads everything'.

Alongside this ideological shift came new regulations from the Central Committee of the China Communist Party designed to institutionalise political control over businesses. For all 97 national-level state firms, the Committee's instructions required that all major business and management decisions must be discussed by the Communist Party cell in a company before being presented to the company's board of directors. These cells very quickly manifested themselves in an estimated 90% of all China's SOEs. They were also, and remain, generally immune from oversight by the courts or regulators, being answerable only to internal Communist Party bodies.

Added to this was that from that point after 2013 all board directors and company executives had the standing instruction to 'execute the will of the Party'. This stricture applied equally to the SOEs, which – in addition to accounting for 26% of China's total imports at that time – also accounted for 25% of its industrial output. Additionally, they held controlling positions in transport, power and other core enterprises, including those relating to the energy sector.

The Biden Administration's View On Iran

The consensus in Iran and its supportive UNSC members, China and Russia, after the US withdrawal from the JCPOA in 2018 under then-President Trump was that any future president from the Democratic Party would probably begin to reverse that decision soon after winning office.

Indeed, John Bolton has stated that when the US withdrew from the JCPOA deal it was John Kerry, former Secretary of State under the previous Democratic President, Barack Obama – under whose leadership the JCPOA had been signed in the first place - who had advised Iran to stay in the deal and just wait it out until Trump was no longer president.

This is exactly what Iran did, confident that a new Democratic President would swiftly reverse Trump's decision to withdraw from the JCPOA. Tehran's belief that this would occur was bolstered by the fact that nearly all of the other major powers in the P5+1 grouping (the US, the UK, France, Russia and China 'plus' Germany) that had put the deal together were still in favour of the JCPOA. Moreover, as this grouping essentially reflected the composition of the Permanent Members of the UNSC – comprised of the US, UK, France, Russia and China – Iran could count on support in that body too.

Additionally supportive of this positive view from Iran, China and Russia were comments made by the Democratic presidential candidate Biden early in his campaigning. Most notably, perhaps, he had said that although Iran remained a '…destabilising actor in the Middle East…that must never be allowed to develop a nuclear weapon… [former-President Trump's abandonment of the JCPOA, with no viable plan to produce a better one] has produced a deep crisis in transatlantic relations and pushed China and Russia closer to Iran [and] … As a result, the United States, rather than Iran, has been isolated.' Like Obama, Biden had echoed the view that the JCPOA was a deal: '…that blocked Iran's paths to nuclear weapons, as repeatedly verified by international inspectors.'

These comments had been taken by Iran, and China and Russia, as clear signals that the US under Biden would be willing to re-enter the JCPOA deal early in his presidency if he were elected, with few adjustments being necessary to the original version of the deal. This would also mean the early dropping of all the sanctions that the US had imposed on Iran, and also effectively on China and Russia, as Tehran's main backers at the time.

At that point, this appeared to be a reasonable enough supposition, but it overlooked two key factors. One of these was that what a US presidential candidate says on his own during his campaign does not necessarily directly translate into the policy of him, his cabinet, and all of the rest of his presidential administration when in office. The second factor was that

Biden had supported the Obama version of the JCPOA but the Obama version of the JCPOA had not been the version that was finally signed.

The Obama version contained in it up to a dozen extra clauses that were extremely tough in terms of their requirements on Iran and in the monitoring that those requirements were being met. These are detailed and analysed in full in the *'Key Players In The Global Oil Market: The US'* section.

US Sanctions Had Weighed Heavily On Iran And Its Trading Partners

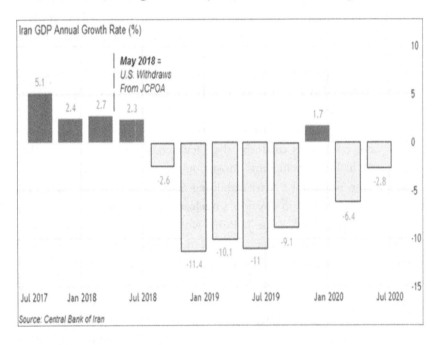

Iran GDP Annual Growth Rate (%)

May 2018 = U.S. Withdraws From JCPOA

Source: Central Bank of Iran

It was also this (Obama) version of the JCPOA, in fact, that Trump and Bolton wanted to see Iran sign up to and the two Republicans thought that the best way of forcing Iran to do this was to have the US pull out of the softer-version JCPOA first. Attesting to this was that if each of the statements from the key players in Trump's presidential team on what should be contained in any new version of the JCPOA were put together, they added up to the original tough clauses in the original Obama version of the JCPOA before it was toned down. It was toned down because of pressure from almost all of the other signatories to the JCPOA – with the exception of the UK – which believed that simply having any oversight in

Iran was better than having none at all and that Iran would never sign up to a deal containing all the clauses of the original Obama version.

It was this original Obama version of the JCPOA that Biden wanted Iran to sign up to or no new deal would be struck and no US sanctions would be lifted. Although there were moments when it seemed to Iran, and to China and Russia, that the US might waive some of these tougher sanctions, Biden's team did not back down.

Iran and its allies did much to increase the pressure on Biden to drop the tougher clauses and to inveigle the US into signing back up to the JCPOA. All of the key measures that they tried to bring to bear on the US, and the US's responses to them, are analysed in full in the '*Key Players In The Global Oil Market: Iran*' section.

However, this programme of incrementally increasing pressure on the US to re-join the softer JCPOA version did not work, and several elements of Iran's actions aimed at trying to force the US back to the negotiating table caused a loss of support for the deal from its previous prime proponents in France and Germany, to add to the longstanding opposition to it of the UK.

Biden's Balancing Act With Iraq

What this tougher line on China and Iran meant for neighbouring Iraq in the short term was that it would have to tread a lot more carefully in its dealings with both countries. This was evidenced in Baghdad's pausing and/or cancellation of the Zhenhua Oil deal for oil exploration and development in the south of the country.

That Iraq was surprised by the scale of fury from the US privately directed at it over the deal, especially as all the deals it had struck with China in the previous few years had gone ahead without any trouble, was implied by the ludicrous official explanation as to why it had been so paused and/or cancelled. To wit, the Iraqis said that the deal was predicated on oil prices remaining at the low end, but with oil prices more stable and perhaps rising the deal could not go ahead.

Even in Iraq, long-running oil contracts – including prepayment ones – had never consisted of a single rigid pricing figure but rather of the reference price for the oil sold being based on a rolling mean average, perhaps over the previous three months, or six months, or maybe even a bit longer. This would automatically factor in a rising price trend or a falling price trend as the base price point, so this explanation made no sense.

Instead, it looked like Baghdad was seeing what the US reaction would be if it did back down, and whether that might involve any financial benefits to it, direct or indirect. In essence, Iraq was just trying to see if it could start playing its usual game with the new US government all over again by sending this signal that it was open to offers from Washington during this suspended relationship period with Beijing. This view appears well-founded as, after a suitable period had elapsed after Baghdad had announced that it was pausing and/or cancelling the Zhenhua Oil prepayment deal, it approved three potentially far-reaching new infrastructure deals that heavily involved China in the heartland of Iraq.

One of these was Baghdad's approval of nearly IQD1 trillion (USD700 million) for infrastructure projects in the city of Al-Zubair in the southern Iraq oil hub of Basra. Judging from comments made by the city's Governor at the time, Abbas Al-Saadi, China's heavy involvement in Phase 2 of the projects was part of the broad-based 'oil-for-reconstruction and investment' agreement signed by Baghdad and Beijing in September 2019. This agreement allowed Chinese firms to invest in infrastructure projects in Iraq in exchange for oil.

The Al-Zubair announcement followed shortly after the awarding by Baghdad of another major contract to another Chinese company to build a civilian airport to replace the military base in the capital of the southern oil rich Dhi Qar governorate. The Dhi Qar region includes two of Iraq's potentially biggest oil fields – Gharraf and Nassiriya – and China said that it intended to complete the airport by 2024. This airport project, it announced, would include the construction of multiple cargo buildings and roads linking the airport to the city's town centre and separately to other key oil areas in southern Iraq.

This, in turn, followed yet another deal being mooted, which would involve Chinese companies building out Al-Sadr City, located near Baghdad, at a cost of between USD7-8 billion, also within the framework of the 2019 'oil-for-reconstruction and investment' agreement.

At the same time as Iraq was making these deals with China, Baghdad looked to offset any negative reaction that the US might have with promises that Iraq would put more distance between itself and Iran. For many years, Iraq – despite its oil and gas riches – had been dependent on neighbouring Iran for around 40% of its power supplies, coming in the form of both gas and electricity imports into Iraq.

When the US-Iraq War ended in 2011, Washington wanted to keep open the possibility that it could rebuild its influence across the country, albeit in a more subtle way than had gone before. Part of this was to be done through acting essentially as Iraq's lender of last resort, giving money to each new prime minister of Iraq who regularly came asking for it.

The other part was trying to allow for a gradual weaning off in Iraq's dependence on Iran for gas and electricity supplies critical to Iraq's power grid. Washington hoped that by employing these two tactics, the historical broad and deep ties between Iraq and Iran might be reduced and that the US might be able to reassert its presence in Iraq over time.

Baghdad (and Tehran) knew exactly what the US plan was and had been manipulating it ever since. This was most obviously done in the matter of securing waivers from the US to continue to import gas and electricity from Iran even after the US had reimposed sanctions on other countries that did this after it had withdrawn from the JCPOA in 2018.

The Iraq method was the following: whoever was prime minister of Iraq went to Washington (usually in the summer, as the Iraqis prefer the Washington climate during that period) to ask for a huge amount of money to bail out Iraq's budget. In return, the Iraq prime minister would promise the US president that Iraq would gradually stop using Iranian energy imports for its power grid, as part of a broader initiative to reduce the power of Iran's political, economic and military proxies in Iraq.

The US would then give Iraq billions more dollars to bail out its budget and also grant it another waiver to import Iranian gas and electricity for a set period (ranging upwards from 30 days). The Iraqis then banked the money and continued to import as much Iranian energy supplies as it had before, if not more. This relationship dynamic is analysed further in the 'Key Players In The Global Oil Market: Iraq' section.

Having appeased Washington somewhat by pausing and/or cancelling the Zhenhua Oil deal, then, not only did Iraq continue to import just as much gas and electricity from Iran as it did before, and then make a series of huge infrastructure deals with China in the south of the country, but also it allowed Beijing to expand its presence in the southern Iraq oil heartland.

More specifically, the middle of 2021 saw a statement from the then-Iraq Oil Minister, Ihsan Abdul Jabbar, that China's State-owned Assets Supervision and Administration Commission (SASAC) had agreed to fund the Fao refinery project that would process at least 300,000 bpd of crude oil in Iraq's oil field-packed southern region that runs into the Fao Peninsula around Basra.

Once Iraq had received the guarantee from China's SASAC that it would guarantee all of the required funding for the strategically critical Fao refinery project, the contracts were awarded to the China National Chemical Engineering Co (CNCEC). These included the construction of the refinery, training, technology transfer, operation, and maintenance. In addition to the heavy Chinese personnel contingent that would be involved in these areas, there would also be even more 'specialist security personnel' from China to 'ensure the safety of the entire site' according to several sources at the time.

Iraq Appeased The US While Allowing China Expansion

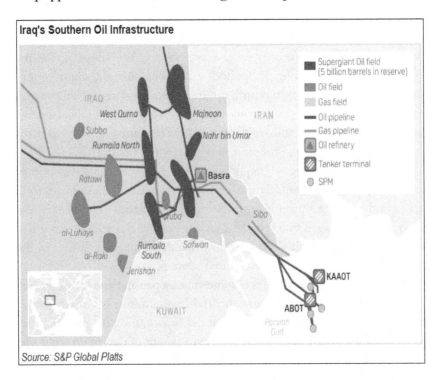

Source: S&P Global Platts

Biden's Policy Towards Saudi Arabia

For Saudi Arabia, Biden's starting point was made clear in broad terms on 2 October 2020 when he said that any presidency of his would seek to: 'Reassess our relationship with the Kingdom [of Saudi Arabia], end US support for Saudi Arabia's war in Yemen, and make sure America does not check its values at the door to sell arms or buy oil.'

Specifically regarding Crown Prince Mohammed bin Salman (MbS) during the same speech – which marked the second anniversary of the murder of expatriate Saudi journalist Jamal Khashoggi that according even to the CIA was carried out on the personal orders of the Crown Prince – Biden appeared to endorse the CIA's findings. He said: 'Two years ago, Saudi operatives, reportedly acting at the direction of Saudi Crown Prince Mohammed bin Salman, murdered and dismembered Saudi dissident, journalist, and US resident Jamal Khashoggi…His offense – for which he paid with his life – was criticising the policies of his government.'

He added, in a worrying twist for MbS personally: 'Today, I join many brave Saudi women and men, activists, journalists, and the international community in mourning Khashoggi's death and echoing his call for people everywhere to exercise their universal rights in freedom.' He concluded: 'America's commitment to democratic values and human rights will be a priority, even with our closest security partners,…and I will defend the right of activists, political dissidents, and journalists around the world to speak their minds freely without fear of persecution and violence.'

These comments, MbS and his advisers noted at the time, could be seen by senior disillusioned Saudis as a clarion call if not to arms then certainly to pushing for a less autocratic style of government at the top of Saudi Arabia's power structure. For MbS personally, these remarks from Biden came at a time when his latest ill-thought-through foray of a second failed oil price war in less than five years had left the ruling Al Saud dynasty facing the greatest existential threat to its continued rule since Ibn Saud had first consolidated his conquests into the Kingdom of Saudi Arabia in 1932.

The Kingdom remained economically damaged, having blown over USD400 billion of its never-to-be-recovered foreign exchange reserves in the two oil wars and faced the prospect of strained budgets stretching into the 2030s. Additionally, its core relationship with the US was at its lowest ebb since the original relationship agreement was formulated in 1945 between then-US President Roosevelt and the Saudi King at the time, Abdulaziz, onboard the US Navy cruiser Quincy in the Great Bitter Lake segment of the Suez Canal.

Such anger was felt in Washington that the Saudis had yet again attempted to destroy, or at least disable, the US shale oil industry in March 2020, that even the pro-MbS former President Donald Trump felt compelled to personally call the Crown Prince on 2 April and tell him that if he did not end the oil price war then the US would withdraw its military support for Saudi Arabia, as highlighted earlier.

Saudi's Self-Destructive Oil Price Wars

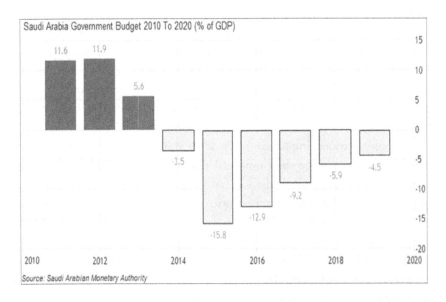

Source: Saudi Arabian Monetary Authority

Given these factors, MbS's personal hold on power had never been more tenuous, particularly with other senior Saudis jostling for position in light of King Salman's extremely poor health. Those looking to re-assert their claim to the throne – most notably Prince Muhammad bin Nayef, King Salman's nephew and the former crown prince – were supported by 500 of the wealthiest Saudis.

These opponents to MbS were then rounded up from 4 November 2017 and held captive in the Ritz-Carlton in Riyadh as part of what his supporters portrayed as a crackdown on corruption. In reality it was a standard criminal shakedown in which those being held were told to hand over USD800 billion to USD1 trillion of their assets to MbS's grouping or else their lives would become a lot worse very quickly.

An almost identical tactic was used in 2020, with the same sort of people rounded up, including again Prince Muhammad bin Nayef, plus most notably as well Prince Ahmed bin Abdulaziz, one of three members of the Allegiance Council (the senior royal organisation that endorses the line of succession), who opposed MBS's appointment as crown prince in place of his cousin bin Nayef in 2017.

One way MbS might have been able to mitigate the negative effects of these actions at that point, as far as the US was concerned, was to give Saudi Arabia's support to Washington's push for its relationship normalisation deals programme – of which Biden was a supporter. MbS was believed at that stage to be more sympathetic to the agreements – and to the ultimate strategic aim of the US and Israel of reducing Iran's power in the region – than King Salman.

Biden knew that back in 2002 it was the Saudis who had launched the 'Crown Prince Abdullah Peace Plan' at the Beirut Arab summit, offering Israel full recognition in exchange for a return to its pre-1967 borders. The new US President, therefore, thought that MbS might be amenable to the idea of not opposing further relationship normalisation deals and then perhaps to publicly supporting them when King Salman died.

However, as 2021 proceeded, any hopes the Biden team may have entertained of such a scenario were dashed as oil prices rose from August/September of that year on expectations of a Russian invasion of Ukraine and as the full effects of the COVID-19 pandemic began to be mitigated more widely across the world.

The Russia-Ukraine War, Post-COVID Order

Although more people died across the world from COVID-19 and its variants in 2021 than in 2020, by the beginning of the second half of 2021 several effective vaccines against the disease had been rolled out widely. Additionally, medical responses to infections had significantly improved. In this sense it can be said that from around that point the scale and scope of the virus across the world was in decline.

Pre-Invasion Deal-Making Strategy From Russia And China

This process, though, overlapped with the beginning of new momentum in the third quarter of 2021 in the deal-making of Russia and China with countries of key strategic interest to them, and to the US. This, at least from Russia's side, was done in the knowledge that an invasion of Ukraine would occur within the coming few months. At the same time, it is difficult to believe that the slew of deals involving China securing further oil and gas supplies were not also connected to some knowledge on Beijing's part of Russia's planned invasion of its neighbour.

Russia Wanted To Ensure Sustained High Oil Prices After The Invasion

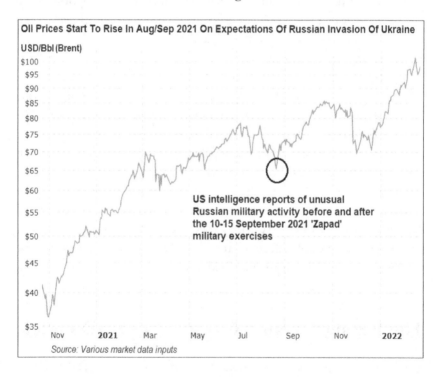

It is all the more difficult to believe as, from the end of August/beginning September 2021, global oil prices began to rise sharply on US intelligence reports that the regular 'Zapad' joint Russia-Belarus military exercises scheduled to take place from 10 September to 15 September might turn into something more real that year as far as Russia's intentions towards

Ukraine were concerned. By the end of September 2021, even more money had flowed into net long oil positions, as further US intelligence reports showed that several Russian units involved in 'Zapad 2021' had not returned to their usual positions but rather were staying very close to the Ukrainian border.

The slew of deals made by Russia and China in this lead-up period from September 2021 to the invasion of Ukraine on 24 February 2022 were all geared towards three purposes. The first was to ensure that any rise in oil prices in the near future was not counteracted by major increases in oil output from other key suppliers, with the obvious candidates being OPEC countries. From Russia's perspective, this meant that higher oil prices would mean ongoing healthy export revenues from its oil and gas exports.

The second purpose was to ensure continued heavy buying of Russian oil and gas from key buyers around the world, to ensure a base level of demand for its production of these products. This was aimed at providing Russia with some corollary political support from these key buyers.

The third purpose was to ensure that Russia's key ally, China, would not have its economy or finances adversely affected by shortfalls in its oil and gas requirements arising from any market turbulence in the coming months. Russia was very keen to keep China onside in what it had planned, both from an economic and political perspective.

Russia's Wide-Ranging Deals With Saudi Arabia

In early September 2021, then, and aimed at addressing Russia's first objective, its Deputy Prime Minister and Energy Minister, Alexander Novak, met with Saudi Arabia's Energy Minister, Prince Abdulaziz bin Salman, to discuss broadening and deepening the two countries' cooperation in the energy sector and others.

This meeting picked up on issues that had first been raised in the aftermath of Russia's support for Saudi Arabia and the OPEC grouping of countries after they had lost the 2014-2016 Oil Price War and needed Moscow's help to bring oil prices back up again so that they could begin to restore their crippled finances. This support from Russia had then been formalised in the then-new OPEC+ alliance.

The framework for the continued expansion of Saudi Arabia's relationship with Russia had been established when President Putin had invited Saudi Arabia's King Salman to Russia in October 2017 - the first visit to Moscow made by a sitting Saudi monarch. It had further been developed during the visits to Moscow by King Salman in 2017 and by Crown Prince Mohammed bin Salman (MbS) in 2019.

At these various meetings, not only was the continuation of the OPEC+ alliance agreed, but also several major deals were made across a wide range of areas, not just the oil sector. Among the USD3 billion or so specific deals announced over that period was an investment by the Saudis of at least USD150 million into Russia's Eurasia Drilling Company and the consideration of Russian petrochemical company Sibur to build a USD1.1 billion plant in Saudi Arabia.

Novak also flagged at the time that Russian gas producer Novatek was in talks for Saudi investors to take part in its Arctic LNG2 project, a follow-up to its USD27 billion plant in the Yamal peninsula. At the same time, it was agreed that Saudi Arabia's sovereign wealth fund, the Public Investment Fund, would establish a USD1 billion fund alongside Russia's sovereign wealth fund, the Russian Direct Investment Fund, which would invest in Russian technology companies.

In the same vein, Russian state-owned hydrocarbons companies Rosneft and Gazprom entered talks with Saudi counterpart Aramco to conduct co-ordinated oil and gas trading operations – bringing in the expertise and non-crossover contacts of Lukoil's Litasco trading operation when required – and to establish a joint research and technology centre.

Even more seriously from the US perspective were two other key points discussed – and agreed in principle - between Russia and Saudi Arabia during these meetings, which immediately yielded results for Moscow.

The first of these was that the Saudis rowed back on their demand that Syria's President Bashar al-Assad be removed from power. The second, and even more extraordinary given its history with the US since the 1945 Agreement, was that Saudi Arabia signed a memorandum of understanding for the purchase from Russia of its S-400 air defence missile systems.

These two latter points can be regarded as the first clear evidence of the significant deal creep that Russia had been looking to leverage since it began co-operation with the OPEC+ deals back in 2016 and, by so doing, to decisively move Saudi away from its longstanding relationship with the US and replacing it with one with Russia (and, by extension, China).

Putin Pushes Through Key Supply Deals With India

Alongside China, India was the major economic force in Asia but, unlike China, its growth trajectory was sharply rising, not gradually falling. As highlighted earlier, India was projected to become an oil and gas buying power to rival, and even surpass, China in the coming years.

India Had Been The US's New Designated Backstop Bid For Oil

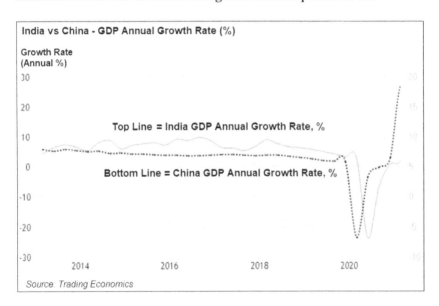

India vs China - GDP Annual Growth Rate (%)

Growth Rate (Annual %)

Top Line = India GDP Annual Growth Rate, %

Bottom Line = China GDP Annual Growth Rate, %

Source: Trading Economics

It was for these reasons, and the ability to play off the longstanding rivalry between India and China, that the US had designated India as being its global backstop bid for oil. This oil would come from countries that aligned with Washington - partly through more planned relationship normalisation deals and partly through other vehicles, in the US vision of its new oil order.

Russia, however, also knew all of this, and in a shock announcement just before Christmas 2021, Moscow stated that a slew of deals had been concluded with India during a visit of Putin himself to Indian Prime Minister, Narendra Modi. There were 28 deals in total, covering a broad range of subjects, including not just oil, gas, and petrochemicals, steel, and shipbuilding, but also military matters.

The main hydrocarbons deal was for Russia, via state-owned oil giant Rosneft, to supply 2 million tonnes of crude to Indian Oil by the end of 2022. Igor Sechin, Rosneft chief executive officer and close friend of Putin, said: 'The signing of a new oil supply contract confirms the strategic nature of the long-term partnership between Rosneft and Indian Oil.'

Rosneft's oil deliveries would be shipped through the Russian Black Sea port of Novorossiisk, with off-loading facilities in India to be built when required. Putin highlighted: 'Both sides reaffirmed their commitment to increasing Russian crude oil production under long-term contracts at preferential prices and increasing LNG [liquefied natural gas] imports to India with the possible use of the Northern Sea Route for energy supplies.' India's Modi added: 'We have set a target of USD30 billion in trade and USD50 billion in investment by 2025.'

In a joint statement from Russia and India it was also confirmed that the two countries had: 'Reiterated [our] intention to strengthen defence cooperation, including in the joint development of production of military equipment." Specifically, according to further official statements, India would produce at least 600,000 Kalashnikov assault rifles - the weapon of choice for terrorists and militias across the Middle East and elsewhere. Even more disturbing for the US, India's Foreign Secretary, Harsh Vardhan Shringla, said that a 2018 contract for the Russian S-400 air defence missile systems was being implemented.

Russia Keeps New Supplies From Iran Under Its Control

In what turned out to be the run-up to its invasion of Ukraine, Russia was very careful to keep control over other major gas suppliers as and when it could, with Iran being a key case in point. From the withdrawal of the US from the JCPOA in 2018 and its reimposition of sanctions regarding Iran after that, there had been intermittent calls from various countries for Washington to re-join the agreement and to gradually lift sanctions, as analysed in depth in the '*Key Players In The Global Oil Market: Iran*' section.

Iran had also done its part to pressure these sympathetic countries, and non-sympathetic ones including the US, to do the same as well, as also analysed in depth in the aforementioned section. In this context, by November 2021 senior politicians in Tehran were directly messaging senior figures in the European Commission in Brussels that the country wanted to talk about the quick resumption of negotiations in order to reactivate the JCPOA before the end of that Iranian calendar (ending on 20 March 2022 in the Gregorian calendar.

Moscow knew that significant turbulence in the global oil markets, especially that marked by upwards spiralling oil prices, would renew calls for the US to re-join the JCPOA to allow for new oil and gas flows to come from Iran, which would help to bring prices back down again. However, Russia's presence in Iran's oil and gas sector dated back a long way and had been steadily growing for decades. One of the key reasons for this was that Moscow wanted to ensure that oil and gas flows from Iran did not challenge the supremacy of Russian flows in its most important target markets, which included Europe. In 2021, then, Russia moved to cement this idea further.

At around the same time as Iranian politicians were messaging their counterparts in the European Union to resume negotiations to reactivate the JCPOA, a deal was finalised to develop Iran's multi-trillion-dollar new gas discovery, the Chalous field. The deal would see Russian companies holding the major share in it, despite Chalous's position unequivocally within the Iranian sector of the Caspian Sea, over which the Islamic Republic has complete sovereignty.

Billions of dollars in additional capital investment were scheduled to come from financial institutions in Germany, Austria, and Italy, as the indications were that Chalous's gas reserves were even greater than initially thought. According to a comment at the time from one of the senior Russian officials involved in negotiating the deal: 'This is the final act of securing control over the European energy market.'

In context, the wider Caspian basins area, including both onshore and offshore fields, is conservatively estimated to have around 48 billion barrels of oil and 292 trillion cubic feet of natural gas in proven and probable reserves. In 2019, Russia was instrumental in manipulating a change in the legal status of the Caspian basins area that meant that Iran's share of the total revenues from the entire Caspian site was slashed.

Specifically, in the original agreements with the then-USSR in 1921 (on 'fishing rights'), then amended in 1924 to include 'any and all resources recovered', Iran had enjoyed a 50-50 split in the financial proceeds from the Caspian with its partner. After the new agreement in 2019, Iran's share had been cut to just 11.875%. Before the Chalous discovery, this meant that Iran would lose at least USD3.2 trillion in revenues from the lost value of energy products across the shared assets of the Caspian Sea resource going forward. Following the Chalous discovery, that amount increased substantially.

Previously, the estimates of Iran and Russia were that Chalous contained around 3.5 trillion cubic meters (tcm) of gas in place. This equated to around one-quarter of the 14.2 tcm of gas reserves contained in Iran's supergiant South Pars natural gas field. The South Pars field already accounted for around 40% of Iran's total estimated 33.8 tcm of gas reserves and about 80% of its gas production.

The Caspian's Massive Realised And Unrealised Potential

The Chalous discovery, however, was soon found to be not just one huge single-field site but a twin-field site, with the two fields nine kilometres apart. 'Greater' Chalous was found to have 5.9 tcm of gas in place and 'Lesser' Chalous 1.2 tcm of gas, giving a combined figure of 7.1 Tcm of gas. Therefore, the new Chalous figures gave Iran a total natural gas reserves figure of 40.9 Tcm, whilst Russia – for a long time, the holder of the largest gas reserves in the world – officially had just under 48 Tcm. However, the Russian figure had not been revised to account for usage, wastage, and gas field degradation for many years so, according to Russian gas industry sources, was around 38.99 Tcm as at the end of 2020. Consequently, the Chalous find, if it panned out as expected, would make Iran the biggest gas reserves holder in the world.

These new estimates led to a change in the plan that had been agreed between Iran and Russia. The plan had been for Iran's side of the development to be led by the Khazar Exploration and Production Company (KEPCO), with the additional principal participation of then-to-be finalised Russian companies. Following the upgrading of the gas reserves estimates in Chalous and spiralling gas prices across Europe in the previous weeks during 2021, the new stake split in the combined Chalous twin-sites was changed to the following: Russia's Gazprom and Transneft together would hold a 40% share, China's CNPC and CNOOC together a 28% share, and South Korea's KEPCO a 25% share only.

Russia's Gazprom would also have overall responsibility for managing the Chalous development and Transneft would do the transportation and related operations. CNPC would undertake much of the financing and providing the necessary banking facilities, and CNOOC would take care of the infrastructure and engineering.

Russia's Transneft then projected that Chalous alone could provide up to 72% of all the natural gas requirements for Germany, Austria, and Italy every year for the full 20 years that the Chalous deal was set to run. Transneft has also reported to Moscow that Chalous alone could supply up to 52% of all of the European Union's gas needs over the period as well.

To gain effective control over these new Iranian gas flows through securing such a stake in Chalous, Russia privately assured Iran that, in addition to development and exploration expertise and some funding, it would also 'seek to support Iran's interests in the matter of the JCPOA and in other matters at the UN'.

Aside from the enormous geopolitical value for Russia in adding the Chalous gas streams to the gas supplies over which it already had control, especially into the European Union countries, Moscow was looking at an enormous financial payoff from its involvement in the field.

Russia calculated that, using an annual mean average figure of USD800 per 1,000 cubic meters of gas, the value of exports from Chalous at a comfortable rate of recovery from the site would be at least USD450 billion over the 20-year duration of the deal, which would coincide with the next 20-year Iran-Russia deal.

After the 20-year deal was up, the agreement then was that the IRGC corporate vehicle Khatam al-Anbiya would take over ownership of Chalous for the next 50 years. Even then it seemed unlikely that this transition away from Russian management would take place, given the value of the Chalous site. Given the likely length of gas recovery at Chalous – and the fact that Russia intended to take less than 10% of it out over the course of its 20-year deal - sources close to the deal estimated the total value of the Chalous gas site at USD5.4 trillion at that stage.

Russia Bolsters Its Presence In Iraq's Oil Sector

Having bolstered its relationships with Saudi Arabia, India and Iran following the Zapad joint exercises with Belarus near the Ukraine border, Russia turned its attention to doing the same with Iraq. Late November 2021 saw Russian oil giant, Lukoil, file a preliminary development proposal with Iraq's Oil Ministry for the Eridu oil field.

Located in Block 10, around 120 kilometres west of Basra in southern Iraq, the preliminary consensus of opinion was that the field contained between 7 and 10 billion barrels of crude oil reserves. This alone would have made it the biggest oil discovery in Iraq in at least 20 years, but subsequent Russian oil industry estimates pointed to reserves of up to 12 billion barrels of oil.

Lukoil's remuneration fee of USD5.99 per barrel was among the highest of all Iraq's awards under its technical service contract model, and likely peak production was estimated at between 250,000 and 300,000 bpd. Lukoil had been awarded a 60% share in the Block in the fourth round of licensing in 2012, along with a 40% stake being given to Japan's Inpex.

The key reason why Lukoil had been slow to move on developing Eridu was that the giant field had been caught up in the Russian oil company's manoeuvrings to get a better deal for the nearby field of West Qurna 2. Towards the middle of 2017, Lukoil had felt that it had done a good job in developing West Qurna 2 in that the field had been steadily producing around 400,000 bpd - about 9% of Iraq's total oil production - for some time. However, Lukoil, which had a 75% stake in West Qurna 2, had already spent at least USD8 billion on developing it, but was only being compensated USD1.15 pb recovered. This was the lowest rate being paid to any IOC in Iraq at that time and was dwarfed by the USD5.50 pb being paid to Gazprom Neft in its development of the Badra oil field.

Lukoil's Real Interest Was In West Qurna

Iraq's Southern Oil Infrastructure

Source: S&P Global Platts

Therefore, when at the end of July 2017 the Iraqi Oil Ministry told Lukoil that it needed to step up production to the higher levels targeted in the later phases, Russia made it clear that in order to be able to do this there would need to be an adjustment of the per-barrel remuneration terms.

In this context, the development plan had been for Lukoil to increase crude oil production to 480,000 bpd in Phase 2, and then to add another 650,000 bpd to the total in Phase 3, which would focus on the deeper Yamama formation. The ultimate target had been adjusted down from the initial 1.2 million bpd to 1.13 million bpd.

However, Russia had secretly known for some time that Lukoil could produce 650,000 bpd already at that point, as it had been running test excavations at that level on and off for weeks. The Iraq Oil Ministry then found this out in August-September 2017 and warned Lukoil that it needed to start drilling to capacity, but Russia again made clear that it wanted better compensation for Lukoil and the Ministry broadly agreed.

Lukoil was assured that the Oil Ministry would expeditiously pay the USD6 billion that it owed the company in unpaid remuneration for oil recovery and for part of the capital outlay to that point, and that a higher compensation rate per barrel would be looked into as soon as was feasible. In addition, the Oil Ministry said that it would allow Lukoil more leeway in its application of the terms of the Development and Production Service Contract for the West Qurna (Phase 2) Contract Area signed by Lukoil on 31 January 2010.

This latter assurance was aimed at allowing the Russian oil firm a more spread-out field investment development program over the length of the contract, which had also been extended from 20 to 25 years, so lowering the average cost to Lukoil anyhow. The Russian company would invest at least USD1.5 billion in the oil field in the following 12 months with a view to raising production from the 400,000 bpd level to 1.13 million bpd.

Although the USD6 billion that Lukoil was owed by the Ministry was subject to ongoing delays, by the end of 2021 the Russian oil firm had decided that it would press on with the development for two key reasons. The first was that after the latest round of threats from Lukoil about withdrawing from West Qurna 2, Iraq's Oil Ministry had told the Russian firm that it was free to do so but that before it did it would have to pay the Ministry billions of dollars in compensation for breaking the contract.

The second was that for some – at that point unknown – consideration in 2021, Russia was very keen to secure its influence in Iraq in order to influence its oil production policy in the coming months. Specifically, Russia wanted as much leverage as possible over Iraq to ensure that any sharp rises in the oil price in the coming period would not be offset by increases in oil production from Iraq.

The danger of this happening had increased towards the end of 2021 as news had reached Moscow that the newly resuscitated Iraq National Oil Company (INOC) had been authorised by the government in Baghdad to directly negotiate with US oil giant, Chevron, for it to develop the long-delayed supergiant Nasiriya oil field.

Russia's efforts in cementing its influence in Iraq in what turned out to be the run-up to its invasion of Ukraine were supported by China. At around the same time as Russia was manoeuvring its position in Iraq's oil business, China secured a contract from Iraq to build a civilian airport to replace the military base in the capital of the DhiQar governorate.

This project, which China said it would complete by 2024, would include the construction of multiple cargo buildings and roads linking the airport to the city's town centre and separately to other key oil areas in southern Iraq. Block 10, in which the Eridu oil field is located, is close by to this planned project, lying in Muthanna and DhiQar, approximately 10 km southwest of Nassiriya city.

China Secures Massive Qatar Gas Supplies Before The West

In fact, from just over one year before Russia's invasion of Ukraine, China had been engaged in a flurry of activity to expand its sources and methods of gas supply. This began in earnest with a series of major deals in March 2021 with the world's top LNG supplier, Qatar.

LNG requires much less infrastructure for delivery than gas delivered through a pipeline, meaning not only that it costs a buyer less to establish the facilities needed to benefit from a regular LNG supply but also that quantities can be increased and decreased at very short notice. In essence, LNG supplies would be the 'swing gas supply' for China, and all other countries, in the event of any global gas supply emergency.

March 2021, then, had seen the signing of a 10-year purchase and sales agreement by the China Petroleum & Chemical Corp (Sinopec) and Qatar Petroleum (QP) for 2 million tonnes per annum (mtpa) of LNG. December 2021 saw another major long-term contract for Qatar to supply China with LNG, on that occasion a deal between QatarEnergy and

Guangdong Energy Group Natural Gas Co for 1 mtpa of LNG, starting in 2024 and ending in 2034, although it could be extended.

Quite aside from ensuring a diversity of gas supply – and very quick supplies if necessary – these deals (and later ones) with China subtly shifted the Emirate at that point into the China-Russia-Iran sphere of influence. The deals brought together in this loose alliance the world's top LNG exporter (Qatar) and one of the world's top holders of gas reserves (Iran). Additionally both of these countries were founding members of the 11-member Gas Exporting Countries Forum (GECF), together with Russia.

The deals also further inextricably linked this huge combined global gas resource with the world's biggest buyer of energy products over the past two decades or more - China.

On every level, those early deals between Qatar and China considerably added to the geopolitical challenge faced by the US-Israel-Arab states alliance in the Middle East that had tentatively started to be established through the relationship normalisation deals process.

China and Russia had always thought that Qatar might be pre-disposed towards joining their bloc, given that it shared its principal gas reservoir asset with neighbouring Iran, a key ally of both major powers. This 9,700 square kilometre reservoir was, and remains, by far the biggest gas resource in the world, holding an estimated 51 trillion cubic metres (tcm) of non-associated natural gas and at least 50 billion barrels of natural gas condensates.

Qatar's 6,000 square kilometre section – the 'North Field' (or 'North Dome') – is the cornerstone to its world-leading LNG exporter status. Iran's 3,700 square kilometre section – 'South Pars – accounts for around 40% of Iran's total estimated 33.8 tcm of gas reserves – mostly located in the southern Fars, Bushehr, and Hormozgan regions – and about 75% of its gas production.

Until Qatar withdrew from OPEC at the beginning of 2019, Iran had been developing its South Pars area at full tilt regardless of all other considerations. Iran had been able to do so with a great degree of impunity, as from 2005 until the end of the first quarter of 2017 Qatar had a moratorium in place on its own further development of the North Field.

Over this period – especially while Qatar was a member of the Saudi-led OPEC grouping – the Emirate had complained that Iran's no-holds-barred development of its South Pars site would damage the future recovery rate in the North Field, although to little avail.

Following the US's withdrawal from the JCPOA in May 2018, senior figures from Iran's Petroleum Ministry and Qatar's Energy Ministry began a series of meetings to agree a new North Field-South Pars joint development plan.

Qatar And Iran Linked Through World's Biggest Gas Field

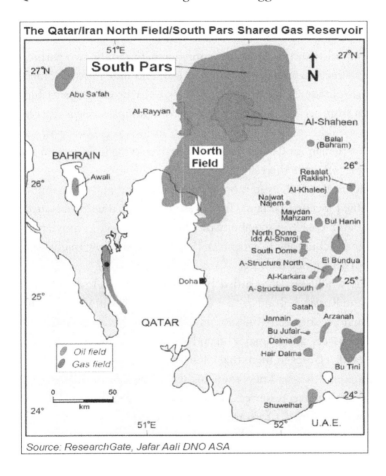

The meetings covered two main areas. First, Iran agreed not to continue with developments on its side of the reservoir in South Pars that might damage Qatar's gas take from its North Field. This left Qatar free to increase its own LNG export volumes with a guaranteed buyer in China.

Iran in the meantime would receive assistance as and when required from Qatar on building out its own LNG capabilities. Second, Qatar agreed to sit down with the Chinese and the Russians to discuss the future co-ordination of gas export destinations for Iranian, Qatari and Russian gas flows, marketing and pricing.

Following this, Qatar did indeed announce that it was to embark on a dramatic expansion in the development of its North Field site, with its state corporate proxy Qatar Petroleum targeting an increase in its LNG production by 2024 to around 110 mtpa from the then-77 mtpa or so, and after that to 126 mtpa by 2027.

Having a unified and co-ordinated approach between the two partners in the world's largest natural gas resource – Qatar and Iran - afforded many other positive outcomes for China and Russia. In broad terms, China would benefit from security of energy supply from this massive gas reserves pool. Russia would benefit from the ability to influence export routes so that a flood of Iranian (or Qatari) gas did not start moving into Europe and undermining is influence there.

An adjunct to this with even more possibilities was that this amount of gas meant more pipelines (certainly from Iran and Iraq in the first instance), which meant an increase in the ability of China and Russia to move men, machinery, and technology to wherever Beijing and Moscow might want to move them on a pipeline route.

All of this would be safeguarded by security personnel sent directly from China and Russia. Oil and gas companies are legally within their rights to station such security staff on sites in which they have an interest to safeguard their assets, and all major oil and gas contracts around the world also have specific clauses in them that allow them to do so.

Both China and Russia knew that this would tie-up considerable US military and intelligence resources, given that the US's huge Al Udeid airbase in Qatar remained a forward operating headquarters of its Central Command (CentComm).

China Strengthens Influence Through FTA And SCO Deals

At around the same time as these deals were being struck by Russia and China with key oil and gas players in the Middle East, Beijing in particular was using its financial leverage – as part of its OBOR project – to specifically extend its political influence in them as well.

One part of this was done informally through a series of meetings with the senior figures of each of these key players, under the pretext of China establishing a Free Trade Agreement (FTA) with the countries of the Gulf Cooperation Council.

In this context, the end of December 2021/beginning of January 2022 saw meetings in Beijing between senior officials from the Chinese government and foreign ministers from Saudi Arabia, Kuwait, Oman, Bahrain, plus the secretary-general of the Gulf Cooperation Council (GCC). At these meetings, the principal topics of conversation were to finally seal a China-GCC FTA and to forge 'a deeper strategic cooperation in a region where US dominance is showing signs of retreat.'

In Saudi Arabia and its close ally, Bahrain, much of the groundwork for a long-lasting shift in the two countries' geopolitical alliances had already been done by China, as mentioned earlier. It was also the case that Oman had been targeted by China in the previous few months in particular, given its much greater significance in the Middle East, and therefore the world, than its 5.4 billion barrels of estimated proved oil reserves (only the 22nd largest in the world) might imply.

The Sultanate's true importance to both China and the US lies in its critical geographical position, which makes it one of the most important oil and gas hubs in the world. Specifically, the Sultanate has long coastlines along the Gulf of Oman and the Arabian Sea offering unfettered access to the markets of the East and the West equally. As such, Oman and its key ports and storage facilities offer the only true alternative in the Middle East to the Strait of Hormuz, controlled by Iran, through which passes at least one third of the world's crude oil supplies.

What China wants from Oman is to control all the major crude oil shipping route chokepoints from the Middle East into Europe that avoid the more expensive and more nautically-challenging Cape of Good Hope route around South Africa and the more politically-sensitive Strait of Hormuz route. This is entirely aligned with Beijing's broad strategic goal encapsulated in its OBOR multi-generational power-grab project.

China already has effective control over the Strait of Hormuz by dint of its all-encompassing 25-year deal with Iran. The same deal also gives China a hold over the Bab al-Mandab Strait, through which crude oil is shipped upwards through the Red Sea towards the Suez Canal before moving into the Mediterranean and then westwards. This has been achieved as it lies between Yemen (which is being disrupted by Iran-backed Houthis, just as China wants) and Djibouti, over which China has also established a stranglehold.

Oman Occupies A Crucial Geographical Location

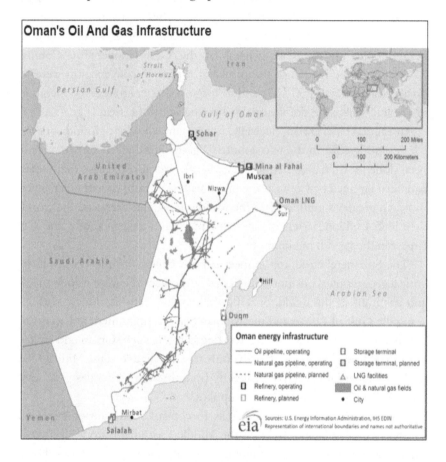

In the lead-up to a big meeting of GCC countries in December 2021, China had been using its standard chequebook diplomacy to expand its presence in Oman. Already accounting for around 90% of Oman's oil exports and most of its petrochemicals exports, China had been quick to pledge a further USD10 billion immediately for investment into Oman's flagship Duqm Refinery Project.

Although further investment from China was notionally geared towards completing the Duqm Refinery, Chinese money was also funnelled towards the construction of an 11.72 square kilometre industrial park in Duqm in three areas - heavy industrial, light industrial, and mixed-use. This enabled China to plant a flag in deeply strategic areas of land in the Sultanate.

The signal that Oman may have moved into the China sphere of influence – the 'Hotel California' of global power alliances ('You can check out any time you like, But you can never leave') – came with comments just before the GCC meetings. In June 2021, Oman's Oil and Gas Minister, Mohammed al-Rumhy, said that the Sultanate wanted to revive plans to import Iranian gas via a pipeline should the JCPOA be reinstated and was also considering extending its pipeline network to Yemen.

This pipeline plan was part of a broader co-operation deal made between Oman and Iran in 2013, extended in scope in 2014, and fully ratified in August 2015. The plan was centred on Oman's importing at least 10 billion cubic metres of natural gas per year (bcm/y) from Iran for 25 years beginning in 2017 (equating to just less than 1 billion cubic feet per day and worth around USD60 billion at the time). The target was then changed to 43 bcm/y, albeit for a shorter period, of 15 years, and then finally to at least 28 bcm/y for a minimum period of 15 years.

According to a statement at the time of the signing of the 2014 memorandum of understanding on the deal from the then-managing director of the National Iranian Gas Export Company (NIGEC), Mehran Amir-Moeini, the Iranian company was already working on the different contracts' mechanisms for the key phases of the project. Principally these comprised the onshore and offshore pipeline sections, the gas pressure and measuring stations in Iran, and the gas receiving facilities in Oman.

The land section of the project would comprise around 200 kilometres of 56-inch pipeline (to be constructed in Iran), to run from Rudan to Mobarak Mount in the southern Hormozgan province. The sea section would include a 192-kilometre section of 36-inch pipeline running along the bed of the Oman Sea at depths of up to 1,340 metres, from Iran to Sohar Port in Oman.

This deal was intended to allow for the completely free movement of Iranian gas (and later oil) via Oman through the Gulf of Oman and out into the world oil and gas markets. Iran was sanctioned at that time as well, and this route would augment the same sort of sanctions-free route that it was operating via Iraq.

It would also allow for the advancement of Iran's planned entry into the global LNG market. Iran had long sought to become a world leader in the export of LNG and this ambition remained intact. To this end, Iran had arranged as part of the 2013/14/15 deal with Oman to utilise at least 25% of the sultanate's own LNG production facilities. Once converted, the Iranian LNG would be loaded onto the specialised LNG vessels for export, in return for commission payments to Oman. This process would begin after the completion of the land and the sea pipelines.

This Oman-based LNG supply would also act as a starting point for any Iran-Pakistan-China pipeline and would augment the other LNG projects that Iran was looking to roll out at that time. Iran's then-recent activities in its huge North Pars gas site did not mark the onset of this process of Iran looking to become a force in the global LNG sector but rather marked a change of tactics due to ongoing sanctions in order to achieve the target laid out nearly 20 years before.

This target was, to become the largest exporter of gas – natural gas, LNG, and liquefied petroleum gas (LPG) combined – to Europe and Western Asia, with a focus on China and later on South Korea, and India. The aim was to double the amount of gas then exported to these two regions within five years of the base facilities being established.

Another highly beneficial synergy for the China-Iran axis of this direct route from Iran to Oman would be that it would coincide with the completion of Iran's equally sanctions-busting Goreh-Jask pipeline, analysed in full in the 'Key Players In The Global Oil Market: Iran' section.

At that point, the Goreh-Jask pipeline was due to come online imminently and would be able to transport at least 1 million bpd of oil from its major oil fields. This would be done via Goreh (in the Shoaybiyeh-ye Gharbi Rural District of Khuzestan Province) to the port of Jask in Hormozgan province, 1100 kilometres away on the Gulf of Oman. The Goreh-Jask pipeline had, of itself, expedited the finalisation of the Iran-Oman gas pipeline, given the infrastructure build-out associated with it.

This included the minimum of 20 huge oil storage tanks that would be built in Oman's Jask. Each would be capable of storing 500,000 barrels of oil in the first phase (10 million barrels total) for later loading onto very large crude carriers (VLCCs) headed from the Gulf of Oman into the Arabian Sea and then out into the Indian Ocean.

The plan was that the storage capacity for Iranian oil in Oman would be increased over the following two years to at least 30 million barrels and that the shipping facilities at Jask would be expanded to allow for extended in-port stays of all sizes of VLCCs. Jask would also see the creation of multiple single-point moorings (SPMs), and other infrastructure features for the import and export of crude oil and other products.

Oman's Link To Iran's Goreh-Jask Pipeline

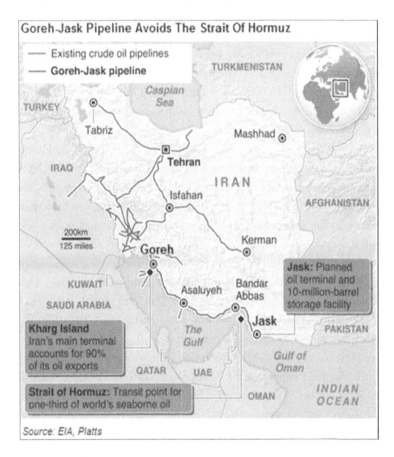

Moreover, according to Oman's Rumhy, Muscat was happy to be a conduit for the gas pipeline that would begin in Iran's supergiant South Pars gas field and run to Sohar in the north of Oman. This pipeline would then link up to the existing pipeline that ran from there to Salalah near the Yemeni border, whereupon it could be extended deeper into Yemen.

Whilst all of this was going on, China and Russia were also extending their influence over targeted Middle Eastern countries through expanding the membership of the Shanghai Cooperation Organization (SCO). The SCO is the world's biggest regional organisation both in terms of geographic scope and of population, covering 60% of the Eurasian continent (by far the biggest single landmass on Earth), 40% of the world's population, and more than 20% of global GDP.

Iran's acceptance in September 2021 into the SCO's full membership grouping, in which it had held 'observer status' only for over 15 years, meant in effect that the seismic, multi-generational 25-year Iran-China deal was set for full roll-out, with Russia firmly alongside both playing its role. It also meant that any new JCPOA deal done with Iran by the then-newish US administration – in the event, for example, of a sudden need to bring new oil flows into the markets to reduce oil prices – would not be worth the paper it was written on.

At that point, the public musings on the JCPOA from the White House were that the US was prepared to return to negotiations on the JCPOA if Tehran was prepared to do the same. Privately, the endgame for Washington was Iran's adherence to several of the tougher clauses that had been drawn up in the original version of the deal, as mentioned earlier, and as also analysed in the *'Key Players In The Global Oil Market: The US'* section.

A final part of what China and Russia were doing toward the end of 2021 was seeking to build out their military foothold in the region. This was to be done not just in the usual places (such as Syria, Iran, Iraq, Lebanon and the Palestinian areas) but also into places that the US considered firmly under its sphere of influence.

One such place was the UAE, which the US considered 'a critical ally' that provided essential support for US troops, aircraft and naval vessels in the Middle East region. Aside from the US's more covert activities across the seven emirates that comprise the UAE, the group of emirates was also host to around 5,000 US military personnel at the Al Dhafra Air Base, just outside Abu Dhabi. A testament to the US's faith in the UAE was that it was also the only Arab nation to have nuclear reactors.

Given its designation as a cornerstone in the US's relationship normalisation deals initiative, Washington's plan had been to build this grouping of oil-rich Middle Eastern oil producers into a cohesive hydrocarbons bloc that functioned within its sphere of influence. This would run in tandem with the US's plan for India to take the place of China in this new global oil market order as the big backstop bid for the oil. Propitiously in this context as far as the US was concerned, the UAE had been the first country to sign a relationship normalisation deal.

However, just before Christmas 2021, news broke that that China had been building a secret military facility in and around the big UAE port of Khalifa. Based on classified satellite imagery and human intelligence data, US officials stated that China has been working for several months to establish 'a military foothold in the UAE.'

The UAE authorities stated that they were not aware of such an extraordinary amount of activity being conducted by China at one of their biggest ports, including month after month of extremely high levels of movement of enormous Chinese ships in and out of it day and night.

At around the same time, news also broke that US intelligence agencies had found that Saudi Arabia had started to manufacture its own ballistic missiles with the help of China.

Russia Makes A Series Of Landmark Deals With China

In early February 2022, Vladimir Putin had his first in-person meeting with his Chinese counterpart Xi Jinping for nearly two years, at the opening of the Winter Olympics ceremony in Beijing, and reiterated that there is 'no limit' to how far Russian and Chinese friendship may go.

At around the same time as this meeting, a slew of huge new cooperation deals in the oil and gas sectors, and beyond, were being announced by state news agencies on both sides. These deals broadly built on the two countries' increasingly coordinated global activities in the previous few years and were geared towards weakening the dominant global power position of the US and then supplanting it in this role.

The oil and gas deals announced between Russia and China included state-owned oil giant, Rosneft, signing an USD80 billion 10-year deal to supply the China National Petroleum Corporation with 100 million metric tonnes of oil over the period (slightly over 200,000 barrels per day), shipped from Kazakhstan to refining plants in Northwest China.

This would occur alongside the other exports of Russian crude oil to China. In 2021, Russian crude shipments via pipelines to China were 40 million metric tonnes (just over 800,000 barrels per day), according to Russian pipeline operator Transneft. None of this would affect the continued flow of Russia's principal crude oil export route to China either - the 80 million metric tonnes per year (circa 1.6 million barrels per day) that went through the East Siberia-Pacific Ocean pipeline that moved oil directly to China, as well as oil supplies via the port of Kozmino.

Russia Deepened Ties With China In Early February 2022

This previous increase in crude oil delivery volumes and mechanisms to China had been put into place by Russia to mitigate the effects of the international sanctions that had been in place against it after its annexation of Crimea in 2014. Russia's takeover of Crimea had been seen by many in the governmental and military hierarchy – including Putin - as a 'trial run'

for a full-scale invasion of the entire country at some point. The 2014 annexation of Crimea had in several key aspects thematically followed a similar manoeuvre by Russia in Georgia in 2008.

This short-lived war in 2008 had followed the Russian-backed creation of two self-proclaimed republics in Georgia (of South Ossetia, and Abkhazia), which Russia then supported militarily on the basis of unsubstantiated claims by Russia that the government of Georgia was persecuting the Russian-aligned inhabitants of the two breakaway republics as part of a wider 'genocide' being committed upon them.

Following these events, Rosneft swiftly developed the Northern Sea Route (NSR), which allowed for the relatively unimpeded delivery of crude oil to Russia's key economic, political, and military partner, China. Rosneft had also been pushing the development of the Vostok Oil Project in Russia's Far North that includes the Vankor cluster, the Zapadno-Irkinsky block, the Payakhskaya group of fields, and the East Taimyr cluster.

Rosneft chief executive officer, Igor Sechin, had also promised that the Vostok Oil project and corollary build-out of the NSR would involve the creation of a 'new oil and gas province' on Siberia's Taymyr peninsula. The entire project would necessitate a total investment of RUB10,000 billion (then-USD135 billion), including two airports and 15 'industry towns'. Sechin had added that Rosneft's Arctic developments would eventually produce 100 million tonnes of oil per year, with 30 million tonnes of oil being sent from the Arctic along the NSR between then and 2024 alone.

In the gas sector, early February 2022 also saw Russian state gas giant Gazprom's sign a deal to supply 10 billion cubic metres per year (bcm/y) to China's CNPC. This built on another supply contract between the two companies signed in 2014 – a 30-year deal for 38 bcm per year to go from Russia to China. This was part of, but significantly augmented, the 'Power of Siberia' pipeline project – managed on the Russian side by Gazprom and on the China side by CNPC – that was launched in December 2019. This, and similar major deals between Russia and China, are analysed in full in the 'Key Players In The Global Oil Market: Russia' section. Gazprom was also in the process of developing the 'Power of Siberia 2' project - with shipments to be sent to China via Mongolia - that would increase gas supply to China by an additional 50 bcm per year.

These developments followed the 50.5% increase year-on-year (y-o-y) in 2021 of Russian gas exports to China. The volume of gas delivered by pipeline during that period increased by 154.2% y-o-y, to 7.54 million metric tonnes, according to January 2022 data from China's General Administration of Customs.

This multi-level cooperation strategy between Russia and China was intended to guarantee financing into Russia from China, regardless of possible sanctions from the US and its allies, including the much-vaunted barring from the Society for Worldwide Interbank Financial Telecommunications (SWIFT) international payments system.

Russia's NSR Was A Sanctions-Circumventing Delivery Mechanism

It was also intended by Russia to bolster the political support that it could expect from China for whatever happened in the future. This was even more important to Russia, as China was also – alongside Russia itself, the US, the UK, and France – one of the five Permanent Members of the UN Security Council.

On the other side of the relationship equation, it would provide China with an increasing proportion of the oil and gas it needed to power its attempt to overtake the US as the world's largest economy by nominal GDP by 2030 at the latest. At that point, China was already the world's largest economy by purchasing power parity, the largest manufacturing economy, and the largest trading nation.

Any interim gaps, both in finance for Russia or in the provision of its oil and gas supplies for China, could be increasingly filled it was thought by the leadership in Moscow and Beijing by the cooperation of politically ambiguous states around the globe, particularly amongst the Middle Eastern oil-producing countries. Not only were they regarded by the two allies as pools of natural energy resources for China's economic growth machine but also their apparent increased willingness to switch away from USD-centric oil and gas markets would gradually neuter the single most effective power that the US held in terms of international financial power exerted through sanctions.

Oil And Gas Prices Spike As Russia Invades Ukraine

As many smart money investors had anticipated in August/September 2021, Russia invaded the rest of Ukraine that it had been eyeing up since its annexation of Crimea in 2014, on 24 February 2022. Global oil prices predictably shot up on the day from around USD90 pb of the Brent benchmark to around USD140 pb. At the same time, the benchmark European gas contract, the Dutch Title Transfer Facility (TTF), jumped from around the EUR72 per megawatt hour (MWh) level that it had been trading the day before to about EUR135/MWh and then moved higher again very quickly to over EUR227/MWh.

These spikes in prices were partly a geopolitical risk premium for a war in Europe involving a major nuclear power that had the potential to escalate around the world. A larger part of the spikes, though, was due to the straightforward supply/demand balance in the oil and gas markets.

This related to Russia's key role in the world oil and gas markets by dint of its huge reserves of both, as analysed in full in the '*Key Players In The Global Oil Market: Russia*' section. Europe in particular, as evidenced by the particularly sharp rise in its benchmark Dutch TTF gas price, had come to rely to a great degree on cheap gas pipelined in from Russia. As at the end of 2021, according to IEA figures, the European Union imported an average of over 380 million cubic metres (mcm) per day of gas by pipeline from Russia, or around 140 billion cubic metres (bcm) for the year. As well as that, around 15 bcm was delivered in the form of LNG. The total 155 bcm imported from Russia accounted for around 45% of the EU's gas imports in 2021 and almost 40% of its total gas consumption.

Russia's Stranglehold Over Europe

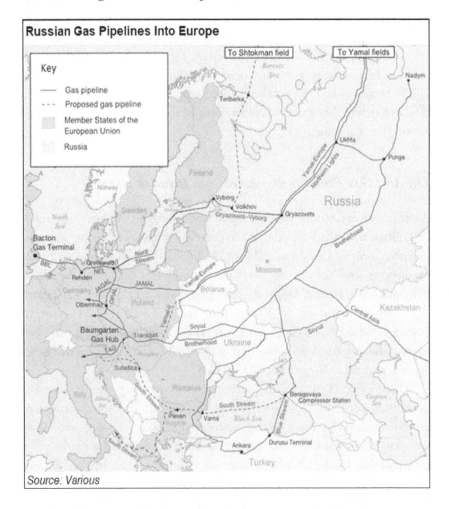

Several central and eastern European countries, including the Baltic states – principally those countries that had been part of the former USSR - were reliant on Russian gas for all or virtually all of their domestic gas supplies.

Crucially, though, it was the case that even the European Union's *de facto* leader and economic powerhouse, Germany, was reliant on Russian gas for around 30-40% of its own commercial and domestic gas needs, depending on the time of year.

Having said this, over and above the immediate security concern of whether Russia might quickly push further westwards into Europe from Ukraine, the consensus of political opinion in the US and Europe in the first day or two of the invasion was that Russia would secure victory in Ukraine within a week at most.

This assessment was based on the longstanding NATO wargaming scenario dating back to the height of Russian power in the Cold War that envisaged Russian conventional forces being able to advance westwards from eastern positions, including in East Germany, to overwhelm NATO forces in Germany within three days.

Russia Made Early Gains In The First Seven Days Of Invasion

If Russia had been able to effect such a victory within a week in Ukraine or had even managed just to secure the capital Kiev within that timeframe, then it is highlight likely that events would have run the same course as they had in Russia's effective invasion of Crimea in 2014.

That is, leading politicians in the West would have made a few condemnatory speeches, more sanctions would have been introduced against Russia, and everything in practice would have continued as before, including huge gas supplies from Russia into Europe, and oil supplies too. In short, it would have been the standard 'Macbeth Response' habitually used by Western politicians in their previous comments on various Russian actions ('a tale told by an idiot, full of sound and fury, signifying nothing').

Within a relatively short time after the first week of the invasion, however, it gradually became clear that, in fact, the Russian military as of 2022 was not the same as it had once been, or that maybe it had not been the same as it had been since the extraordinary success of the Red Army in the Second World War.

It appeared to many that the endemic corruption that had grown into the fabric of the new Russia since the dissolution of the USSR in 1991 had also made rotten its fighting machine. In essence, the Russian forces that had been designated to take Kiev quickly had broken down along the key road that would have led them into the capital, stranded by poor quality machinery, dismal logistical planning, and a paralysed command structure.

It was obvious to the West that if Russia had invaded one of the NATO countries - with the group's advanced C4ISR (Command, Control, Communications, Computers, Intelligence, Surveillance and Reconnaissance) systems and air power capabilities - then this entire invasion convoy, stretching for over 40 miles, would have been destroyed within two or three hours at most. It was also obvious to the West that if Ukraine could hold the Russians off with the limited resources it had, then this might be an excellent opportunity to engage Putin in a proxy conflict, albeit delicately done, given Russia's still-usable nuclear threat.

This, though, would mean three things. First, it would be necessary to keep Russia in Ukraine, which would not be difficult, given that Putin had personally staked his reputation on a victory there. All that needed to be done was to supply Ukraine with what it wanted in terms of arms, provided that none of these supplies would push Putin into the use of a nuclear device, even a battlefield nuclear weapon.

To circumvent the Russian leader's decision-making process towards this end, the White House made it known early on to the Kremlin that if

Russia did use a nuclear device anywhere – including in Ukraine, and including any of the territories subsequently claimed by Russia - then NATO would destroy all Russian military and quasi-military assets in and around Ukraine, including in Crimea, with conventional weapons.

Second, it would also be necessary not just to try to bring oil and gas prices down in the very short term but also to replace Russian supplies of gas especially, and then oil, into Europe, given the continent's high level of dependence on them.

By May, Russia Had Lost In The North And Fallen Back To The South

This would require considerable efforts by the US to inveigle Germany, in particular – as the effective leader of the European Union and as a highly dependent user of Russia gas – to toe the line. It would also require a similar level of effort on the part of the US and its key allies, including the UK and major European Union member states, to leverage their relationships with other global suppliers of gas and oil to plug these supply gaps.

This second factor, though, led into a third element, which would be key to redrawing the global oil market order yet again, but this time for much longer. This third factor was that Russia's invasion of Ukraine would give the US and its allies an opportunity to see exactly which side of the fence long-time geopolitical waverers would jump. This would include not just Russia's obvious geopolitical ally, China, but also all of those countries that had moved towards the Russia-China sphere of influence in the previous few years, especially since the US withdrawal from the JCPOA deal in 2018 and its subsequent withdrawals across the Middle East.

Securing Alternative Gas Supplies Quickly Was Key

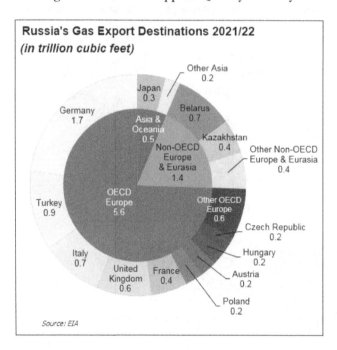

Biden Seeks To Clarify Saudi Arabia's Position

With several strategies already being discussed by senior US and European Union officials to address the gas supply shortfall problem both in Europe and elsewhere, President Biden's remaining priority was to address sharply rising oil prices. As highlighted earlier, these have a direct and profound effect not just on the economies of developed countries, including the US and all its principal allies, but also on the political fortunes of incumbent US presidents.

Biden at that point was facing critical mid-term elections in November that would be key to the fortunes both of himself, should he wish to seek re-election, and, if he did not, then to any chosen successor from the Democratic Party.

Top of the list of these 'floating' Russian allies – perhaps not yet true allies but simply using the appearance of being so to use as leverage with the US - was Saudi Arabia. Since the 1973 Oil Crisis, the US had been looking to make itself independent of the whims of Middle Eastern countries – especially Saudi Arabia – for its energy needs. After the rise of the US shale gas and oil sectors in the early 2010s especially, and the 2014-2016 Oil Price War instigated by Saudi Arabia to destroy or at least disable those sectors, the US relationship with the Kingdom was finished in spirit.

The final nail in the coffin of any residual goodwill left over from the original 1945 Agreement between the US and Saudi Arabia came in the form of Russia's crucial support for OPEC's oil production cut at the end of 2016, aimed at increasing oil prices to try to restore its member states' finances after the War.

This had turned into the OPEC+ grouping, with the 'plus' principally being Russia and the OPEC states having been increasingly used by Moscow since then as an adjunct to the Kremlin's broadly anti-US geopolitical agenda. The US's lack of willingness to put up with any further games playing from Saudi Arabia was evidenced by its multi-pronged hostility towards Riyadh during the next oil price war, also instigated by the Kingdom, in 2020.

The direct threat was made by the White House to the Saudis that the US would withdraw all its military and financial support from them if the war persisted, which could result in the removal of the royal family from power and/or war with one or more of Saudi Arabia's neighbours. Additionally, moves were advanced in Washington to pass the long-threatened 'NOPEC' legislation. This legislation is examined in depth in the *'Key Players In The Global Oil Market: The US'* section but suffice it to say here that such legislation would severely damage Saudi Arabia economically and geopolitically.

Since the end of the 2014-2016 Oil Price War, then, Saudi Arabia had drifted inexorably first into the orbit of influence of Russia and then also into that of Moscow's partner in seeking to define a 'non-unipolar' world order, as they put it – China. Nonetheless, the US still had enormous investments in Saudi Arabia, including military ones, and it was not unreasonable to expect Saudi support at a time of extreme crisis.

The specific support required after 24 February 2022 was for Saudi Arabia to increase its oil production so that prices were brought down to levels that did not fuel global inflation. This, in turn, would lead to a series of interest rate rises that would, in turn, damage economic growth and possibly tip several leading global economies into recession.

The Saudis had done the same thing many times over the years when it had suited them and were perfectly capable of doing so again. Discounting the self-aggrandising comments from Riyadh in the previous years of the Kingdom's ability to pump 12 million bpd if it wished – these inaccurate claims are analysed in depth in the '*Key Players In The Global Oil Market: Saudi Arabia*' section – the fact remained that, at a push, Saudi Arabia could sustain production of around 10 million bpd for some time.

The US Looked To Saudi For Help In Bringing Oil Prices Down

Saudi Arabia Crude Oil Production 1999-2022 (in '000s of barrels per day)

Source: OPEC

Additionally positive in terms of bringing global oil prices down was that Saudi could persuade its fellow OPEC members to similarly increase their oil production to the same end. In short, it was not much for any president of the US to ask the Saudis.

Perhaps Biden and his advisers grouped around the main phone in the Oval Office in late February 2022 had expected some to-ing and fro-ing in debate from the Saudi side over how much extra oil should be pumped, or perhaps over how long extra supplies were expected to continue into the global oil market. However, it is absolutely the case that not one of them expected the Saudis to not even deign to take the call from Biden in the first place, but this is exactly what happened.

Moreover, shortly after Saudi Crown Prince Mohammed bin Salman (MbS) had refused to even take Biden's telephone call to discuss Saudi Arabia increasing oil production to bring oil prices down, the UAE's Sheikh Mohamed bin Zayed al Nahyan (MbZ) did exactly the same. The humiliation by the UAE was even more surprising to Washington than that from Saudi Arabia, as the UAE had been a special focus for the previous two years. It had been designated by the US as a key part of the regional re-weighting of allies to counterbalance Saudi Arabia's drift to the East.

The UAE had been the first country to sign a relationship normalisation deal with Israel, brokered by the US, and had been a key link in the US building up of India as the substitute for China as the big backstop bid in the global oil market. It was true that the US had discovered just a few weeks before that China had been building a secret military facility in and around the UAE's Khalifa port, but Washington had chosen ultimately to believe that this had perhaps been an oversight by the UAE as its government had said.

In Saudi Arabia's case, not only had the Kingdom apparently actively sought to humiliate Biden, and by extension the US and its allies, by refusing to take the telephone call, but just afterwards MbS had also re-affirmed his and his country's commitment to the standing OPEC+ agreement with Russia. These reaffirmation comments were made by MbS in a private conversation to French President Emmanuel Macron but were quickly reported by the Saudi Press Agency, which meant that they had the blessing of MbS himself to be publicly leaked.

MbS had sought to couch this extraordinary re-assertion of his country's alliance with Russia in terms of the 'the Kingdom's keenness on the stability and balance of oil markets'. However, this idea was quickly undermined by the announcement that the ongoing modest rise of 400,000 barrels per day in collective output seen over the previous few months would continue, despite the economic damage being done to many developed economies by rising oil and gas prices.

Covering all of its new alliance bases, Saudi Arabia's state-owned oil giant, Saudi Aramco, then announced towards the end of March 2022 that it was looking at several further opportunities to expand its downstream dealings with China, via its state-controlled company, Sinopec. Any such deals with Sinopec would augment the joint Saudi Arabia-China refining and petrochemical complex that the two countries were looking to build at that point in northeast China.

It was clear at the onset of the rising trend in oil and gas prices when Russian invaded Ukraine that the longer these prices stayed high, the greater the economic damage that would be done to US-allied industrialised countries that were not self-sufficient in energy supplies. China could still rely on cheap Russian oil and gas supplies.

Biden's Other Short-Term Options To Lower Energy Prices

In Europe these rising prices might also mean increasing political fragmentation in the resolve to punish Russia for its attempted land-grab of Ukraine. It was likely that such fragmentation would not just stay focused on what possible sanctions might be brought against Russia - with the implications for retaliatory oil and gas stoppages from Moscow that this might lead to - but it might also lead to fractures in the cohesive response to the Ukraine invasion from NATO as a security alliance.

In the US, in addition to the economic damage that would be done by sustained high oil and gas prices, and the security threat to NATO that might come from a disunited approach to Russia by disparate European countries, there were domestic political considerations for incumbent President Biden.

Given historical precedent, as analysed in full earlier, sustained high oil and gas prices might well tip the US into recession and the election prospects for a sitting president and his party in this scenario were grim. At that point in March 2022, Biden and the Democrats were facing crucial mid-term elections in around nine months.

With Saudi Arabia and the UAE, and by extension OPEC as a group, refusing to help the West to bring oil and gas prices down by increasing their own supplies of each, Biden had four other main options to attempt to bring them down in the short term by US-centric efforts alone.

Biden Needed To Bring Energy Prices Down Fast

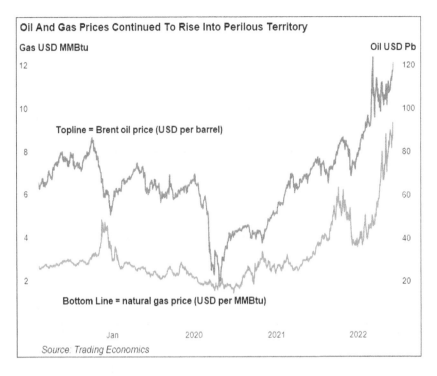

Oil And Gas Prices Continued To Rise Into Perilous Territory

Gas USD MMBtu — Oil USD Pb

Topline = Brent oil price (USD per barrel)

Bottom Line = natural gas price (USD per MMBtu)

Jan / 2020 / 2021 / 2022

Source: Trading Economics

The first option was to commit to a sustained release of oil from the US's Strategic Petroleum Reserve (SPR). An initial 30 million barrels of oil were released from the SPR around this time, as part of a globally coordinated release of over 60 million barrels led by the IEA.

However, crucially in this regard, US Energy Secretary Jennifer Granholm said on 9 March that it may have to do the same again, depending on market conditions. Only a day before that, IEA executive director, Fatih Birol, stated that the organisation was ready to release as much oil as was needed and that 60 million barrels were only 4% of IEA members' total strategic oil reserves.

The second option was to conclude a new iteration of the JCPOA with Iran, or at least some temporary working version of it until a more thoroughly constructed longer-term version could be phased in. The full details of the negotiating points pertaining to the JCPOA at this time are analysed in the '*Key Players In The Global Oil Market: The US*' section, but the key fact at that point in March 2022 was that such a deal could bring oil and gas prices down significantly very quickly.

The First Option Was To Announce SPR Releases

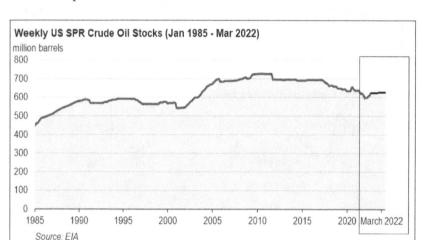

Weekly US SPR Crude Oil Stocks (Jan 1985 - Mar 2022)
Source: EIA

Specifically in this scenario, it was thought that Iran could see an 80% recovery of full production within six months and a 100% recovery within 12 months, with Iranian production increasing by as much as 1.7 million bpd (including 200,000 bpd of condensate and LPG/ethane), in a six- to nine- month period from when sanctions were lifted, prompting a quick 5-10% fall in the oil price.

For obvious reasons, Moscow was busy trying to destroy or delay the chance of this happening. Russian Foreign Minister, Sergei Lavrov, on 5 March, demanded 'written guarantees' that Western sanctions over Ukraine 'will by no means affect our right to free and full-fledged trading, economic, investment, military and technical cooperation with Iran.'

Russia remained one of the five countries that constituted the United Nations Security Council that had signed the original JCPOA, along with Germany, and Moscow's signature would still be required for any new full version of the JCPOA to go ahead, despite its actions in Ukraine.

However, as news emerged that a new temporary form of JCPOA might be signed between all the Western sponsors of the deal – omitting

Russia and, if necessary, China as well – the Russia-sponsored elements of Iran's IRGC made additional attempts to sabotage a new deal. This included an attack on a US consulate complex in the northern Iraqi city of Erbil.

Russia Still Held One Of The Key UNSC Permanent Memberships

Composition Of United Nations Security Council (as at 1 March 2022)

ASIA, PACIFIC
2 seats

USA

RUSSIA

5 permanent members, who have veto power.

FRANCE

UNITED KINGDOM

CHINA

AFRICA
3 seats

10 non-permanent members with no veto power, each elected for two years.

LATIN AMERICA AND THE CARIBBEAN
2 seats

EASTERN EUROPE
1 seat

WESTERN EUROPE AND OTHERS
2 seats

Apart from procedural matters, 9 out of 15 votes are required for a decision to be valid, including agreement or abstention by the P5. In the absence of formal approval, abstentions are understood as a politically ambivalent "endorsement" of the Council's decisions.

CSS Analyses in Security Policy, No. 262, May 2020

Sources: UN, Tages-Anzeiger

The third option open to US President Biden to bring oil prices down was to partially lift the US-centric sanctions on Venezuela, which has the highest oil reserves in the world - at 304 billion barrels.

Laying the groundwork for this strategy was the release by Venezuela of two jailed US citizens following talks with a high-level US delegation in Caracas. White House Press Secretary, Jen Psaki, confirmed that 'energy security' was one of the issues that had been raised at the talks in the Venezuelan capital.

In the first instance, if US sanctions had been partially lifted allowing for oil exports to resume from Venezuela, then the expectations were that they would go to the US itself to compensate for lost supplies from Russia, following Washington's recent ban on oil imports from there. This, though, would have caused a ripple effect in the global oil and gas supply/demand complex that would have softened these energy prices.

The fourth option for Biden, although it was unlikely to yield significant increases in oil production in the very short term, was to encourage US oil firms, shale or otherwise, to increase their production. In the third week of March 2022, US Energy Secretary,, Jennifer Granholm, said that Biden's administration had already started taking steps that should result in a 'significant increase' in domestic energy supply by the end of the year.

According to Granholm in March, the US was working to identify at least 3 million bpd of new global oil supply, with assurances from several high-level oil and gas executives that their companies were set to dramatically increase investments and bring new rigs online.

China's Accidental Contribution To Lowering Energy Prices

Although by the time of Russia's invasion of Ukraine it can be said that COVID-19 was broadly in decline across the world, with the roll-out of several effective vaccines against the disease and treatments for those who were infected, the situation in China was very different.

China had adopted a 'zero-COVID' strategy to handling the disease, as had several other countries at the onset of the virus, to greater or lesser degrees. However, China's version of zero-COVID was particularly strict, an interpretation backed personally by President Xi. He regarded the country's ability to survive COVID-19 without assistance from other countries, and then to quickly prosper afterwards, as a matter of patriotic pride. He said: 'We must adhere to scientific precision, to dynamic zero-COVID…Persistence is victory.'

Under China's interpretation of the zero-COVID strategy, each strand of the 'Find, Test, Trace, Isolate and Support' (FTTIS) policy inherent in the zero-COVID model was implemented with the utmost rigour. In practical terms, this meant at its most extreme iteration locking down entire cities in China, including its major economic centres.

Just a week or so after Russia had launched its invasion of Ukraine, China saw the largest wave of COVID-19 infections since those across Wuhan in early 2020, with the new cases focused across its northeast and coastal regions, mostly in the Jilin and Shandong provinces.

At that point, although the rhetoric coming from various Chinese authorities did not signal any softening in the official zero-COVID containment strategy in the near term, the previous December had seen a refinement of the strategy to one incorporating the idea of 'dynamic clearing'. This provided local governments with a little more flexibility in imposing restrictions, allowing daily increases in symptomatic cases to be capped at around 200 on a national basis.

Oil Prices Softened On China's March 2022 COVID-19 Case Spike

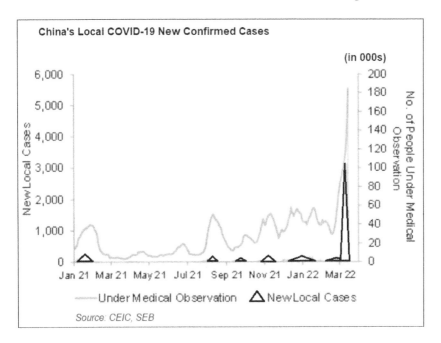

Even back then, though, there were clear limits to this flexibility. China's still-aggressive approach to tracing possible exposures to the virus put more than 184,000 individuals under medical observation in isolation within two weeks of a major new outbreak in March 2022.

The potential loss of a significant element of demand from China – the world's biggest net importer of crude oil and associated products – served to take the edge off the rising trend in oil prices that had occurred following Russia's invasion of Ukraine. Oil prices then looked softer still with news at the end of March that the economic powerhouse city of Shanghai, population 26 million, had been placed in a two-stage lockdown. This was then followed in early April by news that the authorities in other cities, including Ningbo (population 4.2 million) and the capital Beijing (22 million) had begun implementing limited restrictions to curb the spread of the virus.

Again, at that point, there had been hopes of a softening in the zero-COVID policy, stoked by the publication in the second week of April from the Chinese Center for Disease Control and Prevention (CCDC) of a guide that outlined measures for quarantining at home. These measures seemed to indicate the possibility that those people suffering from very mild symptoms or none at all, but having tested positive for COVID, might be able to quarantine at home rather than having to go to centralised state-run facilities to do so. Hopes that such measures might be introduced, however, were dashed when the CCDC in a later clarification simply reiterated the previous set of strict zero-COVID policies.

At that point, the bearish effect on global crude oil prices of the 'China COVID' factor was highlighted by OPEC in its report wherein it cut its global oil demand forecast for 2022 by 480,000 bpd. At almost the same time, the same reasoning was given by the IEA in the lowering of its global demand outlook for 2022 by 260,000 bpd.

Even then, though, the IEA warned that although crude oil prices had come back down from recent highs (trading at that point around the USD110.00 pb of Brent level), they still: 'Remain troublingly high and are a serious threat to the global economic outlook.' This was even before further spikes in oil prices prompted by ongoing talks about a bullish-for-prices ban on Russian oil.

The end of April 2022 saw further announcements from China of mass testing for the virus being rolled out across Beijing, and other cities, including Hangzhou (population 12.2 million). By the beginning of May, some analysts had calculated that the effect of ongoing lockdowns in China was reducing crude oil demand from it by around one million barrels per day, with no indication of when or how this decline would end.

Even before the transmission of COVID surged in mid-March, several major banks had regarded China's 2022 economic growth target of 'about 5.5 percent', as China had indicated, as too ambitious and the big data releases in April showed that they were right.

April's official Purchasing Managers' Index (PMI) – the key indicator that shows the state of a country's manufacturing activity (with a reading above 50 showing an expansion and below 50 marking a contraction) came in at just 47.4 for the month, the lowest level since February 2020.

China's own National Bureau of Statistics (NBS) senior statistician, Zhao Qinghe, stated that: 'The production and operation of... enterprises have been greatly affected [by COVID-related actions].' Although the waves of the Omicron variant of COVID that were sweeping across China at that time appeared to have peaked by the middle of April, it remained the case that mobility across the country had stayed low and economic stimulus measures had been rendered less effective.

China COVID-19 Resurgence Put A Temporary Brake On Oil Price Rises

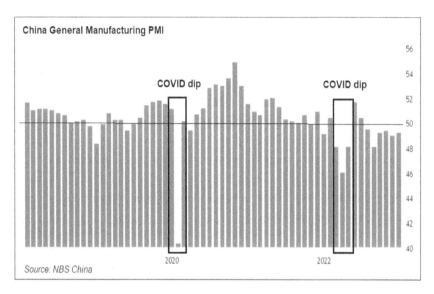

Moreover, with the zero-COVID policy still in place, further lockdowns looked inevitable during the remainder of 2022. These looked likely to be exacerbated in their negative effects by the ongoing severe healthcare limitations across China, including the low vaccination rate and insufficient numbers of hospitals and staff.

Given the nationalistic element involved in China's application of its zero-COVID policy, as espoused by Xi, the country had also refused international offers from all major vaccine-producing countries to make such supplies available to it, despite having no effective vaccine of its own. China also did not have an effective post-infection anti-viral, again despite offers from several countries to make such supplies and post-infection treatments available to it.

With President Xi so closely associated with the strict zero-COVID policy it was difficult to see any change to the rigour of its implementation in the run-up to the 20th National Congress of the Chinese Communist Party due to be held in October 2022.

Oil Price Swings In Early Aftermath Of Russia's Invasion

In broad terms, after the initial spike in the Brent benchmark on the news that Russia had invaded Ukraine, oil prices seesawed on two primary factors.

The primary bullish factor for prices was the prospect of major supply shortfalls. In the short term, these were expected to come from logistical disruptions in the supply of oil and gas from Russia due to the ongoing invasion of Ukraine. In the medium term, if the Russia-Ukraine War continued past the first month, then the supply disruptions were expected to continue as sanctions of some sort or another would be placed on Russia and perhaps on those energy supplying countries that supported it as well. In the long term, it was expected that some sort of compromise solution would be effected with Russia, with oil and gas supplies additionally sourced from other suppliers.

The offsetting part of this bullish trade outlook was that some new supplies could be brought into the market for an unspecified time through SPR releases from the US and from other IEA member countries and others. New supplies could also possibly come through new deals done directly with major suppliers not allied to Russia.

Precisely which countries these were varied during the different phases of the Russia-Ukraine War, although at various points they included all the major suppliers of oil and gas in the Middle East and beyond. There was also the emergency backstop possibility that interim deals might be done with countries sanctioned by the US and its allies to bring new oil and gas supplies online as quickly as possible, most notably with Iran and Venezuela.

The primary bearish factor for prices was the prospect of major demand reductions. One of these remained further COVID-19 outbreaks in China. The other was the likelihood of demand destruction resulting from reduced economic growth, perhaps tipping into recession, across several of world's largest economies as interest rates were repeatedly hiked to combat energy price-driven inflation. This factor in oil prices increased in importance the longer the war in Ukraine kept oil prices high.

Oil Price Swings In The Aftermath Of Russia's Invasion Of Ukraine

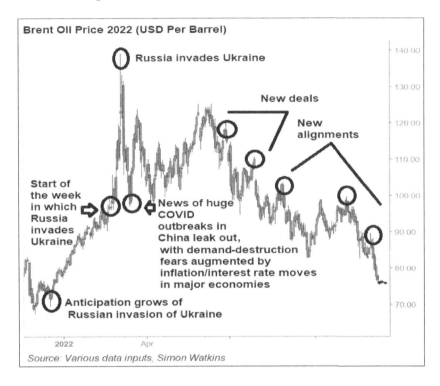

As it was then, Brent crude had seesawed from around the low USD80 pb level on the Monday of the week in which Russia had first invaded Ukraine to around the USD140 pb level, and then back down again to around the mid-USD90 pb levels in early March as news of China's new COVID-19 infections came into the market.

It then swung with extreme daily volatility between the high-USD90 pb levels to the mid-USD120 pb levels until it started to trend decisively down from around the second week in June. This downswing was based on announcements of new deals and initiatives being struck and on an apparent change in the attitudes towards Russia's invasion of Ukraine of several major oil market players.

China's 'No Limit' Friendship With Russia Develops Limits

By far the most notable of these changes in attitudes came from China. As mentioned earlier, just three weeks before Russia invaded Ukraine, President Putin had held his first in-person meeting with his Chinese counterpart Xi Jinping for nearly two years, at the opening of the Winter Olympics ceremony in Beijing. After this meeting, China and Russia had issued a joint communiqué on 4 February in which they had stated that: 'Friendship between the two States [China and Russia] has no limits, there are no forbidden areas of cooperation'.

At around the same time as this meeting, several huge new cooperation deals in the oil and gas sectors and beyond had been announced by state news agencies on both sides. These deals had broadly built on the two countries' increasingly coordinated global activities in the previous few years geared towards weakening the dominant global power position of the US and then supplanting it in this role.

However, within a week of the Russia-Ukraine war having spread to Ukraine's major cities, Xi held urgent talks with Putin and advocated peaceful negotiations between Russia and Ukraine. At the same time, China's then-Foreign Minister Wang Yi told senior European officials that China respects countries' sovereignty, including Ukraine's, while adding that Russia's concerns about NATO's eastward expansion should be properly addressed.

Such a swift public intervention by China to clearly state its view on respecting other countries' sovereignty - when this was precisely what Russia's invasion of Ukraine had not done - shocked Putin, according to senior sources close to the Russian president. He had been certain before the invasion that China would stand by Russia whatever it did, in line with the 'no limit' friendship joint communiqué released so recently.

China, for its part, according to the same sources, had not been kept fully informed by Putin of what Russia had intended to do in Ukraine in terms both of the sequence of actions and their timing. For China, the optimal approach to increasing its power, and that of its allies – including Russia – was the steady accretion of influence through economic and political deals, as exemplified through the stealth strategy inherent in its OBOR programme.

In terms of the European phase of this programme, what China wanted Russia to do was to continue to increase the dependence of European states, principally Germany, on cheap and plentiful supplies of Russian gas, and also oil, whilst additionally broadening and deepening its relationships with key political and business figures across the region.

China Wanted Russia To Increase Its Influence In Europe Gradually

In this context, China had been very pleased with the progress of the second Nord Stream pipeline that would take Russian gas direct into Germany. Beijing anticipated further similar developments in the following few years would mean that Russia's influence over Europe would be ingrained into the fabric of its economic and political systems by 2027.

By this time, China also anticipated that its own OBOR-related efforts would have secured interests in key infrastructure in the north and south of Europe. One notable example of what China was looking to do more broadly in Europe came in 2016 when Greece allowed the China Ocean Shipping Company (Cosco) to secure a 67% stake in the country's major port of Piraeus in Athens. President Xi described Cosco's investment in Piraeus as an 'exemplary project'. He added: 'Piraeus is an important hub for China's fast land-sea link with Europe, and for connectivity between Asia and Europe'.

China had similar ambitions in Germany, with the intention being for Cosco to acquire a 35% stake in Germany's Hamburg Port, which would have allowed it to become a 'preferred hub' for Cosco in Europe. The idea received a high degree of personal backing from German Chancellor, Olaf Scholz, who stressed the importance of strong trade ties between China and Germany.

However, shortly after Russia's invasion of Ukraine, objections from several German, European and US organisations became louder, resulting in Cosco only being allowed a 24.9% stake in Hamburg Port. China was also looking to expand its OBOR-related footprint into other key European states, both in the south and in the north before Russia's invasion of Ukraine made the advancement of these projects in the way China had envisaged much more difficult.

China's stealth approach to the accretion of power and influence in target countries – founded on the mixture of economic and political elements inherent in the OBOR programme – was also the one favoured for its eventual 'repatriation' of Taiwan.

Xi knew when he met Putin in early February 2022 that neither country, even working together (and even when the myth of the 'invincible' Russia Army was still intact), could defeat the US and its allies militarily at that point. Therefore, he had always been careful not to overstep the carefully drawn-up boundaries between the US and China on what China (or the US) could do relating to Taiwan.

This is based on the highly precise terms involved in all the pertinent agreements and understandings between China and the US relating to the 'One China' position. This is that: the US 'recognises' the People's Republic of China (based in Beijing) as the sole legal government of China, but only 'acknowledges' the Chinese position that Taiwan is part of China.

This is why, in the same 4 February 2022 joint communiqué between China and Russia, virtually at the top of the document was the statement:

'The sides call on all States to [...] protect the United Nations-driven international architecture and the international law-based world order, seek genuine multipolarity with the United Nations and its Security Council playing a central and coordinating role, promote more democratic international relations, and ensure peace, stability and sustainable development across the world'.

The joint communiqué had also made the point – aimed at what China (and Russia) saw as military interference by the US and its allies in the internal affairs of other countries - that: 'Some actors representing but the minority on the international scale continue to advocate unilateral approaches to addressing international issues and resort to force; they interfere in the internal affairs of other states, infringing their legitimate rights and interests, and incite contradictions, differences and confrontation, thus hampering the development and progress of mankind, against the opposition from the international community'.

The problem for China was that having laid down its supposed endgame in its international ambitions and the methods by which it wanted to achieve it – and having contrasted those with the methods it saw the US and its allies as using - its own principal geopolitical ally, Russia, had done much worse by launching a full-scale invasion of a sovereign territory, unprovoked and unwanted by its people.

China's attitude to Russia following the invasion became more cautious, then, and this was reflected in the attitudes to Russia of those countries whose primary allegiance in the China-Russia bloc had always been primarily to China, not to Russia. Publicly, although Beijing refrained from calling Russia's actions in Ukraine an 'invasion', and abstained in a UN Security Council resolution vote that would have deplored Russia's aggression against Ukraine at the time, it reiterated several times that it respected the 'sovereignty and territorial integrity of all countries'.

Europe's Early Reticence On Russian Energy Sanctions

Given these more cautious attitudes on Russia's invasion of Ukraine from several of Russia's previously stalwart allies, including China, the opportunity for the US and its allies to sanction Russia effectively around the globe appeared considerable.

The US and its closest NATO allies knew that the most effective method to punish Russia for its invasion in the medium and long term – and to even possibly manoeuvre President Putin into peace talks sooner rather than later – were sanctions focussed on two key areas, both of which had to function properly in order to be effective.

The first area was to ban the Russian state, Russian companies, and key Russian individuals, from using the US dollar in their transactions. Effectively functioning as the global reserve currency and the currency in which the oil and gas markets are denominated, such a ban on the use of the US dollar would be potentially catastrophic over time for the Russian economy and perhaps even to Putin's political standing in the country. The second area was to ban Russian oil and gas exports to as many of its key markets as possible. Oil and gas export revenues historically accounted for nearly half of Russia's government budget, and even more when taking into account tangential goods and services to the oil and gas sectors.

The US on its own could put into place the mechanisms involved in banning the use of the US dollar by the people and sectors it wanted, particularly with the ready support of the UK's key financial markets that were home to a large proportion of foreign Russian money.

However, for the ban on Russian oil and gas exports to work, the US and its core allies would need to persuade Germany to back the sanctions as well. Not only was Germany a huge buyer of Russian gas, especially, and also oil, but it was also important politically as the effective leader of the European Union.

It is apposite to note at this point that there was enormous pushback from the 27 country European Union alliance over reimposing sanctions on Iran after the US unilaterally withdrew from the JCPOA in May 2018, as analysed in full in the *'Key Players In The Global Oil Market: Iran'* section.

Germany had also been at the forefront of several EU initiatives designed to circumvent the mainly US-led sanctions before 2018, specifically during the phase of heightened sanctions from 2011/2012. Shortly after the US announcement of its withdrawal from the JCPOA deal in May 2018, the EU had moved to impose its 'Blocking Statute' that made it illegal for EU companies to follow US sanctions.

At around the same time, Germany's then-Foreign Minister, Sigmar Gabriel, had warned: 'We also have to tell the Americans that their behaviour on the Iran issue will drive us Europeans into a common position with Russia and China against the USA.' Shortly after that, Germany was a key mover in the EU's introduction of a special purpose vehicle – the 'Instrument in Support of Trade Exchanges' – that would act as a clearing house for payments made between Iran and EU companies.

Europe Had A High Dependence On Russian Oil

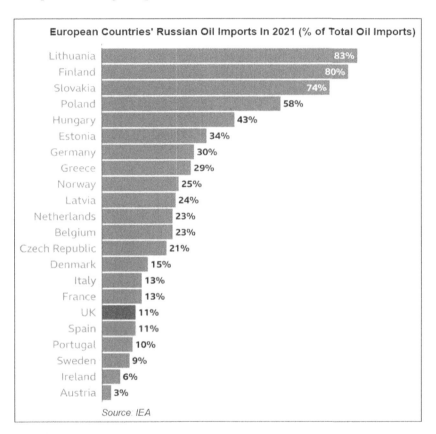

European Countries' Russian Oil Imports In 2021 (% of Total Oil Imports)

- Lithuania 83%
- Finland 80%
- Slovakia 74%
- Poland 58%
- Hungary 43%
- Estonia 34%
- Germany 30%
- Greece 29%
- Norway 25%
- Latvia 24%
- Netherlands 23%
- Belgium 23%
- Czech Republic 21%
- Denmark 15%
- Italy 13%
- France 13%
- UK 11%
- Spain 11%
- Portugal 10%
- Sweden 9%
- Ireland 6%
- Austria 3%

Source: IEA

On the oil side of the equation back in early 2022, prior to the invasion of Ukraine, Europe was importing around 2.7 million bpd of crude from Russia and another 1.5 million bpd of oil products, mostly diesel. Even before the EU's 27 member states met on 8 May 2022 to discuss pushing forward with the US-proposed ban on Russian oil, Hungary and Slovakia had made it clear that they were not going to vote in favour of it.

According to figures from the IEA, Hungary imported 43% of its total oil imports in 2021 from Russia, while the figure for Slovakia was even higher, at 74% of all its oil imports in the same year. Other EU countries also heavily reliant on oil from Russia's Southern Druzhba pipeline (that ran through Ukraine and Belarus) also made it clear that they were not willing to support the ban on Russian oil exports.

The most vocal of these were the Czech Republic (68,000 bpd of its 2021 oil imports came from Russia) and Bulgaria. The government in Sofia was almost completely dependent on gas supplies from Russia's state-owned oil giant Gazprom, and its only refinery was owned by Russia's state-owned oil giant, Lukoil, providing over 60% of its total fuel requirements. Other EU member states that were also especially dependent on Russian oil imports were Lithuania (185,000 bpd, or 83%, of its 2021 total oil imports) and Finland (185,000 bpd, or 80%, of its total oil imports).

Even compromise proposals offered by the EU of allowing Hungary and Slovakia to continue to use Russian oil until the end of 2024 (and the Czech Republic until June 2024) were not enough to remove their opposition to the idea of the proposed EU ban on Russian oil at that point.

In fact, the only real flurry of activity in terms of a concerted effort by any group within the EU during those early weeks after Russia invaded Ukraine was aimed at ensuring that Russia did not stop supplying its member states with either oil or gas, due to their not being able to pay in the way Moscow preferred. This followed the 31 March decree signed by President Vladimir Putin that required EU buyers to pay in roubles for Russian gas via a new currency conversion mechanism or risk having supplies suspended.

According to an official guidance document sent out to all 27 EU member states on 21 April by its executive branch, the European Commission (EC): 'It appears possible [to pay for Russian gas after the adoption of the new decree without being in conflict with EU law],... EU companies can ask their Russian counterparts to fulfil their contractual obligations in the same manner as before the adoption of the decree, i.e. by depositing the due amount in euros or dollars.' The EC added that existing EU sanctions against Russia also did not prohibit engagement with Russia's Gazprom or Gazprombank beyond the refinancing prohibitions relating to the bank.

Several EU member states made it plain that they would veto any EU proposal to ban Russian oil (or gas) imports – and all 27 EU member states must vote in favour of such a ban for it to come into effect. Additionally, the EC sent out crib notes on how best to continue to pay for Russian oil and gas imports, effectively to bypass any sanctions on them, including those from the US.

Germany was also set to be hit hard itself by any ban on Russian oil in the first instance, being the recipient in 2021 of the most crude oil from Russia of any country in the EU – an average of 555,000 bpd, or 30% of its total oil imports in that year, according to the IEA.

Germany Had An Even Higher Dependence On Russian Gas

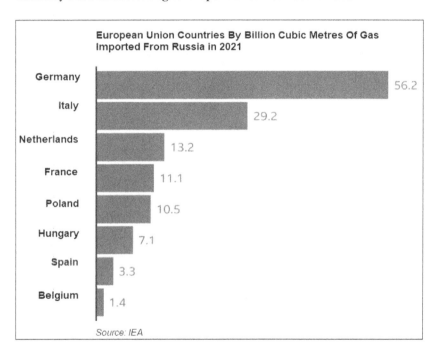

Comments from German Economics Minister, Robert Habeck, that Berlin was prepared for a ban on Russian energy imports were overlain with considerable detail about how Germany had still not been able to find alternative long-term fuel supplies for the Russian oil that came by pipeline to a refinery in Schwedt operated by Russia's state-owned oil giant Rosneft. He concluded that fuel prices could rise and that an embargo 'in a few months' would give Germany time to organise itself in this regard.

The EU's view on the gas side of the Russian energy import equation was in the same vein and based on the same sort of reliance on these imports from Russia as it had for oil. As at the end of 2021, according to IEA figures, the European Union imported an average of over 380 million cubic metres (mcm) per day of gas by pipeline from Russia, or around 140 billion cubic metres (bcm) for the year as a whole. As well as that, around 15 bcm was delivered in LNG form.

The total 155 bcm imported from Russia accounted for around 45% of the EU's gas imports in 2021 and almost 40% of its total gas consumption. Germany itself was reliant on Russian gas for around 30-40% of its own commercial and domestic gas needs, depending on the time of year.

Qatar Becomes A Key 'Swing' Energy Supplier For Europe

It was vital to the interests of the US and its European allies – both from the security perspective of NATO and from the intertwined economic perspective of the EU, the UK, and the US – that substitute sources of gas and oil be found as quickly as possible.

Plans were being put into place for Europe to reduce its gas and oil needs for Russia over time, and in the interim to attempt to reduce their energy usage as winter 2022 approached. However, the reality was that without new energy supplies flowing into the continent before and during winter, any political resolve the EU had to implement meaningful energy sanctions against Russia was liable to break.

One country that emerged early on front and centre of the new global energy order in this context was Qatar, the world's leading LNG exporter at the beginning of 2022 and for many years before, barring a brief period when it was overtaken by Australia.

LNG remained the most flexible form of gas for buyers, being readily available in the spot markets and able to be moved very quickly to anywhere required, unlike gas or oil sent through pipelines. Unlike pipelined energy as well, the movement of LNG does not require the build-out of vast acreage of pipelines across varying terrains and the associated heavy infrastructure that supports it. In essence, LNG supplies are the 'swing gas supply' in any global gas supply emergency.

Qatar has several key factors to its advantage as far as Western buyers in urgent need of energy are concerned. The first is that it already has huge gas reserves – the third-largest in the world (after Russia and then Iran), at

872 trillion cubic feet (Tcf). Not only had it recouped its world number one LNG exporter spot by the beginning of 2022, but it was also in the process of increasing its LNG production by 2024 to around 110 million mtpa from 77 million mtpa or so, and then to 126 million mtpa by 2027.

The second factor in its favour from the Western perspective was that although its geographical position between Saudi Arabia and Iran had inclined it towards a politically neutral geopolitical stance since it gained independence from the UK in 1971, in recent years there had been significant trouble between it and Saudi Arabia. On 5 June 2017, Saudi Arabia had led the UAE, Bahrain and Egypt into severing diplomatic relations with Qatar. It had additionally banned Qatar-registered aeroplanes and ships from utilising their air and sea space and had also blocked Qatar's only land crossing.

In January 2019 Qatar left the Saudi-led OPEC, after 60 years as a member, with Saad Sherida al-Kaabi, Qatar's minister of state for energy affairs and president and chief executive officer of Qatar Petroleum, saying that the decision was: 'Not political, it was purely a business decision for Qatar's future strategy towards the energy sector.' With Saudi Arabia increasingly regarded by the West as a neutral country at best, and one increasingly aligned with Russia and China, Qatar appeared to be an even more promising prospect as an emergency energy supplier into Europe.

May 2022, then, saw Qatar sign a declaration of intent on energy cooperation with Germany aimed at becoming its key supplier of LNG. These new supplies of LNG from Qatar would come into Germany through existing importation routes augmented by new infrastructure approved by the German Bundestag on 19 May. This would include the deployment of four floating LNG import facilities on its northern coast, and two permanent onshore terminals, which were under development.

These plans would run in parallel with, but were likely to be finished significantly sooner than, the plans for Qatar to also make available to Germany sizeable supplies of LNG from the Golden Pass terminal on the Gulf Coast of Texas. QatarEnergy holds a 70% stake in the project, with the US's ExxonMobil holding the remainder. The Golden Pass terminal's estimated send-out capacity is projected to be around 18 million mtpa of LNG and the facility is expected to be operational in 2024.

Around one month after this declaration of intent on energy cooperation with Germany was signed by Qatar, the Emirate signed new partnership deals with France's TotalEnergies and Italy's Eni for the USD30 billion North Field Expansion project. According to statements from Qatar's Energy Minister al-Kaabi, the French oil and gas supermajor would have a 25% stake in the project, with no other company to have a higher stake. The same terms were announced for the Eni partnership deal.

Qatar Was Seen As The Top 'Swing' Gas Producer After Russian Invasion

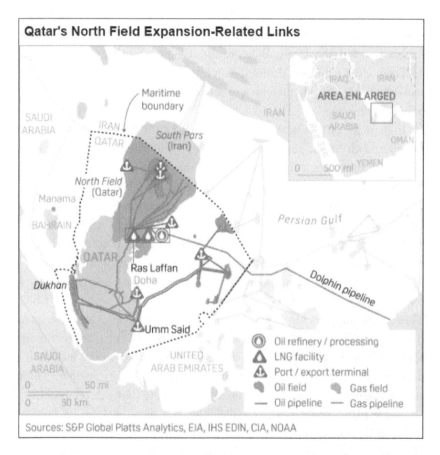

Qatar's North Field Expansion-Related Links

Sources: S&P Global Platts Analytics, EIA, IHS EDIN, CIA, NOAA

TotalEnergies' chief executive officer, Patrick Pouyanne, highlighted that the company's 25% stake would be for one 'train' (liquefaction and purification facility) of the project. Al-Kaabi confirmed that, as Qatar has a unified approach, in which all four trains are considered to be one unit, TotalEnergies' 25% stake in one virtual train would give it around a 6.25% holding in the whole four trains. The same terms would apply for Eni.

European And US IOCs Work To Secure New Energy Flows

These new deals with Qatar dovetailed into the determined push early after the Russian invasion of Ukraine by selected European major oil and gas companies to act as spearheads for securing new oil and gas supplies for their countries. France's TotalEnergies, Italy's Eni, and the UK's Shell and BP were at the vanguard of these approaches for European countries. They were bolstered by direct and indirect support from several of their US counterparts, most notably early on by Chevron and ConocoPhillips.

For France, TotalEnergies signed a series of such deals early on after 24 February 2022 and laid the groundwork for several more deals. July saw the French oil and gas giant sign a partnership agreement with the Abu Dhabi National Oil Co. (ADNOC) that included cooperation in trading, product supply, and carbon capture, utilisation and storage.

For ADNOC, the deal was in line with its target of increasing its crude oil production to 5 million bpd, from around 4 million bpd at that point, by 2030. The UAE state oil firm had reiterated its intention of spending USD127 billion between then and 2026 on projects related to this growth target, and to achieving growth in other commercial areas as well. In this vein, it had already attracted by the middle of 2022 just over USD64.5 billion in foreign investments since 2016 by monetising several of its assets.

For the US and its allies, given the drift of the UAE towards the China-Russia alliance from around the time that the US withdrew from the JCPOA with Iran, any such deals by Western companies were extremely notable. The broader importance of this deal with the UAE, and with similar deals made by TotalEnergies at around the same time, was subtly acknowledged in the French company's official comments on the deal. '[The agreement includes] the development of oil and gas projects in the UAE to ensure sustainable energy supply to the markets and contribute to global energy security,' it said.

The July 2022 deal also came after the signing of the UAE-France Comprehensive Strategic Energy Partnership, which also focused on securing energy supply for France going forward. Concerns about the negative effects for France of the then-mooted bans on Russian energy came from France's economy minister, Bruno Le Maire, who said: 'Let's prepare for a total cut-off of Russian gas.'

Although France received at that point slightly less than 20% of its gas imports from Russia – much less than several other EU states - its LNG imports fell by nearly 60% month-on-month in June, to around 1.06 million metric tonnes. This last fact also explained why TotalEnergies had been so busy at that point in Qatar, putting it in prime position to win, as it did, one of the highly prized partnership deals with the Qatari government to develop the huge offshore North Field East gas project.

Although Germany has long been seen as the leader of the EU, in the matter of world-class energy companies it has been left wanting. France - having pushed for the 'Treaty of Paris' in 1951 (which can be seen as the precursor to the European Economic Community and then to the EU itself) – had long seen itself as the ideological leader of the EU and in TotalEnergies it had a truly world-class international oil company.

From the economic, political, and energy perspectives of the US and EU, then, what TotalEnergies was doing was much more than any of those single elements on their own. Given France's long history in the Middle East – the most active European country for many years, together with the UK – its companies were also in a position to leverage decades-old contacts and networks of influence to secure the necessary meetings with the key people in key areas to advance its agenda.

The combination of these factors was perhaps most evident in Total Energies' huge, four-pronged deal in Iraq; a country that in many ways had sought to distance itself from the US and its most apparent allies, including the UK. In this context, July 2022 had also seen TotalEnergies reiterate its commitment to the US$27 billion deals agreed in 2021 with Iraq's Oil Ministry, and the company was set to move into its 'execution phase' at some point during the year.

The first of these phases would address the completion of the Common Seawater Supply Project (CSSP). This project is covered in full in the *Key Players In The Global Oil Market: Iraq'* section but it is apposite to note here that the CSSP was, and still is, absolutely crucial in enabling Iraq to reach its longer-term crude oil production targets of 7 million bpd, and then even 9 million bpd and perhaps 12 million bpd.

The second of the projects also was, and remains, a matter of high importance and urgent necessity: to collect and refine associated natural gas that was being burned off at the five southern Iraq oilfields of West Qurna

2, Majnoon, Tuba, Luhais, and Artawi. This would have three key advantages, although all are interlinked.

Iraq's CSSP Build Out Was Critical To Future Oil Output Increases

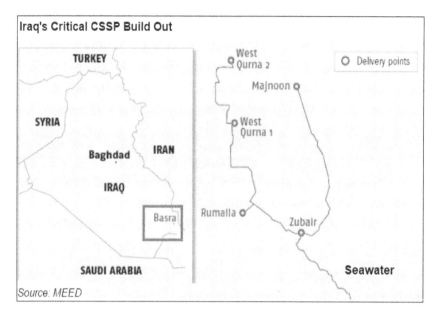

First, it would allow Iraq to make some progress on its commitment to the United Nations and World Bank 'Zero Routine Flaring' initiative - aimed at ending by 2030 the routine flaring of gas produced during the drilling of oil. At that time, Iraq flared the second largest quantity of gas in the world (after Russia) – some 17.37 billion cubic metres.

Second, much of this collected – not burnt off – gas could be used by Iraq for its own domestic power purposes (the above-mentioned amount of gas, if collected, could power around three million homes day and night, year in, year out).

Third, and most important from the perspective of the US and its allies, this would in turn reduce Iraq's dependence on Iran for energy for its power grid.

The penultimate project involving TotalEnergies, would be to increase the crude oil output of the giant Artawi oil field up to 210,000 bpd of crude oil, from the then-circa-85,000 bpd. The fourth project would be to construct and operate a 1,000-megawatt solar energy plant in Iraq.

The US And Its Allies No Longer Need A New Iran Deal

With major new oil and gas supply deals already yielding new energy flows into Europe and other US security allies, and storage levels of oil and gas well on the way to being full ahead of winter, there was no need to accommodate Iran's demands to secure a new iteration of the JCPOA.

This point, around the middle of the third quarter of 2022, marked the beginning of a hardening view by the US and its key security allies that it was only by bolstering its key alliance structures – NATO and its fewer formal equivalents in Asia – that their political, military, economic and energy security could truly be safeguarded.

The idea of Europe as a fully-functioning entity that could survive – never mind prosper – in a world in which Russia would likely continue to salami-slice pieces of it away from the whole if it was successful in Ukraine was increasingly regarded as fanciful.

The failure of the US and Europe to act decisively in Georgia in 2008 and then in Crimea in 2014 had meant that Russia felt able to invade Ukraine with little fear of significant action being taken against it. Moreover, after each of these events, the US's and Europe's trade with Russia had not been affected seriously either.

Therefore, if Russia succeeded in Ukraine then there was no reason for it not to do the same in the next European country of its choice, and then the one after that, and so on. Even if it failed, given the previous world order, then it would have lost nothing in trying.

It was also obvious to both the US and Europe that not only could things never go back to the way they were before with Russia – which meant bolstering their abilities to survive and prosper as, effectively, a standalone unit – but also the same would have to be done with their allies in the Far East. This was because it was also obvious to all three elements of this new world order alliance – the US and its allies in Europe and the Far East – that China was watching every aspect of what happened with Russia's invasion of Ukraine for future reference for its own ambitions in Taiwan, elsewhere in Asia, and beyond.

The JCPOA deal with Iran, then, which was deeply insinuated in the China-Russia sphere of influence, could have no place in this new US-centric architecture and from the same time as this view hardened among the US and its allies around the middle of the third quarter of 2022,

Washington took an uncompromising view on Tehran's demands. This view was supported in full by Europe.

The view of the US and its allies was not one founded primarily on the subtle vagaries of the global energy market. It was one instead founded on whether Iran wanted to be part of its alliance or that of China-Russia and there was no middle ground afforded it in terms of deciding.

Although the ebbs and flows connected to the JCPOA are analysed in full in the '*Key Players In The Global Oil Market: Iran*' section, it is illustrative here to state the US's uncompromising position, and why it took it. The US's intransigence over a new iteration of the JCPOA looked like it was based on a mere technicality but, in fact, it went to the very foundation of what the Islamic Republic of Iran was.

The point in question was that Iran demanded as a prerequisite for future negotiations on the JCPOA that the US remove its designation of its Islamic Revolutionary Guards Corps (IRGC) as a 'Foreign Terrorist Organisation' (FTO). This designation had been placed on the group in 2019 during former US President Donald Trump's term in office.

For Tehran, not only does the IRGC function as the guardian of the spirit of its 1979 Islamic Revolution but it is also the principal mechanism through which Iran can spread its own particular brand of Islamic faith across the world through whatever means it deems necessary. These means include the bankrolling and the logistical and materiel support by Iran of multiple military and political proxies across the globe, many of which are deemed as terrorist organisations by the US and its allies.

These activities require funding - almost always ultimately converted into US dollars or gold. For this reason, the IRGC had been allowed to access every layer of Iran's business and financial networks since 1979 to the point where by 2022 it was inextricably ingrained throughout the entire fabric of Iran's economy.

Estimates at the time were that the IRGC has placed top commanders at the heart of more than 200 Iranian companies. Even back at the beginning of 2016 – around the same time as Implementation Day of the first JCPOA - Emanuele Ottolenghi, a senior fellow with the foundation for Defense of Democracies testified before a sub-committee of the US's House Committee on Foreign Affairs that the IRGC had significant ownership shares in 27 companies that were publicly traded on the flagship

Tehran Stock Exchange. This constituted a minimum of 22% of its total value, at the time USD15.8 billion between them.

According to Ottolenghi in 2016, the IRGC was active in the Iranian oil, gas, petrochemical, automotive, transportation, telecommunications, construction, and metals and mining sectors, among others. Additionally, the US Office of Foreign Assets Control, in September 2012, described the National Iranian Oil Company itself as an 'agent or affiliate' of the IRGC and subject to sanctions under 'Iran Threat Reduction Act'.

By Mid-Q322 The US Was Happy To Let Iran Die A Slow Death

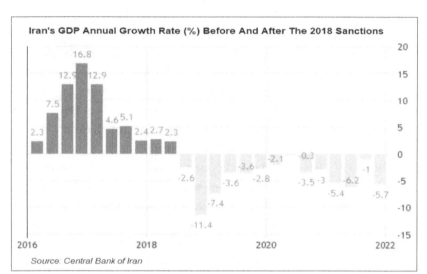

The IRGC and its related entities and proxies were also at the very heart of Iran's nuclear programme, the ultimate intention of which had always been to create nuclear weapons and to eventually pair them with long-range ballistic missiles.

Therefore, by designating the IRGC as an FTO and targeting it by all means available in this context, the US was seeking to hit at the very source of the IRGC's power and, by extension, of Iran's ability to project its influence across the globe.

The US - during the very short talks with Iran in 2022 on the subject of removing the FTO designation of the IRGC - stated that it might be prepared to do so on the specific proviso that Iran signed up to the rules and regulations of the Financial Action Task Force (FATF) and then to becoming a fully-regulated and constantly-monitored FATF member.

The FATF has 40 active criteria and mechanisms in place to prevent money laundering - an activity that is vital to the IRGC's activities across the world. It also has nine criteria and mechanisms in place to do the same for the financing of terrorism and related activities - again, a core of the IRGC's role in promoting Iran's brand of Islam around the globe.

The FATF also has swingeing powers to wield against individuals, companies, or countries who transgress any of its standards and is extremely aggressive in using them by degrees, depending on whether the sanctioned entity is on its 'grey' or 'black' list.

In sum, either the FTO designation stayed, and Iran faced the gradual destruction of its economy through ongoing sanctions, or it signed up to the FATF and faced the gradual destruction of the IRGC. By that point, the US did not care which option it chose, as it regarded the choice as being essentially, 'either you're with us or you're against us and we don't much care either way'.

US's 'NOPEC' Threat Increases On Saudi Arabia

Much the same view was taken by the US and its allies about Saudi Arabia too, given the Kingdom's extreme unhelpfulness in bringing energy prices down, the refusal of Crown Prince Mohammed bin Salman to take President Biden's telephone calls on such issues, and its unwillingness to condemn Russia's actions in Ukraine.

One key threat on which the US had relied in the past to try to keep Saudi Arabia aligned broadly to Washington's foreign policy objectives was the implementation of the 'NOPEC' Bill. As the US played out its non-negotiating game with Iran over the JCPOA, it also rekindled the NOPEC threat against Saudi Arabia.

The NOPEC Bill is analysed in full in the *'Key Players In The Global Oil Market: The US'* section, together with the circumstances and methodology of its various deployments against the Saudis. In this instance, though, early May 2022 saw the passing of the NOPEC Bill by a US Senate committee and it was the surest sign to that point that Washington had finally run out of patience with Saudi Arabia and OPEC.

The ante was huge for Saudi Arabia, OPEC, and OPEC+'s key member, Russia, as the NOPEC Bill in essence has a broad mandate allowing it to declare it illegal to artificially cap oil production or to set prices. OPEC was specifically mandated upon its foundation in 1960 to 'co-ordinate and unify the petroleum policies' of all of its member states – effectively fixing oil prices, just like a cartel.

A Cartel By Any Other Name, As Far As NOPEC Is Concerned

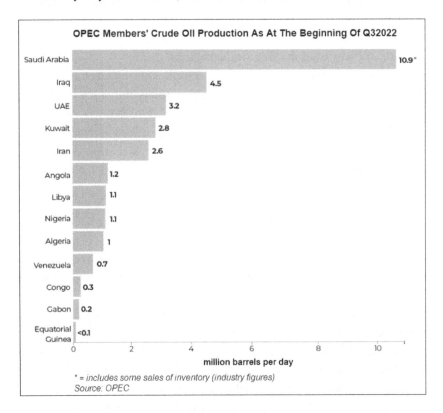

OPEC's cartel-like appearance is further enhanced by the facts that its members account for around 40% of the world's crude oil output, about 60% of the total petroleum traded internationally from their oil exports and just over 80% of the world's proven oil reserves. The NOPEC Bill, if fully enacted, would immediately dramatically inhibit any and all actions or statements from OPEC specifically, and its key members, and its *de facto* leader Saudi Arabia. This would include coordinated oil production cuts or increases and statements relating to where the organisation or any of its key members, including Saudi Arabia, forecast production levels or oil prices might be in the future.

It would also immediately remove the sovereign immunity that existed in US courts for OPEC as a group and for its individual member states. This would leave Saudi Arabia open to being sued under existing US anti-trust legislation, with its total liability being estimated at USD1 trillion of investments in the US alone.

For Saudi Arabia, it would also mean that the effective value of its flagship oil and gas giant, Saudi Aramco, could go to zero, given that the company is the key corporate instrument used to manage the oil flows of the effective leader of the world's *de facto* oil cartel.

Although Saudi Aramco is not directly involved in making OPEC policies, the anti-trust legislation of the US and UK can point to the company as being collusive in price-fixing through the adjustment of its output to help manage oil prices and through statements and guidance from its key corporate officers about future oil production levels of the company and its price expectations.

This view of Saudi Aramco as a proxy of the Saudi Arabian state was not undermined by its part privatisation, as only a tiny percentage of its shares were floated in the IPO in December 2019. Its enduring status as a state proxy even after its IPO was made clear at the time of the offering by statements from leading company and government officials that the company would remain operationally directed by the government of Saudi Arabia. Indeed, Saudi Aramco's chief executive officer, Amin Nasser, said at the time of the IPO that Saudi Aramco's oil and gas production decisions were 'sovereign matters that would remain with the government'.

The eventual enactment of the NOPEC Bill would also mean that trading in all Aramco's products – including oil – would be subject to the anti-trust legislation, meaning the prohibition of sales in US dollars. It could further mean the eventual break-up of Aramco into smaller constituent companies that are not capable of influencing the oil price, if the Saudis could offer up no other way of complying with the anti-trust laws.

The NOPEC Bill had come very close to being fully enacted before, most notably in February 2019 when it was passed by the US's House Judiciary Committee, which cleared the way for a vote on the Bill before the full House of Representatives. On the same day, Democrats Patrick

Leahy and Amy Klobuchar and – most remarkably – two Republicans, Chuck Grassley and Mike Lee, introduced the NOPEC Bill to the Senate.

The passing of the Bill in May 2022 in the Senate Judiciary Committee by 17 votes to 4, sponsored by senators including Republican Chuck Grassley and Democrat Amy Klobuchar, was another key milestone towards its finally being enacted and passing into law. From the May 2022 vote, the option was open to President Biden, or his successors, to move the Bill to the full Senate and House and, if also passed in those two houses, to go to the President to be formally signed into law.

Saudi Reiterates Its Commitment To The OPEC+ Group

Despite the clear message from the US and its allies given through the vote on the NOPEC Bill, Saudi Arabia shortly afterwards reiterated its commitment to the OPEC+ group of oil producers and, by extension, to Russia. Early June 2022 saw Russian Foreign Minister, Sergei Lavrov, and his Saudi counterpart, Prince Faisal bin Farhan, meet at length in Riyadh. Afterwards they released statements highlighting: 'The level of cooperation in the OPEC+ format.' The two ministers also underlined the: 'Stabilising effect that tight coordination between Russia and Saudi Arabia in this strategically-important area has on the global hydrocarbon market.'

The OPEC+ alliance then announced a theoretical increase in crude oil production - of 648,000 bpd in July and August, instead of by 432,000 bpd as previously agreed. However, in practice - as it also included Russian exports that were already banned by the US and in the process of being banned in the EU - the increase was meaningless. Subsequent Saudi assurances that any deficit in Russia's output caused by the ban would be met by other OPEC states was similarly meaningless in practical terms, given enduring question marks over the true crude oil production capabilities of several OPEC countries, most notably of Saudi Arabia itself.

Any residual notion that Saudi Arabia might be trying to alleviate the economic problems of many countries resulting from high oil prices was dispelled over the weekend following the meeting between Lavrov and bin Farhan. The Kingdom raised its official selling price for its flagship Arab Light crude deliveries to Asia for July to a USD6.50 pb premium to the average of the Oman and Dubai benchmarks. This was an increase from a premium of USD4.40 pb for deliveries in June. The net effect of OPEC+'s production increase, therefore, would be zero, which Saudi Arabia, Russia, and all other OPEC members, knew perfectly well.

Russian Crude Oil Production Was Bouncing Back

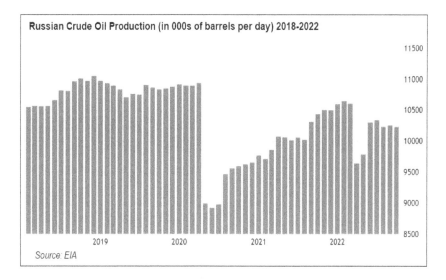

Source: EIA

Two key questions arose from this: the first was, why did Saudi Arabia feel able to disregard the threat from the US and its allies that it should not continue to be a key part of keeping oil prices high? The second was, why was Saudi Arabia persisting in its alliance with Russia, despite its actions in Ukraine and the likely global fallout from it?

The answer to the first question goes back to the key reason behind the Saudis launching the two previous oil price wars. This was, in the most basic terms, that the Saudis could not afford to be part of the US alliance so far as it pertained to energy prices any longer. The US, as analysed earlier, wanted oil prices within the USD40/45-75/80 pb of Brent range. Saudi Arabia could not make money at even the USD80 pb price at the top of that range but equally it could not endure another oil price war that featured prices as low as the USD40 pb level of that range either.

Saudi Arabia needed oil prices at above USD84 pb minimum for years in order to repair the damage done from the previous two oil price wars and to ensure its own future. This was even more necessary, given the greater necessity to bolster its own defences on every level (from hardware through to intelligence capabilities) that would come from a fully rogue Iran if, as seemed likely, no new JCPOA deal was done. Russia, in the aftermath of its invasion of Ukraine in February, also wanted all the money it could get from its oil at high prices. It additionally knew that high prices of oil and gas were causing economic damage to the US and its allies and political damage as well to their governments.

This partly answers the second question as well as to why Saudi Arabia was persisting in its alliance with Moscow. The fact was that Russia could provide all the support that Saudi and OPEC lacked in terms of its genuine crude oil capabilities. It could add lots of barrels quickly and subtract them quickly too. Whether it did so through official or unofficial sales channels made no substantive difference to the global oil market, as such a sizeable addition or subtraction of barrels in the market would ultimately ripple through to its pricing matrix in any event.

Additionally, Russia still had an enormous capability in its intelligence organisations and networks that stretched all the way across the Middle East and into all other major theatres of potential conflict. This remained an extremely useful resource for the Saudis. Russia also had a broad and deep relationship with Saudi Arabia's nemesis, Iran, so the Saudis believed that this too could be used to keep Iran in check as far as the Kingdom was concerned, especially in the event of no new JCPOA deal being struck.

And finally, Russia also enjoyed a similarly multi-layered relationship with China, which the Saudis thought would allow them to further leverage their burgeoning relationship with Beijing. It was true that, as a net importer of oil, China broadly wanted oil prices kept at the lower end of recent historical ranges. However, the Saudis knew that Beijing was happy to live with higher prices for the time being, given the damage that high prices were doing to the US and the boost to China's own prestige and to its sphere of influence that having Saudi Arabia increasingly aligned to it – rather than to the US - meant.

Saudi Arabia's relationship with Beijing would also allow Riyadh growing access to the biggest consumer of oil and products in the world, to further intelligence networks, to military hardware and software, and to support in the United Nations Security Council (UNSC) as and when required. As mentioned earlier, of the five Permanent Members of the UNSC, Russia and China held two positions between them, and France was seen by the Saudis virtually as a neutral in this context. China, like

Russia, also had a very broad and deep relationship with Iran, which again could be utilised by the Saudis to keep any threats to it from Tehran neutralised.

China's Short-Term Pain For Long-Term Gain Trade With Saudi Arabia

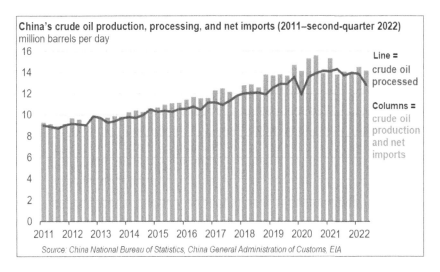

China's crude oil production, processing, and net imports (2011–second-quarter 2022)

Source: China National Bureau of Statistics, China General Administration of Customs, EIA

Saudi Intensifies Its Cooperation With China

From the moment that China offered Saudi Crown Prince MbS a face-saving way out of the Aramco IPO disaster that he had created for himself, as highlighted earlier, the relationship between the two countries had grown ever stronger. As mentioned above, Saudi Arabia appeared determined to stick with Russia, despite its invasion of Ukraine, and in tandem with this – and as part of the tangential relationship between Russia and China – Saudi Arabia's own relationship with China continued to broaden and deepen over the same period.

A little under a year before the Russian invasion of February 2022, Saudi Aramco's chief executive officer, Amin Nasser, had spent several days at the annual China Development Forum hosted in Beijing, during which time he stated: 'Ensuring the continuing security of China's energy needs remains our highest priority - not just for the next five years but for the next 50 and beyond.'

At that point in the first quarter of 2021, Aramco had a 25% stake in the 280,000 bpd Fujian refinery in southern China through a joint venture with Sinopec. Several other joint projects between China and Saudi Arabia that had been agreed in principle were delayed due to a combination of factors. These notably included the ongoing effects of COVID-19, Aramco's crushing dividend repayment schedule (analysed in full in the in the *Key Players In The Global Oil Market: Saudi Arabia'* section), and concern from both countries – especially China – on how Washington might react to this clear threat to the US's own long-running interests in Saudi Arabia.

However, one year later, and just a few months after the Russian invasion of Ukraine, Aramco's senior vice president downstream, Mohammed Al Qahtani, announced the creation of a 'one stop shop' provided by his company in China's Shandong.

He said: 'The ongoing energy crisis, for example, is a direct result of fragile international transition plans which have arbitrarily ignored energy security and affordability for all.' He added: 'The world needs clear-eyed thinking on such issues. That's why we highly admire China's 14th Five Year Plan for prioritising energy security and stability, acknowledging its crucial role in economic development.'

The megaproject in Shandong, which is home to around 26% of China's refining capacity and is a key destination for Saudi Aramco's crude oil exports, would broadly involve the flagship Saudi oil and gas giant creating 'stronger ties with the world's largest oil exporter [that] will enhance China's energy security, especially as we work on increasing our production capacity to 13 million barrels per day,' according to Al Qahtani.

Aside from the fact that Saudi Arabia could not then, and still cannot, produce anywhere near 13 million bpd of crude oil (analysed in full in the in the *Key Players In The Global Oil Market: Saudi Arabia'* section), closer cooperation between Aramco and China of the sort evident in Shandong would mean Saudi Arabia investing heavily in the build-out of a large, integrated downstream business across the country. This, in turn, would mean a heavy Saudi presence in the region and a mirroring of that heavy presence by Chinese personnel in Saudi Arabia in reciprocal projects.

Extremely shortly after the Shandong deal had been signed, a multi-pronged memorandum of understanding (MoU) was signed between Saudi Aramco and the China Petroleum & Chemical Corporation (Sinopec).

As the president of Sinopec, Yu Baocai, himself put it: 'The signing of the MoU introduces a new chapter of our partnership in the Kingdom…The two companies will join hands in renewing the vitality, and scoring new progress, of the Belt and Road Initiative [BRI] and [Saudi Arabia's] Vision 2030.'

The scale and scope of the MoU was enormous, covering deep and broad co-operation in refining and petrochemical integration, engineering, procurement and construction, oilfield services, upstream and downstream technologies, carbon capture and hydrogen processes.

Crucially for China's long-term plans in Saudi Arabia, it also covered opportunities for the construction of a huge manufacturing hub in King Salman Energy Park that would involve the ongoing, on-the-ground presence on Saudi Arabian soil of significant numbers of Chinese personnel: not just those directly related to the oil, gas, petrochemicals, and other hydrocarbons activities, but also a small army of security personnel to ensure the safety of China's investments.

It is extremely apposite to note that by this stage China and Russia's increasing influence over their two prize assets in the Middle East - Sunni Saudi Arabia and Shia Iran - was such that they had been able to engineer a series of secret meetings between the two countries.

At the beginning of September 2022 Iran's newish President, Ebrahim Raisi, stated that there had been five rounds of meetings between high-level personnel from Tehran and Riyadh in the previous few months. In fact, the two countries had been meeting relatively regularly ever since the US ended its combat mission in Iraq toward the end of 2021.

The first public signal that a rapprochement of sorts between the two arch-Middle East rivals might occur at some point came from Saudi Crown Prince, Mohammed bin Salman, at the end of April 2021. He stated very publicly that he sought: 'A good and special relationship with Iran…We do not want Iran's situation to be difficult; on the contrary, we want Iran to grow… and to push the region and the world towards prosperity.'

This comment followed what it transpired had been four previous meetings in the Iraqi capital of Baghdad between senior figures from the Iranian and Saudi regimes, the first of which was personally brokered by then-Iraq Prime Minister, Mustafa al-Kadhimi. The existence of these talks was subsequently confirmed by an Iraqi government official, although neither Riyadh nor Tehran formally acknowledged them at the time.

The positive comments towards Iran from MbS came at around the same time that Aramco let it be known that it was in the process of broadening and deepening its relationship with Beijing, with the comment from its chief executive officer Amin Nasser, as highlighted earlier, that: 'Ensuring the continuing security of China's energy needs remains our highest priority – not just for the next five years but for the next 50 and beyond.'

The Two Key Islamic Forces In The Middle East

Saudi Arabian And Iranian Influence Across The Middle East

Source: FT

Russia Moves To Increase Its Iran-Iraq Influence

Whilst China was expanding its influence further across the Middle East through initiatives founded initially on money given to targeted countries, Russia was doing the same in states where it had the longer-running relationships, including Iran and Iraq.

In June 2022, three events occurred in just over a week involving either Iran or Iraq separately, or together, that put Russia back front and centre in the Middle East, to the detriment of the US. In order of timing, these events were: a series of meetings between Russia's veteran foreign minister, Sergei Lavrov, and Iran's senior political and military figures, including President, Ebrahim Raisi; the withdrawal from the Iraqi parliament of the country's long-time *de facto* leader, Moqtada al-Sadr, and his 73-member political bloc, the largest group in the legislative body; and, the agreement of a new cooperative roadmap between Iran and Iraq.

On the first point, prior to the withdrawal of the US from the JCPOA in 2018, Moscow had used the loosening up of restrictions in the run up to that agreement being struck in 2015 to dramatically increase its presence in Iran. In the energy sector alone, initial field exploration and development agreements had been signed by Gazprom Neft for the Changouleh and Cheshmeh-Khosh oilfields, Zarubezhneft for the Aban and Paydar Gharb fields, and Tatneft for the Dehloran field. These had been additional to those contained in the previous memoranda of understanding (MoU) signed by Lukoil and the National Iranian Oil Company (NIOC) centred on studies of the Ab Teymour and Mansouri oil fields.

Even more significant had been the concomitant signing of a 22-point MoU by Iran's deputy petroleum minister, Amir-Hossein Zamaninia, and Russia's deputy energy minister, Kirill Molodtsov. These points had included not just the plans for exploration and extraction of oil but also for the transfer of gas, petrochemical swap operations, and the manufacture of oil equipment with local Iranian engineering firms. They had also included the transfer of technology in the refinery sector.

Discussions in 2018 had also been underway for adjunct developments to this 22-point MoU that included the dual use of Iranian seaports and airports by Russia for both civilian and military purposes. These plans, however, were suspended due to the US withdrawal from the JCPOA in May of that year. They had later been rolled into the same concept of dual use contained in the landmark 25-year agreement between Iran and China, as analysed in depth in *'Key Players In The Global Oil Market: Iran'* section.

At the meeting in June 2022, however, Lavrov and Raisi discussed expanding cooperation across all fields, in line with the original 22-point MoU. This also included logistical cooperation for the movement of goods, including where oil and gas and related products, both from Iran to Russia and Russia to Iran. It also included elements of the special dual use civilian and military cooperation that had been agreed four years before. Iran's foreign ministry itself noted that Lavrov's visit was aimed at: 'Expanding cooperation with the Eurasian region and the Caucasus.'

The June 2022 discussions further advanced the idea raised at the earlier meeting on 19 January 2022 between President Putin and President Raisi of Russia finally providing Iran with the long-promised S-400 missile defence system and with the Sukhoi Su-35 fighter jets that Russia had also been promising for many years.

The bulk of Iran's payments for these items were to be made through favourable oil and gas sector deals given to Russian companies. However, Russia had also perennially linked these military hardware requests from Iran to other of its own security concerns across the Middle East, with Syria, in particular, an area in which Iran and Russia had long sought to come to a decisive working arrangement.

To Russia, its ongoing presence in Syria served several strategic functions. The main one was that it made it more difficult for the US to advance its own plans in the Levant region, either alone or with its NATO ally Turkey and its broader ally Israel.

In its narrowest sense, the Levant region includes Iraq, Israel, Jordan, Lebanon, Palestine, parts of Turkey, Cyprus and Syria Itself. In its broader sense, the region also includes Libya, Egypt and parts of Greece. There were several reports around this time that in order to keep Russia's military positions in the area fully secured whilst its own resources were being used in Ukraine, Iran's IRGC occupied them.

On the second point, relating to Iraq's al-Sadr, the radical cleric had long seen as his principal political philosophy unifying all of Iraq - including the semi-autonomous region of Kurdistan in the north - and keeping foreign influence, including both Iran's and the US's – at a minimum.

In the lead-up to his withdrawal from Iraq's parliament, and the subsequent withdrawal of the 73 members of his faction from it, al-Sadr had been looking to create the country's first true majority government since the fall of Saddam Hussein in 2003. This was to have been done through an alliance made with the bloc of Iraq's Speaker of Parliament, Mohamed al-Halbousi, and the Kurdistan Democratic Party (KDP).

The key problem for al-Sadr was that if this were successful, it would have excluded the Iran-controlled Coordination Framework from any legitimate power, and Russia too, given al-Sadr's extreme dislike of any foreign interference in Iraqi affairs. Russia had controlled Iraq Kurdistan's oil sector since 2017 and looked to build on that to extend its influence in the south of the country. This would enable it to form effectively one client state of Iran-Iraq, and al-Sadr's plan if it had succeeded would have destroyed that.

A Vital Key To The Middle East And Europe

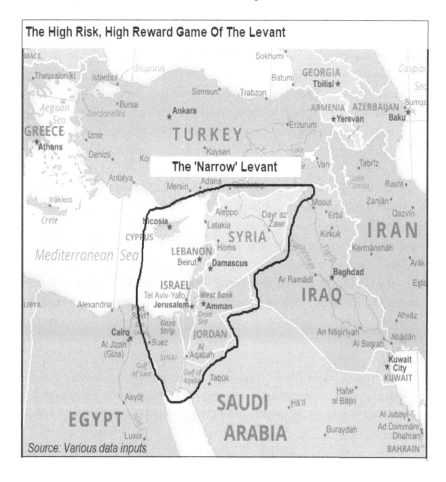

It was the Kurdish grouping (the KDP) that stopped al-Sadr's plan, as it side-stepped the usual convention relating to distributing political positions that would have seen the Patriotic Union of Kurdistan present the presidential candidate by just presenting its own candidate. Therefore, everything was back to the way it was before, with no clear power figure in Iraq, which is exactly the way Iran and Russia want it.

On the third point, relating to the new cooperative roadmap between Iran and Iraq, with no clear leader in sight in Baghdad, Tehran was quick to announce several major initiatives between the two countries. One of the most important methods of securing power across the Middle East remained the consolidation of control of the energy distribution grid – not just the movement of electricity but of oil and gas too. Russia had already seen in Europe the power that came from making countries reliant on its oil and gas exports, and the US also knew full well the power that Iran had over Iraq by dint of its ongoing supply of electricity and gas to Iraq.

In June 2022, then, Iraq's Deputy Minister of Oil for Exploration, Bassem Mohammad Khazir, stated that a roadmap should be prepared for the future steps and goals of Iraq and Iran, adding: 'Another important issue is Iranian technology and products…For example, this country already has a high capacity in many sectors such as power cables, pipes and fittings and up-to-date technologies that can be transmitted to us.'

He added: 'The CEO of the National Iranian Oil Company emphasised the issue of training and transfer of technology and technical equipment in his remarks…The issue of transfer of expertise and technology is very important, and we should be able to cooperate in this field.'

This new roadmap also had obvious synergies with the range of deals that had been discussed between Russian Deputy Prime Minister Alexander Novak and senior Iranians at the end of May 2022. These had included energy, agricultural, and transport projects and further cooperation in the financial and banking sector, oil, gas, petrochemicals, and nuclear energy.

Less than a month later, President Putin arrived in Tehran (for the second time since he ordered the invasion of Ukraine on 24 February), just after Russia's state gas giant, Gazprom, had signed a USD40 billion MoU with the NIOC.

Among other deals contained in the MoU, Gazprom pledged its full assistance to the NIOC in the USD10 billion development of the Kish and North Pars gas fields with a view to their producing more than 10 million cubic metres of gas per day. The MoU also contained details of a USD15 billion project to increase pressure in the supergiant South Pars gas field on the maritime border between Iran and Qatar.

According to the MoU, Gazprom would additionally be involved in the completion of various LNG projects and the construction of gas export pipelines. This was designed by the Kremlin to give it even more control over future gas supplies coming out of Iran that might have found a home in southern Europe initially, before being transported north, to help alleviate the ongoing gas supply crunch in major European countries.

By also becoming more deeply involved in the huge South Pars gas field Russia had also positioned itself to disrupt LNG supplies coming out of Qatar and destined for Europe. It is apposite to recall here that the South Pars field is one part of the two parts that comprise by far the biggest gas reservoir in the world, with the other part belonging to Qatar.

Strategically important as well was that Gazprom's focus on expanding Iran's LNG capabilities came at exactly the time when dramatically increasing LNG supplies was vital for European states to compensate for shortfalls in gas supplies resulting from bans on Russian gas imports. This was plainly identifiable as a tried-and-tested KGB/FSB strategy for success that relied on a combination of gradually increasing pressure on an enemy and then just waiting for as long as it took for him to have choice but to give up.

At that point in July 2022, Europe was struggling with energy storage levels and eyeing the prospect of severe shortages in the upcoming winter. There had been unprecedented warnings in Germany from local authorities of the need for households and businesses to cut energy usage going into the winter. At the same time, the EU's proposal that member countries cut gas use by 15% to prepare for possible supply cuts from Russia had seen fierce opposition from at least 12 of the 27 member states.

On the other side of the coin, Russia was earning more from energy exports at that point than it had before it invaded Ukraine. Specifically, according to several reports on the subject, Russia had earned around USD97 billion in revenue from fossil fuel exports in the first 100 days of the Ukraine conflict (from 24 February to 3 June) and this level of exports was ongoing. The European Union made up 61% of imports for these products from Russia, worth approximately USD59 billion. In short, Russia's revenues from gas and oil exports – the prices of which had shot up after the invasion - still exceeded the cost to it of the Ukraine war.

Additionally positive for Russia at that point was that the rouble was at an eight-year high, and Moscow's exports of gas accounted for only two percent of Russia's GDP. In short, Russia at that point it seemed could afford to wait it out, but the EU could not.

The China-Russia Relationship Shifts Around Q32022

For several years after the USSR collapsed in 1991 – around the same time as China began its turbo-charged drive for economic growth (when productivity gains overtook capital as the most significant source of national growth) - Russia and China were broadly equal partners in their alliance, with Russia having the edge in leadership terms. From around the mid-2000s, it might be said that the leadership position was beginning to move significantly in China's favour.

By 2007, according to World Bank figures and based on a revision from China's government of its growth figures for that year from 11.9% to 13%, the country had overtaken Germany in GDP terms to be the third ranked economy. China's GDP that year was USD3.4 trillion versus Germany's USD3.3 trillion, after the US and then Japan. At the same time, the Russian economy was in decline, and was increasingly dependent on sales of oil and gas to other countries for its prosperity.

Aside from looking like it would seriously challenge the US economy itself on a selection of economic and trading metrics sooner rather than later, China had also established itself as the key buyer in the global energy industry. This meant that, all other factors aside, Beijing was a key customer – perhaps the key customer even at that stage – of Russia's core business.

China Was Set To Challenge The US Sooner Rather Than Later

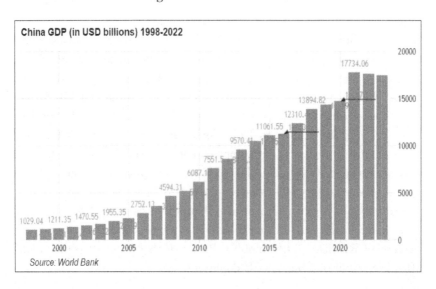

China GDP (in USD billions) 1998-2022

As analysed in depth in the *'Key Players In The Global Oil Market' 'Russia'* and *'China'* sections, Beijing broadly took a more cautious approach to its plans to translate this economic power into geopolitical power than Moscow ever had. For China, this approach was founded on the levers of financing implicit in its 'One Belt, One Road' programme. For Russia, a more direct approach involving territorial acquisition (either through occupation or political interference) had always been the more favoured approach, as evidenced from Cuba in an early instance through to Venezuela most latterly, among many others.

Russia Was In Steady Decline

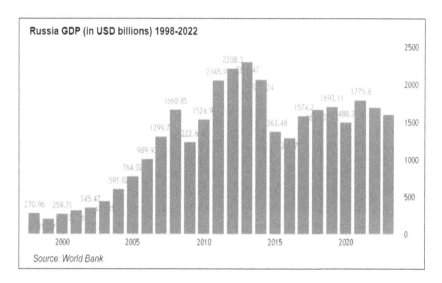

Russia GDP (in USD billions) 1998-2022

Source: World Bank

By the third quarter of 2022 – around six months after Russia had launched its invasion of Ukraine – China was still taking a much more cautious approach to the situation than had been implied in the pre-invasion comments that the friendship between Russia and China had 'no limits'. At the beginning of September 2022, President Putin again met President Xi.

In the run-up to the series of meetings between the two presidents, Putin had made four comments that together perfectly encapsulated what the central problem for Russia was that he wanted to address with Xi. First, he laid out what he thought the broad aim of the Russia-China partnership should be, which was to challenge the US's ongoing efforts to create a unipolar world. Putin added: 'Attempts to create a unipolar world have recently acquired an absolutely ugly form and are completely unacceptable.'

Second, while stating that he 'appreciate[d] the balanced position of our Chinese friends in connection with the Ukrainian crisis,' Putin went on to imply that this balanced position was not what Russia wanted from China. He said: 'We understand your questions and concern about this [Ukraine, although this was not specified by Putin],' before moving on to the subject of Western provocation of China in the Taiwan Strait.

Third, he expressed some exasperation over China's unwillingness to not fully support his view of what the Russo-China partnership should be, as outlined in point one, despite previous discussions where he had gone through it all: 'During today's meeting, we will of course explain in detail our position on this issue [the invasion of Ukraine], although we have talked about this before.'

Fourth, Putin picked up again on Western provocation of China in the Taiwan Strait and made an offer consistent with his view of what the Russo-China partnership should involve. It was also a direct signal to Xi of what he wanted from China, in terms of the type of support that Russia would be willing to give if China was in the same situation as he felt Russia was in the matter of Ukraine. He said: 'For our part, we adhere to the principle of one China…We condemn the provocation of the US and their satellites in the Taiwan Strait.'

This meeting between Putin and Xi – the thirty-ninth since Xi became China's president in 2013 – was not a specially convened arrangement between the two men but rather took place on the side-lines of the meeting of the Shanghai Cooperation Organization (SCO) summit in Uzbekistan. Aside from its vast scale and scope, as mentioned earlier, the SCO can reasonably be said to believe in the idea and practice of the 'multi-polar world'. Indeed, this idea had been the centrepiece of the declaration signed in 1997 between then-Russian President, Boris Yeltsin, and his then-China counterpart, Jiang Zemin.

However, for China, caution in dealing with the US and its allies at that point was still the optimal policy for it, which was the message that Putin received. Xi was well aware that although China was not economically that far behind the US in terms of a straight head-to-head GDP comparison - with the US's economy in 2021 totalling USD22.9 trillion and China's around USD5 trillion behind that - the US had nonetheless been an economic superpower for well over 100 years.

Xi knew when he met Putin back in September 2022 that this meant that Washington had been spending a lot more money on a lot of things – military, technology, global political connections - for a lot longer than Beijing. Even then, the US's military spending per annum was more than double that of China's, at just over USD800 billion spent in 2021, compared to just under USD300 billion spent by Beijing. In short, in a direct non-nuclear confrontation with the US, Beijing would lose and would lose quickly, and China knew that it had to tread carefully until it was in a stronger position to challenge the US directly.

Given these factors, then, China's 'balanced position', as Putin exasperatedly called it, could be summed up in one phrase: become the world's leading economic power as quickly as possible while building up military capabilities, but avoid any direct confrontations with the US during that time that would threaten those objectives.

There was an economic balance for Xi to maintain when it came to Russia and the rest of the world. It was true that although Russia accounted for only 2.9% of China's total imports, Moscow had resolutely stepped up to the plate in 2021 when China had faced an energy crunch.

Following that, by 2022 Russia accounted for 20.1% of China's total coal imports, and its share of China's imported crude oil had steadily risen to 15.6% by the end of 2021 from 11% in 2014. Russia's strategic importance to China was bolstered again with the 30-year contract for Russia to supply gas to China through its new Far Eastern pipeline. This had followed the earlier installation of the Power of Siberia-1 pipeline that had begun pumping supplies in 2019.

Putin was also in the process of seeking to boost those already-high levels of oil and gas exports to China, possibly with another pipeline (a 'Power of Siberia 2') to China via Mongolia. Indeed, also at the SCO meeting in September 2022 during which Xi and Putin had their discussions, Mongolian President, Ukhnaagiin Khurelsukh, said that he supported the construction of such oil and gas pipelines.

This said, while Russia had become an increasingly important source of energy for China, its total trade with the country paled in comparison to China's trade links with the US and the European Union. According to the figures at that point in 2022, among China's top trading partners, the EU accounted for 15.3% of China's total trade, followed by the US with 12.5%.

China Was Still A Long Way Behind The US Where It Counted

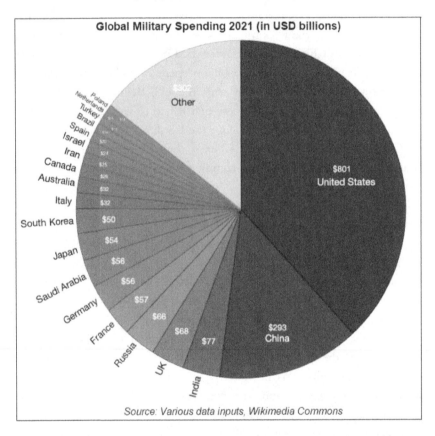

Global Military Spending 2021 (in USD billions)

Source: Various data inputs, Wikimedia Commons

This balancing act between the US, Europe, and Russia by Xi was echoed in the practical policies adopted by Chinese institutions in their dealings with Russia at the time. As sanctions against Russia mounted, there were reports that some of China's largest state-owned banks were limiting financing for transactions of Russian commodities. There were also reports that some Chinese banks had stopped issuing USD-denominated letters of credit related to Russian commodities. Nonetheless, Chinese yuan-denominated financing for Russian commodities was still available, albeit with a higher level of scrutiny attached to it.

China And Russia Move To Disrupt US Dollar Dominance

Another key topic in the Putin-Xi meetings on the side-lines of the September 2022 SCO summit was the continuation of moves between Russia and China to end of the US dollar's hegemony in the global oil and gas markets.

Just prior to this meeting, Russian and Chinese hydrocarbons giants, Gazprom and China National Petroleum Corporation (CNPC) agreed to switch payments for gas supplies to roubles (RUB) and renminbi (RMB) instead of US dollars. In the first phase of the new payments system, this would apply to Russian gas supplies to China via the 'Power of Siberia' eastern pipeline route that totalled at minimum 38 billion cubic metres of gas per year (bcm/y). After that, further expansion of the new payments scheme would be rolled out.

Although ongoing international sanctions against Russia over its invasion of Ukraine in February had provided the final impetus for this crucial change in payment methodology, it had been a core strategy of China's from at least 2010 to challenge the US dollar's position as the world's reserve currency and as the principal currency in which global oil and gas markets were denominated. As touched on earlier, China has long regarded the position of its renminbi currency in the global league table of currencies as being a reflection of its own geopolitical and economic importance on the world stage.

Back at the G20 summit in London in April 2010, then-governor of the People's Bank of China (PBOC), Zhou Xiaochuan, had flagged the notion that the Chinese wanted a new global reserve currency to replace the US dollar at some point. He had added that the RMB's inclusion in the IMF's Special Drawing Rights (SDR) reserve asset mix would be a key stepping-stone in this context. At that time, at least 75% of the then-USD4 trillion daily turnover in the global foreign exchange (FX) markets, as determined by the Bank for International Settlements (BIS), was accounted for by the 'Big Four' international currencies: the US dollar (USD), the Eurozone's euro (EUR), the British pound (GBP), and the Japanese yen (JPY).

Aside from dominating daily FX markets turnover, currencies in the SDR also dominate in the payment, reserves, and investment currency functions in the global economy. Enormous media fanfare in China followed the RMB's inclusion in the SDR mix in October 2016, when it was assigned a weighting of 10.9% (the USD had a 41.9% share, the EUR 37.4%, GBP 11.3%, and JPY 9.4%). As of 2022, the RMB's share in the SDR mix had risen to 12.28%, which China still regards as not truly befitting its rising superpower status in the world.

A Reflection For Beijing Of China's Global Standing

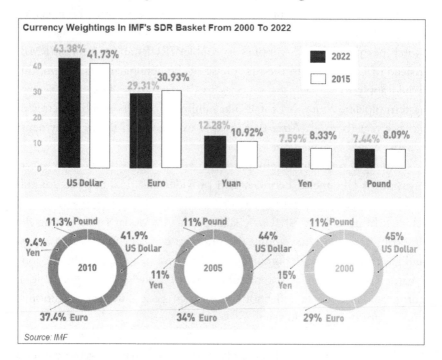

China has also long been acutely aware of the fact that, as the largest annual gross crude oil importer in the world since 2017 (and the world's largest net importer of total petroleum and other liquid fuels since 2013), it is subject to the vagaries of US foreign policy tangentially through the oil pricing mechanism of the US dollar.

This view of the US dollar as a weapon was powerfully reinforced after Russia's invasion of Ukraine and the accompanying US-led sanctions that followed. The most severe of those – as with sanctions on Iran from 2018 – related to exclusion from use of the US dollar.

The former executive vice-president of the Bank of China, Zhang Yanling, said in a speech in April 2022 that those US dollar-related sanctions against Russia would: '[...] cause the US to lose its credibility and undermine the [US] dollar's hegemony in the long run.' She further suggested that China should help the world 'get rid of the dollar hegemony sooner rather than later.'

Russia itself had long held the same view on the advantages for it of removing the US dollar's dominance in global hydrocarbons pricing. However, while China was unwilling to overtly challenge the US during the height of its Trade War under the highly unpredictable former US president, Donald Trump, it could do little about it on its own.

A sign of Russia's intent, though, came just after the US reimposed sanctions in 2018 on its key Middle Eastern partner, Iran. The chief executive officer of Russia's Novatek, Leonid Mikhelson, said in September of that year that Russia had been discussing switching away from US dollar-centric trading with its largest trading partners such as India and China, and that even Arab countries were thinking about it. He had added: 'If they [the US] do create difficulties for our Russian banks then all we have to do is replace dollars.'

At around the same time, China launched its later highly successful Shanghai Futures Exchange with oil contracts denominated in yuan. Such a strategy was also tested initially at scale in 2014 when Gazprom Neft started to trade cargoes of crude oil in Chinese yuan and roubles with China and several buyers in Europe.

This idea again resurfaced following the various rounds of sanctions imposed on Russia and led by the US, focused on the use of the US dollar. Almost as soon as they were introduced, Russian President Vladimir Putin signed a decree requiring buyers of Russian gas in the EU to pay in roubles via a new currency conversion mechanism or risk having supplies suspended. Putin's threat on accepting only rouble payments nearly succeeded in exploiting existing fault lines running through the US-led NATO alliance, as major EU consumers of Russian gas scrambled to work out how to appease these payment demands, without overtly breaking sanctions.

Saudi Supports Russia With A Huge Oil Production Cut

Despite some degree of caution being exercised towards the US and its allies by Russia's key geopolitical ally, China, its key energy ally, Saudi

Arabia, clearly indicated its support for Moscow by leading OPEC into a huge production cut just after the meeting of Xi and Putin.

At the October 2022 OPEC meeting, Saudi Arabia and its fellow member states collectively cut their crude oil production by two million bpd, a gigantic decrease.

Saudi Supported Russia With A Huge OPEC Oil Production Cut

OPEC & OPEC+ Oil Output Cut Announcement Oct 2022 (000 bpd)			
	August 2022 Required Production	Voluntary Adjustment	Voluntary Production
Algeria	1,055	-48	1,007
Angola	1,525	-70	1,455
Congo	325	-15	310
Equatorial Guinea	127	-6	121
Gabon	186	-9	177
Iraq	4,651	-220	4,431
Kuwait	2,811	-135	2,676
Nigeria	1,826	-84	1,742
Saudi Arabia	11,004	-526	10,478
UAE	3,179	-160	3,019
Azerbaijan	717	-33	684
Bahrain	205	-9	196
Brunei	102	-5	97
Kazakhstan	1,706	-78	1,628
Malaysia	594	-27	567
Mexico	1753	0	1,753
Oman	881	-40	841
Russia	11,004	-526	10,478
Sudan	75	-3	72
South Sudan	130	-6	124
OPEC 10	26,689	-1,273	25,416
Non-OPEC	17,167	-727	16,440
OPEC+	43,856	-2,000	41,856

Source: API

Market expectations had been for a possible cut of around one million bpd, with a very remote possibility of one and a half million bpd, if OPEC decided to ignore all its Western allies' arguments against such a reduction.

The October 2022 cut was the largest crude oil production reduction since the 9.7 million bpd decrease in May 2020, which was implemented expressly to rescue oil prices from the once-in-a-lifetime threat posed to them at the height of the COVID-19 pandemic. The October cut was set to last for 14 months, until December 2023.

The huge reduction in crude oil output from Saudi Arabia and its OPEC brothers occurred despite repeated pleas from the US that such a cut would lead to three outcomes that it saw as exceptionally dangerous for the world at that point. First, it would add further impetus to the energy price-led surge in global inflation that had caused rising interest rates around the world that were, in turn, crimping economic growth.

Second, it would significantly boost the state revenues of Russia, as a major exporter of crude oil and gas, enabling its invasion of Ukraine to continue for longer, costing more lives and increasing the likelihood of escalation into a global nuclear war. And third, it increased the chances that sitting US President Joe Biden would do poorly in the November mid-term elections. This would make his government less likely to be able to deal effectively with the Russian- and Chinese-led security challenges that the world would face during the remainder of his presidency.

The immediate impact on crude oil prices of the October production cut by OPEC was not as dramatic as many had feared, but it had the potential to become very serious indeed, given that it coincided with two other market factors, of which the Saudis were well aware. The first of these was that the long-running program of releasing one million bpd of crude oil from the US's Strategic Petroleum Reserve (SPR) – begun with the specific intention of bringing oil prices down in order to dampen inflationary pressures across the West - were scheduled to end in the same month as the cut was announced.

The second factor was that a European Union (EU) ban on seaborne imports of Russian crude was scheduled to go into effect on 5 December 2022. At the same time, the G7 group of major industrialised nations was also looking at the mechanics of placing a price cap on Russian energy exports – oil in the first instance and then perhaps gas.

Aside from knowing the huge upwards pressure that this historically enormous cut in crude oil supply would place on the global oil price, Saudi Arabia was also fully aware of the huge political ramifications of the cut for the US, for Europe, and for Russia.

Senior EU energy security figures conveyed to leading OPEC countries that cutting crude oil production at that particular point could be disastrous for several proposed EU energy policies relating to Russian oil and gas sanctions, but these entreaties were ignored.

The most senior figures in the Saudi government, including Crown Prince Mohammed bin Salman, also know exactly what these cuts and continued high energy prices might mean for President Joe Biden in his upcoming mid-term elections.

The US's Furious Reaction To The Saudi-Led Production Cut

According to senior sources in the White House at the time, the President and his closest advisers viewed the massive oil output cut from OPEC and OPEC+ announced in October as being directly led by Saudi Arabia, in conjunction with Russia. They also saw the cut as a direct comment from Saudi Arabia's highest leadership on what it thought of the US president, of the US's democratic process, and of its stand with its allies against the Russian invasion of Ukraine.

Given the history of Saudi Arabia's manoeuvres in the global oil market since it had launched the Second Oil Price War in 2014, the October 2022 oil production cut, despite US pleas not to do so, should not have surprised Washington, and yet it did. The US was infuriated because it thought the cut was a direct attack on it and its allies against Russia, and it was right.

Initially, US officials condemned the decision as 'short-sighted' but then White House National Security Advisor, Jake Sullivan, and National Economic Council Director, Brian Deese, called it out for what it was, saying in a joint statement: 'At a time when maintaining a global supply of energy is of paramount importance, this decision will have the most negative impact on lower- and middle-income countries that are already reeling from elevated energy prices.'

They added that the Biden administration would consult with the US Congress on potential measures that would strike at OPEC's control over oil prices, and this would include moving to the next stage of the 'NOPEC' Bill legislative process, as examined earlier. The NOPEC bill had passed the Senate Judiciary Committee in May, having also passed a House committee in 2021.

Senate Majority Leader, and Democrat, Chuck Schumer also stated just after the October 2022 oil production cut announcement that: 'What Saudi Arabia did to help [Russian President Vladimir] Putin continue to wage his despicable, vicious war against Ukraine will long be remembered by Americans…We are looking at all the legislative tools to best deal with this appalling and deeply cynical action, including the NOPEC Bill.'

Following this and indicating cross-party support for a new aggressive approach to Saudi Arabia, Republican Senator Chuck Grassley, an original sponsor of the NOPEC bill, said that he would attach the measure as an amendment to the then-forthcoming National Defense Authorization Act.

Underlining the seriousness with which the US viewed what Saudi Arabia had done in the October 2022 oil production cut, President Biden himself said that: 'There's going to be some consequences for what they've done, with Russia [supporting oil prices by leading OPEC's 2 million barrel per day (bpd) collective output cut]…I'm not going to get into what I'd consider and what I have in mind. But there will be – there will be consequences.'

Just before Biden's comments, John Kirby, the national security council spokesperson, echoed official doubts on the future of the US-Saudi security relationship, as he said that Biden believed that the US ought to 'review the bilateral relationship with Saudi Arabia and take a look to see if that relationship is where it needs to be and that it is serving our national security interests,…in light of the recent decision by OPEC, and Saudi Arabia's leadership [of it].'

Saudi Further Shores Up Its Relationship With China

Given the US's furious response to the Saudi Arabia-led October 2022 oil production cut that had been done in conjunction with, and in support of, Russia, Riyadh quickly moved to shore up its relationship with China.

Since Saudi Arabia's drift towards China had begun in earnest following its face-saving offer to MbS relating to the Aramco IPO in 2017 (covered in part earlier and also in full in the *'Key Players In The Global Oil Market: Saudi Arabia'* section) a slew of deals between Riyadh and Beijing had followed. Alongside those, Saudi Arabia had also supported several of China's broader geopolitical initiatives, including its desire to see its renminbi currency challenge the longstanding dominance of the US dollar in the world, both as its effective reserve currency and as the primary denominating currency of the global oil and gas markets.

Saudi Arabia Reiterated Its Long-term Commitment To China

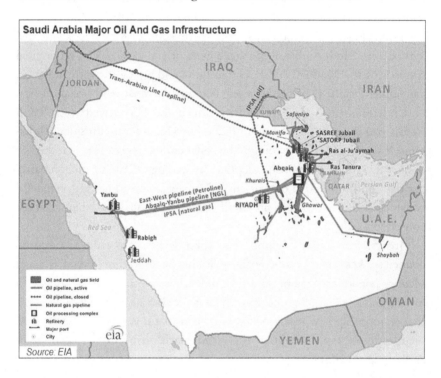

Back in August 2017, as touched on earlier, the idea had first been publicly mooted at government level by the then-Saudi Vice Minister of Economy and Planning, Mohammed al-Tuwaijri, who had told a Saudi-China conference in Jeddah that: 'We will be very willing to consider funding in renminbi and other Chinese products.'

By the third quarter of 2022, there had been a noticeable further shift by Saudi Arabia towards China in all areas, including the multi-pronged MoU signed in August between Saudi Aramco and the China Petroleum & Chemical Corporation (Sinopec).

As the president of Sinopec, Yu Baocai, himself had put it: 'The signing of the MoU introduces a new chapter of our partnership in the Kingdom…The two companies will join hands in renewing the vitality and scoring new progress of the Belt and Road Initiative [BRI] and [Saudi Arabia's] Vision 2030.'

Moving into the fourth quarter of 2022, Saudi Arabia reiterated its commitment to China as its 'most reliable partner and supplier of crude oil,' along with broader assurances of its ongoing support in several other areas. This was in line with the earlier comments from Aramco chief executive officer, Amin Nasser that: 'Ensuring the continuing security of China's energy needs remains our highest priority - not just for the next five years but for the next 50 and beyond.'

This, and several other comments around that time in the same vein highlighted elsewhere in this book, appeared to confirm that Saudi Crown Prince Mohammed bin Salman had come to regard the US as just another one of its partners in a new global order that would see Beijing and its allies share the leadership position with Washington, before attempting to surpass it. In this view, it appeared that MbS saw the US as a partner just for its security considerations, with no meaningful *quid pro quo* on Saudi Arabia's part, whilst regarding China as its key partner economically and Russia as its key partner in energy matters.

Early November 2022 saw Saudi Arabia state that, in addition to continuing in its role as China's partner of choice in the oil market, the two countries would continue 'close communication and strengthen co-operation to address emerging risks and challenges,' according to a joint communiqué from Saudi Energy Minister, Prince Abdulaziz bin Salman and Beijing's National Energy Administrator, Zhang Jianhua. In the context of crude oil, according to Chinese Customs data, Saudi Arabia delivered 1.76 million bpd in shipments to China over the January to August 2022 period. This marked an increase in Saudi Arabia's market share to 17.7% from 16.9% a year earlier.

Additionally, at around the same time, the two countries pledged not only to continue discussions on developing joint integrated refining and petrochemical complexes but also, crucially, to cooperate on the use of nuclear energy. This was flagged by Saudi Arabia and China as being 'the peaceful use of nuclear energy'.

However, given the news just a year before that US intelligence agencies had found that Saudi Arabia was manufacturing its own ballistic missiles with the help of China – and given China's long-running and extensive 'assistance' to Iran's nuclear ambitions - ongoing US fears about what

Beijing's endgame might be in building out the nuclear capabilities of key states in the Middle East were elevated.

A month later, in December 2022, Crown Prince Mohammed bin Salman hosted a series of meetings in Riyadh between China's President Xi Jinping and the leaders of countries in the Arab League. The Arab League comprises Algeria, Bahrain, Comoros, Djibouti, Egypt, Iraq, Jordon, Kuwait, Lebanon, Libya, Mauritania, Morocco, Oman, Palestinian Authority, Qatar, Saudi Arabia, Somalia, Sudan, Syria, Tunisia, United Arab Emirates and Yemen.

Whatever the pretext for this gathering, its ultimate mission was clearly stated at the series of meetings in January 2022 between senior officials from the Chinese government and foreign ministers from Saudi Arabia, Kuwait, Oman, Bahrain, plus the secretary-general of the Gulf Cooperation Council (comprising Bahrain, Kuwait, Oman, Qatar, Saudi Arabia, and the United Arab Emirates).

At both sets of meetings the principal topics of conversation were to finally seal a China-GCC Free Trade Agreement (FTA) and to forge a 'deeper strategic cooperation in a region where US dominance is showing signs of retreat'.

Also at the December 2022 meetings, President Xi Jinping and Crown Prince Mohammed bin Salman signed a China-Saudi partnership pact with King Salman, demonstrating still-deepening ties. The new pact pledged 'cooperation' in just about everything a country does, including finance and investment, innovation, science and technology, aerospace, oil, gas, renewable energy, and language and culture.

Xi then identified two 'priority areas' that he believed should be addressed as quickly as possible. The first was the transition to using the Chinese renminbi in oil and gas deals done between the Arab League countries and China. The second was to bring nuclear technology to targeted countries, beginning with Saudi Arabia.

On the first of these thinly-veiled programs to shift the centre of global power away from the US and towards China, Xi said that the Shanghai Petroleum and Natural Gas Exchange would be 'fully utilised in RMB [renminbi] settlement in oil and gas trade.'

The trade-off for countries in the Arab League, the GCC, and any countries in the MENA region not covered by these organisations, was clearly reiterated by Xi, and it was all to do with money. 'China will continue to import large quantities of crude oil on a long-term basis from GCC countries, and purchase more LNG,' he said. He added: 'We will also strengthen our cooperation in the upstream sector, engineering services, as well as storage, transportation and refinery of oil and gas.'

Turning to the second of Xi's urgent priorities – bringing nuclear technology to the Arab League and GCC countries, starting with Saudi Arabia – there was a peculiar timing attached to the statement, given the discovery just before Christmas 2021 by US intelligence agencies that Saudi Arabia was manufacturing its own ballistic missiles with the help of China.

At that point in late 2022, the only Arab nation to have nuclear reactors was the UAE. However, Washington had also been surprised to find – also around Christmas 2021 - that China had been building its own secret military facility in and around the UAE port of Khalifa. Based on classified satellite imagery and human intelligence data, US officials stated that China has been working to establish 'a military foothold in the UAE'.

Meanwhile, Saudi Arabia had stated several times that it wanted to add around 17 gigawatts (GW) of nuclear capacity by 2040 and, to this end, wanted to bring two nuclear reactors with a combined capacity of 3.2 GW online by 2030. Previously, the Kingdom had been in talks to acquire nuclear technology from the US under the '1-2-3' protocol.

As highlighted in 2019 by then-US Energy Secretary, Rick Perry, Saudi Arabia had told the US that it wanted to go ahead with a full-cycle nuclear programme, including the production and enrichment of uranium for atomic fuel. The US had made it clear that in order for US companies to participate in Saudi Arabia's project, Riyadh would need to sign an accord on the peaceful use of nuclear technology with Washington. The '1-2-3' protocol was intended to limit the enrichment of uranium for arms purposes. China does not have such a protocol in place for Saudi Arabia.

China's Bearish To Bullish COVID-19 Pressure On Oil Prices

Whilst this tug-of-war between the US and its allies and China-Russia and its allies was in full swing, China was continuing to fight its own ongoing battle over how best to handle COVID-19.

A sharp drop in crude oil prices at the beginning of September 2022 had come on the back of news that China had extended a COVID-19 lockdown in Chengdu, the capital of the southwestern province of Sichuan, for the majority of its 21 million residents. This served as a clear reminder of the capacity for such news to cause a significant drop in oil prices, based on expectations of sudden sharp drops in demand from China, the world's biggest net importer of crude.

China's Zero-COVID Policy Was Destroying Its Economic Growth

China Annual GDP Growth (% per quarter) January 2020 To December 2022

Source: National Bureau of Statistics China

At the point headed into the fourth quarter of 2022, there was still no sign whatsoever that China's 'zero-COVID' policy - in which ultra-tight lockdowns were introduced across entire cities immediately that a relatively miniscule number of COVID-19 cases were identified – would be softened. Even before the extension of the Chengdu lockdown, 44 million people in China were already in lockdown elsewhere across the country.

The zero-COVID policy remained fully backed by President Xi himself, who continued to regard it as a matter of national honour for China to deal with the virus in its own way, with no medical help accepted from any other country. Ahead of the 20th National Congress of the Chinese Communist Party due to be held in October 2022, there appeared to be very little chance of a change being made to the rigour with which the zero-COVID policy was enforced.

Around a month after that 20th National Congress, though, with the COVID case outlook still uncertain across China and economic growth estimates for Q42022 and for full-year 2023 subject to regular downwards revisions by analysts around the globe, Xi did allow an initial easing of the zero-COVID policy.

In terms of specific negative ramifications for China's economic growth, the key Purchasing Managers' Index (PMI) for factory activity fell unexpectedly in October, to 49.2, a decrease of 0.9 from the previous month, and indicative of an outright contraction. In line with this, China's crude oil imports for the first three quarters of the year fell 4.3 percent year on year to mark the first annual decline for the period since at least 2014.

On 11 November 2022, the Chinese government unveiled 20 changes to the zero-Covid policy that had been in place for around three years. One such change was that travellers from abroad would require one negative polymerase chain reaction (PCR) test within 48 hours of boarding a flight to China instead of two. Another was that foreign travellers would have to quarantine for eight days, rather than 10, and another was that inside China people considered 'close contacts of close contacts' of COVID-19 carriers would no longer need to quarantine.

Crucially as well the new guidelines also forbade mass testing unless 'it is unclear how infections are spreading' in an area. This said, the same day that these announcements were made, municipal officials in Beijing were still requiring many of the city's residents to be tested daily, more often than in previous weeks. Moreover, as of just over a month before these 20 changes to China's COVID-19 policy were announced, 26 out of 31 regions had seen severe outbreaks of the disease.

The associated drop in demand from the world's longstanding big buyer in the global oil market, though, was exactly what the US and its allies wanted. It would act to reduce the effects of the toxic combination of ballooning inflation powered largely by soaring energy costs, and repeated sharp increases in interest rates to combat this trend. At the same time, concerns had increased that higher-for-longer interest rates might tip developed market economies into recession.

In this context, US economic quarter-on-quarter growth fell from 3.7% in Q1 2022 to 1.8% in Q2 and the same again in Q3, as inflation rose to around 40-year highs of over 8%, and the Fed Funds rate was hiked to 3.75-4.00%. German economic growth saw the same pattern of decline, from 3.6% in Q1 to 1.7% in Q2 and to 1.2% in Q3, and so did the UK's, from 10.9% in Q1 to 4.4% in Q2 and to 2.4% in Q3.

As dictatorships throughout time have found, they are most vulnerable at the precise moment at which they relax their pressure on their people, even by the tiniest degree, and so it was with President Xi's slight relaxation of the zero-COVID policy. By late November 2022, Xi was facing a wave of public protests against the still-tight COVID-19-related restrictions across the country. They were of a scale and scope of seriousness not seen since those of the mid-1980s that culminated in the 1989 massacre in Tiananmen Square.

A Toxic Mix Driven By Rising Energy Prices After Russian Invasion

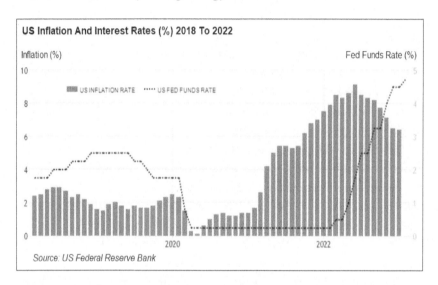

The latest round of these protests at that time began after at least 10 people burned to death in an apartment fire in the city of Urumqi, the capital of eastern Xinjiang province, with many blaming COVID lockdown rules for delaying any response from the emergency services. According to several live television reports at the time, the protests spread to several big cities, including Shanghai and Beijing, with protesters shouting 'Step down, Xi Jinping! Step down, Communist Party!'.

President Xi found himself caught between the metaphorical rock and a hard place. On the one hand, if he stuck to anything close to zero-COVID restrictions – at that point, basically any meaningful restrictions at all – then his power in the Communist Party apparatus (and therefore, China) might well begin to erode. The public discontent against him would add to the economic pressure against him, both resulting from his ongoing strict handling of COVID-19.

On the other hand, though, if he meaningfully loosened China's COVID-19 control measures, then it was highly likely that vast numbers of China's people would die, resulting in exactly the same appalling scenario that China would face if it stuck to tight control policies for the disease.

The reason why vast numbers of deaths would result from any meaningful lifting of the strict COVID-19-related controls was that China still lacked at that time a highly effective vaccine against the disease or any variant thereof. This was despite offers from all major vaccine-producing countries to make such supplies available to it.

China also did not have an effective post-infection anti-viral, and it still refused to buy in such supplies from foreign suppliers, again despite offers from several Western countries to make such anti-viral and post-infection treatments available to it. China's lack of focus on vaccines and anti-viral medicines, even during the long periods of strict and extensive lockdowns, meant that the country still had vast numbers of its people without any vaccination against any variant of the disease (even its own CoronaVac vaccine). China also had a critical shortage of intensive care units (ICUs).

In sum, at that point in the fourth quarter of 2022, there were around 263 million people in China over the age of 60 and 35 million people over the age of 80, with people of these ages known to be particularly vulnerable to COVID-19 and its variants.

According to data from several sources, of the over-80s, only around 66% of these had been vaccinated at that point, with only about 40% having had three shots of any vaccine. According to medical details from the Hong Kong COVID-19 outbreak in February 2022, China's CoronaVac shot had the equivalent efficacy of mRNA vaccines only after three doses. This left around 37 million of the over-60s vulnerable to similar COVID-19 outbreaks on the mainland. The huge shortage of intensive care unit (ICU) beds across China would exacerbate the negative effects of such outbreaks.

Ultimately, Xi decided to loosen the COVID-19 restrictions still further toward the end of December 2022 and the last COVID-19 containment measures were lifted on 8 January 2023.

It was, and remains, extremely difficult to gauge the subsequent level of infections and deaths from COVID-19 and its related strains, as China's

National Health Commission (NHC) stopped publishing daily COVID-19 case data on 25 December 2022, a practice that had been in effect since 21 January 2020.

However, during a press conference in early January 2023, Kan Quancheng, a senior official in Henan - China's third most populous province – revealed that nearly 90% of people there had been infected with COVID-19 and its related strains by that point. This equated to around 88.5 million people in just that province.

China Still Had A Critical Shortage Of ICU Beds

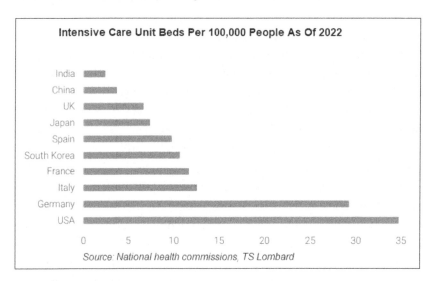

This said, at some point – and many smart money investors were predicting the end of the first quarter of 2023 or thereabouts – COVID-19 and its related variants would peak in China as it had done at various points in other countries before, and China's economy, and its demand for oil, would return in full.

To lay more groundwork for this, China's annual Central Economic Work Conference (CEWC) signalled in the middle of December 2022 that boosting growth would be the priority in 2023. Investments in research and development in high tech sectors would be increased in particular. The CEWC called for greater market access for foreign capital especially in modern services industry, although it added that the long-term policy direction of greater self-reliance in key sectors was to be continued.

In President Xi's New Year 2023 speech as well there was a focus on creating stronger economic growth again for China, although the thrust of what he said appeared to be geared towards removing previous COVID-19-related obstacles to growth rather than towards policies that would aggressively drive it. Several smart money investors and analysts predicted that this phase of growth recovery – to above 5.0% at least – would be a cyclical recovery, led by household consumption mainly of services.

As such, they predicted a 5-8% increase in net oil import volumes in China over 2023 but thought as well that this this was unlikely to cause oil prices to surge as they had during previous economic growth spurts, especially as China continued to buy oil at a discount from Russia.

Russia Deals With Price Caps Against It

Following Russia's invasion of Ukraine, various bans and price caps were introduced on its hydrocarbons products by differing groups of the US and its allies. The most important of these were from the G7 group of countries (comprising Canada, France, Germany, Italy, Japan, the UK, and the US) and from the EU (which is also a 'non-enumerated' additional member of the G7), plus Australia.

The broad aim of these bans and price caps was to reduce Russia's hydrocarbons' revenue streams to limit its ability to keep fighting in Ukraine, and also to punish it in a wider sense for instigating the war there. Legislation and guidance effective as of 5 December 2022 banned seaborne imports of Russian oil and introduced a general oil price cap for its oil at USD60 per barrel. EU prohibitions on vessels and other maritime services needed to transport Russian petroleum products also came into force on 5 February 2023.

The price caps also sought to partially balance the interim energy needs of the various member countries of each of the aforementioned alliances with the punitive elements of the sanctions on Russia, given its status as one of the biggest suppliers of oil and gas in the world. A corollary consideration was that retaining Russian oil and gas in the global supply and demand mix would help to keep prices for these resources at 'manageable' levels whilst a broader long-term transition away from Russian oil and gas was structured. This transition in large part would be predicated on securing supplies of oil and gas from alternative vendors to Russia, preferably those allied to the US-Europe axis.

For Russia's part, on 27 December 2022 President Putin signed a decree on countermeasures against the introduction of the price cap on Russian oil and oil products. The decree banned the sale of oil and oil products if the sales contract was based on a price cap, although the decree allowed Russia the right to make exceptions to the application of this rule.

In many ways – aside from what these various bans by both sides meant longer-term for the balance of the new global oil market order – all these prohibitions would have little effect on oil and gas flows around the world or their pricing. As with all matters relating to the global oil market there would be two basic versions of 'reality' to consider: the official version and the unofficial version.

Officially, some pricing-in of the supply risk attached to the bans and caps, and Russia's reaction to them, appeared to be justified. Russia's Deputy Prime Minister, Alexander Novak, said on 23 December 2022 that Russian oil output might fall 5-7% because of the G7's sanctions. OPEC expected Russian liquids output to decline by 850,000 million bpd, to average 10.1 million bpd in 2023. The IEA forecast that Russian crude oil production would drop by 1.4 million bpd in the period.

Unofficially, there was no reason to expect any meaningful drop in Russian oil or oil products output in 2023 for several reasons. The first was that Russia was still making a lot of money from each barrel of oil it produced, whether it was sold at a discount to the benchmark or not. Consequently, it remained in Russia's interests to keep production going at the usual pre-Ukraine War levels to maximise its government revenues.

In this context, for a very long time, Russia had a budget breakeven price per barrel of Brent oil equivalent of around USD40 - about the same as the best of the US shale oil producers. Given the drain on its government finances that Russia's invasion of Ukraine had created, this figure had risen substantially. However, the fact remained that Russia's oil sector was still intrinsically profitable on a standalone corporate basis at oil prices above USD40 pb. With the USD60 pb cap in place, this was a very healthy profit.

It was also apposite to note at that point that the 30% or so discount on Russian oil demanded by some major buyers since the Ukraine war began – most notably, China and India - was a discount from the market price of oil, not from the price cap. With Brent trading around that point at about USD80 pb, Russia was receiving around USD56 pb for its oil from those buyers. This was still a healthy profit on a standalone operational basis for the major Russian oil producers. In fact, therefore, the USD60 pb G7 oil price cap was actually higher than the effective price that Russia could obtain for its oil in the open market.

Another element to factor into the unofficial reality of the global oil supply/demand mix at that stage was that Russia could still work around any price caps or sanctions that the G7 or any other group cared to put into place through the myriad of sanctions-avoiding mechanisms put into place by Iran since it first came under various sanctions in 1979.

Indeed, in December 2018 at the Doha Forum, Iran's Foreign Minister, Mohammad Zarif, had stated that: 'If there is an art that we have perfected in Iran, [that] we can teach to others for a price, it is the art of evading sanctions.' As analysed in depth in the *'Key Players In The Global Oil Market: Iran'* section, there were several of these tried-and-tested methods that Russia could borrow from Iran.

To get more oil into Europe at better prices than the price cap allowed, for example, Russia could use the basic shipping-related method of disabling – literally just flicking a switch – on the 'automatic identification system' on ships that carried Russian oil. Simply lying about destinations in shipping documentation was another tried-and-trusted method used by Iran, as highlighted by Iran's own former Petroleum Minister, Bijan Zanganeh, when he said in 2020: 'What we export is not under Iran's name. The documents are changed over and over, as well as [the] specifications.'

Once oil from anywhere, using the above-mentioned methodology, had arrived at the less rigorously policed ports of southern Europe that needed oil and/or oil trading commissions - including those of Albania, Montenegro, Bosnia and Herzegovina, Serbia, Macedonia, and Croatia - it could easily be moved into Europe's bigger oil consuming countries, including through well-established routes in Turkey.

For Asian-bound shipments, including those to China, the reliable method for moving sanctioned Iranian oil, also available to Russian oil, had involved Malaysia (and to a lesser degree Indonesia). In this method, tankers bound ultimately for Asia engaged in at-sea, or just-outside-port, transfers of Iranian oil onto tankers flying the flags of other countries.

The only possible stumbling block for Russia in how much oil it could move in such a way was how many ships it could gain access to. At that point around the end of December 2022, Russia could secure very quickly at least three quarters of the shipping needed to move its oil as usual to established buyers, a figure that rose to 90% within a few weeks after that.

Before the invasion of Ukraine, according to IEA figures, Russia was exporting around 2.7 million bpd of crude oil to Europe, and another 1.5 million bpd of oil products, mostly diesel. Globally, Russia's total oil exports just prior to the invasion were 7.8 million bpd, two-thirds of which were crude and condensate, also according to the IEA. Therefore, using the likely scenario range above, the global oil markets would only lose between 0.78 million bpd and 1.95 million bpd of pre-Ukraine invasion levels of Russian oil, even with the cap in place, regardless of all other factors at the time.

However, even this amount of supply loss from Russia seemed extremely unlikely, as Iran possessed a huge fleet of tankers, part of which could be made available to Russia, as did China and Hong Kong, and India, among others. The commonly cited 'problem' of shipping and cargo protection and indemnity insurance was also spurious, as such insurance could easily be covered from all the countries mentioned, as it was when such shipping insurance-related sanctions were placed on Iranian oil tanker fleets by the US.

Russian Crude Oil Production Had Steadied And Begun To Rise Again

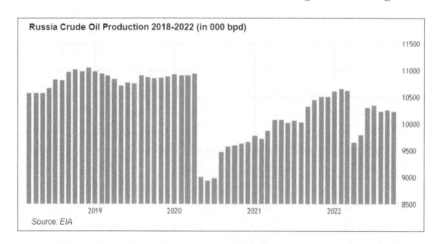

Given all of this, then, it seemed that Putin was firing off verbal warnings about the USD60 pb price cap not because that cap would do Russia any significant damage – at least in the short-term – but rather to prevent the G7 and/or Europe deciding to bring the price cap down to the levels originally mooted. These levels were between USD20-30 pb of Brent equivalent, which would absolutely have put Russian oil sales into genuine loss-making territory.

Europe Continues To Diversity Its Energy Suppliers

One year on from the onset of Russia's invasion of Ukraine, things looked a lot different in the global energy markets than they had both before it and during its early stages. There had been three key factors that had led Russian President Vladimir Putin to believe that Russia could invade Ukraine and get away with it, just as it had done with its invasion of Georgia in 2008 and its invasion of Crimea in 2014, but none of them had worked out as Putin had envisaged.

The first was that the endemic corruption that had spread throughout the country since Putin had become acting president on 31 December 1999 – which had always played a key part in the operational style of the KGB/FSB of which he was a part – had meant his view on the likely outcome of an invasion of Ukraine had been skewed by wrong information on many levels. One crucial such piece of information was that there was no willingness on the part of the Ukrainian people to trade in their sovereignty in any way. Consequently, they would not welcome any attempt by Russia to 'repatriate' the country into any idea of a 'Greater Russia'.

Another crucial piece of information that had not been relayed to Putin, it seemed, was that the corruption in his armed forces had left the Russian military a shadow of its former Second World War self. Many commanders at all levels had conspired to strip and sell off much of the Russian military's machinery, technology, and ammunition, among other items. This conspiracy of corruption had also left the Russian military without an effective wartime command structure.

The upshot of all of this was that the Russian military would have to fight for all gains in Ukraine in a war for which it was no longer truly prepared in any meaningful way. Logically, in turn, this also meant that the idea given to Putin that the Russian military as of 2022 would succeed in securing control over Ukraine within three days was plain wrong.

The practical impossibility of securing control over Ukraine within a short period would additionally result in the US and its key allies being able to support Ukraine's fightback in an ongoing struggle. Moreover, the longer Ukraine was able to resist Russian military advances, the more the US and its allies would see an opportunity in Ukraine to engage in actions that would deter Russia from making any plans to invade other European countries, especially those that were part of the NATO security alliance.

This delay in securing control over Ukraine would also gradually strengthen what Putin had regarded as being the weak link in the European security equation that would have smoothed the way for the invasion. This was the continent's reliance on cheap and plentiful supplies of Russian gas and oil, as touched on earlier. As time went on without Ukraine falling to Russia, all of those countries that had been reliant on Russian energy supplies found temporary short-term measures to fill the gaps in Russian supplies. By the beginning of 2023 they were continuing to consolidate new supplies and new suppliers to manage their longer-term energy needs.

Germany, upon which Putin had focused much of his attention, given its status as the economic powerhouse and *de facto* leader of the European Union, had seemed the most likely of the EU states to take an appeasement approach to Russia's invasion of Ukraine. Aside from its huge gas and oil imports from Russia, Germany - along with Putin's other perceived weak link in Europe, France - had been instrumental in formulating the 'Minsk 2' agreement in February 2015. This agreement, among other contiguous policies aimed at appeasing Putin, had enshrined the idea of autonomy for the Russian separatist-held regions of Donetsk and Luhansk within the Ukraine constitution. Germany had also been the most vociferous opponent to the US's reimposition of sanctions on Iran after Washington's unilateral withdrawal from the JCPOA in May 2018.

However, relatively early on after Russia had first invaded Ukraine, Germany found new sources of gas supply with Qatar, with the help of the US, as highlighted above. Since those early deals with Qatar, new deals with new suppliers for Germany began to appear. For example, news emerged towards the end of 2022 that Germany was in advanced talks to sign a long-term deal for LNG from Oman, with the initial amounts touted as being in the 0.5-1 million tonnes per annum range.

Additionally, February 2023 saw the Abu Dhabi National Oil Co. (ADNOC) deliver 137,000 cubic metres of LNG – its first to Germany –

to the Elbehafen floating storage regasification unit (FSRU) LNG terminal in Brunsbüttel. This was flagged back then as likely to be one of many further deliveries, according to ADNOC Gas's acting chief executive officer, Ahmed Alebri, who said: 'ADNOC Gas stands ready to provide further shipments of this key transition fuel to our partner, RWE and German industry.' The US had made it very clear after discovering in December 2021 that China had been building a secret military facility in the UAE's Khalifa Port that it looked forward to a new phase in its relationship with the UAE.

Europe Moved Quickly To Plugging The Russian Energy Supply Gaps

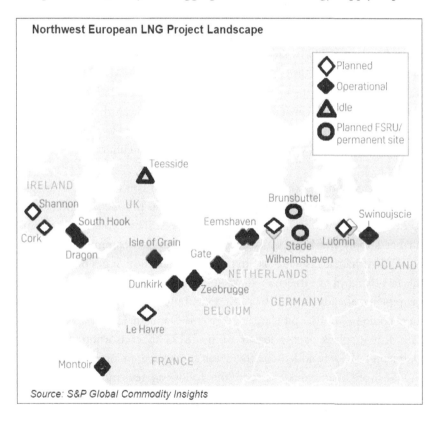

Source: S&P Global Commodity Insights

Brunsbüttel was the third FSRU to begin operations in Germany after the startup of the Wilhelmshaven facility in December 2022 and the Lubmin unit in early January 2023. Germany's economy ministry said at that point that it expected Germany to have 37 billion cubic metric tonnes per annum of LNG import capacity available by 2024.

Germany was not the only country from which EU member states secured new energy supplies, though. Libya was the target of several approaches by Italy's Eni and France's TotalEnergies. The end of January 2023 saw an announcement that the Italian firm was to sign an agreement with Libya's state-owned National Oil Corporation (NOC) that would see it invest around USD8 billion to produce about 850 million cubic feet per day (mmcf/d) from two offshore gas fields in the Mediterranean Sea. The deal – as stated by the NOC's chairman, Farhat Bengdara - would involve the renewal of an existing agreement originally struck in 2008, which had then been subject to delays due to the ongoing civil war in the country.

At that point, Eni was already producing gas in Libya from its Wafa and Bahr Essalam fields, operated by Mellitah Oil & Gas, a joint venture between the Italian company and the NOC. Gas from the fields was then transported to Italy through the 520-kilometre eight billion cubic metres per year (bcm/y) capacity Green Stream pipeline that crosses the Mediterranean Sea and lands in Gela in Sicily. This deal was part of several initiatives launched by the government in Rome to eliminate Russian gas by 2025.

Bengdara said that the USD8 billion deal with Eni would be a key part of Libya's refocusing its efforts on boosting its gas production and tapping some 80 trillion cubic feet of proven reserves. This would be potential further supply for Europe. According to previous comments from the NOC chairman, ideas were also in place to install another gas pipeline from the east of Libya to Greece to augment the potential export capacity of the gas pipeline already in place from Libya to Italy. In addition, Bengdara said there could be another pipeline linked to the Damietta LNG plant in Egypt, with Eni in place as the leader of the SEGAS consortium that owns Damietta LNG. He added that there was also a program of drilling offshore and onshore that would start in the following few months under the leadership of Eni and the UK's BP.

These plans for Libya's gas sector were announced in tandem with its plans for the development of its oil sector, with Bengdara stating that Libya wanted foreign investment to boost its oil production up to 2 million bpd in the following three to five years. According to industry figures, Libya -

which did not have an OPEC quota at that point - pumped 1.17 million bpd in December 2022.

European countries in particular know that there remains huge natural oil and gas resources potential in Libya. Before the removal of its longstanding leader, Muammar Gaddafi, in 2011, Libya had easily been able to produce around 1.65 million bpd of mostly high-quality light, sweet crude oil and production had been on a rising production trend, up from about 1.4 million bpd in 2000.

Europe Looked To The Eastern Mediterranean For New Gas Supplies

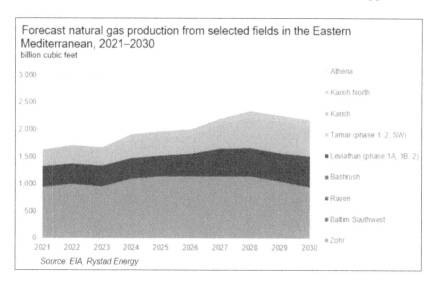

Forecast natural gas production from selected fields in the Eastern Mediterranean, 2021–2030
billion cubic feet

Source: EIA, Rystad Energy

Although this output was well below the peak levels of more than 3 million bpd achieved in the late 1960s, the NOC had plans in place before 2011 to roll out enhanced oil recovery (EOR) techniques to increase crude oil production at maturing oil fields. Given this plan, there appeared scope to increase crude oil production up to the 2.1 million bpd targeted by Libya's minister of gas and oil, Mohamed Aoun, and to hit the informal interim target of 1.6 million bpd by the end of 2023. Libya still has around 48 billion barrels of proved crude oil reserves – the largest in Africa.

Eni had another huge success around the same time – in conjunction with US hydrocarbons giant, Chevron – with a major new gas discovery in the 1,800 square kilometre Nargis offshore area concession in Egypt. Chevron and Eni each hold a 45% stake in Nargis offshore concession, with Egypt's Tharwa Petroleum Co. holding the remaining 10%. This discovery followed the announcement in December 2022 that Chevron had hit at least 3.5 trillion cubic feet of gas with its Nargis-1 exploration well in the eastern Nile Delta, about 60 kilometres north of the Sinai Peninsula.

The US Saw The Strategic Significance Of The Eastern Mediterranean

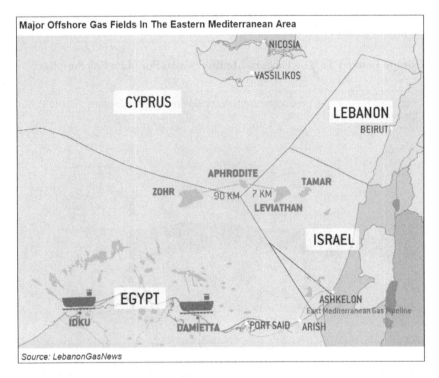

Source: LebanonGasNews

Chevron, along with most notably ConocoPhillips, had established itself at that point as being at the vanguard of the re-engagement of the US in several highly strategic regions across the Eastern Mediterranean. These efforts were aimed at boosting the supplies of gas especially, but also, oil to replace lost Russian supplies.

Chevron had only entered the Egyptian upstream sector in 2020 but by the end of 2022 was operating the huge Leviathan and Tamar fields in Israel and the Aphrodite project in the offshore Cyprus area. According to the president of Chevron International Exploration and Production, Clay Neff in 2022: 'The East Mediterranean has abundant energy resources, and their development is driving strategic collaboration in the region.'

The previous strategic collaboration in the region worthy of note was concentrated around China, Russia, and Iran's efforts to rope in its core countries – including Egypt – into their vision of how the area should be configured. A central strand in this strategy was the creation of a 'unified power grid' – in every sense of the words – as analysed in depth in the *'Key Players In The Global Oil Market: Iran'* section.

Pan-Arab Power Grid Was Full Of Promise For China, Russia And Iran

Pan-Arab Power Grid Initial Connectivity Projections

Source: Atlantic Council

In essence, the idea ran along the same lines as former US President Theodore Roosevelt's view on how to maintain power: 'If you've got them by the balls, their hearts and minds will follow.' In this context, if one country can shut off the ability of other countries' citizens to cook, and to heat and light their houses and offices, then they will be highly receptive to any suggestions that the country might make.

The attempt to exert control over the wider Middle East's power grid by China, Russia, and Iran had been going on for some years prior to that point in late 2022/early 2023. An announcement was made in 2022 that

Egypt and Jordan were increasing their cooperation in gas delivery projects inside Jordan, with Egyptian expertise. Just prior to this, it was announced that Iraq had agreed to re-start the export of crude oil from Iraq's Kirkuk to the refinery at Zarqa in Jordan. Electricity supply originating from Iran was also factored into this deal, given that Iran had historically supplied Iraq with 30-40% of all its electricity, and had just signed the longest-ever deal between it and Iraq to continue to do so.

At around the same time, Iraq's then-Electricity Minister, Majid Mahdi Hantoush, announced that plans had been finalised for the completion of Iraq's electricity connection with Egypt within the next three years. This network was to be bolstered by the parallel network connections that Iran had consolidated through direct electricity and gas exchanges. These, said Iran's then-Energy Minister, Reza Ardakanian in 2019, would be part of the overall project to establish a joint Arab electricity market. The establishing of broad and deep cooperation in oil, gas, and electricity was a key part of the wide-ranging '25-Year Comprehensive Cooperation Agreement' between China and Iran.

Consequently, the series of gas discoveries in Egypt and elsewhere in the Eastern Mediterranean by companies from the US and its allies (with Israel also a dominant force in the area) not only drove a wedge between Egypt and the idea of a unified Middle East power grid beholden ultimately to China but also provided a new source of gas into Europe as and when required. In this context, the activities of US companies in the area were complemented not just by Eni, but also notably by France's TotalEnergies, and by British firms, including BP and Shell.

A Sign Of Strain In Saudi Arabia's Relationship With Russia?

To many oil market watchers, the decision on 1 February 2023 by OPEC+ to stick to its previously agreed oil production cut quota of 2 million bpd was made regardless of concerns in the West that energy prices were still at levels that fuelled inflation, pushed interest rates higher and catalysed economic slowdowns. However, it was crucial to note that the decision to maintain that cut - due to run until the end of 2023 - represented only around 2 percent of the then-recent historical mean average of supply in the global oil market.

Additionally crucial to note was that oil prices at that point were at levels that barely helped Saudi Arabia in budgetary terms at all, with a fiscal breakeven oil price forecast of around USD78 pb of Brent in 2023, compared to about USD80 pb of Brent in the previous year.

Highly significant as well was that those prices were way below the level that Russia wanted, and would have been strongly lobbying for, given its fiscal breakeven oil price at that time of just over USD114 pb of Brent, up from around USD64 pb before its invasion of Ukraine. So, the question for oil traders to have really asked at that stage was, to invert the earlier Chinese comment on Russia: had Saudi Arabia's relationship with Russia reached its limits?

February's OPEC Deal Surprisingly Did Nothing To Help Russia

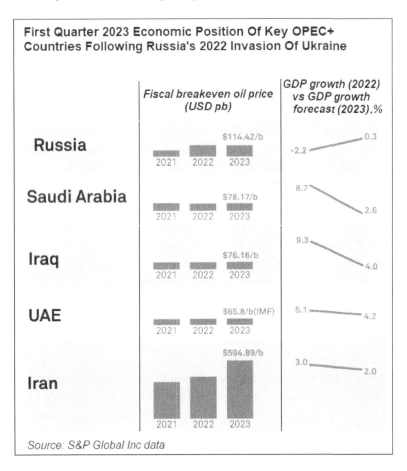

First Quarter 2023 Economic Position Of Key OPEC+ Countries Following Russia's 2022 Invasion Of Ukraine

Source: S&P Global Inc data

Given the deterioration in the relationship between Saudi Arabia and its former principal superpower ally, the US, since Riyadh had instigated the Second Oil Price War in 2014 – specifically aimed at destroying or at least disabling the then-nascent US shale energy sector – there had been every reason to expect Saudi Arabia to press OPEC for deeper cuts in collective oil production. These would have put more upwards pressure on oil prices towards the elevated levels that Russia needed to begin to balance its fiscal position.

Only a few months before, Saudi Arabia had been perfectly happy to do precisely that through the original gigantic cut in production that it had been able to orchestrate through it OPEC brothers and Russia. That huge production cut had been done despite extreme pressure from the US on Saudi Arabia not to do it. The US had rightly argued that the mammoth cut in oil production would fuel inflation, which would fuel interest rate rises, which would dampen economic growth, which might lead to recessions in several of the world's leading economies. The US had also rightly argued that it would effectively lead to more funding for Russia's war in Ukraine.

What had changed at the top of the Saudi power structure was an awareness of the need to hedge its geopolitical position, given what had been happening to Russia both in Ukraine and internationally as a result of its presence there. According to several senior sources connected to the energy security apparatus of the EU and the US, the senior Saudis saw Russia's omni-shambolic invasion of Ukraine as a signal that President Vladimir Putin may have lost some of his former shrewdness as a supreme geopolitical operator and that his country may no longer be the major military and political force that it had once been.

In tandem with this, Saudi Arabia had also seen, and privately been made aware of, China's own similar growing reservations about Putin and his country over the course of the war, as analysed in even more depth in the 'Key Players In The Global Oil Market: China' section. By that point in early 2023, it was perhaps China that Saudi Arabia viewed as its chief superpower ally, certainly in the economic sense.

Russia was still important to Saudi Arabia from an energy perspective, particularly in the context of the OPEC+ grouping. The US it seemed was regarded merely as having a part to play in Saudi Arabia's security considerations and also as leverage through which the Kingdom could gain even more support from China. The situation with the US was not static, though, as Saudi Arabia wanted to make sure that all of its options remained intact for future use if needed. It remained the case, however, that it was to China that Riyadh had made decades-long major commitments spanning the range of energy, business, financing, and political cooperation.

India Flouts US Plan And Continues To Support Russia

Early in March 2023, India stepped up its negotiations with the US aimed at continuing to import as much oil from Russia as it required, regardless of in-place sanctions against Moscow and further sanctions planned for the near future. This ran in tandem at that point with India's ongoing refusal to vote in favour of United Nations' resolutions that condemned Russia for its invasion of Ukraine.

The US's Plans For India In The New Oil Order Were Not Working Out

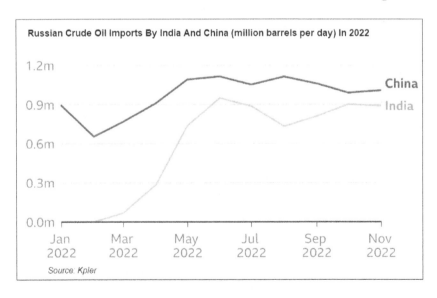

Just a few months before, on a visit to Moscow, India's Foreign Minister, Subrahmanyam Jaishankar, stated: 'For us, Russia has been a steady and time-tested partner and, as I said, any objective evaluation of our relationship over many decades would confirm that it has served both our countries very, very well.'

Around the same time in March 2023 that India was negotiating with the US to allow it to continue to import Russian energy, Jaishankar also met with his Chinese counterpart, Qin Gang, during which both countries agreed to promote the improvement of relations between them.

Back in 2020/2021, when the U.S. was rolling out its 'relationship normalisation deals' with Middle Eastern states as a counterbalance to ever-increasing Russian and Chinese influence in the region - and wanted to use India as an alternative to China's backstop bid for oil - Washington would not have believed how the situation with India appeared to be playing out.

The US had certainly got one thing right in its calculations back then, which was that India's economic growth rate would cause a surge in its demand for energy to power that expansion. Although economic growth had suffered during the height of the COVID-19 pandemic, the prospects that India could act as a genuine substitute for Chinese demand in the global energy markets remained bright.

By that point, India was the world's third-largest energy consuming, on the back of rising incomes and improving standards of living. Energy use across the country had doubled since 2000, with 80% of that demand still being met by coal, oil and solid biomass. In the coming years, according to the IEA, millions of Indian households would buy new appliances, air conditioning units and vehicles, whilst at the same time the country was set to become the most populous in the world.

During this process, India was set to add the equivalent of a city the size of Los Angeles to its urban population each year. To meet growth in electricity demand over the following 20 years, India would need to add a power system the size of the European Union to what it already had in place, the IEA added. In sum, India was projected to make up the biggest share of global energy demand growth over the next two decades, at 25%.

Several major new deals between India and the UAE – for which the US had also expected much, following its relationship normalisation deals initiative of 2020 – had been predicated on India becoming the substitute global oil (and other energy sources) demand alternative to China.

Despite the 28-deal bonanza signed between India and Russia just before Christmas 2021, as analysed earlier, the US had still believed that India could be induced in some way or another into moving gradually back in the direction that it wanted in its intended new global order of things. After all, Washington reasoned, India was a core member of the

'Quadrilateral Security Dialogue' (Quad) alliance, also featuring the US, Australia and Japan and had regularly taken part in the annual 'Exercise Malabar' of armed forces from the Quad member countries. China had several times referred to the Quad as the 'Asian NATO'.

One key problem, though, had become much clearer to Washington as time had gone by in terms of India's view on the ordering of its international relationships. This was that despite the China-Russia alliance, the first country to which India had historically turned for protection from its key regional rival, China, was, in fact Russia.

Even before the military proposals contained in the 28-deal extravaganza signed just before Christmas 2021 between India and Russia were revealed, India had much in the way of military assistance – hardware and software – from Russia. India was also a full member of the Russia-China dominated Shanghai Cooperation Organisation. Economically as well, although the growth trajectory of the following 20 years looked very healthy for India, in the shorter-term it needed to fully bounce back from COVID-19-related damage. To do this, India was determined to secure the cheapest energy supplies that it could, and one such source of these was its longstanding ally, Russia.

At that point in the aftermath of its invasion of Ukraine, Russian oil was very cheap indeed, trading at a discount to the Brent benchmark of at least USD30 pb. It was true that these purchases could be construed by the US and its allies as being supportive of Russia – which they were, in the broadest sense of the relationship between New Delhi and Moscow. However, it was also the case that India could argue that it was just buying the cheapest oil it could get to help to repair its economy after the COVID-19 pandemic.

Regardless of the reason, though, India's imports of crude oil from Russia had soared at a time when the key aim of the US and its allies – as in large part exercised through sanctions on its energy sector - was to isolate President Putin to cause financial repercussions for his actions in Ukraine. According to industry figures, by the end of 2022 there had been a sevenfold year-on-year increase in India's buying of Russia crude oil – up to 700,000 bpd, from 100,000 bpd in 2021.

Additionally, the end of February 2023 saw Russian LNG giant Novatek state that it was open to accepting payments in Indian rupees for any LNG term deal that it signed with Indian gas companies. Novatek's chairman, Leonid Mikhelson, added at that time that his company was in talks with India's state-owned gas utility GAIL and other large Indian energy firms for LNG term deals in this context.

China Remains Cautious But Eyes Future Opportunities

Up until Russia invaded Ukraine on 24 February 2022, it was generally accepted wisdom that China would not attempt to overtly challenge the US's authority across the world for around five to 10 years, given the technological, economic, and military deficit between the two countries. Then again, up until Russia invaded Ukraine, few had believed that the longstanding rhetoric of Russia's leadership about Ukraine just being one part of Russia rather than a sovereign independent state would turn into the reality of war. Once Russia had invaded Ukraine, though, high-level officials in the US's and Europe's security apparatus began very seriously to wonder if the timing had shifted in favour of China's making an early move in a similar vein in Taiwan.

Militarily, it was obvious very soon after Russian forces moved into Ukraine that although the military forces of the US and its allies were not directly fighting in the war themselves, most of the allied countries were committed to providing resources to Ukraine to help in its war effort against Russia. This included not just military hardware but also extensive intelligence, logistics, and command resources. It was also obvious to these allied countries – and to China – that a major attack on a site in a distant sphere of the world from Europe, would significantly stretch these resources further.

There was also a key political reason why China's President Xi Jinping might want to expedite any plans he had to invade Taiwan sooner rather than later, the US and its allies thought at that point. President Xi was attempting to secure an unprecedented third term as General Secretary of the Chinese Communist Party at the 20th National Congress of the Chinese Communist Party, scheduled for some time in October or November 2022. Securing a third term would provide the basis for him to effectively become president for life. To achieve this, though, he was going to have to make various changes to China's constitution. This, in turn, would require the unwavering support of all elements of China's military and of the most nationalist politicians in the country. And one thing that both groups agreed on was that Taiwan was just a part of China rather than being an independent state, and it always had been. Moreover, just ahead of the scheduled National Congress meeting, a major live fire exercise was planned by China around Taiwan, in much the same way as the 'Zapad' military exercises had taken place just before Russia's invasion of Ukraine.

Would China's Military Exercises Go The Same Way As Russia's Had?

China's Planned Live-Fire Drills Around Taiwan - August 2022

China had obviously been watching and analysing every angle at play since Russia had begun its invasion of Ukraine, and several factors had become clear. The most important one from China's perspective was that although many countries in the West – especially those from the NATO security alliance - had supported Ukraine's fight against Russia through the provision of weapons, intelligence, and broader logistical resources, there had been no direct on-the-ground military support of Ukraine, in Ukraine, by NATO military forces. Indeed, NATO had not even sought to enforce a 'no-fly' zone across Ukraine, partly because there was only a fuzzy legal justification to do so – as Ukraine was not a member of NATO – but more appositely because it feared escalation into a nuclear war with a major nuclear power.

Both reasons, Beijing saw, would also apply to the West's likely response to an invasion of Taiwan by China, First, Taiwan was not a member of NATO or any similar Asia-Pacific version of it; and second, the risk of escalation into a nuclear war with major nuclear power China was also very real. In terms of some sort of 'justification' for an invasion of Taiwan by which China could seek to undermine the collective resolve of the West in its response, it could use the same one that Russia had used with some early success in distorting the conflict narrative in Ukraine. Specifically, China could say, just as Russia had done, that it was seeking to 'repatriate' a land that had long been part of the greater whole.

One key factor that Russia had going for it in its invasion of Ukraine that China would not have had if it had invaded Taiwan was that Russia possessed all of the energy supplies that it needed to keep its critical infrastructure running, regardless of any sanctions brought against it by any country. An added benefit for Russia, which would have worked in the opposite way for China, was that the rise in energy prices that resulted from Russia's invasion of Ukraine had boosted its energy revenues. As mentioned above, Russia earned just under USD1 billion per day from oil and gas exports during the first 100 days of the war in Ukraine – so around USD97 billion in total – whilst the cost to it of fighting the war over that first 100-day period was just under USD88 billion.

Turning a profit was unlikely to have been at the top of President Xi's agenda in any plans to invade Taiwan at that point, but ensuring China's energy security in such an event certainly would have been. However, China had long been strengthening its energy security both through its expanded activities in the Middle East connected to its 'One Belt, One Road' programme and through its broadening and deepening of its energy links to Russia. The building of direct energy infrastructure links between China and Russia had been extremely extensive in the previous few years in both the oil and the gas sectors. Moreover, in the weeks just before and just after Russia's invasion of Ukraine, China bought massive extra quantities of Russian oil, on top of the levels previously required in its regular usage pattern. According to industry data, China bought a record quantity of Russian crude oil in May 2022, increasing purchases by around USD1 billion more than in April, to just under USD7.5 billion. This was more than double the amount that China bought from Russia in the same period of 2021.

Crucially as well, trading between China and Russia in their local currencies – rather than the US dollar - had increased dramatically in the previous few years. As the chief executive officer of Russia's Novatek, Leonid Mikhelson, had said back in September 2018, Russia had been discussing switching away from USD-centric with its largest trading partners, such as China and India, and even Arab countries had been thinking about it. 'If they [the U.S.] do create difficulties for our Russian banks then all we have to do is replace dollars,' he had added. At around the same time, China launched its subsequently extremely successful Shanghai Futures Exchange with oil contracts denominated in yuan.

Additionally, as the US dollar had become increasingly used as the cornerstone of international sanctions against countries that the US and its allies wanted to punish, so the incentive had grown for a shift by those countries to convert more FX reserves into yuan. In Russia's case, earlier restrictions imposed following the annexation of Crimea in 2014 led to the significant diversification of Russia's foreign reserves away from US dollars and into the Chinese yuan. Specifically, of Russia's USD643 billion reserves just before it invaded Ukraine in 2022, the share of US dollars had fallen to 16.4%, from 44.4% in 2014. Over the same period, Russia had made cumulative purchases of almost USD78 billion worth of Chinese yuan, meaning that the yuan's share of Russian FX reserves at that point had risen to 13.1%.

Although China's initial official response to Russia's invasion of Ukraine had been quite guarded, an early indicator of Beijing's true feelings on it came at the beginning of April 2022 when China's Foreign Ministry spokesperson, Zhao Lijian, had laid the blame for Russia's invasion of Ukraine squarely at the feet of the US. 'As the culprit and leading instigator of the Ukraine crisis, the US has led NATO to engage in five rounds of eastward expansion in the last two decades after 1999,' he had said during a virtual summit call with leaders of the European Union.

Shortly afterwards, China had warned the US against any moves that 'adds fuel to the flames' in Ukraine and its then-Foreign Minister, Wang Yi, had called again on the West to take account of Moscow's concerns about NATO expansion. This rhetoric had been echoed again on President Xi Jinping's birthday – 15 June – when he had taken part in a lengthy telephone conversation with Russian President, Vladimir Putin. During this talk, according to Russian news sources in the first instance: 'Xi had pledged China's ongoing support for Russia... [and] President Xi had noted the legitimacy of actions taken by Russia to protect itself in the face of challenges to its security created by external forces.'

Concomitant with all these developments had been a surge in the number and seriousness of Chinese security threats against Western powers at domestic levels. This had been noted by the director of the US's principal domestic security intelligence service, the FBI - Chris Wray – and his opposite number in the UK, the director-general of MI5, Ken McCallum.

On the first ever occasion that the two most senior figures in the US's and UK's domestic security intelligence services had shared a public platform together, Wray had warned that China was 'drawing lessons from what's happening with Russia and its invasion of Ukraine.' McCallum had said that at that point in 2022 MI5 was running 'seven times as many investigations into Chinese activity of concern' than it had been as recently as 2018.

The FBI's Wray had added: '[were China] to forcibly take over Taiwan … it would represent one of the most horrific business disruptions the world has ever seen.' He had concluded that: 'We've seen China looking for ways to insulate their economy against potential sanctions trying to cushion themselves from harm if they do anything to draw the ire of the international community. In our world, we call that kind of behaviour a clue.'

As the war in Ukraine went on, though, and the resolve of the US and its allies hardened to support Ukraine and resist Russia's actions there, China shifted its tone and actions markedly. For several reasons analysed in earlier sections, China's previously stated 'no limits' relationship with Russia turned into one that suddenly had a lot of limits indeed.

In essence, Beijing moved to a more – overtly, at least – neutral position in order to lower the risk of its being caught up in political and economic spillovers from the Russian invasion of Ukraine and anything approaching direct confrontation with the US and its NATO allies. In practice, this involved China maintaining normal ties with Russia but avoiding being seen to help its war efforts; doing nothing to alienate the US, Europe, or any allies thereof; and avoiding undertaking any actions that might lead it to being the subject of secondary sanctions and economic damage.

None of these stances, though, have precluded China from continuing to seek to expand its influence in areas of influence around the world that are of particular interest to it from the political, economic and military perspective. The principal mechanism for this accretion of power in all these areas remains its 'One Belt, One Road' programme for the many reasons, and in the many ways, examined earlier in this section and also in the later *'Key Players In The Global Oil Market: China'* section as well.

The Middle East remains one such area of key interest to China, principally for its vast oil and gas resources that are essential for the fuelling of its economic growth into the future. The region is also of interest to China because it has been a key part of the US's political, economic and military focus around the globe over the past several decades. Given these twin factors, China is likely to continue to take a path that inexorably builds up its influence across the region whilst not placing it in a direct confrontation with the US and its allies.

A case in point in this context was China's role in the re-establishment of relations between arch-regional rivals Iran and Saudi Arabia in March 2023. As analysed in detail above, at the beginning of September 2022 Iran's then-newish President, Ebrahim Raisi, stated that there had been five rounds of meetings between high-level personnel from Tehran and Riyadh in the previous few months. In fact, the two countries had been meeting relatively regularly ever since the US ended its combat mission in Iraq toward the end of 2021.

The first public signal that a rapprochement of sorts might occur at some point between the two Middle East rivals – Shia Iran and Sunni Saudi Arabia - had come from Saudi Crown Prince, Mohammed bin Salman, at the end of April 2021. He had stated very publicly that he sought: 'A good and special relationship with Iran…We do not want Iran's situation to be difficult; on the contrary, we want Iran to grow… and to push the region and the world towards prosperity.'

This comment followed what it transpired had been four previous meetings in the Iraqi capital of Baghdad between senior figures from the Iranian and Saudi regimes, the first of which had been personally brokered by then-Iraq Prime Minister, Mustafa al-Kadhimi. The existence of these talks was subsequently confirmed by an Iraqi government official, although neither Riyadh nor Tehran formally acknowledged them at the time.

The March 2023 announcement, then, was not a surprise in and of itself but what was surprising was the degree to which China allowed itself to be publicly cast as the key broker in the deal. Beijing had correctly judged that because the deal was of the peaceful variety, the US could not say too much negatively about it, although White House national security spokesperson, John Kirby, did observe tersely that, 'This is not about China'.

At the same time, though, the Iran-Saudi announcement would clearly be seen by the world as potentially one of the biggest such deals done in the Middle East for many, many years. It was, in short, just the sort of far-reaching geopolitical coup that the US had wanted to achieve in its 'relationship normalisation deals' programme.

The deal also put China in an ideal position to begin to effect other far-reaching shifts in the geopolitical alliances of all other countries in the Middle East, given that each of them had formerly been broadly allied to either Iran or Saudi Arabia. Indeed, China's top diplomat, Wang Yi, described the deal as a victory for dialogue and peace, adding that Beijing would 'continue to play a constructive role in addressing tough global issues'.

This position would also be very useful for securing political backing in the region and energy supplies ahead of any action China might take in Taiwan. In February 2023, the director of the US's CIA, William Burns, revealed that Chinese President Xi Jinping has instructed his country's army 'to be ready by 2027 to conduct a successful invasion' of Taiwan. He added: 'Now, that does not mean that he's [President Xi] has decided to conduct an invasion in 2027, or any other year, but it's a reminder of the seriousness of his focus and his ambition'. He concluded: 'It's very much in our interest […] to make clear […] that we are deeply opposed to anyone trying to change that unilaterally, especially by the use of force'.

Part Two: Key Players In The Global Oil Market

Saudi Arabia

In the aftermath of two failed oil price wars in less than ten years, Saudi Arabia's position within both the global oil market and OPEC is the most uncertain it has ever been. Not only has Saudi Arabia undermined its core 1945 Agreement with the US but it has also lost the trust of many of its fellow OPEC members as the organisation's effective leader.

It now finds itself walking a metaphorical tightrope between the US on the one side and China and Russia on the other, with everything at stake should it fail to maintain this balance.

Saudi Arabia's Delicate Balancing Act Between East And West

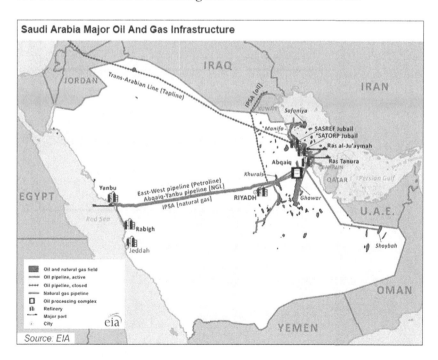

1945 Agreement With US Broken And Price Range Required

The core 1945 Agreement between the US and Saudi Arabia was essentially that: the US will receive all the oil supplies it needs for as long as Saudi Arabia has oil in place, in return for which the US will guarantee the security of Saudi Arabia (and, by extension, of the Al Saud ruling family).

By the end of the 2014-2016 Oil Price War, the agreement had effectively been changed to: the US will receive all the oil supplies it needs for as long as Saudi Arabia has oil in place, in return for which the US will guarantee the security of Saudi Arabia (and, by extension, of the Al Saud ruling family), *provided that Saudi Arabia does not attempt to interfere with the growth and prosperity of the US shale oil sector or the US economy as a whole.*

For Saudi Arabia, this new caveat meant that Washington wanted oil prices to trade between a floor of USD40-45 per barrel of Brent and a ceiling of USD75-80 per barrel of Brent for the economic and political factors analysed in the previous section.

Saudi Could Not Survive Within The US's Oil Trading Band

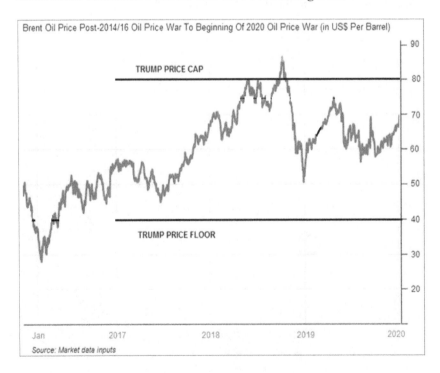

Brent Oil Price Post-2014/16 Oil Price War To Beginning Of 2020 Oil Price War (in US$ Per Barrel)

TRUMP PRICE CAP

TRUMP PRICE FLOOR

Source: Market data inputs

The key problem for the Kingdom in this new global oil market order was that after the end of the Second Oil Price War it had a budget breakeven price per barrel of Brent of much more than the US's 'acceptable' ceiling price for Brent. This higher breakeven price was set to endure for several years.

For this reason, it had again tried in 2020 to destroy or at least disable for as long as possible the US shale oil sector but had again failed. These failures had only served to strengthen the US's resolve to 'not put up with any more crap from the Saudis', as they put it, and to rigidly enforce this oil price trading band.

One of the key mechanisms that the US might use to do this in the future, as discussed at length in the previous section, was to threaten to withdraw all military support from Saudi Arabia, which would have left it vulnerable then to attacks from its regional neighbours, particularly Iran.

The other key mechanism was the enactment of the 'NOPEC' bill, which would have left Saudi Arabia as a country open to lawsuits of all kinds, most notably related to the '9-11' terrorist attacks. The bill's enactment would also have left the Kingdom's entire hydrocarbons sector vulnerable to being banned from using US dollars and to having Saudi Aramco broken up into smaller 'non-cartel-like' parts.

The 'NOPEC' Act Could Reduce Aramco's Value To Zero

The 'No Oil Producing and Exporting Cartels' (NOPEC) Bill, if passed into legislation to become an 'Act', would open the way for sovereign governments to be sued for predatory pricing and any failure to comply with the US's antitrust laws. The bill represents a modification of the US's existing antitrust laws (particularly the Sherman Antitrust protections) that specifically allows for OPEC, its key members (including its *de facto* leader Saudi Arabia), and its national oil companies (including Saudi Aramco), to be sued.

Litigation could be brought on any basis that related to anti-competitive practices that sought to limit the world's supply of petroleum, with the consequent impact of that on global oil prices. The legal basis for judging the aforementioned entities as being complicit in activities that were in direct opposition to antitrust practices – that is, those that were in keeping with the practices of a cartel – appeared compelling. OPEC was specifically created in 1960 to 'co-ordinate and unify the petroleum policies' of all of its member states – effectively fixing oil prices, in the exact manner of a cartel.

OPEC Is A Cartel As Far As The NOPEC Bill Is Concerned

OPEC Members' Crude Oil Production As At The Beginning Of Q32022

Country	million barrels per day
Saudi Arabia	10.9*
Iraq	4.5
UAE	3.2
Kuwait	2.8
Iran	2.6
Angola	1.2
Libya	1.1
Nigeria	1.1
Algeria	1
Venezuela	0.7
Congo	0.3
Gabon	0.2
Equatorial Guinea	<0.1

million barrels per day

* = includes some sales of inventory (industry figures)
Source: OPEC

OPEC's cartel-like appearance is further enhanced by the facts that its members account for around 40% of the world's crude oil output, about 60% of the total petroleum traded internationally from their oil exports and just over 80% of the world's proven oil reserves.

The NOPEC Bill, if enacted, would immediately inhibit any and all actions or statements from OPEC specifically, and its key members, and its leader Saudi Arabia. This would include coordinated oil production cuts or increases, and statements relating to where the organisation or any of its key members, including Saudi Arabia, forecast production levels or oil prices might be in the future.

For Saudi Aramco it could also mean a drop in its effective value to zero, given that the company is the key corporate instrument used to manage the oil flows of the *de facto* leader of the world's *de facto* oil cartel. Although Saudi Aramco is not directly involved in making OPEC policies, the company can be seen as being collusive in price-fixing through the adjustment of its output to help manage oil prices and through its statements and guidance about its future oil production levels and its price expectations.

This view of Saudi Aramco as a proxy of the Saudi Arabian state was not undermined by its part privatisation, as only a tiny percentage of its shares were floated in the IPO in December 2019. Its enduring status as a state proxy even after its IPO was made clear at the time of the offering by statements from leading company and government officials that the company would remain operationally directed by the government of Saudi Arabia. Indeed, Saudi Aramco's chief executive officer, Amin Nasser, said at the time of the IPO that Saudi Aramco's oil and gas production decisions were 'sovereign matters that would remain with the government'.

The eventual enactment of the NOPEC Bill would also mean that trading in all Aramco's products – including oil – would be subject to the antitrust legislation, meaning the prohibition of sales in US dollars. It could further mean the eventual break-up of Aramco into smaller constituent companies that were not capable of influencing the oil price.

The 'NOPEC' Act Would Also Expose Saudi's Terrorist Links

The fact that the NOPEC Bill would also immediately remove the sovereign immunity that existed in US courts for OPEC as a group and for its individual member states would leave Saudi Arabia itself open to being sued, with its total liability being estimated at USD1 trillion of investments in the US alone.

Over and above ay commercial litigation brought against the country by US corporates, Saudi Arabia could also be faced with a deluge of civil actions brought on the basis of its alleged links to several acts of terrorism committed either in the US or on US citizens outside the US. Chief amongst these possible legal actions were those connected to the 9/11 terrorist attacks in New York and the 7/7 terrorist attacks in London, to name but two of the most high-profile events.

Crucially in this context, on 28 September 2017, the US Congress overrode former President Barack Obama's veto of the Justice Against Sponsors of Terrorism Act (JASTA), making it possible for victims' families to sue the government of Saudi Arabia. Within weeks of this, there were seven major lawsuits in federal courts alleging Saudi government support and funding for the 9/11 terrorist attack on the US. Although Saudi Arabia has denied longstanding suspicions of involvement in the attack, 15 of the 19 hijackers were Saudi nationals.

That Saudi Arabia might have been involved in these attacks, directly or indirectly, should have come as no surprise to anyone who knows anything about the Kingdom. Notably in this context, 2010 saw the publication in various news media, including the BBC, of several lengthy documents that highlighted such potential links between Saudi Arabia and various terrorist organisations.

One of these was a leaked classified memo from then-US Secretary of State, Hilary Clinton, in which she warned that donors in Saudi Arabia were: 'The most significant source of funding to Sunni terrorist groups worldwide.' She added that these Sunni groups included al-Qaeda, the Taliban and Lashkar-e-Taiba.

The Aramco IPO Had Been Key To MbS's Rise To Power

The run-up to the landmark IPO of Saudi Aramco is analysed in depth here for five key reasons. First, it highlighted the lack of basic understanding of many of the most senior Saudis about how the global oil market works in practice. Second, it underlined how a major force in the global oil markets could be hijacked by those at the top of the government who, due to this lack of understanding, could cause chaos in both their own country and to other countries significantly connected to the oil sector. Third, there are plans to offer more of Aramco at some point, as well as other major Saudi hydrocarbons-sector companies, so understanding the deficiencies of Saudi Arabia in this regard is necessary to understanding the scope of trading possibilities available. Fourth, these plans will occur amidst the certainty that sooner or later the Saudis will do exactly the same thing as they did in 2014-2016 and in 2020 – that is, launch another extraordinarily ill-thought-through oil price war. And fifth, even before the new offerings, there is plenty of scope to make money shorting various Saudi assets.

It is vital to understanding everything that followed the Saudi Aramco IPO saga to recall that the idea to float part of Saudi Arabia's flagship oil company had come from the then-Deputy Crown Prince Mohammed bin Salman (MbS). MbS had only been appointed to this position in April 2015, whilst it was Muhammed bin Nayef (MbN) who had been named as the Crown Prince in the same month. This had followed the death in January 2015 of King Abdullah and the accession to the throne of King Salman. MbN was a grandson of the founding king of Saudi Arabia, Abdulaziz, and enjoyed considerable support from many senior Saudis.

Prior to his appointment as Deputy Crown Prince, MbS had been minister of defence just after the Houthis took control of northern Yemen in late 2014 and it was he who had ordered air strikes against the Houthis and the imposition of a naval blockade. MbS had secured the support required from the majority of senior Saudis by assuring them that under his supervision the war against the Houthis would be won very quickly, but this had proven to be incorrect.

As a result of this intervention, and of similar actions in MbS's tenure as minister of defence, the German intelligence service, the Bundesnachrichtendienst (BND), leaked an abridged internal-only assessment report of MbS to various trusted members of the press that stated: 'Saudi Arabia [under MbS] has adopted an impulsive policy of intervention.' It went on to describe MbS in terms of being a political gambler who was destabilising the Arab world through proxy wars in Yemen and Syria.

At the same time as all this was happening, a power struggle was ongoing between the powerbase of former King Abdullah, whose supporters favoured MbN, and the powerbase of the new King Salman, whose supporters favoured MbS. The potential switch – involving the possible replacement of MbN with MbS as Crown Prince – can be regarded in large part as a function of the extreme domestic rivalry between these two factions, and also of the US wanting to have a more aggressively anti-Iran figure in charge in Saudi Arabia when King Salman died.

Central to MbS winning over senior Saudis from the opposing faction in the run-up to his replacing MbN as Crown Prince on 21 June 2017 had been his idea to float a stake in Saudi Aramco through an IPO. In theory, the idea had a number of positive factors going for it that would benefit MbS.

First, it would raise a lot of money – exactly how much depended on the size of the stake to be sold – part of which could be used to offset the economically disastrous effect on Saudi Arabia of the 2014-2016 Oil Price War. Second, it would likely be the biggest ever IPO, thus boosting Saudi Arabia's reputation and the breadth and depth of its capital markets. And third, the money coming directly from the sale and from the increased capital pool of Saudi capital markets could be used as part of the 'National Transformation Program' (NTP) 2020 - in turn part of Saudi's 'Vision 2030' development plan – that sought to diversify the Kingdom's economy away from its reliance on oil and gas exports.

MbS's Big Idea To Securing His Position As Crown Prince

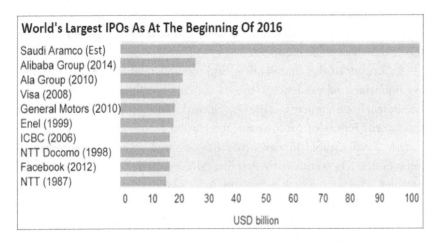

After a few months of further discussion, MbS assured senior Saudis that he could ensure the flotation of 5% of the company, which he believed would raise at least USD100 billion in much-needed funds for Saudi Arabia. It would also make the Saudi Aramco offering by far the biggest IPO in history. This, in turn, place a valuation on the entire company of at least USD2 trillion.

Additionally, MbS assured the senior Saudis, the company would be listed in one or two of the most prestigious international stock exchanges in the world, such as the New York Stock Exchange (NYSE) and the London Stock Exchange (LSE). These would further project Saudi Arabia's presence as an international player in financial markets globally, and not just in the oil sector. The concurrent listing of part of the IPO shares on Saudi Arabia's own domestic stock exchange, the Tadawul, would also – as MbS highlighted to the senior Saudis - involve the local population in the fortunes of the country's commercial jewel-in-the-crown and make them aware of Saudi Arabia's great success on the world financial stage.

However, almost immediately that the process to float part of Saudi Aramco began, questions started to emerge from international investors targeted by MbS's advisers to be big buyers of Saudi Aramco stock in the IPO. These doubts and questions are relevant to this day, both in terms of key data related to Saudi Arabia's oil sector and to Saudi Aramco, and more broadly to how they led to a sustained shift by Saudi Arabia away from the US and its allies and towards the China-Russia sphere of influence.

Core Assumptions About Saudi's Oil Industry Are Wrong

Aside from the aforementioned threats from the US hanging over Saudi Arabia, with obvious knock-on effects to the attractiveness of the Saudi Aramco IPO, the more that international financiers looked into the details of Saudi Aramco, the more it became clear to them that Saudi Arabia had long been highly exaggerating several key metrics relating to its oil sector.

This had been known for several years by a few oil industry observers (and had been highlighted by me as well from 2014 in many articles in various oil sector publications and in my early books on the global oil industry). These distorted figures had apparently been produced in order to bolster Saudi Arabia's status in the world, as this status was almost solely dependent on its position as a leading oil producer.

Among the most serious exaggerations from Saudi Arabia were figures relating to its crude oil production capacity, its 'spare capacity', and its oil reserves levels. On the other side of the equation, the breadth and depth of the relationship between the Saudi state and Saudi Aramco, particularly relating to the ownership of its oil concessions and to the control of oil its oil production policy, had been significantly underplayed.

Other oil producing countries had done the same thing over the years, including the UAE, which had claimed unchanged reserves of 92.3 billion barrels of oil from 1988 to 2004 despite having extracted 14 billion barrels of that oil and having made no new oil finds during that period. However, with its senior role in the global oil markets and its leadership of OPEC, senior oil figures in the West had expected more of Saudi Arabia on the transparency front.

Saudi Arabia's Crude Oil Reserves Number Is Questionable

At the beginning of 1989, Saudi Arabia claimed proven oil reserves of 170 billion barrels. Just one year later, and without the discovery of any major new oil fields, the country claimed proven oil reserves of 257 billion barrels, an increase of 51.2%. Shortly afterwards, Saudi Arabia's proven oil reserves increased again, this time to just over 266 billion barrels, again without the discovery of any major new oil fields. This level of proven oil reserves increased once more in 2017, to 268.5 billion barrels, again with no new major oil finds being discovered.

At the same time as these increases in Saudi Arabia's claimed proven oil reserves were being announced – despite there being no new major oil finds at all during that period – the country was also extracting and then selling an average of 8.162 million barrels per day (bpd). This figure was the factual average crude oil production from Saudi Arabia's oil fields from 1973 to the beginning of 2017, when the idea of the Saudi Aramco IPO first became widely known. Incidentally, the factual average from 1973 to the beginning of 2023, is 8.24 million bpd.

Therefore, from 1990 (the year in which Saudi Arabia's claimed proven oil reserves jumped from 170 billion barrels to 257 billion barrels), to 2017 (the year when Saudi Arabia was claiming proven oil reserves of 268.5 billion barrels), it had drilled out, physically removed from the ground and sold an average of just over 2.979 billion barrels of crude oil every year.

Therefore, from the beginning of 1990 to the beginning of 2017, Saudi Arabia had drilled out, physically removed from the ground and sold 80.43 billion barrels of crude oil. Therefore, if Saudi Arabia 's original claimed proven oil reserves of 170 billion barrels at the beginning of 1989 had stayed the same – without being increased in 1990, despite no new major oil finds at all during that period – then the country's crude oil reserves would currently be around 89.57 billion barrels, and not the still-stated 268.50 billion barrels.

The reconciliation of this rise in crude oil reserves figures with the production figures over the same period is a mathematical impossibility, regardless of any realistic improvements in recovery rates across the fields that may have been effected at various points.

Saudi's Official Reserves And Production Numbers Did Not Stack Up

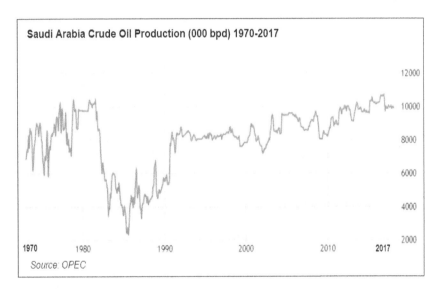

Saudi's Spare Capacity Figure Is Not As It Might Appear

The true extent of Saudi Arabia's extreme exaggerations about its claimed proven oil reserves only began to be revealed to a wider audience when serious questions about its claims relating to its spare capacity bubbled up, and this occurred during the 2014-2016 Oil Price War. To put this into context, the EIA defines spare capacity very specifically as production that can be brought online within 30 days and sustained for at least 90 days.

Saudi Arabia stated for decades that it had a spare capacity of between 2.0 and 2.5 million bpd. This implied – given the widely-accepted (but also wrong, as highlighted above) belief that Saudi had pumped an average of around 10 million bpd for many years – that it had the capacity to ramp up its production to about 12.5 million bpd in the event of unexpected disruptions elsewhere.

However, as the 2014-2016 Oil Price War dragged on and reached new heights of economic devastation both for Saudi Arabia and its OPEC colleagues, the Kingdom could on average produce no more than just over 10 million bpd – very rarely managing to hit above 10.5 million bpd in the two-year duration of the War. The obvious question that gained traction among an increasingly sceptical wider audience was a simple one: if Saudi had the ability to pump up to 12.5 million bpd – as it repeatedly implied it could - then why did it not do this, given that the core aim was to destroy the US shale sector, crashing prices by producing as much oil as possible?

The answer was very simple: it was producing the most crude oil that it could, based on its true oil production figure of around 8 million bpd. Given this true base figure, an extra 2.5 million bpd equalled 10.0-10.5 million bpd, the very figure Saudi Arabia just about managed to achieve during the 2014-2016 Oil Price War.

In one of my earlier books - *'An Insider's Guide To Trading The Global Oil Market'* - it was established that Saudi's true spare capacity at an unsustainable maximum output of 10.5 million bpd was at that time, at most, 0.5 million bpd. This was a huge difference in oil production and spare capacity terms to the figures frequently repeated by Saudi Arabia around the time that it was beginning to pitch to savvy international financiers MbS's idea for an IPO of Saudi Aramco.

Consequently, and in the same way that it has tried to do ever since – most notably around the time of the 2019 Houthi attacks on its oil facilities and during the 2020 Oil Price War – the Saudis attempted to obfuscate these true production and spare capacity figures with semantic trickery. Senior Saudis spoke of 'capacity' and of 'supply to the market' rather than of 'output' or 'production'. These two different sets of terminology do not mean the same thing at all.

'Capacity' (and its synonym, as far as the Saudis are concerned, 'supply to the market') does not equate to just to production but also includes the utilisation of crude oil supplies held in storage at any given time in the Kingdom. It also appears to mean to Saudi Arabia any supplies that can be withheld from contracts and re-directed into those stored supplies. During the 2014-2016 Oil Price War, Saudi nearly drained its storage facilities of oil and cut back on oil supply contracts with non-priority clients. Capacity (or supply to the market) can also apparently mean, at least as far as Saudi Arabia is concerned, any supplies of similar crude oil grades to its own that Saudi Arabia can buy from other OPEC members – either directly or through brokers – that it can then pass off as its own supplies. to buy through brokers in the spot market and then pass it off as its own oil supplies.

In reality, the true meaning of 'production' and 'output' in the international oil market is crude oil that actually comes out of the ground through drilling and production at the wellheads. And 'spare capacity', as mentioned above, means, according to the EIA, 'production that can be brought online within 30 days and sustained for at least 90 days'.

Misdirection In Action After The 2019 Houthi (Iran) Attacks

All of these obfuscation techniques were in evidence after the 14 September 2019 aerial attacks on Saudi Arabia's massive Abqaiq oil processing facility and Khurais oil field – launched either by Houthi 'rebels' in Yemen or by Iranian operatives in Yemen and/or in Iran.

In reality, the attacks caused a long suspension of 5.7 million bpd from Saudi Arabia. This equated to well over half of Saudi Arabia's actual crude oil production capacity, not the fantastical capacity figure that Saudi had long stated for geopolitical power purposes, as highlighted above.

Early on after the attacks, it was clear that several senior Saudi officials did not know how the oil market worked or any details of Saudi's oil industry, or they were simply happy to make misleading comments. One such statement came from Saudi Arabia's then-new Oil Minister, Prince Abdulaziz bin Salman, just after the attacks. He said that the Kingdom planned to restore its production capacity to 11 million bpd by the end of September and recover its full capacity of 12 million bpd two months later.

As already mentioned, Saudi had never sustained true crude oil production of over 10.5 million bpd for more than a month or two to that point, and the figures being quoted by Abdulaziz bin Salman were either deliberately misleading (in order to protect its reputation as a reliable oil supplier, especially to its target clientele in Asia) or ignorant (he did not know the difference between production and capacity). Either way, it was not what might be expected of a credible Oil Minister of a credible oil producer. These comments also did not play well with the international financiers that Saudi was targeting for the Saudi Aramco IPO.

Additionally undermining any faith that the oil market or international financiers might have in either Saudi Arabia or its flagship oil company were further statements from senior Saudis that the Abqaiq and the Khurais facilities were expected to return to their nominal capacity by 16 September (just two days after the attacks). This was later changed to a statement that restoring full production would take 'weeks not days'.

In reality, whatever Saudi's actual capacity, there was absolutely no way that it can even have made an accurate assessment at that stage after the attacks of how long it would take to get back to any particular capacity level. They could also not have made an accurate assessment of how long it might take for meaningful repairs to take place within that timeframe. In the real world, in which the West's oil industry and its financiers work, it would take engineers several weeks just to assess the damage after an incident of that scale.

Instead, what the Saudis did to keep exports up was draw down supplies to its domestic industry and reduce the amounts it was sending to domestic refineries. One big refinery, SASREF, brought forward its planned maintenance for later in the year to just after the attacks and other refineries began operating at much-reduced run rates. Many buyers were also warned of significant delays, while others were offered swaps with other grades. Specifically, a number of customers of Saudi's Arab Light and Arab Extra Light grades – the grades most affected by the attacks – were offered Saudi's Arab Medium or Arab Heavy as substitute grades.

Additionally, several refineries were told by Aramco that their rolling orders for Arab Extra Light crude could not be supplied until further notice but could be switched for either Arab Medium or Arab Heavy, depending on the set-up of the refinery. Others looking for their usual monthly supply of Arab Light were told that this would be switched to Arab Heavy as a substitute for September loading at least.

The other measure that Saudi took was looking to buy Iraq oil grades, which are close to the key export grades that Saudi ships to various destinations, including Asia. Reportedly, Aramco Trading Company aggressively checked prices and lot sizes for Iraqi crude with various oil trading houses in the aftermath of the attacks and were looking at shorter-term potentially rolling contracts.

The supreme irony was that a cornerstone strategy that was used by Iran to circumvent reimposed US sanctions against it (as was also the case in the previous periods of sanctions) was to rebrand its oil into Iraqi oil, by the methods analysed earlier, which made it impossible to identify which oil came from Iraq or Iran. Consequently, in looking to plug the supply gaps created by the Houthi attacks (sponsored by Iran), Saudi Arabia had ended up buying a considerable volume of Iranian oil rebranded as Iraqi oil, thus boosting the bank accounts of the very people that were ultimately behind the attacks on its own oil infrastructure – that is, Iran's IRGC.

Aramco's Oil Concessions Are Not Its Own

Compounding the scepticism of international financiers at the time that the Aramco IPO was being pitched by Saudi Arabia – which endures among many in the oil market to this day – was lack of clarity over whether the listed Aramco would actually own its oil and gas concessions, and its oil wells, after the intended IPO. There were also corollary questions on whether it would be Aramco (directors and shareholders, including the new shareholders via the IPO) that made the decisions on how much oil it produced at any given time.

The answer, as provided at the time by Saudi Aramco's chief executive officer, Amin Nasser, did not enhance the attractiveness of the IPO to any of the targeted international investors back then, and have been a major cause for concern from interested parties since. Nasser stated that although the IPO would include the concessions, the actual wells: '…will still be owned by the government … this is the same as before, and there are no changes to that.'

He also stated that Aramco's oil and gas production decisions were sovereign matters that would remain with the government. In practical terms, then, this meant that if Saudi Arabia decided that it was going to try again to destroy the US shale oil industry as it did between 2014 and 2016 by crashing the oil price through overproduction then Saudi Aramco shareholders would see huge losses in the value of the shares. This, of course, was exactly what happened when Saudi Arabia decided to do exactly that in 2020.

Aramco's Oil Fields' Position In The 2017 Build-up To The IPO

Major Oil Fields In Saudi Arabia And Production As Of 2017			
Field	Location	Production capacity as of 2017 (million b/d)	Crude grade
Ghawar	onshore	5.8	Arab Light
Safaniya	offshore	1.2	Arab Heavy
Khurais	onshore	1.2	Arab Light
Manifa	offshore	0.9	Arab Heavy
Shaybah	onshore	1	Arab Extra Light
Qatif	onshore	0.5	Arab Light
Khursaniyah	onshore	0.5	Arab Light
Zuluf	offshore	0.68	Arab Medium
Abqaiq	onshore	0.4	Arab Extra Light
Source: Saudi Aramco			

This, in turn, reinforced the already burgeoning scepticism around how much independently verified data about the company's oil reserves and operations would be given to existing and future investors, its board structure, minority shareholder rights, and other matters related to company strategy once the IPO had been done.

Funding Source For Socio-Economic And Vanity Projects

Compounding these concerns was the fact that throughout its history Aramco has been used by the government as a funding source for various socio-economic projects that were nothing to do with its core businesses of oil (and gas) production. Recent examples at that time included developing a USD5 billion ship repair and building complex on the east coast, working with General Electric on a USD400 million forging and casting venture, and even creating the King Abdullah University of Science and Technology.

Whatever the views of individuals on such projects, international investors had zero interest in putting money into a company that spent enormous amounts of its money on ventures that stood no chance of making a profit – in short, activities that were profoundly shareholder-value destructive. Moreover, at the time that the IPO had been initially mooted, there was no indication that this practice would stop, with the USD500 billion Neom project being a case in point.

The USD500 billion investment – a sizeable portion of which was destined to come from Aramco's profits (and, therefore, from the would-be capital gain of its shareholders) was the idea of MbS. If and when it is completed, it will be a new city (and surrounding area) spanning some 26,500 km^2 (10,200 sq. miles) – around the same size as the country of Belgium – in the far north of Saudi Arabia's Red Sea coastline.

According to its own advertisements, Neom will be 'An Accelerator of Human Progress' that may include such features as an artificial moon, glow-in-the-dark beaches, flying drone-powered taxis, robotic butlers to clean the homes of residents and a Jurassic Park-style attraction featuring 'animatronic' lizards. Predictably, this idea was not well-received either by would-be international investors during preliminary meetings to discuss the prospects for international listing of Aramco in the UK and the US.

The Desperate Search For An International Listing Site

Given this agglomeration of negative factors, it was little wonder that there was very little interest from any major international stock exchange to host any part of the Saudi Aramco IPO.

The New York Stock Exchange (NYSE) had been one of the original top-two favoured candidates, alongside the London Stock Exchange (LSE), given the two bourses' reputation as the most liquid, most traded and most prestigious stock exchanges in the world. Early on, though, a number of major problems began to bubble up for a listing of any Saudi company, and particularly the omni-toxic Aramco, in the US.

A key early sticking point was Saudi Arabia's perceived links with the 9/11 terrorist attacks, as mentioned above, which was then augmented by

Saudi Arabia's continued bombing of Yemen, the international ostracising of Qatar, and the kidnapping and forced resignation of Lebanon's then-President Saad Hariri, allegedly by Saudi elements. The negative backdrop for Saudi Arabia in the US, and for the listing of Saudi Aramco on the NYSE, worsened further after the murder of dissident Saudi journalist Jamal Khashoggi, which even the CIA said would never have been done without MbS's personal go-ahead.

Saudi Was Eyeing The Top Western Bourses For Aramco In 2017

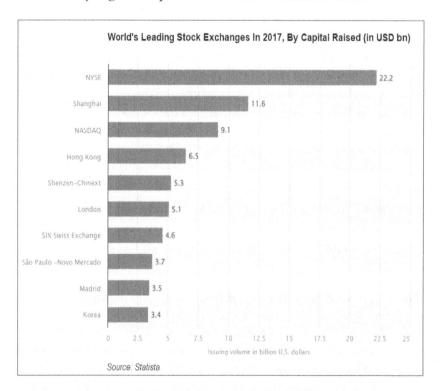

World's Leading Stock Exchanges In 2017, By Capital Raised (in USD bn)

NYSE	22.2
Shanghai	11.6
NASDAQ	9.1
Hong Kong	6.5
Shenzen-Chinext	5.3
London	5.1
SIX Swiss Exchange	4.6
São Paulo –Novo Mercado	3.7
Madrid	3.5
Korea	3.4

Issuing volume in billion U.S. dollars

Source: Statista

Given this, Saudi Arabia looked for a time at the UK's LSE as the prime foreign listing destination. This followed a trip to Saudi Arabia by then-LSE chief executive officer Xavier Rolet and then-UK Prime Minister Theresa May. The problem with this from the UK's side (aside from the same antitrust concerns as in the US) centred on the fact that such a listing for Saudi Aramco would have required the creation of a new category of listing in order to accommodate Aramco, given its lack of transparency.

More specifically, historically companies looking to list on the LSE had could do so either through a 'premium' (formerly 'primary') or 'standard' (formerly 'secondary') listing. According to LSE rules, a premium listing - that would be included in the benchmark FTSE 100 index – would have meant Aramco having to allow potential investors full access to the company's books, giving minority investors a vote on an independent board of directors, and allowing them to approve transactions between the company and its controlling shareholder – the Saudi government – none of which were likely to occur.

However, a standard listing would have meant that Saudi Aramco would not be in included in the FTSE 100, being relegated instead to the second tier of companies alongside mid-cap UK firms and family-controlled foreign firms.

The compromise solution – which followed the Rolet-May trip – was to have been the creation of a new category of listings for large international companies that may not have met the premium listing standards but was more prestigious and more appealing to investors than the 'standard' category. Clearly, though, simply changing the name of a listing type would not alter the fact that it did not in reality meet the standards expected from FTSE 100-listed companies in terms of rigorous reporting, operational transparency and accountability to shareholders, even minority ones.

Indeed, after this possible compromise solution leaked into the media a number of major pension and insurance funds commented that there were still 'very big governance issues' around how much independently verified data pertaining to the company's oil reserves would be given, its board structure and the small portion of the company being listed.

With both of the major exchanges out of the running as international listing destinations for Aramco, Canada's Toronto Stock Exchange (TSE) made a pitch for the IPO. It was rejected by MbS because of its small size relative to the bigger exchanges and the fact that its value was already dominated by oil companies.

This latter point meant that a drop in the oil price would in itself negatively affect Aramco's TSE valuation over and above any company-specific factors. Hong Kong was also for a time a front-runner, given its close links to Chinese money and Chinese oil and gas buyers, but the burgeoning protest movement against Chinese rule by Hong Kong residents subsequently marginalised its appeal.

The Hotchpotch Solution To The Saudi Aramco IPO

Following the failure to find a prestigious international listing destination for any of the Saudi Aramco IPO, China made a face-saving offer to MbS to buy the entire 5% stake for USD100 billion in a private placement, as mentioned in the previous section. One advantage from MbS's perspective was that, as it was a private placement, no details regarding the sale would be released to anyone, unless he specifically authorised it.

Another major advantage from his perspective was that the deal would have allowed him to go to the senior Saudis and tell them that he had managed to achieve every one of the objectives for the IPO that he had laid out when he had first pitched it to them, except for the international listing element. Specifically, 5% of the company had been sold, the price for that stake had been USD100 billion, and the valuation, therefore, for the whole company had been placed at USD2 trillion.

The key reason, as mentioned earlier, why MbS did not take China's offer was that at that point back in 2016 and later when China made the same offer again, King Salman and other senior Saudis were not ready to decisively alienate the US and to do away with the political and military security that it afforded them.

Given this, MbS's IPO team had to work through a hotchpotch of solutions to try to sell as much of the 5% that he had originally promised to anyone who would have it in whatever way they could. The bankers who were advising on the issue were also acutely aware of the fact that it would be their banks that would have to buy up any unsold shares, as the underwriters of the IPO. Consequently, the compromise was reached that only 1.5% of Saudi Aramco could be sold at a price level that came close to the level at which the whole company would be valued at USD2 trillion.

Even this amount, though, was extremely difficult to sell. To attempt to get rid of these shares, Saudi banks were 'encouraged' to offer retail customers of theirs loans at a 2-to-1 ratio for every riyal that they invested in Saudi Aramco (compared to an average leverage ratio limit of 1 to 1 previously). Given this, the Saudi public ended up buying around one third of the total 1.5%, which was an unprecedentedly large proportion of any Saudi IPO to that point. Additionally, according to various reports, many of those senior Saudis who had been rounded up, imprisoned and tortured in the Ritz-Carlton in 2017 were also encouraged to buy the Aramco shares.

These 'carrot and stick' strategies were also employed on those Middle East countries with close links to Saudi Arabia that either wanted something positive (more co-operation in the oil and gas sector, for example) or wanted to avoid something (such as Saudi's severing of relations and subsequent blockade of Qatar in 2017).

Consequently, the sovereign wealth funds and similar entities of virtually all of Saudi's allies bought significant stakes in the Aramco IPO, as did the funds of those countries who sought to gain geopolitical advantage by exploiting Saudi Arabia in the future (China and Russia). The final part of the offering was bought – in line with the underwriting contracts for the offer – by the international banks advising on the offer.

The Toxic Dividends Legacy Of The Aramco IPO

A key part of inducing financial institutions in particular to buy any of the Aramco shares offered in December 2019 IPO was the assurance from the Saudi government that, whatever happened, it would guarantee a USD75 billion dividend payment in 2020, split equally over each quarter. This was more than five times larger than Apple's then dividend pay-out, which was already among the biggest of any S&P 500 company.

Even after all of this, the 1.5% of Saudi Aramco was listed at SAR32 (USD8.53) per share. This figure was notable for two key reasons. First, it was just enough to allow the Aramco IPO to become the biggest ever - raising USD25.6 billion compared to Alibaba's then-record USD25 billion in 2014. Second - and much more important – it still meant that MbS had not reached his desired USD2 trillion implied valuation for Aramco as a whole, with the company's implied value being USD1.7 trillion instead.

Adding to Aramco's troubles was that MbS's massive, guaranteed dividend pay-outs coincided with a period that saw the onset of the COVID-19 pandemic (at the very end of 2019) and the instigation of another oil price war by Saudi Arabia (in the first quarter of 2020), both as analysed in full in the previous section.

In practical terms for the Saudi finances, what all this meant was that Saudi Aramco's finances suffered a massive hit. For the first half of 2020, the company saw a 50% plunge in net profit and at the beginning of November 2020 it reported another massive drop in profits of 44.6% for the third quarter of 2020, showing a fall to SAR44.21 billion (USD11.79 billion) from SAR79.84 billion in the same period in 2019.

At the same time as it was incurring these huge drops in profits, Aramco was also having to meet the enormous dividend payments that had been guaranteed by the Saudi government in order for it to sell at least a respectable minimum number of shares in the disastrous IPO in the first place. Specifically, the overall dividend guaranteed was USD18.75 billion per quarter - USD75 billion for a full year.

In sum, the first two dividends together for the first two quarters of 2020 – USD37.5 billion – had far outstripped Aramco's total free cash flow of USD21.1 billion for the same period. The profits number for the third quarter, meanwhile, covered just 62.88% of the dividend payment, never mind any other expenses or investment for projects ongoing or planned that Aramco may have had in mind. To put this even more clearly: Aramco's entire profit for the third quarter of 2020 could not even cover the dividend it owed for the same quarter - not even two-thirds of it.

The knock-on effect of these gigantic, guaranteed dividend payments was a severe cutting back on spending on ongoing and planned projects by Saudi Aramco. Aramco's chief executive officer, Amin Nasser, alluded to further budget cuts over and above the USD15 billion cut in Aramco's annual capital spending announced just after the first half profits figures were unveiled. This took the total in such planned spending down from around USD40 billion to about USD25 billion. Further reports stated that even this US$25 billion figure was set to be reduced by another USD5 billion, taking the total capital spending in 2020 from an initially planned USD40 billion to USD20 billion.

As a result of the slide in Aramco's profits in just the first three quarters after the IPO in December 2019, the once much-vaunted flagship USD20 billion crude-to-chemicals plant at Yanbu on Saudi's Red Sea coast had been indefinitely suspended. The similarly high-profile purchase of a 25% multi-billion-dollar stake in Sempra Energy's liquefied natural gas (LNG) terminal in Texas was also apparently under threat.

In the same vein, according to various sources, Aramco had suspended its key USD10 billion deal to expand into mainland China's refining and petrochemicals sector, via a complex in the north-eastern province of Liaoning. This would have seen Saudi supply up to 70% of the crude oil for the planned 300,000 barrels per day refinery. In sum, it appeared that all of Aramco's principal projects aimed at diversifying Saudi Arabia away from the relatively zero added-value pursuits of just pumping and selling crude oil were subject to review and/or outright suspension.

The chances of those projects being resuscitated with money from other Saudi government departments looked minimal, as Saudi Arabia's second oil price war, of 2020, had decimated the country's finances just as the previous 2014-2016 Oil Price War had. Figures released at the end of September 2020 showed that Saudi Arabia's economy contracted 7% year-on-year (y-o-y) in the second quarter of 2020, with the Kingdom's private sector showing a negative growth rate of 10.1%, while the public sector recorded negative growth of 3.5%.

Saudi's oil revenue in the first half of that year was 35% lower than a year earlier, while non-oil revenue fell by 37%. Moreover, in the second quarter of 2020 alone, the Kingdom's petroleum refining activities recorded a 14% y-o-y drop. All of this resulted in a current account deficit of SAR67.4 billion (USD18 billion), or 12% of GDP, in Q22020 compared with a surplus of SAR42.9 billion, or 5.8% of GDP, a year earlier, according to Saudi Arabia's General Authority for Statistics.

Therefore, Aramco found itself in the position of having little choice but to continue to fund the dividend payments to its own shareholders by taking on more debt. This was in direct contrast to the influx of new money that Crown Prince Mohammed bin Salman had said would flow into Aramco and then more broadly into the Saudi Tadawul stock market following the 'landmark IPO'. In essence, Aramco had been left to take on debt to pay the people who had bought its shares.

The debt that Aramco took on to pay the dividend payments that had been guaranteed by the Saudi government was in the form of newly new bond issues. However, the company's ability to even be able to continue to do that looked increasingly limited. The November 2020 bond sale by Aramco had looked to raise USD8 billion from the five-part debt deal, which it did, but crucially it attracted just USD48.1 billion in orders for the sale, less than half of the amount that it had received for its debut bond sale in 2019 when it had raised USD12 billion. Even more indicative of increasing investor caution at that time in taking on more exposure to Saudi risk – especially that of the increasingly indebted (bonds plus dividend obligations plus revolving credit lines) Aramco – was that in 2019's bond sale Aramco was able to price the bonds at a tighter spread to the benchmark than Saudi sovereign debt but in the November 2020 bond sale Aramco's bonds were priced wider.

This toxic dividend legacy for Aramco added further weight to the Saudi view that it could no longer survive and prosper within the oil pricing constraints that the US wanted, as had been first effectively delineated in the 'Trump Oil Price Range'. The Aramco IPO debacle had also brought China much more into a positive focus as far as MbS was concerned and paved the way for a rapid broadening and deepening of Riyadh's relationship with Beijing.

This Sino-Saudi relationship also complemented the burgeoning relationship with Russia that Saudi Arabia had constructed at the end of the 2014-2016 Oil Price War. This had been intended in the very first instance to be a temporary measure needed to bring oil prices back up – through coordinated production cuts by OPEC and Russia - to levels at which Saudi Arabia could begin to repair its finances in the aftermath of that war. Given the success of the coordination, though, and Saudi Arabia's - and OPEC's - awareness that their failure in the 2014-2016 Oil Price War had severely damaged their reputation and credibility in the global oil markets, this relationship with Russia had very quickly been formalised into the 'OPEC+' grouping.

Over time, as analysed in full in the previous section of this book, it appeared that MbS had come to regard the US as just another one of its partners in a new global order that would see Beijing and its allies share the leadership position with Washington, before attempting to surpass it. In this view, it seemed that MbS saw the US as a partner just for Saudi Arabia's security considerations, with no meaningful quid pro quo on Saudi Arabia's part, whilst regarding China as its key partner economically and Russia as its key partner in energy matters.

Even in matters of security, though, China saw an opportunity to cement its relationship with Saudi Arabia further, to add to what had already been effected in this regard by Russia (as analysed in the '*Key Players In The Global Oil Market: Russia*' section). The March 2023 resumption of relations deal between Saudi Arabia and Iran, brokered by China, had removed several security threats to Riyadh in one fell swoop, although it was uncertain how long that would remain the case. The deal had also been done without the US's input, marginalising Washington further from its former core interests in the Middle East.

Iran

Irrespective of any political considerations, which will be examined in depth shortly in this section, Iran remains a great oil and gas power, the full potential of which has yet to be fully realised. It has an estimated 157 billion barrels of proven crude oil reserves, nearly 10% of the world's total and 13% of those held by OPEC.

As great as its oil reserves are, its gas reserves are even greater, with Iran having estimated proven natural gas reserves of 1,193 trillion cubic feet (Tcf), second only to Russia, 17% of the world's total, and more than one-third of OPEC's. Additionally, Iran has a high success rate of natural gas exploration, in terms of wildcat drilling, which is estimated at around 80%, compared to the world average success rate of 30-35%.

Still Full Of Untapped Potential

Huge Oil And Gas Reserves But Low Recovery Rates

Despite the extraordinarily high success rate of wildcat drilling for both gas and oil, the recovery rate from drilled wells has been extraordinarily low by comparison. In the matter of oil, for example, the recovery rate at even the most easily exploitable fields in Iran, such as those in the hugely oil-rich West Karoun cluster, has been between 3.5 and 5.5% for many years. By contrast, the average recovery rate at comparable fields in Saudi Arabia is currently around 50% and there are plans to increase this to at least 70% in the coming three years or so.

However, it is crucial to note that this disparity is not due to any technical difficulty in extracting either oil or gas from the ground in Iran. In fact, focusing on oil again, Iran has the lowest 'lifting cost' (the cost of extracting oil or gas) of any country in the world, at only USD1-2 pb (excluding capital expenditure), alongside Iraq and Saudi Arabia.

Instead, this low rate of recovery has been almost entirely due to factors connected to various international sanctions that have been in place against Iran on and off ever since the beginning of 1979. This year marked the Islamic Revolution in Iran and the coincident takeover of the US Embassy in Tehran by Iranian revolutionaries who then held captive 52 US diplomats and other citizens for 444 days (from 4 November 1979 to 20 January 1981).

From that point, sanctions against Iran of varying types and various severity were in place against Iran by either the US or European Union or other G7 countries, or any combination thereof, until they began the process of being eased, with the adoption of the Joint Comprehensive Plan of Action (JCPOA) – colloquially 'the nuclear deal' – on 20 July 2015. This long period of sanctions meant that Iran's ability to recover its oil or gas reserves in an efficient and expeditious way was severely hindered by a lack of the required machinery, technology, materials, expertise, and high-level corporate logistical processes to do so.

It is apposite to note at this stage that before the US's unilateral withdrawal from the JCPOA in 2018, and the subsequent reimposition of sanctions against Iran, several international oil companies (IOCs) presented realistic plans to Iran's Petroleum Ministry detailing how they would increase the average rate of recovery at the West Karoun fields in the first instance. The plans detailed a relatively easily achieved increase in the rate of recovery to at least 12.5% within one year, to 20% within two years and to at least 50% within five years.

With over 67 billion barrels of oil in place in place across the West Karoun oil fields, the Petroleum Ministry has stated several times that each 1% improvement in the rate of recovery would increase recoverable reserves by 670 million barrels or some USD33 billion in revenues even with oil at USD50 a barrel.

Even More Reserves In The Caspian

Iran also holds a further estimated 2 trillion cubic feet (Tcf) of proven and probable natural gas reserves onshore and offshore in the Caspian basin. However, very shortly after the US withdrew from the nuclear deal in 2018, Russia engineered a new legal agreement over the rights of the five countries that border the Caspian – the 'littoral states', comprising Russia, Iran, Kazakhstan, Turkmenistan and Azerbaijan – in which Iran came off the worst.

On the face of it, little of any meaningful consequence was decided in the 'Convention on the Legal Status of the Caspian Sea' agreement signed by littoral states at that time. The public agreement only stipulated that relations between the littoral states would be based on the principles of national sovereignty, territorial integrity, equality among members and the non-use of threat of force.

Publicly, the agreement also refrained from specifically going into details about share allocations in the resource, and although it referred to the Caspian as legally a 'sea', it also referred to it having provisions that gave it 'a special legal status'. What was generally not known, though, was that there was a second part to the deal that might yet prove explosive for relations between the perennially fractious Caspian states.

In general terms, the oil and gas resources prize in the Caspian that has been fought over since the dissolution of the USSR in 1991 is huge. The wider Caspian basins area, including both onshore and offshore fields, is conservatively estimated to have around 48 billion barrels of oil and 292 Tcf of natural gas in proven and probable reserves.

Around 41% of total Caspian crude oil and lease condensate (19.6 billion barrels) and 36% of natural gas (106 Tcf) exists in the offshore fields, according to this data. An additional 35% of oil (16.6 billion barrels) and 45% of gas (130 Tcf) is estimated to lie onshore within 100 miles of the coast, particularly in Russia's North Caucasus region.

Potentially Huge Further Iranian Reserves In The Caspian

The remaining 12 billion barrels of oil and 56 Tcf of natural gas are believed to be variously located further onshore in the large Caspian Sea basins, mostly in Azerbaijan, Kazakhstan and Turkmenistan. The area accounts for an average of 17% of the total oil production of the five littoral states that share its resources, on average totalling 2.5-2.9 million barrels per day.

Before the new agreement was signed, oil output targets for each country were set three months in advance, with all revenues – usually at least 95% in US dollars and euros but with some local currencies in the mix – paid into a central Caspian oil account, which was then split in equal proportions of 20% between the five littoral states. However, almost permanently since 1991, the five littoral state partners had been in dispute over what percentage each should have of the overall production, and this had been focused on pinning down the Caspian's exact legal status as being defined either as a 'sea' or a 'lake'.

If it was designated a sea then coastal countries would apply the 'United Nations Convention on the Law of the Sea' (1982), in which event each littoral state would receive a territorial sea up to 12 nautical miles, an exclusive economic zone up to nautical 200 miles and a continental shelf. In practice, this would have meant that countries such as Turkmenistan and Azerbaijan would have been given exclusive access to offshore assets that Iran would not have been able to access.

If it was designated a lake – and this was the informal designation before the latest agreement – then the littoral countries could have used the international law concerning border lakes to set boundaries. According to this part of the law, each country effectively possessed 20% of the sea floor and surface of the Caspian.

Prior to the latest deal, the main areas of dispute were the boundaries between the Azeri, Turkmen and Iranian sectors, with Iran having long held ambitions to develop oil and gas resources in the Caspian. This would have included the development of the then-new Sardar-e Jangal field. Although it had originally been discovered in 2002 - at a time when Iran's total share of the Caspian gas take was assumed to be around 11 Tcf at best – it had been in the process of true development since 2012.

However, the new gas field found at 700 metres depth off the shore of the northern province of Gilan in the Caspian, contained total proven gas reserves of around 50 Tcf, around 10 times more gas than the Shah-Deniz field of Azerbaijan, with which Iran had been locked in dispute for years.

In addition, in 2012 a routine exploration of the Sardar-e Jangal site had led to the discovery of an oil layer slightly deeper – at 728 metres – that was estimated to hold two billion barrels of quality crude. Of this, at least 500 million barrels was thought to be recoverable.

Following the 2015 nuclear deal, Iran had hoped to license Caspian exploration blocks under its Iran Petroleum Contract (IPC) framework and to actively pursue the development of the Sardar-e Jangal field.

In order to lay the legal groundwork for this development, prior to the new agreement, Iran had engaged lawyers to challenge the established 20% share that each littoral state had informally agreed upon. The matter had been further complicated by a core dispute over territoriality. According to Iran, the Sardar-e-Jangal field was located in Iran's share, so Azerbaijan had no claim at all on the field. However, based on some previously reached agreements between Russia and Kazakhstan on dividing the basin by a line equidistant from the five coastlines, Azerbaijan claimed that Sardar-e-Jangal was, in fact, a shared field.

Iran had argued that the geology favoured Azerbaijan having easier access to greater reserves, so Iran proposed that for two neighbouring states there should be a compensatory adjustment clause so that the one that had easier access to greater reserves should receive a maximum reduction of 2.5%. In this context, this caveat would have meant 17.5% for Azerbaijan, whilst the neighbour received an extra 2.5% - so, 22.5% in total for Iran.

Azerbaijan's view that the 20% status quo should prevail was backed by its ally, the US. Russia also did not want to change it because it could lose its 20% share and this, crucially, provided a large proportion of the only hard currency it was generating at the time, given then-ongoing sanctions since the annexation of Crimea in 2014.

Underpinning these Caspian rights negotiations from Russia's perspective were strategic considerations over where Iran's oil and, especially, gas, supplies went in the world. Specifically, as analysed in first section of this book, Russia did not want Iranian gas flows especially competing with its own gas flows into Europe, as it was based on these flows that Russia was seeking to build its influence across that continent.

These flows, and the corollary build-out of the infrastructure to support them – notably the series of pipelines from Russia into Europe – allowed Russia the platform to cement crucial relationships with key players in politics, finance, and the energy sector, across several major European countries that could be leveraged later on for whatever purposes Russia had in mind. They had already been used very effectively by that point to contain the political and economic fallout for Russia from its annexation of Crime in Ukraine in 2014.

Shortly after the US withdrew from the JCPOA in 2018, Russia had joined China in securing control over much of Iran's oil and gas sector as part of the wider 25-year deal made between Beijing and Tehran. This deal is analysed in full in the *'Key Players In The Global Oil Market: China'* section but in a broad sense it effectively led Iran into becoming a client state of China in the first instance, and of Russia to a lesser degree.

Russia's Network Of Gas Power Across The West

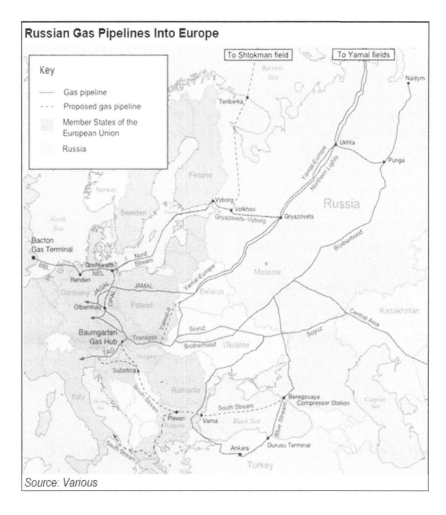

With Iran already secured as far as Russia was concerned, Moscow's view on the Caspian resources was to skew the new allocations more in favour of those countries that had yet to be persuaded back into its sphere of influence. Such a country at that time from Russia's perspective was

Azerbaijan, a former USSR state but one that had repeatedly been seen as potentially allying with the US instead. Russia already had Kazakhstan on side, and it remained confident that Turkmenistan could be brought on side too. This meant that Russia could continue to thwart the construction of the Washington-backed Trans-Caspian Pipeline (TCP) - originating in Turkmenistan - that it saw as another direct threat to its dominance of the European gas supply market.

Consequently, in the then-new Caspian agreement it was Russia that was the prime mover in having the Caspian designated as a sea, not as a lake. Russia argued that because it had recently opened up the channel from the Volga River into the Caspian ('to prevent the levels dropping', according to Russia), the Caspian no longer conformed to the legal definition of a lake (that is, a localised water deposit standing independent of any river that serves to feed it), which meant that it was now a sea.

This meant, effectively, that Russia could divide up the share as it saw fit, and the way it saw fit was to benefit its existing ally, Kazakhstan, which was awarded a 28.9% share under the redrawn agreement, and its targeted ally, Azerbaijan, which received a 21% stake. Russia benefited from a slight increase, to 21%, while Turkmenistan's share went down to 17.225%, as it was seen as a softer touch by Russia. Most stunningly, Iran's share under the redrawn Caspian agreement went down to just 11.875%.

This smallest share of all stood in stark contrast to the 50-50 split with the USSR that Iran had enjoyed as from the original agreement made in 1921 (on 'fishing rights') and amended in 1924 to include 'any and all resources recovered.' This switch from 50% to just over 11% meant that Iran would lose at least USD3.2 trillion in revenues from the disputed and lost value of the Caspian's energy products from that point.

2013 To 2016's Apparent Pro-West Tilt Rewarded By JCPOA

A move towards a seemingly more Western-friendly leadership in Iran occurred on 3 August 2013 with the election to the presidency of Hassan Rouhani. Although Rouhani was often referred to as a 'moderate', that was not really the case in the truest sense of the word. Certainly, he was keen to re-engage with the West, but this was based on economic and financial considerations for Iran and not on some deeper ideological basis that might have included embracing anything other than the notion of Iran as a true Islamic state. In this sense, there was no difference between Rouhani and his group of supporters and the more overtly Islamic elements in Iran's political and religious architecture, including the Islamic Revolutionary Guards Corps (IRGC), who are commonly referred to as 'hardliners'.

All of these groups – political, religious and military – are firmly rooted in and supportive of the Islamic and revolutionary ideals that were the foundation stone for the creation of the Islamic Republic of Iran in 1979. The only difference between any of them lies in the nature of their engagement with the West, which itself is a function of how willing any of these groups are to 'play the game' with the US and its core allies.

Consequently, the clear differentiation of the labels of 'moderate' and 'hard-line' when it comes to different political groups in Iran is not grounded in reality, with both groups seeking to achieve the same ends but through different means. The increasing use, though, of these terms – 'moderate' and 'hard-line' – has been exploited by Iran since 1979 to leverage the West into certain negotiating positions and certain deals by playing up the West's fear of 'further empowering the hardliners' or 'undermining the moderates'.

This said, the broader Iranian population believed that by pursuing the more Western-friendly policies advocated by Rouhani, long-standing economic sanctions against Iran would be removed. They also believed that following the removal of these sanctions a huge wave of Western investment would flow into the country.

This was set to occur once the JCPOA had been adopted on 20 July 2015 between Iran and the P5+1 group of nations (US, UK, France, Russia and China plus Germany). The practical guardians of the 1978/79 overthrow of the Shah – the IRGC – were willing to give this approach a try at the time, albeit for their own multi-layered reasons. The adoption of the JCPOA at that point – predicated essentially on Iran pledging not to pursue nuclear weapons in exchange for sanctions being dropped by the West – resulted in a slew of initial in-principle agreements being made.

This agreement was then formally implemented on 16 January 2016, whereupon even more high-profile, high-value deals started being agreed in principle by Western firms with Iran. These were understandably focused on the oil, gas and petrochemicals sectors, given Iran's huge reserves of both.

JCPOA Was Predicated On Iran Downscaling Its Nuclear Programme

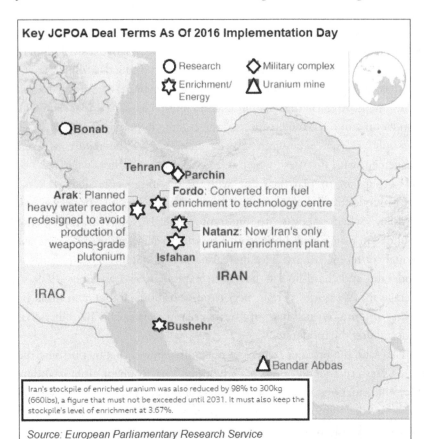

Key JCPOA Deal Terms As Of 2016 Implementation Day

○ Research   ◇ Military complex

☆ Enrichment/   △ Uranium mine
Energy

○ Bonab

Tehran ○◇ Parchin

Arak: Planned heavy water reactor redesigned to avoid production of weapons-grade plutonium

Fordo: Converted from fuel enrichment to technology centre

Natanz: Now Iran's only uranium enrichment plant

Isfahan

IRAN

IRAQ

☆ Bushehr

△ Bandar Abbas

Iran's stockpile of enriched uranium was also reduced by 98% to 300kg (660lbs), a figure that must not be exceeded until 2031. It must also keep the stockpile's level of enrichment at 3.67%.

Source: European Parliamentary Research Service

The Devil In The JCPOA Details That Threatened The IRGC

Rouhani secured his re-election in 2017 on the promise of the continued economic benefits and others, including greater social freedoms, that the JCPOA would bring to Iran. These ideas polled very well with Iran's broadly young and well-educated demographic.

They were not as popular with the IRGC, however, for three key reasons. First, the IRGC saw itself as the guardian of the spirit of the original Islamic Revolution of 1979 that had been the foundation for the Islamic Republic of Iran. Second, the IRGC saw itself as the principal mechanism through which Iran spread its own brand of Islamic faith across the world through whatever means necessary. Third, as these means involved the expensive bankrolling of multiple military and political proxies across the globe, the IRGC had built up a vast financial empire that it controlled in order to fund these activities.

Rouhani's 2017 Victory Was Secured On The Continuation Of The JCPOA

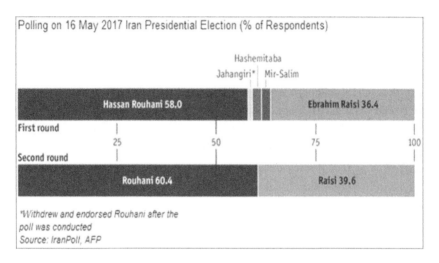

It had been clear to the IRGC from the outset of Iran's negotiations in 2013 with the West towards the JCPOA that some or all of these key elements in its power would come under threat at some point. However, early on in President Rouhani's discussions with senior IRGC commanders about what a future JCPOA might mean for Iran, the impression was given that little would change for the IRGC in the short- to medium-term, if ever.

Rouhani assured the senior commanders that the IRGC would be able to keep its organisational structure as it had always been, and that it would be able to continue to operate independently in all the areas in which it had done so before. The senior IRGC commanders were also told by Rouhani that nothing significant would change in terms of the IRGC's financial organisation either.

However, towards the second half of 2017 – as US President Donald Trump was turning his focus even more on the JCPOA after nearly a year in office - Rouhani had little choice but to agree to US demands that in order to keep the agreement in place the power of the IRGC needed to be reduced. A key part of this was the idea that the IRGC should be assimilated into Iran's regular army and, in so doing, begin the process of the IRGC divesting all elements of its financial empire.

This was in line with Trump's negative view of the deal, and that of other key members of his early (and later) administration's. Indeed, almost immediately that Trump formally took over as president on 20 January 2017, it was clear that disassembling the JCPOA would be a top priority of his new administration.

A large part of Trump's view was attributable to reports from the hawkish elements of his defence and intelligence staff that Iran was using the JCPOA to secretly renege on key elements of its commitments. Another part was due to Trump's desire to destroy a flagship achievement of Barack Obama's presidency 'out of spite', according to various sources.

The suggestions that Rouhani felt pressured to make towards the end of 2017 regarding the future of the IRGC, then, were essentially a function of the US at that point calling his bluff on how far he would go to trade the economic benefits of the JCPOA for a significant scaling back of the IRGC's influence across all areas of Iran.

In response, the IRGC began a series of highly provocative military manoeuvres, including a series of missile tests, which it knew would incense the US, as such testing would have been prohibited under the terms of the original JCPOA draft. The full details of the original draft JCPOA deal are analysed in the 'Key Players In The Global Oil Market: The US' section.

In September 2017, the IRGC conducted a very high-profile ballistic missile test and then, between February and August 2018, Iran conducted another seven high-profile missile test flights: one Khorramshahr, two Shahab-3 variants, one Qiam and three Zolfaghar ballistic missiles. Even according to the president of the United Nations Security Council, these were 'in violation of resolution 2231' because the missiles were all category I systems under the Missile Technology Control Regime and capable of carrying nuclear warheads.

Iran also displayed various missile systems at a military parade, including the S-200 and S-300 Russian-made systems, the Talash missile system, the Mersad optimised missile system, the Kamin portable missile system and the Skyguard missile system. Also on display were long-range missile launchers, including the domestically-produced Nasr system, and the al-Sabehat submarine. All of this was designed specifically to cause the US to pull out of the JCPOA.

The US's Reaction To The New Ballistic Missile Tests

The idea being publicly floated in Washington late in 2017 as an additional step to censuring Iran over the new missile testing was to officially designate the IRGC as a foreign terrorist organisation (FTO). The effects of doing this would have been extremely negative not just for Iran but also for all of those countries in Europe and Asia that, after the lifting of most sanctions in January 2016, had been on a mission to get a foothold in the great hydrocarbons play. If the FTO designation had been put through at that point then it would effectively have rendered meaningless in all practical terms the JCPOA agreed in July 2015.

Although the IRGC's Al-Quds Force, its elite unit responsible for foreign and covert operations, had already been designated by the US Treasury as an FTO in 2007, such a designation of the entire IRGC would have resulted in much broader and deeper implications, given its status not just as Iran's most powerful security entity but also as a group that had control over large stakes in Iran's economy (analysed in depth in the first section of this book).

First off, as required by the Anti-Terrorism and Effective Death Penalty Act (AEDPA) of 1996 and as implemented by the Foreign Terrorist Organizations Sanctions Regulations (FTOSR), US financial institutions are required to block the property and interests in property of FTOs and to report to the Department of Treasury the existence of such blocked funds. Also, pursuant to Executive Order 13224 and the Global Terrorism Sanctions Regulations (GTSR), practically all FTOs also are designated as Specially Designated Global Terrorists (SDGTs), meaning that all US persons – including US citizens, US lawful permanent residents, persons located within the United States and entities organised under US law and their foreign branches – are also required to block their property and interests in property.

Severe though that was, it was by no means the worst part of an FTO designation for the IRGC. The AEDPA makes it a criminal offence to provide 'material support' to a designated FTO and explicitly provides that this prohibition has extraterritorial application. This last part means that jurisdiction exists where 'after the conduct required for the offence occurs an offender is brought into or found in the United States, even if the conduct required for the offense occurs outside the United States.' A violation of this is taken extremely seriously. Individuals face up to 20 years' imprisonment and penalties of up to the greater of USD250,000 for every single violation or twice the monetary gain from the activity. Companies are subject to penalties of up to USD500,000 per violation or twice the monetary gain from the activity.

Designating the IRGC as an FTO would also exacerbate the uncertainties around dealing with Iranian companies with potentially murky ties to the IRGC. For example, if a European company were to engage in a major transaction with an Iranian company indirectly owned or controlled by senior IRGC officers, the question would hang over it as to whether that company could be charged with providing material support to an FTO, as the AEDPA does not shed much light on this, defining 'material support' only broadly.

There were three reasons why the US delayed the FTO designation of the IRGC. First, it wanted to allow Rouhani some time to effect the rolling in of the IRGC into the army and the divesting of its business assets – basically to test whether he would even try to do it. Second, the damage to US commercial interests that this would cause would be significant. Third, the Shi'ite militias backed by Iran and advised by IRGC commanders were playing a vital role on the ground in the fight against ISIS in Iraq in 2017.

This latter point was also cited by those who advocated FTO designation on the basis that, with the war against ISIS possibly entering its final phase, the time was right to re-assert US influence in Iraq, given the high level of blood and treasure expended by the US in the country over the previous two decades. There was further pressure for increased sanctions against Iran unsurprisingly from the US's historical allies Israel, Saudi Arabia and other Gulf states. Amongst other longstanding issues these countries wanted the US to act against Iran's support for Lebanese militant group Hezbollah, the Houthi rebels in Yemen and Shi'ite opposition to the Sunni regime in Bahrain, plus they feared Iran's nuclear ambitions in the region.

At that stage in 2017, President Trump's intentions were impossible to predict. On the one hand, major US commercial interests took the view that the opportunities in Iran remained enormous. On the other hand, these interests recognised that Iran was as a very volatile entity that could do something at some point that might undermine their reputation. Trump's comments on the JCPOA were also equivocal. On the one side, he frequently described the JCPOA deal as a 'disaster', 'ranking among the worst deals in US history'. On the side, though, he also often said that he wanted to 'improve' the JCPOA deal, rather than tearing it up. Indeed, he added: 'We have a horrible contract, but we do have a contract.' The different elements involved from the US's perspective in withdrawing from the JCPOA, and towards Iran in general, are analysed in the *'Key Players In The Global Oil Market: The US'* section of this book.

US Withdrawal From The JCPOA Became A Trump Priority

Ultimately, Trump went with the first instinct on Iran – highly encouraged by his Secretary of State, Mike Pompeo, and National Security Advisor, John Bolton - that either Iran should sign up to a much tougher version of the JCPOA (the one Obama originally wanted, as analysed in the *'Key Players In The Global Oil Market: The US'* section) or the US should effect regime change in the country. This would be done initially by reimposing a full spectrum of sanctions on Iran to cripple its economy and to cause popular unrest sufficient to topple the country's political leadership. In either event, the catalyst would be the US pulling out of the in-place JCPOA, which is what it did on 8 May 2018.

Despite the continued support of all the other P5+1 group of countries (the UK, France, Russia, China plus Germany) for JCPOA, plus nearly all of the remainder of Europe and Asia, the US's hold over business dealings and transactions done in US dollars – the world's reserve currency – meant that in practical terms, all companies that used the US dollar or had any dealings with the US were unwilling to go ahead with deals with Iran. Consequently, all the big deals agreed by Western companies with Iran were cancelled and/or indefinitely postponed.

For around a year afterwards, until April 2019, the US continued to extend waivers for eight of Iran's key customers – China, India, Japan, South Korea, Taiwan, Turkey, Italy and Greece – to import oil and gas from Iran, as they were deemed to be in urgent need of these supplies. Iraq's waiver to import electricity and gas from Iran for power needs was also continued.

In early 2019, though, two key factors changed that made the decision to not extend the waivers possible. One of these was the shift in Russia's view on extending its agreement to cut its oil production in tandem with OPEC. Russia's Finance Minister, Anton Siluanov, said that Russia and OPEC might decide to boost production to fight for market share with the US. 'There is a dilemma: what should we do with OPEC – should we lose the market, which is being occupied by the Americans, or quit the deal?' he underlined. This came on the back of similar expressions by several Russian oil companies, notably Rosneft – closely aligned to Russian President Vladimir Putin's personal financial interests – that objected to losing market share to the US by dint of the then in-place oil production cuts. In purely budget terms, as highlighted by Putin in November 2018, an oil price of around USD60 pb 'suits us fine.' He went on to remind his audience at a Moscow investment conference that Russia's fiscal policy was framed around a USD40 per barrel price for oil.

How Far Would Iran's Real Oil Exports Fall With Sanctions Reimposed?

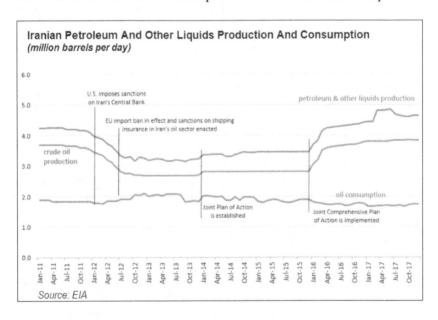

The second factor that changed in early 2019 was Saudi Arabia's apparent willingness to dampen down any dramatic spikes in the oil price resulting from a much greater cut in Iranian oil in the market. In this context, Trump spoke over the telephone to Saudi Arabia's Crown Prince Mohammed bin Salman, to discuss ways of 'maintaining maximum pressure against Iran.'

In the conversation, Salman pledged to increase Saudi's oil supply by whatever amount was taken off the Iranian supply and even more if necessary to compensate for at least some of the shortfalls from Venezuela and Libya. There was scepticism in some parts of the White House over these promises – after all, King Salman made the same promise in the previous May, in the context that his country alone could increase production sufficiently to bring oil prices down, as Trump wanted, but had not been able to pump any more than just over 10 million bpd.

Nonetheless, focused on its policy of causing as much damage to Iran as quickly as possible, the US ended all of the waivers to import Iranian oil (except for Iraq's), believing that oil market dynamics had shifted sufficiently to allow it to impose its 'zero oil exports' policy on Iran in full. According to the official White House statement released at the time: 'President Donald J. Trump has decided not to reissue Significant Reduction Exceptions [waivers] when they expire in early May [2019] … this decision is intended to bring Iran's oil exports to zero, denying the regime its principal source of revenue.'

The tactic looked fine on paper but in practice all it did was to open the way for Russia to step into the oil supply void left by Iran's exclusion in the oil market. This added to the void the US had left in the Middle East politically, militarily and economically and, because the US had effectively made Iran a criminal state, it left it with nothing to lose by becoming the renegade oil and gas superpower firmly allied to Beijing and Moscow.

The US Went After The IRGC With An FTO Designation

At around the same time as the waivers were ended, the US finally designated the IRGC as an FTO and also sanctioned 14 individuals and 17 entities linked to Iran's Organization of Defensive Innovation and Research ('SPND' acronym in Farsi). This followed the sanctioning in 2008 of SPND's head, Mohsen Fakhrizadeh.

In the US's view, the SPND – in collusion with the IRGC – had continued to work on the Iran's nuclear weapons programme so that it could be officially picked up again whenever Iran saw fit. Indeed, the SPND, working together with the IRGC, had become expert in continuing its nuclear weapons research under the cover of a range of quickly changing front companies. These could operate unhindered in the international business community by pretending that they were engaged in legitimate non-sanctioned business activity, including accessing traditional finance, credit and banking facilities. The notion that the Iranian regime needed to be changed as soon as possible based on this enduring nuclear threat permeated up to Vice President Mike Pence, who – when referring to the widespread domestic protests in Iran at that time – said: 'The world missed an opportunity last time to confront the regime, but not this time.'

However, this view of the relative readiness of Iran's nuclear weapons programme to take up where it had left off before the JCPOA was not one entirely shared by the CIA, nor by its Head of Iran Mission Center, Michael D'Andrea. His analysis was usually taken extremely seriously by the Presidential Administration not just because of his position but also because he had overseen the US's sharp-end counter-terrorism operations after the 9/11 attacks. This had included the hunt for Osama bin Laden, which had earned D'Andrea the nickname of 'the Dark Prince.' He had even been the key figure in organising the elimination of one of Hezbollah's leaders, Imad Mougniyeh, in Damascus in 2008, when he was Head of the CIA's Counterterrorism Center, which he had been from 2006. The US's Director of National Intelligence, Dan Coats, shared D'Andrea's view, testifying just prior to the US withdrawal from the JCPOA that there was no indication that Iran was attempting to develop a nuclear weapon and that Tehran remained in compliance with the 2015 nuclear deal.

Another Blow For Rouhani In The 2020 Elections

From the moment that the JCPOA had been adopted in 2015 by Iran and the P5+1 group of nations, the Islamic Republic had teetered between being a more Western-friendly regime or a more pro-Russia and China one. The strong showing in the 2020 four-yearly parliamentary elections of the 'Principlist' faction, comprising religious conservatives supported by the IRGC, portended a decisive shift towards the latter model of regime, reinforced by the earlier US withdrawal from the JCPOA in May 2018.

It is true that the specific powers of Iran's 290-member parliament (Majlis) are not as extensive as those of the parliaments of many other countries, but it is also true that with at least 220 members being very conservative the result of the 2020 election would have enormous repercussions for Iran's foreign and domestic policies for years to come. This much more conservative outlook is already entrenched in the fact that all the legislation passed by Iran's parliament then needs to be approved by the Guardian Council of the Constitution. This is a 12-member body that acts in the manner of a general constitutional overseer, with half of its membership always being Shia theologians directly chosen by the Supreme Leader himself.

The other six members are lawyers selected by the head of the judiciary, who is, in turn, also directly appointed by the Supreme Leader. In practical terms, then, Iran's parliament has tended to deal with domestic issues only, albeit not those related to state security. The bigger picture issues, such as foreign policy (including major policy programmes relating to the oil and gas sector) are decided in practice between the senior commanders of the IRGC and the President and his closest allies, with the resulting recommendation being made to the Supreme Leader, who then formally makes the decision.

The strong showing of the highly conservative anti-West elements in the 2020 parliamentary elections, then, laid down a marker by the IRGC that although some rapprochement with the West might be tolerated – provided that it was deal-specific and not part of a broader effort to try to moderate Iran – in reality it was more likely that Iran would continue to drift into the geopolitical orbit of China and Russia. This had been evidenced from the middle of 2017, with deals being cancelled by Western companies and then taken up by Russian or Chinese ones.

The parliamentary elections of 2020 appeared to highlight that the electorate had tired of the lack of real economic results that came to them from Rouhani's re-engagement with the West. Moreover, with Rouhani not allowed under the constitution to run in 2021's presidential elections, those who thought that re-engagement with the West was Iran's best bet for economic and/or social improvement did not have a recognisable figurehead for their cause.

Moreover, as evidenced by the subsequent formal accession to the presidency in August 2021 of Ebrahim Raisi, the US's attempt to cause some sort of change in Iranian politics towards a more pro-West engagement by continuing to squeeze its economy only appeared to encourage a more nationalistic anti-West view across the core electorate.

Europe's Determination To Keep Dealing With Iran

In broad terms, many European Union countries, including its core states of Germany and France, believed that keeping Iran within the confines of the JCPOA was a preferable approach to effectively leaving Iran to do as it pleased. This pro-JCPOA stance also meant specifically that the West could exert some control over Iran's nuclear programme, including regularly inspecting its nuclear programme sites.

In Germany's case, this desire to remain in the JCPOA was also partly personal assertion of both anger and independence toward the US from its longstanding Chancellor, Angela Merkel. She had been incensed by the revelations in 2013 from former CIA operative, Edward Snowden, that the US's National Security Agency (NSA) had been spying on various European leaders, including Merkel herself. This was particularly appalling for Merkel as she had grown up in Communist East Germany in which the Stasi secret police had engaged in widespread spying against every aspect of its citizens' lives, even recruiting one or more members of a family to spy on the others.

The Blocking Statute

Consequently, very shortly after the US announcement of its withdrawal from the JCPOA deal, the EU's foreign policy chief, Federica Mogherini, said that the JCPOA agreement: 'Is not a bilateral agreement ... so it is clearly not in the hands of any president of any country in the world to terminate [it] ... The president of the United States has many powers, but not this one.'

Shortly after that the then-German Foreign Minister, Sigmar Gabriel, warned: 'We also have to tell the Americans that their behaviour on the Iran issue will drive us Europeans into a common position with Russia and China against the USA.'

At the same time, the EU moved to impose its 'Blocking Statute' that made it illegal for EU companies to follow US sanctions. This statute had four principal mechanisms that could be utilised by European companies to potentially great effect. First, there was the 'nullification of court decisions' that invalidated the effect in the EU of decisions made by any foreign court or administrative body.

This would include, for example any and all of the US's re-imposed sanctions on Iran in the aftermath of Washington's unilateral withdrawal from the JCPOA. Second was the 'clawback provision' that allowed for any European companies and individuals affected by new US sanctions on Iran to recover damages in EU courts.

Third was the 'obligation to inform' that obliged companies to comprehensively document business dealings with Iran and to notify the European Commission (EC) of any financial consequences of a measure blocked in the Annex. This typically would relate to new unilateral US Office of Foreign Assets Control (OFAC) sanctions on Iran. Fourth, the 'obligation of non-compliance', which simply meant that any companies that violated the Blocking Statute – by following the US's re-imposed sanctions on Iran – could be legally sanctioned by any EU Member State.

INSTEX

Moves were also made by the EU to introduce a special purpose vehicle – the 'Instrument in Support of Trade Exchanges' (INSTEX) – that would act as a clearing house for payments made between Iran and EU companies doing work there.

Based in Paris, managed by a former senior German banker, and with a supervisory board headed by the UK, culpability had been divided between the three key European powers of France, Germany and the UK. This had been done because, although it was supposedly only going to handle transactions in food, medical devices, medicine and similarly humanitarian-sounding products, it was clear that payments for many other products could also go through it.

This was not lost on the US which quickly sent a warning to these countries that INSTEX, as well as anyone associated with it, could be barred from the US financial system if and when the US deemed fit.

Specifically, the letter from the US under-secretary of treasury for terrorism and financial intelligence, Sigal Mandelker, to INSTEX President, Per Fischer, on 7 May 2019 read: 'I urge you to carefully consider the potential sanctions exposure of INSTEX [as] engaging in activities that run afoul of US sanctions can result in severe consequences, including a loss of access to the US financial system.'

Where There's A Will, There's A Way Around Any Sanctions

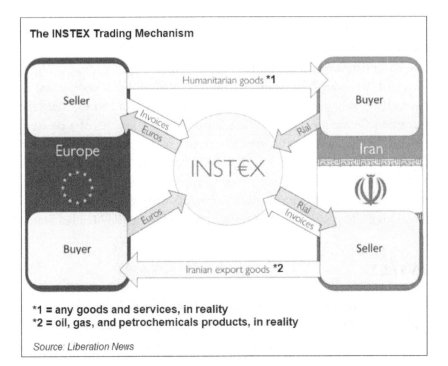

The INSTEX Trading Mechanism

Seller
Europe

Buyer
Iran

Buyer
Europe

Seller
Iran

INST€X

Humanitarian goods *1
Invoices / Euros
Rial
Rial / Invoices
Euros
Iranian export goods *2

*1 = any goods and services, in reality
*2 = oil, gas, and petrochemicals products, in reality

Source: Liberation News

Banks

This said, with Germany especially keen to look the other way on Iran, billions of dollars of money owed to the Islamic Republic for pre-sanctions oil and gas supplies (and other money from post-sanctions oil and gas supplies) made their way back to the country, despite US measures.

For a long time, Turkey's Halkbank and Germany's Europäisch-Iranische Handelsbank were two of the major global mechanisms by which money for oil sales was funnelled back to Iran. Germany additionally made it clear to Iran after the new US sanctions were introduced that Commerzbank and Austria's Oberbank would also be factored into the system in the future to enable payments to be made.

Indeed, Austria – especially the branches of various European banks operating there – became a key clearing centre for European money destined for Iran. It had had long functioned in the same manner for

European money destined for Russia or the other way around (Russian money looking to find a route into the major stock markets of the West, especially into the various indices of the FTSE). The same sort of history pertained to Turkey (and to various banks in the Turkish-controlled Northern Cyprus).

The Rhetoric And Reality Of Iran Sanctions

The key point here from the oil perspective is that the more crude oil that made it way past sanctions and into the global oil market, the more downwards pressure was brought to bear on the oil price, all other factors remaining equal. In the era of the Trump presidency in which the role of sanctions changed from being an instrument of policy to being the policy itself, this was particularly true.

It is reasonable to believe that the continued export of many millions of barrels per day from sanctioned countries – that, by dint of the sanctions, had to be offered at discounts to official oil market prices – had a dampening effect on global oil prices. It is also evident from observations over that period that this widespread sanctioning of countries – at the same time as the US had signalled its desire and willingness to withdraw from engagement in the Middle East in any meaningful sense – opened the way for the massively increased economic, political and military presence in the region by China and Russia.

In terms of honing methods by which sanctions could be circumvented, Iran is a past-master, having been sanctioned by various countries on and off ever since the 1979 Islamic Revolution in the country. As highlighted earlier its ability to do this had become a matter of some pride, as underlined by Iran's Foreign Minister, Mohammad Zarif: 'If there is an art that we have perfected in Iran, [that] we can teach to others for a price, it is the art of evading sanctions.'

In precisely this context, even a full year after the re-imposition of sanctions in 2018 on Iran by the US, there was a huge divergence between the rhetoric of the US on how effective its sanctions were in choking off crude oil exports from Iran and the reality of how much oil Iran was actually selling. The US early on had stated that its aim was to reduce Iran's oil sanctions 'to zero' and statements out of Washington since sanctions were re-imposed in earnest at the end of 2018 were a virtual countdown of various benchmark levels through which Iran's oil exports supposedly dropped from their previous position of around 2.5 million bpd. These culminated in the first few months of 2019 in headline comments from the US of 'below 2.0 million', 'below 1.5 million', 'below 1 million' and so on. On the other side of this version of reality was the fact that China on its own was importing nearly 1 million bpd from Iran, and the trend was rising rapidly as the global oil market discounts on Iranian oil increased.

China's Rising Oil Imports Continued To Include Iranian Supplies

China's Crude Oil Imports (Left hand scale in millions of bpd) 2010 To 2019
Source: CEIC, OPEC

Even after the US refused to extend China's waiver on importing Iranian oil in May 2019, China continued to increase its oil imports from Iran. Figures from China's General Administration of Customs (GAC) at the end of August 2019 showed that China had imported 926,119 bpd of Iranian oil in July, up 4.7% month on month, from an already high base.

According to various oil industry sources in Iran, the actual figure was much higher, with excess barrels being kept in floating storage in and around China without having gone through Customs. This meant that they did not show up on Customs data but were there nonetheless, effectively as part of China's Strategic Petroleum Reserve.

Rather like for Iran, China had always regarded any US sanctions as a fun puzzle to solve. The US learned early on – when it tried to sanction a Chinese company in 2012 – that Beijing would not be playing according to anyone's rules but its own. As highlighted in the first section of this book, the key factor at play in China's ability to ignore US sanctions on Iranian oil was the lack of exposure of its firms at that time to the US financial infrastructure, particularly to the US dollar. Another key factor was the ease with which Chinese companies could set up new special purpose vehicles to handle ring-fenced areas of their businesses to allow for special situations, such as sanctions.

As a corollary of this operational independence, China also made no secret that it was going to use its Bank of Kunlun as the main funding and clearing vehicle for its dealings with Iran. The Bank of Kunlun had considerable operational experience in this regard, as it had been used to settle tens of billions of dollars' worth of oil imports during the UN sanctions against Tehran between 2012 and 2015. Most of the bank's settlements during that time were in euros and Chinese renminbi and in 2012 it was formally sanctioned by the US Treasury for conducting business with Iran. This sanctioning had no effect on the Bank of Kunlun's operations either then or subsequently.

Standard Ways That Sanctions On Iran Are Circumvented

The aforementioned oil export numbers – and the numbers that continued after those - did not include sizable exports through other tried-and-tested methods that had been successfully operated by Iran during the previous global sanctions period against it. They were, as mentioned in the first section of this book, also adopted by Russia following the imposition of various sanctions against it after the invasion of Ukraine in February 2022.

The most tried-and-trusted methods by which Iran evades sanctions are firstly, and at the most basic level, 'rebranding' Iranian to Iraqi oil simply by switching the stickers on the sides of the tanker trucks moving oil across the enormous and porous border between the two countries. Compounding the difficulty in distinguishing unsanctioned Iraqi oil from sanctioned Iranian oil is that the two countries share many oil fields.

Indeed, the oil on the Iraqi side of the border is often being drilled from the same reservoirs as the oil being drilled on the Iranian side, and sometimes through long-distance horizontal directional drilling. Even if the Americans or their trusted appointees stationed people at every single rig in every single shared field in Iraq they would not be able to tell if the oil coming out it was from the Iraq side or the Iranian side.

Some notable examples of shared reservoirs and fields are Iran's Azadegan oil reservoir (split into North and South fields) that is exactly the same reservoir upon which sits Iraq's Majnoon oilfield. The same feature applies to Azar (on the Iran side)/Badra (on the Iraq side), Yadavaran (Iran)/Sinbad (Iraq), Naft Shahr (Iran)/Naft Khana (Iraq), Dehloran (Iran)/Abu Ghurab (Iraq), West Paydar (Iran)/Fakka/Fauqa (Iraq), and Arvand (Iran)/South Abu Ghurab (Iraq). There are many other shared fields as well between Iran and Iraq.

Another reliable sanctions side-stepping technique is the disabling – literally just flicking a switch – on the 'automatic identification system' (AIS) on ships that carry Iranian oil, as is just lying about provenance, destinations or specific cargo types in shipping documentation. Iran's own former Petroleum Minister, Bijan Zanganeh, publicly highlighted this very practice when he said in 2020: 'What we export is not under Iran's name. The documents are changed over and over, as well as [the] specifications.'

In Europe, this oil – all of which was discounted from the benchmark after the US reimposed sanctions on Iran in 2018 in price – goes into some of the less rigorously policed ports of southern Europe that need oil and/or oil trading commissions, including those of Albania, Montenegro, Bosnia and Herzegovina, Serbia, Macedonia and Croatia. From there, the oil can easily be moved across borders to Europe's bigger oil consumers, including through Turkey. There are also plenty of buyers in Asia aside from China for Iran's high-quality oil, including India, Pakistan and Malaysia.

Malaysia (and to a lesser degree Indonesia) also allegedly plays a key role when required in forwarding oil exports to China, with tankers bound ultimately for China engaging in at-sea or just-outside-port transfers of Iranian oil onto tankers flying other flags. Iran had also been able to re-flag its vessels under the flag of Panama, until the US began to vigorously enforce its shipping sanctions. In addition, as highlighted in the furore over the Adrian Darya 1 tanker and similar vessels, Iran continued to be a major supplier of oil to Syria.

All of this occurred even after the US also reimposed sanctions on Iran's two key tanker firms – the National Iranian Tanker Company (NITC) and the Islamic Republic of Iran Shipping Lines (IRISL). These huge shipping companies continued to offer oil cargoes not just at a substantial discount to the benchmark oil price but also offered – as a further incentive to buyers - cost, insurance and freight (CIF) cargoes at free-on-board (FOB) pricing. In tandem with this, Iran continued to offer protection and indemnity (P&I) insurance through the 'Kish P&I Club', among other such entities.

The Goreh-Jask Pipeline Sanctions-Avoidance Mechanism

Aside from these methods by which Iran had effectively avoided US and other sanctions before the JCPOA had been announced in 2015, Iran had been careful to work as well on new mechanism to avoid sanctions in the future – specifically, pipeline routes. The work on these routes continued even as the JCPOA was fully operational because the IRGC believed that their continued work on Iran's nuclear programme – including the development of the corollary ballistic missile programme – would eventually lead to the end of that agreement and the reimposition of sanctions at some point.

Pipeline routes ensure that a greater sustained volume of oil (or gas) can be pumped and that this can only be disrupted through more dramatic actions than the simple matter of intercepting very large crude carriers (VLCCs) or similar. Indeed, truly disrupting pipeline flows would require major acts of sabotage, which would be construed by Iran as acts of war. If such an act was tracked back to the US (including anything done by Israel) then such sabotage would open the way for all types of attacks against US military and even selective civilian targets anywhere in the world.

Additionally advantageous for countries laying pipelines in other countries is that the countries laying the pipelines can station large numbers of personnel around the pipeline locations. Such personal can include management, technicians and workers of the oil or gas company involved but also a very heavy presence of 'security' personal to safeguard the pipeline.

At the top of the list of Iran's pipeline programme was the game-changing oil pipeline that would be able to transport oil from its major fields via Guriyeh (or 'Goreh') - in the Shoaybiyeh-ye Gharbi Rural District of Khuzestan Province - 1,100 kilometres to the port of Jask, in Hormozgan province on the Gulf of Oman. This 42-inch Guriyeh-Jask pipeline was absolutely crucial to Iran's ability to continue to circumvent US-led sanctions against it whether imposed in 1979, 2018 or any time thereafter, and to consolidate its burgeoning customer base in Asia – and to its key superpower sponsor, China, in particular.

The Goreh-Jask Pipeline Was Crucial To Iran's Sanctions Strategy

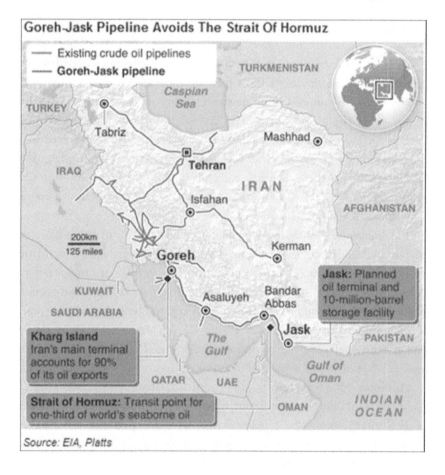

The Guriyeh-Jask pipeline would allow Iran to freely move at least 1 million bpd of its own crude oil anywhere in the world, with a continued focus on China initially. This would be done by moving the oil first across Iran and to Jask and then out through the Gulf of Oman, thus avoiding the perennially fractious geopolitical hotspot of the Strait of Hormuz in the Persian Gulf. At the same time, this safe route for Iran's oil out into the

Gulf of Oman would allow the Islamic Republic to disrupt all other oil supplies that transited through the Strait of Hormuz (around 35% of the world's total) whenever it wished to do so.

In the first instance, the oil to be pumped from Goreh would be drawn from the cluster of resource-rich oil fields in the West Karoun area, including the supergiant fields of North Azadegan, South Azadegan, North Yaran, South Yaran and Yadavaran. These fields were the main focus of Iran's programme at that time to increase the mean average rate of recovery from its key oil sites from around 4.5% to at least 12% within two years. To recap, for every 1% that the rate of recovery from West Karoun is increased, the recoverable reserves increase by 670 million barrels.

Once the oil was in Jask, it would be stored in any of the 20 storage tanks available, each capable of storing 500,000 barrels of oil in the first phase. These could then be loaded onto VLCCs headed from the Gulf of Oman and then sail out into the Arabian Sea and onwards to the Indian Ocean. The second phase would see an expansion to an overall storage capacity of 30 million barrels.

These VLCCs would be accommodated in shipping facilities costing around USD200 million in the first phase. In addition, a single point mooring (SPM) loading system with a capacity of 7,000 square metres per hour of loading capacity was in position in Assaluyeh, southern Iran, which would enhance the gas condensate loading capacity of the field. This SPM will allow for the handling of liquid cargo, such as petroleum products, for tanker ships.

The plan was to have several other SPMs installed in the south, in the Gulf of Oman, as they are very useful in areas where a dedicated facility for loading or unloading liquid cargo is not available. These SPMs would operate in a similar manner to those of Iran's neighbour, Iraq, in that they would be located many kilometres away from the onshore facilities, connected to them by a series of sub-sea pipelines and able to handle the biggest of VLCCs.

The logistical model that Iran had in place prior to the Goreh-Jask pipeline to move its oil out into the world before the pipeline was completed in 2021 was not sustainable. Around 90% of its oil for export had been loaded at Kharg Island – with most of the remaining loads going through terminals on Lavan and Sirri – making it an obvious and easy target for the US and its proxies to cripple Iran's oil sector and therefore its economy. Even before US sanctions were re-imposed in May 2018 the Kharg terminal was not ideal for use by tankers as the narrowness of the Strait of Hormuz meant that the vessels had to travel very slowly through it. This resulted in higher transit costs and delays in revenue streams.

The Goreh-Jask pipeline, and the phase 1 plans of its corollary projects, was fully completed in 2021. For oil traders, the completion of the Goreh-Jask pipeline meant that blockades of the Strait of Hormuz by Iran – which would cause oil prices to go up very fast – would be a more likely occurrence from that point. Blockading the Strait of Hormuz is also one of the easiest mechanisms for Iran use to retaliate for an increase in sanctions against it by the US and its allies, or for any other reason.

The Iran-Pakistan Pipeline

The Iran-Pakistan Pipeline (IPP) would allow for the stationing of Iranian security personnel – or IRGC – on Pakistani soil, which is of considerable strategic interest for Iran and for the IRGC. This fact has not been lost on the US and its core allies, or on India, Pakistan's arch-regional enemy. This is a key reason why, so far, little progress has been made on the pipeline by Pakistan, despite the original deal - the Gas Sales Purchase Agreement (GSPA) – having been signed in 2009.

This plan was for the GPSA to run for 25 years, following a three-year construction time for Pakistan to put down its part of the pipeline, which is a 781-kilometre pipeline from the Iranian border to Nawabshah. The completion date for the entire project was to have been December 2014, with full operations beginning on 1 January 2015. At that point, Pakistan was to have started receiving at least 750 million standard cubic feet of gas from Iran daily.

At that point in 2009 and for several years thereafter, there was every sign that the pipeline would go ahead as planned. Pakistan had little to lose from the US. Washington had long accused it of being a duplicitous partner, supporting the Haqqani guerrilla insurgency in Afghanistan and Al Qaeda globally against US forces, despite taking hundreds of billions of dollars in aid payments. In this vein, just after the first wave of the new sanctions were rolled out on 7 August 2018, Pakistan's Foreign Office spokesman Muhammad Faisal said that: 'We are examining the implications of the US's re-imposed sanctions on Iran, however, Pakistan, being a sovereign state, reserves the right to pursue legitimate economic and commercial interests while respecting the international legal regime.'

Iran's Ever-Changing Pipeline Plan To The East

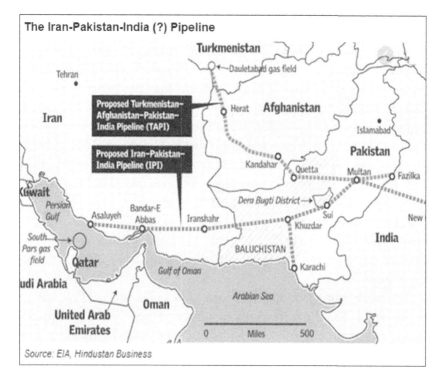

The Iran-Pakistan-India (?) Pipeline

Source: EIA, Hindustan Business

Later, in his inaugural speech as Pakistan's new prime minister, Imran Khan called for improving ties with the country's immediate neighbours, including Iran, from whose president, Hassan Rouhani, he also accepted an invitation for an early state visit to Tehran. Bubbling back up to the top of the list of practical initiatives that were being advanced seriously at that point was the Iran-Pakistan gas pipeline, which Khan personally backed and had made a priority project.

In practical terms, Pakistan certainly needs all the sustainable energy sources it can get. As it stood back then, the country had seen domestic natural gas production stagnate at around 4 billion cubic feet per day (Bcf/d) against demand of more than 6 Bcf/d, which had led to repeated load shedding in many major cities of up to 15 hours a day. Moreover, the supply and demand disparity looked set to become even worse, as industry estimates projected that Pakistan's domestic gas production would fall nearer to 2 Bcf/d by the end of 2021, due to aging infrastructure. At the same time, demand was projected to rise to around 8 Bcf/d by the same time, driven by rising demand from the power, industry and domestic sectors as the economy continued to grow by around 5% per year.

According to Pakistan's Ministry of Energy (MoE), the planned 0.75 Bcf/d of gas that would flow through the Iran-Pakistan pipeline – originating from Iran's supergiant South Pars natural gas field - would add around 4,000 megawatts (MW) of electricity into the Pakistan grid. The cost of the pipeline at the onset of the project was estimated at around USD3.5 billion, although USD2.5 billion of that had already been spent in the 900-kilometre stretch on Iran's side that had been completed early.

Over and above the energy supply consideration alone, the IPP has a high degree of geopolitical importance for both Iran and Pakistan, and therefore to China, Russia and the US as well. For China, there is a threefold motivation. First, it plans to integrate the IPP into the USD50 billion-plus China Pakistan Economic Corridor (CPEC) project, with Gwadar earmarked to be a key logistical node in China's 'One Belt, One Road' initiative.

Second, it wants to keep Iran as one of its key suppliers of oil and gas in the future. And third, it regards supporting those who the US opposes as being a central plank of its foreign policy, over and above the short-term tactic of wrong-footing the US wherever possible. This is all part of the broader shift in recent years in China's foreign policy towards the US as it seeks to assert itself regionally and tries to establish a wider global role for itself. During the same time, the US has moved from the 'constructive engagement' of the Clinton, Bush and Obama administrations to regarding China as a 'strategic competitor'.

For Russia, the motivations are no less imperative and its initial pledge to assist Pakistan has been on the table since March 2012. Back then, officials from Pakistan's MoE went to Russia for talks with state-controlled gas giant, Gazprom, to discuss a range of co-operation agreements. It was agreed that the Russian firm would help finance and construct the IPP. A key part of Russia's willingness at that point to see this pipeline taking Iranian gas to Asia was Moscow's wish to keep the gas market in Europe dependent on Russia only.

Added to this, though, was that Russia saw the IPP as offering surrounding countries a viable alternative to the long-awaited and US-backed Turkmenistan-Afghanistan-Pakistan-India (TAPI) pipeline. A pipeline for Iranian gas, and later oil, running through Central Asia was a core strategy for Russia to exert its increasing influence in the Middle East. It was also seen by Russia as a key to consolidating its presence in central and eastern Europe to the one side and Asia to the other, particularly with a view to building on its already extensive energy relationship with China.

The US clearly sees the IPP in the same way, as it has from the start tried to stymie progress on the pipeline. In January 2010, despite Iran being close to completing its side of the IPP pipeline, the US formally requested that Pakistan abandon the project in return for which it would receive assistance from Washington for the construction of an LNG terminal and for the importing of electricity from Tajikistan through Afghanistan's Wakhan Corridor. Although the IPP agreement came back into effect briefly, July 2011 saw the US interfere again in the corporate proxy shape of energy giant ConocoPhillips, which began mediating the notion of an LNG supply deal between Pakistan and then-US ally Qatar. Ultimately, this formed the basis of the 15-year agreement for Qatar to export LNG to Pakistan, signed in February 2016.

In the past, progress on the IPP was also negatively impacted by questions over the pricing of Iran's gas supply to Pakistan, but this matter was largely resolved in June at the eighteenth Shanghai Cooperation Organization (SCO) summit. At that time, the Iranians had been asking for a price of 14% of the Brent/JCC oil benchmark price, whilst Pakistan wanted 11%, so they agreed to meet in the middle at 12.5%.

This compromise was a signal that both countries were looking to move forward on the IPP project, as part of a much broader co-operation policy. Then-Iranian President Rouhani spoke of much wider 'co-operation and co-ordination' between the two countries to 'expand defence co-operation' especially in border areas. One of these Pakistan shares with India and another it shares with Afghanistan.

He then condemned the relocation of the US embassy in Israel to the highly sensitive Jerusalem site and the US's recognition of the site as Israel's capital. This view was fully supported by Pakistan's then-President, Mamnoon Hussain. Hussain also highlighted that his country could be of use to Iran in terms of 'banking relations' – that is, getting around the US financial sanctions – and underlined Pakistan's support for JCPOA, urging all parties to abide by it.

Given the IPP's enormous geopolitical importance, then, it is little wonder that at the beginning of 2023, Iran told Pakistan that it should move ahead and complete the construction of its part of the IPP by March 2024 at the latest. Iran argued correctly that the JCPOA was still in force legally, despite the US having withdrawn from it. Iran also reminded Pakistan that under the original agreement, Pakistan was liable to pay USD1 million per day to Iran as of the original start date for IPP operation (1 January 2015). As of the beginning of 2023, this penalty amount totalled around USD2.9 billion.

Iraq's Pipelines Used By Iran

Iran and Iraq do not just share several key oil (with associated gas) fields, making it impossible to determine which oil is Iranian in origin and which Iraqi. The two countries also have significant linkage across the pipeline network that runs across them. A key piece of this latter cooperation is the Baghdad-owned oil pipeline that runs from Kirkuk in the northern semi-autonomous region of Iraq's Kurdistan to the Turkish port of Ceyhan. This pipeline allows for the transport of 'Iraqi' oil into southern Europe.

The original Kirkuk-Ceyhan Pipeline or Iraq-Turkey Pipeline (ITP) consisted of two pipes which theoretically had a nameplate capacity of 1.6 million bpd combined. This is split into 1.1 million bpd for the 46-inch (1,168-mm) diameter pipe and 500,000 bpd for the 40-inch (1,016-mm) line. Later though, the Kurdistan Regional Government (KRG) constructed its own single side-track, from the Taq field through Khurmala, which joins the Kirkuk-Ceyhan pipeline in the border town of Fishkhabur. This has a nameplate capacity of 700,000 bpd. In parallel with this is the planned Iraq-Iran oil pipeline that would move oil from Kirkuk to Iran's Abadan refinery initially before being moved for export.

In a similar vein is the Iraq-Syria oil pipeline that was initially discussed in June 2017 and then agreed in July of that year, alongside the plans for the Iran-Iraq-Syria pipeline, moving Iranian, and later Iraqi, gas from South Pars to Syria and then into Europe. As originally envisioned, the pipeline would stretch 800 km from Kirkuk to Banias in Syria, via Haditha, with an initial nameplate capacity of 300,000 bpd. Russia was involved in the original plans for all of these pipeline ideas in Iraq.

Iraq's Pipeline Network Augments The Shared Fields With Iran

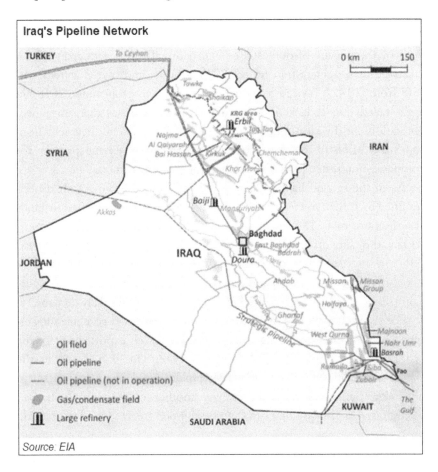

The first of these plans was agreed in principle in 2007 but then annulled in 2009 when no progress had been made by Russian company Stroytrangaz, a subsidiary of hydrocarbons giant Gazprom. The second, agreed in September 2010, involved building two new pipelines. One of these would be for heavy crude – at a planned capacity of 1.5 million bpd, from the northern Baiji area – and the other would carry light crude – 1.25 million bpd capacity – from the southern fields of Majnoon, Halfaya, Badra, Ahdab and East Baghdad.

At that point the preferred route was from Basra to the Jordanian port of Aqaba, again via Haditha, traversing the ever-volatile Anbar province, although discussions persisted on this USD4.5 billion, 1,680-km double conduit – one for oil and one for gas. This would transport 1 million barrels of oil and around 258 mmcf (7.3 mcm) per day to the coastal town.

The agreement to proceed had been made in 2013 but was then delayed both by the paucity of domestic or international investment required for the build-own-operate-transfer (BOOT) contract and by the activities of ISIS from 2014. A revised route via Najaf was then proposed in 2016 but again failed due to lack of international investment, as did subsequent reiterations of the idea until December 2019 saw an announcement from Iraq's Oil Ministry that it had completed the prequalifying process for companies interested in participating in the pipeline project.

As of the second half of 2020, crude oil imports from Iraq had been resumed by Jordan in the amount of at least 10,000 bpd in the first instance at a discount of USD16 to the Brent crude oil price, reflecting transport costs and quality differential. These supplies – which had been suspended earlier in the year due to the price crash following the 2020 Oil Price War – began from Baiji in Iraq direct to the Jordan Petroleum Refinery Company (JPRC) and constituted around 7% of Jordan's daily demand.

For Iraq – and Iran – the Jordan pipeline offers two core advantages. First, it provides another alternate Iraq/Iran oil export line to the historically vulnerable Strait of Hormuz route. This would add to the export capabilities of the Goreh-Jask pipeline and plans to roll out a pipeline to Syria as well. Second, it gives another 'cover' route for Iranian oil disguised as Iraqi oil that can then be shipped freely around the world.

LNG Development Focused On North Pars

Iran has long been looking at further monetising its huge gas resources – and securing further geopolitical power – by becoming a top global exporter of LNG. Its neighbour, Qatar, with which Iran shares the world's biggest gas reservoir – the North Field (on the Qatar side)/South Pars (on Iran's side) site – had long been the world's top LNG exporter, despite losing the spot briefly to Australia. At the beginning of 2021, with Asian spot LNG prices having risen to unprecedented levels in January due to cargo shortages in February, transportation bottlenecks, supply outages and record winter temperatures boosting end-user demand – and the outlook remaining extremely robust – Iran believed the time was right to move full ahead with its long-term strategy to become a leading global LNG supplier.

Given the contractual obligations for much of the gas from the supergiant South Pars field – both for domestic use and as part of the 25-year deal with China (fully analysed in this section shortly) - a key focus for this in the short-term was to be the North Pars non-associated natural gas field. Its first exploration well was completed in 1967 and for the next 23 years, before the discovery of supergiant South Pars field in 1990, North Pars was the largest gas reservoir in Iran. Propitiously for the speed of development of North Pars, not only were the spot prices of LNG set to remain at the historical high-end but also Iran had virtually completed all phases of its South Pars development by that point.

Located 120 kilometres southeast of the southern Bushehr Province, the North Pars gas field has around 59 trillion cubic feet (about 1.67 trillion cubic metres) of gas in place, with a conservatively estimated recoverable volume of gas of approximately 47 trillion cubic feet. The gas itself is lean and sour, with a condensate gas ratio of 4 barrels (0.64 cubic metres) per 1,000 cubic feet and it contains around 6,000 parts per million of hydrogen sulphide and 5% carbon dioxide. The first design to operate this field had been approved in 1977 but, after the drilling of 17 wells and the installation of 26 offshore platforms, the development of North Pars was suspended due to the 1979 Islamic Revolution in the country and the subsequent war with Iraq from 1980-1988.

However, a study of the state of North Pars by Iran at the end of 2020 determined that the field was still in a highly workable state for a quick push to significant gas output. Specifically, it was established, at least 100 million cubic metres per day (mcm/d) of output could be achieved within less than 12 months of proper development – with all the gas recovered to be channelled into LNG production of at least 20 million metric tonnes per annum (mtpa).

Iran also set itself the task of gradually bringing on further phases of North Pars in the following seven years, all to be directed towards building out its LNG capabilities and to developing several other major gas fields partly with the same aim. These included most immediately Golshan, Ferdowsi, Farzad A, Farzad B and Kish.

In context, after the development hiatus, September 2006 saw the China National Offshore Oil Corporation (CNOOC) sign a memorandum of understanding with the National Iranian Oil Corporation (NIOC) to develop the North Pars site. This was then extended in December 2006 to incorporate the development of a four-train (an LNG liquefaction and purification facility) complex with a 20 mtpa capacity.

Later, when China had proven slow on moving forwards with this development – and others in Iran – but before US and EU sanctions against Iran were ramped up in 2011/12 forcing its suspension of the project, German chemicals giant Linde Group took over the main developments of Iran's LNG programme. Within a relatively short time, Linde Group had 60%-completed a USD3.3 billion flagship LNG export facility near Tombak Port that was set to produce at least 10.5 mtpa of LNG, with expectations that it would take less than a year to finish. After sanctions were lifted again in 2016, Iran awarded Linde, whose liquefaction process the facility's first two trains were intended to use, a 'sweetener' contract when it signed the first petrochemical co-operation deal between Iran and Germany - a Front End Engineering Design (FEED) contract for the olefin unit of Kian Petrochemical.

Floating LNG And Mini-LNG Plans

Iran also decided at around the same time to move ahead with plans to construct floating LNG facilities, especially near Europe. In-principle deals to do this had been struck with Italy's Eni and Spain's Cepsa to take both oil and LNG when it became available from Iran.

Similar plans were being discussed between Iran and Greece's state-run gas supplier, Depa, to form a new firm that would build and run a floating LNG storage and re-gasification facility at Alexandroupolis in the north of Greece. The expansion of the Revythousa re-gasification terminal near Athens was also being looked at as a potential entry point for Iranian gas.

Both facilities would have been connected to two international pipeline systems: the Trans Adriatic Pipeline and the Gas Interconnector Greece-Bulgaria links. Indeed, the scale of Iran's original LNG plans can be gauged from the fact that prior to 2011/12 it was in negotiations with a number of international oil companies about LNG-related projects, including Total, Petronas, Repsol and Royal Dutch Shell. All of these companies – and many others – had previously also had agreements with Iran as part of its fourth 'Five Year National Develop Plan' (2005-2009) that aimed to produce 70 mtpy of LNG from the North Pars, South Pars, Ferdowsi and Golshan gas fields.

However, even after the scaling up of sanctions in 2011/12 – and worsened after the US withdrawal from the JCPOA in 2018 - caution amongst European firms about engaging with Iran in such projects understandably increased. In the interim period when the JCPOA was still in place, Iran had been working on a plan to install a network of 'mini-LNG' complexes with the help of South Korea.

Late in 2018, South Korea's Minister of Land, Infrastructure and Transport, Kim Hyun-mee, agreed the finer points on its LNG co-operation with Iran's Petroleum Minister, Bijan Zangeneh, which included Exim Bank's initial EUR8 billion credit line to Iran and another EUR2.3 billion from two other South Korean companies.

These mini-LNG complexes have production capacities ranging from 2,000 to 500,000 tons of LNG per year. This compares to a typical large scale plant capacity of between 2.5 and 7.5 million tons per year. Consequently, mini-LNG complexes benefit particularly from being both relatively quick to start up and being locatable almost anywhere, even in very remote gas fields.

Using Oman's Unused LNG Capacity At Qalhat

Iran also looked at that time at the idea of utilising about 25% of Oman's total 1.5 million tons per year LNG production capacity at the Qalhat plant. This was part of the broader co-operation deal made between Oman and Iran in 2013, extended in scope in 2014, and fully ratified in August 2015 that was centred on Oman's importing at least 10 billion cubic metres of natural gas per year (bcm/y) from Iran for 25 years.

The deal was to have begun in 2017, with the amount equating to just less than 1 billion cubic feet per day and worth around USD60 billion at the time. The target was then changed to 43 bcm/y to be imported for 15 years, and then finally altered to at least 28 bcm/y for a minimum period of 15 years.

Iran Could Use Oman's LNG Facilities As Well

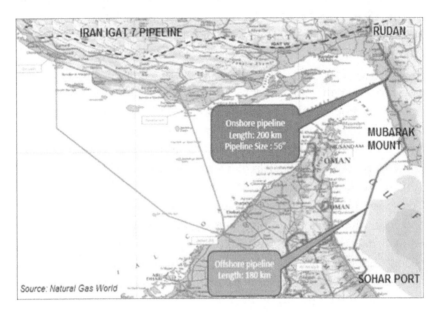

According to a statement at the signing of the 2014 deal from the then-managing director of the National Iranian Gas Export Company (NIGEC), Mehran Amir-Moeini, the Iranian company was already working on the different contract mechanisms for the key phases of the project.

Specifically, the land section of the project would comprise around 200 kilometres of 56-inch pipeline (to be constructed in Iran), to run from Rudan to Mobarak Mount in the southern Hormozgan province. The sea section would include a 192-kilometre section of 36-inch pipeline along the bed of the Oman Sea at depths of up to 1,340 metres, from Iran to Sohar Port in Oman.

This deal was intended to allow for the completely free movement of Iranian gas (and later oil) via Oman through the Gulf of Oman and out into the world oil and gas markets. The route was designed to allow Iran the same sanctions-free flows that it was operating via Iraq.

From Oman's side, all the preliminary work related to seabed surveys, design of the pipeline and its accessories and the compressor stations was completed some time ago. The depth of the subsea pipeline had been increased in August 2016 due to the heightened political tensions between Saudi Arabia and Iran resulting in a plan modified to avoid the territorial waters of Saudi/US ally, the UAE.

Once the gas had made its way to Oman, the technicalities of Iran becoming an LNG supplier were extremely straightforward, as it would just involve utilising a portion of the Sultanate's unused LNG production capacity at the Qalhat plant. The original plan, according to Alireza Kameli, managing director of the National Iranian Gas Export Company (NIGEC), would have entailed Tehran utilising about 25% of Oman's total 1.5 million tons per year LNG production capacity to produce Iranian LNG. This would then have been loaded on to the specialised LNG transport vessels for export to European and Asian markets, in return for commission payments to Oman.

Prior to the withdrawal of the US from the JCPOA in 2018, there was no shortage of international oil and gas firms companies looking to take part in the Iran-Oman pipeline. France's Total, Germany's Uniper and E.ON, South Korea's KOGAS, Japan's Mitsui, and Royal Dutch Shell had all expressed serious interest in being involved, among others.

Give the potentially sanctions-busting nature of the project, though, the US included this Iran-Oman LNG project in its efforts to prevent Iran from meaningfully expanding its hydrocarbons export routes into the booming market of Asia. Before the dispute between Saudi and Qatar erupted again, the US's main alternative for Oman was that it increased its uptake of gas from Qatar, via the existing Dolphin Pipeline that runs from Qatar to Oman through the UAE, or in LNG form, but it refused. Oman's desire to re-energise the plans for the Iran-Oman gas pipeline was fanned by the UAE's demands for an increasingly large fee for allowing the transit of gas from Iran through its waters, again part of the US strategy to persuade Oman to take its gas from Qatar.

The completion of the Iran-Oman subsea pipeline would allow Iran to realise its ambitions to expand gas exports to Asia, both via an extension to the pipeline to Pakistan (analysed above) and in LNG form. Overall, Iran's plan before sanctions were broadened out again after 2018 was to become the largest exporter of gas – natural gas, LNG and liquefied petroleum gas (LPG) combined – to Europe and Western Asia, with a focus on China, South Korea and Pakistan.

Russia's Gazprom Plan For Iranian LNG

With US sanctions firmly back in place in 2018, though, Oman backed away from the plan, although Muscat stated that it would only be for as long as sanctions remained in place on Iran. It was immediately replaced in Iran's LNG plans by Russia's Gazprom, which signed two MoUs with the NIOC concerning the rollout of a two-fold joint strategy regarding gas.

The first part was a gas cooperation roadmap between the two companies, and the second part detailed the construction of Iranian LNG facilities in partnership with Iran's Oil Industry Pension Fund. Initially, this would allow Gazprom to, in effect, take over from Linde on the existing 60%-complete LNG complex and later to be integral in the construction of the mini-LNG complexes. Gazprom would take payment for its work from the sale of gas both from this complex and from part of the output from fields feeding gas into it.

At that time it was envisaged that the North Pars LNG development would need around USD16 billion in investment – comprising USD5 billion in the upstream sector and USD11 billion in the downstream sector (mainly LNG plants) – to achieve at least the first phase LNG output of at minimum 100 mcm/d and the drilling of the 46 wells that this would entail. This is still the ballpark figure that Iran is working with.

Consideration is now also being given by the Petroleum Ministry and NIOC to making the North Pars site the focus of a new bigger energy hub, concentrated on the production of LNG. This would allow for international state-owned companies of China and Russia in particular to engage in a series of projects joining up their South Pars operations with their North Pars ones.

The Iran-China 25-Year Deal

At the end of August 2019, Iran's Foreign Minister, Mohammad Zarif, paid a visit to his China counterpart, Wang Li, to present his Chinese hosts with a road map on the China-Iran comprehensive strategic partnership that had been signed in 2016. Some of this updated agreement echoed many of the points in the previous agreement and was made public. Many of the key specifics of this new understanding, however, were not released to the public but marked a seismic shift in the balance of the oil and gas sector, and in the geopolitical balance of superpowers, in the Middle East. This deal – the 'Iran-China 25-Year Comprehensive Cooperation Agreement' – was first revealed in a global exclusive by me, in a feature article published on 3 September 2019 for Petroleum Economist.

The deal – which remains in effect to this day - is that China will invest a total of USD400 billion into Iran up to 2043 (that is, 25 years from 2018). The first USD280 billion of this will go to developing Iran's oil, gas and petrochemicals sectors, with the amount to be front-loaded into the first five-year period of the 2018 deal. The understanding is that further amounts will be available in each subsequent five-year period, subsequent to both parties' agreement. There will be another USD120 billion of investment, which again can be front-loaded into the first five-year period, for upgrading Iran's transport and manufacturing infrastructure. Again this is subject to increase in each subsequent five-year period should both parties be in agreement.

In exchange for this, Chinese companies will be given the first option to bid on any new oil and gas field developments and on any stalled or uncompleted developments. Chinese companies will also have the first option to either build or become involved with any and all petrochemicals projects in Iran, including the provision of technology, systems, chemicals and personnel required to complete such projects.

China will also have first call on any and all of the oil, gas and petrochemicals produced and will be able to buy these at a minimum guaranteed discount of 12% to the six-month rolling average price of comparable benchmark products, plus another 6-8% of that metric for risk adjusted compensation.

In addition, China will be granted the right to delay payment for up to two years and, crucially, it will be able to pay in soft currencies that it has accrued from doing business in Africa and the Former Soviet Union (FSU) states. Effectively, given the exchange rates involved in converting these soft currencies into hard currencies that Iran can use internationally, China is looking at another 8-12% discount, which means a total discount of around 32% on all of its oil gas, and petrochemicals purchases from Iran.

Another positive factor in the deal for China is that it will be allowed to become involved in a broader-based build-out of Iran's transport and manufacturing infrastructure. This will allow China to utilise the currently cheap labour available in Iran to build factories that will be designed and overseen by big Chinese manufacturing companies with identical specifications and operations to those in China. The final manufactured products will then be able to access Western markets through new transport links planned, financed and managed by China.

China's Multi-Generational Land And Sea Power-grab OBOR Project

One Belt One Road (And Previous Silk Road) Routes

Source: The Economist Group

In this context, China sees Iran as being an absolutely vital country in its key geopolitical multi-generational project, 'One Belt, One Road' (OBOR) economic plan for three key reasons. First, Iran is closely involved in the affairs of those countries that constitute the Shia crescent of power – Jordan, Lebanon, Syria, Iraq and Yemen – which allows China to hold the US in check in those areas; second, it is a direct route into Europe, via both Turkey and the FSU states and Russia; and third, it has huge oil and gas reserves currently going cheap.

Indeed, in the same week in August 2019 that the new 25-year deal was presented to Iran's Supreme Leader, Ali Khamenei, its First Vice President, Eshaq Jahangiri announced that Iran had signed a contract with China to implement a project to electrify the main 900-kilometre railway connecting Tehran to the north-eastern city of Mashhad, close to the border with Turkmenistan. Jahangiri added that there are also plans to establish a

Tehran-Qom-Isfahan high-speed train line. Adjunct to this is the plan to extend this upgraded network to the northwest through Tabriz, home to a number of key sites relating to oil, gas and petrochemicals, and the starting point for the Tabriz-Ankara gas pipeline.

China Secured Influence Over The Shia Crescent Of Power Through Iran

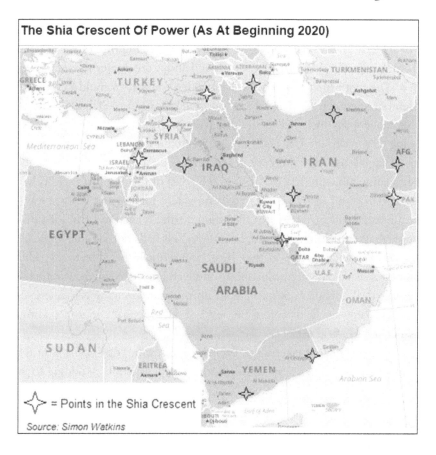

Ultimately, the Mashhad-Tehran high-speed train link will be a key part of the 2,300-kilometre New Silk Road that links Urumqi, the capital of China's western Xinjiang Province, to Tehran, and connecting Kazakhstan, Kyrgyzstan, Uzbekistan and Turkmenistan along the way. After that, the Chinese plan is to extend the railway links through Tabriz into Turkey and then Bulgaria, and then into the rest of southern Europe. This, in turn, will require the co-operation of Russia, as it regards these states as its own backyard, so the 25-year agreement has in place a clause in which in addition to China being offered first option on new or stalled and uncompleted oil and gas field developments, at least one Russian company will also have the option to be involved on equally advantageous discount terms as China.

Iran's Benefits From The 25-Year Deal With China

For its part, the Iranians were, and still are, expecting three key positives from the 25-year deal with China over and above the money to be invested in it. The first is that China is one of just five countries to hold Permanent Member status on the United Nations Security Council (UNSC). Russia, also tangentially included in the deal, holds another, with the remainder going to the US, the UK and France. To circumvent any further ramping up of sanctions – and originally to encourage the US to come back to the negotiating table on the JCPOA - Iran by dint of this deal with China had secured two out of five UNSC votes on side. The fact that Zarif showed up unexpectedly at the 2019 G7 summit at the invitation of France may imply that, at that point at least, Iran thought it had another vote as well.

The second positive is that Iran might finally be able to expedite increases in oil and gas production from several of its key fields. Within the 25-year deal is China's agreement to up the pace on its development of Iran's flagship gas field project, Phase 11 of the supergiant South Pars non-associated gas field (SP11).

However, having taken over French supermajor Total's 50.1% in the field when the French firm withdrew due to US sanctions – adding to its previous holding of 30% – China National Petroleum Corporation (CNPC) made little immediate progress on development due to tensions surrounding the trade war with the US. This meant, as analysed in the first section of this book, that China had to tread carefully in its developments in Iran. This it has done through the aforementioned use of its 'contract-only' exploration and development models. China's efforts after the Trade War tensions had died down were then hampered by the invasion of Ukraine by its key ally, Russia.

China also agreed to increase the production from its oil fields in the West Karoun area – including North Azadegan and Yadavaran – by an additional 500,000 bpd by the end of 2020, to 1 million bpd. Progress on this target, though, aside from the two factors mentioned above, was additionally undermined by the onset of COVID-19 in 2020.

The third and final positive for Iran is that China agreed to continue the steady increase in imports of Iranian oil that had already been seen since the new 25-year deal was first mooted after the US did not extend China's waiver on importing Iranian oil in May 2018. It is apposite to recap here that official figures from China's General Administration of Customs (GAC) regarding imports of oil from Iran are much lower than the true figures, as millions of barrels are kept in floating storage in and around China, without having gone through Customs. The fact that they have not gone through Customs means that that they do not show up on Customs data but nonetheless they are imports and they are in China, held effectively as part of China's Strategic Petroleum Reserves.

The Added Military Element To The 25-Year Deal

At the end of June 2020, another element that has the potential to change the entire balance of geopolitical power in the Middle East was added to the Iran-China 25-year deal. At that point, Iran's Supreme Leader, Ali Khamenei, agreed to the extension of the existing deal to include new military elements – which were proposed by the same senior figures in the IRGC and the intelligence services that proposed the original deal – and this involves complete aerial and naval co-operation between Iran and China, with Russia also taking a key role.

The plan – if and when fully implemented – would include Sino-Russian bombers, fighters and transport planes having unrestricted access to Iranian air bases, beginning with purpose-built facilities next to the existing air bases at Hamedan, Bandar Abbas, Chabahar and Abadan. The bombers to be deployed would be China-modified versions of the long-range Russian Tupolev Tu-22M3s, with a manufacturing specification range of 6,800 kilometres (2,410 km with a typical weapons load). The fighters to be used would be the all-weather supersonic medium-range fighter bomber/strike plane, the Sukhoi Su-34, and the newer single-seat stealth attack Sukhoi-57. In August 2016, Russia used the Hamedan airbase to launch attacks on targets in Syria using both Tupolev-22M3 long-range bombers and Sukhoi-34 strike fighters. At the same time, Chinese and

Russian military vessels would be able to use the dual use facilities at Iran's key ports at Chabahar, Bandar-e-Bushehr and Bandar Abbas.

These deployments would be accompanied by the roll-out of Chinese and Russian electronic warfare (EW) capabilities. This would encompass each of the three key EW areas – electronic support (including early warning of enemy weapons use) plus electronic attack (including jamming systems) plus electronic protection (including against enemy jamming). Based originally around neutralising NATO's Command, Control, Communications, Computers, Intelligence, Surveillance and Reconnaissance (C4ISR) systems, part of the new roll-out of software and hardware from China and Russia in Iran would be the Russian S-400 anti-missile air defence system to counter US and/or Israeli attacks.

The Krasukha-2 and -4 systems would also feature in the overall EW architecture, as they proved their capabilities in Syria of countering the radars of attack, reconnaissance and unmanned aircraft. The Krasukha-2 can jam Airborne Warning and Control Systems (AWACS) at up to 250 km and other airborne radars such as guided missiles, whilst the Krasukha-4 is a multi-functional jamming system that not only counters AWACS but also ground-based radars. Both are mobile, and an entire EW brigade can consist of as little as 100 men.

Part of the new military co-operation includes the continuation of the exchange of officer-level personnel and specialised technicians between Iran, and China and Russia, which has been going on for several years. This cross-training is linked to the fact that Iran's EW system can easily be tied into Russia's Southern Joint Strategic Command 19th EW Brigade (Rassvet) near Rostov-on-Don. One of the Russian air jamming systems is planned to be based in Chabahar and would be capable of completely disabling the UAE's and Saudi Arabia's air defences, to the extent that they would only have around two minutes of warning of a missile or drone attack from Iran.

One indication of what Iran hopes to receive in return for its co-operation with China and Russia came in the first half of 2020 when Zhang Jun, China's permanent UN representative, told the US in a statement to the Security Council: 'To stop its illegal unilateral sanctions on Iran [...] The root cause of the current crisis is the US's withdrawal from the Iran nuclear deal in May 2018 and the re-imposition of unilateral sanctions against Iran.' He also opposed the US's push for the extension of the UN arms embargo on Iran, which expired in October 2020.

'This has again undermined the joint efforts to preserve the JCPOA,' Zhang said, and added: 'The [JCPOA] agreement was endorsed by the UN Security Council [UNSC] and is legally binding.' He concluded: 'We urge the US to stop its illegal unilateral sanctions and long-arm jurisdiction and return to the right track of observing the JCPOA and Resolution 2231 [of the UNSC].'

Iran's EW System Can Tie Into Russia's SJSC 19th EW Brigade

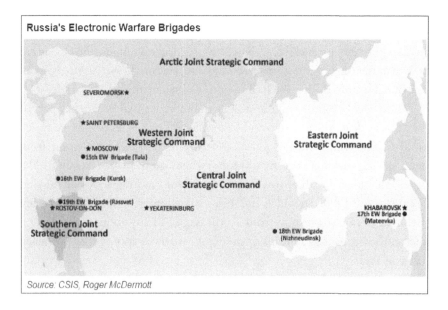

Source: CSIS, Roger McDermott

Co-operation With North Korea On ICBM Technology

Following the end of the 13-year United Nations embargo on Iran buying or selling weapons on 18 October 2020, serious discussions between China and Iran resumed in earnest about the deployment in Iran of North Korean weaponry and technology in exchange for oil. Most notably this would include Hwasong-12 mobile ballistic missiles, with a range of 4,500 kilometres, and the development of liquid propellant rocket engines suitable for intercontinental ballistic missiles (ICBMs) or satellite launch vehicles (SLVs). This would all be part of a broader triangular relationship co-ordinated by Beijing and further facilitated by the then-imminent launch of a new digitised currency system by China.

This sort of co-ordination – between North Korea and Iran and between North Korea, Iran and China – was nothing new, although its resumption at such a scale and in such products was. Over the first five-year period from the onset of Iran's ballistic missile program in 1987, Iran bought up to 300 Scud B missiles from North Korea. Pyongyang, though, did not just sell Iran weapons but it was also instrumental in helping Iran to build out the infrastructure for what has become an extremely high-level ballistic missile programme, beginning with the creation in Iran of a Scud B missile plant that became operational by the end of 1988. This early-stage co-operation in this area between North Korea and Iran also included Iranian personnel travelling to North Korea for training in the operation and manufacture of these missiles and the stationing of North Korean personnel in Iran during the build out of missile plants.

This model of knowledge and skills transference had been a key part of the 25-year deal between Iran and China since it had been first agreed back in 2016. The simple idea of paying North Korea in oil was also far from new, having been a key method by which Iran helped to fund the development of North Korea's more powerful Nodong series of missiles as early as the 1990s, in which Iran has a vested interest. Oil shipments are the number one suggestion from North Korea to any country that has oil and wants weapons as a means of payment for any weaponry that Pyonyang has available.

The Hwasong-12, first revealed internationally in a military parade on 14 April 2017 celebrating the birthday anniversary of North Korea's founding President, Kim Il-sung, fits neatly into Iran's overall military strategy. This is founded on the fact that decades of sanctions have left the Islamic Republic with an inability to adequately defend itself against attacks from hostile aircraft or missiles with its own air force. This has left its massive standing army as the primary deterrent for land invasion and its own missile defence systems as the primary deterrent for aerial attacks.

On the other hand, though, the Islamic Republic is aware that any major long-range missile attack on any foreign power allied with the US will end in disaster for it. As former US Secretary of State Henry Kissinger once said: 'The threat of committing suicide is a poor deterrent to being murdered.' Consequently, Iran has consistently stated since 2017 – by order of the Supreme Leader, Ali Khamenei – that it will limit itself to developing ballistic missiles with a maximum range of 2,000 kilometres.

Clearly, the Hwasong-12 has a range of double this but, crucially from Iran's political impact modelling, this was never likely to make its relationship with the US worse. The US wanted more specific prohibitions on ballistic missiles in a new JCPOA to be drawn up at the beginning of 2018 – as analysed later – but that did not happen, so it withdrew the relevant clauses.

Iran believed at the time in 2019 when it again increased its involvement with North Korea's latest missile technology that the next US President, be it Trump again or Biden, would want to do a deal to get some form of JCPOA back on track. From that perspective, then, being able to offer the withdrawal of its interest in the Hwasong-12 missile programme would be a useful negotiating tool. At the same time, though, there was the threat that the Hwasong-12 IRBM (intermediate range ballistic missile) could be upgraded through the addition of an 80-ton thrust engine to either the Hwasong-14 (two-stage, 10,000 km range) or the Hwasong-15 (two rocket engines cluster in first stage, 13,000 km range) ICBMs.

This 'upgrade' would always be regarded by the US as a serious proposition, as there have been signals over the years that Iran might already have been working on such a higher-powered rocket booster configuration. According to a New York Times report from December 2011, the previous month had seen the destruction of a supposed development site in Iran for long-range solid-propellant missiles. This was the first public indication that Iran was working on such systems that would need much more energetic propellants than used in either Iran's Fateh-110-based solid-propellant short range ballistic missiles or the Sejil medium range ballistic missiles.

Press reports in May 2018 indicated that the programme continued at a new location where ICBM-class solid rocket motor production facilities and evidence of ground testing of ICBM-class motors had been detected. Indeed, various reliable sources since 2013 have suggested that Iran has been receiving cooperation from North Korea in the development of a large, liquid-propellant rocket engine suitable for ICBMs or Space Launch Vehicles (SLVs) and a US Treasury Department sanctions' notice from January 2016 refers to Iranian work on a North Korean '80-ton rocket booster.'

China, for its part, has been warned by the US in the past for failing to adhere to the Missile Technology Control Regime in supplying missile equipment and technology to several countries, which is why it has frequently used North Korea as an agent to do so.

It is obvious, however, that there are many benefits for China in seeking to expedite the movement of such missile technology from North Korea to Iran as part of the 25-year deal's military component. First, as Iran is paying North Korea in oil it takes some financial pressure off China in its obligations to its neighbour. Second, it cements China's clear position to the US as having influence over not just one but two nuclear and near-nuclear states. Third, it further binds Iran (and the rest of the Shia crescent of power, especially Iraq) into China's geopolitically game-changing 'One Belt, One Road' project. Fourth, it creates a counterpoint of influence and power in the Middle East akin to the US-Israel axis. And fifth, it will shift more of the US's attention on the Persian Gulf and away from the Asia-Pacific region that China regards as its backyard of power.

Playing The 'Resistance Economy' Model For Profit

Alongside the ongoing development of its huge West Karoun oil fields, the completion of the supergiant South Pars gas programme and the completion of the crude oil transfer pipeline from Goreh to Jask (which is now done, as analysed above), Iran's core focus in any sanctions environment was to optimise the output and revenues from its already world-scale petrochemicals sector. This sector had always been key to Iran's 'resistance economy' model, the concept of generating value-added returns by leveraging intellectual capital into business development wherever possible.

In late 2020, having hit several key targets, Iran's petrochemicals sector was encouraged to generate further income and capital for the Islamic Republic through listing on the country's stock market, the Tehran Stock Exchange (TSE). In basic terms, a total of USD11.5 billion-worth of petrochemicals projects were to be launched in Iran by the end of the Iranian calendar year ending on 20 March 2021. This was to add at least 25 million tons to the country's annual production capacity, bringing it up to at least 90 million tons per annum (mtpa) and within a hair's breadth of the 100 mtpa production target that is due to be achieved by the end of 2025. This target was subsequently achieved ahead of time.

The first of this new slew of projects was the petrochemicals complex at Miandoab, which came onstream in 2020. At the official launch of the Miandoab, Iran's then-Petroleum Minister Bijan Zanganeh said the next phase of the country's petrochemicals sector development would consist of 17 new projects by the end of 2021. This would enable at least a doubling of the value of the sector to Iran to USD25 billion by the end of the 2021 Iranian calendar year, and to at least USD37 billion by March 2026.

Central to the build-out of this key strategic business area for Iran was the process of 'indigenising' the production of key catalysts involved in petrochemicals' manufacture. This process was always a pre-requisite in the multitude of contracts signed by Iran with foreign companies after the JCPOA was first agreed in 2015. The idea was made very clear when the deputy petroleum minister for international affairs and commerce, Amir-Hossein Zamani-Nia said: 'Direct investment is highly favoured by Iran's petroleum ministry but, before that, Iran's oil industry is in need of technologies and project management.'

Working in Iran's favour as well in terms of continuing to build out its petrochemicals sector – aside from the ongoing financial, technology and personnel support of China and Russia – was that from a legal perspective, Iran's petrochemicals sector had always occupied a grey area as far as sanctions were concerned. When the previous set of major sanctions were at their height in 2011/12, Iran's petrochemical industry was the subject of US and EU sanctions, and the only way for Iran to sell such products 'legally' was to customers outside the US and EU

At that time, secondary sanctions were in place in the US on any person worldwide that purchased, acquired, sold, transported or marketed Iranian-origin petrochemical products, or provided goods or services valued at USD250,000 or more (or USD1 million over a 12-month period) for use in Iran's production of petrochemical products. In the EU there was a ban on the import, purchase or transportation of Iran-origin petrochemical products and on the export to Iran of certain equipment for use in the petrochemical industry.

In stark contrast to the previous sanctions era, however, in the aftermath of the US's unilateral withdrawal from the JCPOA in May 2018 there were no EU sanctions specifically on Iran's petrochemicals sector, nor were there plans to impose them. From the US's perspective, it cannot exert jurisdiction for 'primary' sanctions unless US persons are involved – notably US banks and US employees.

To capitalise on this grey area for foreign investment, Iran redesigned the contracts on offer for foreign firms wishing to invest specifically in its petrochemicals sector. The new contracts sought to address the previous situation in which investors needed to deposit as a pledge at least 130% of the capital investment amount required in a project. According to Iran's National Petrochemical Company (NPC), the new contracts replaced the excess deposit idea with one in which the NPC takes the role of quasi-transactional guarantor. The NPC then retains a lien against future petrochemical products to be produced by petrochemical plants that are under construction. On the one hand, then this acts as a pledge for repayment of private sector loans to banks and on the other it gives assurance to the banks through which the money is funded that repayment will be made. For its part, NPC would retain at least a 20% share in new and under-construction petrochemical plants projects.

Floating petrochemical companies' shares is considered by Iran to be as good an idea as any to broaden and deepen the country's capital pool. The petrochemicals sector generate revenues for Iran of around 15 to 16 times more per tonne of product than crude oil. Also, based on current contract terms, petrochemicals produce rates of return of 30-35% against 12-15% in the upstream segment, and petrochemical companies have often distributed relatively high dividends among shareholders. The Pars, Nouri and Shahid Tondguyan petrochemical companies were among the first petrochemical companies to list on the stock market, opening the way for more companies to do so, with at least six of them holding the extra cache of being subsidiaries of the Persian Gulf Petrochemical Industries Company (PGPIC). According to the latest data, PGPIC has about a 40% share of Iran's petrochemicals market and accounts for the same proportion of Iran's petrochemicals exports.

Overall Solid Fundamentals Of The TSE

It has been said by various smart money funds that global investors are never going to see a country of the size and sophistication of Iran open up again from such a low base. This was the prospect back when the JCPOA was signed in 2015 and it remains the prospect as and when US sanctions against Iran are eased again. To recap at this point, although many countries are supporting the sanctions reimposed by the US after its unilateral withdrawal from the JCPOA in 2018, the JCPOA deal per se still stands.

On demographics alone, the investment fundamentals of Iran are at least as attractive as any emerging market. The population is around 80 million – about the same as former premier investor darling Turkey, more than any of the long-running investment favourites in Eastern Europe and around three times that of Saudi Arabia. Iran also has a large middle class, easily comparable to both Turkey and Saudi, with an 88% overall literacy rate comparable to the 95% each in Turkey and Saudi Arabia.

Essentially, Iran has everything Turkey had when it was top of all global emerging markets investor lists before the security troubles kicked in but with the added bonus of having 10% of the world's oil reserves and nearly 20% of its gas reserves to boot. Moreover, despite – or because of – the hydrocarbons-related sanctions present over long periods since 1979, Iran's economy has been forced into becoming significantly more diversified than any of its Middle East neighbours.

From a technical markets' perspective, the Tehran Stock Exchange (TSE) – and its main index the TSE Dividend & Price total return Index (TEDPIX) - has several advantages over many emerging markets' bourses in general, and to those of the Middle East in particular. It is not just that Iran has a much more diversified sectoral business base than any of its neighbours that places it at such a regional advantage but also the fundamental structures of its market are built on much sounder foundations. In this context, the level of market volatility for the TSE is likely to remain considerably more moderate than investors in emerging markets might usually expect.

Many emerging market bourses are characterised by having a heavy presence of small ('retail') investors and this type of investor tends to chop in and out of the market often and quickly. This leads to wild market moves – as is seen from time to time in China's stock markets, for example – that but Iran has a totally different investor base. Key to this was the way in which Iran went about its privatisation process, targeting it towards steadier types of target investors; the pension funds of civil servants and the military, and 'Justice shares' to be held by major domestic funds that could then be distributed amongst the wider population as a means to make them feel invested in the country's economic future. The pension funds are very long-term investors, as they tend to be anywhere in the world, which will hold on to stocks in almost any market circumstances for 10, 20, 30 years. The funds that hold the 'Justice shares' are beholden to keep them for the people for the duration so, unlike the indigenous participants in many emerging market bourses, Iran's core investor base is in it for the long term, which means very limited volatility.

Regarded For A Long Time As A Sleeping Giant Of An Index

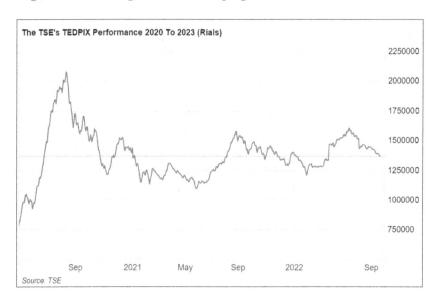

The TSE's TEDPIX Performance 2020 To 2023 (Rials)

Source: TSE

Iran already has a relatively well-developed stock market, with a daily turnover of around USD160 million and a wide range of companies in different sectors constituting a market capitalisation of around USD120 billion on an average price to earnings ratio of only around five or six times. Moreover, unlike until recently in Saudi Arabia, Iran has long allowed foreign investors to directly participate in its benchmark index, with any individual or institutional foreign investor allowed to own up to 10% of the equities in any listed company of the Exchange. Although the total foreign investors' ownership ceiling is 20% in any listed company, foreign investors can apply for a license to own above these portfolio management levels and even to fully take over a listed company, a highly unusual scenario in the region, and indeed in many emerging market countries.

Sukuk And China-Backed Bond Schemes

Although Iran has for some time been in no position to raise a sizeable amount of capital through a Western-oriented traditional bond denominated in a mainstream currency, its prospects in the global Sharia-compliant bond (sukuk) market are better and plans have been put into place to exploit this type of bond. Middle Eastern countries have often used this model of bond issuance in the past when they have been uncertain of how a more conventional bond issue would be received by investors due to negative economic circumstances.

Targeting such a specialised investor base as well has the advantage that the pricing for sukuk is generally lower than for a conventional bond issued by the same country and, given the rising interest rates trajectory in the US, the premium that such countries would have to pay over US Treasuries would be high. Therefore, the appeal of the sukuk for Iran will be in large part determined by its spread – nominal value – not against the usual benchmarks but rather against sukuk alternatives as well as high-yield bonds issued by Iraq, Mongolia, Kazakhstan and even Pakistan. However, US sanctions inserted a significant additional discount in the computation of yield, spread and pricing.

Part of Iran's appeal to the sukuk investment community – which ranges from the UK (the first Western country to issue a sukuk), through Germany and Turkey (key European hubs for sukuk) to Malaysia (the biggest sukuk centre in the world) – is that it is a truly Islamic issuer. The investment universe of sukuk – which, under Sharia law, should avoid investment in activities that are speculative, involve uncertainty, pay interest, are unjust to participants or are connected to prohibited businesses (such as gambling, alcohol and the sale of certain foodstuffs) – became a lot more sceptical of purported Sharia-compliant offering during the Great Financial Crisis that began in 2007/08.

The Accounting Auditing Organisation for Islamic Financial Institutions (AAOIFI) – the Islamic finance standards watchdog – said as long ago as February 2008 that the repurchase undertakings found in around 85% of apparently Sharia-compliant bond- and equity-fund structures that were based on 'mudaraba' and 'musharaka' principles violated the Islamic duty to share risk. After this, the issuance of these two types of bonds fell over that year by around 83% and 63% respectively, even at a time when these 'less risky' Islamic finance products should have benefitted markedly from chaos in Western financial systems.

Iran, though, will always issue fully Sharia-compliant bonds, in keeping with its Islamic Republic status. Buyers of these bonds might well, for example, share in the underlying asset of oil flows from selected oil fields, thus sharing risk and reward, and no interest would be made directly in the form of yield payments. Instead, investors would receive periodic payments of their share of profits on the principal amount invested, as laid down in their certificates of ownership from the issuer. When the bonds matured, the sukuk holder would also receive back the principal amount invested. The paper would also carry with it an implicit government guarantee, as they would be issued either by the government itself or by the quasi-sovereign entity the National Iranian Oil Company.

Because of these rigid strictures, the appeal of sukuk – as expressed in pricing and breadth of investor interest – transcends the issue of credit rating, which is normally central to the success and pricing of a conventional bond issue. The Islamic bond universe – which has increased in size from around USD10 billion of total investable assets in 1975 to over an estimated USD115 billion of total investable assets – judges sukuk by their individual Islamic credentials and the underlying assets involved.

Given that the underlying asset in Iran would likely be a share in oil flows from some pre-announced oil fields this would mitigate any concerns over foreign currency credit ratings. There would likely be interest from state-clients of Iran as well as their corporations who would see a premium in participating in the scheme, most notable amongst them Chinese and Russian entities, the Qataris, Malaysia and India, as they would see both the financial appeal and the political leverage holding of the bond may offer them. Based on the dynamics of previous issuances, the spread would need to be about 10-15 basis points higher than Iraq has aimed for. In addition, there is a lot of investable money both in Iran and with Iranians abroad.

As part of its 'One Belt, One Road' initiative, China has also seen a number of sukuk issues from state entities as a key part of its strategy of building a network into the world's main centres of Islamic finance – the Middle East and Southeast Asia - in which Sharia-compliant assets account for as much as a quarter of total banking assets. China already had plans in place before the US withdrawal from the JCPOA to act as a book-runner for Iranian sukuk issues. There were further plans for China to be the coordinator for a new bond issue, structurally designed between it and Iranian risk experts. The Peoples Bank of China (PBOC) would act as sole lead underwriter and principal distributor of the bond, and the structure would involve the Iranian government, or state vehicle, issuing a bond through the PBOC, which would be backed by the Chinese central bank, either in renminbi or another currency pegged at a specific rate to the renminbi. Crucially for broadening out its appeal to as wide a foreign investor pool as possible, the China-run bond would carry with it the option not only to be redeemed in rials but in euros as well. The bond holder could decide on redemption day the currency preferred for repayment, given the prevailing spot rate, so eliminating much of the illiquid currency risk.

Iraq

There are four key things to know about Iraq from which spring all of its problems since the removal by the US of Saddam Hussein in 2003. First, it has greater oil potential than any country in the world, including Saudi Arabia. Second, it has been – and is still – prevented from realising this potential by exceptional levels of endemic corruption at all levels of government, administration and business. Third, it is intimately tied into the dominant neighbour, Iran, through political, economic and military factors. Fourth, it is effectively split into two parts - southern Iraq, governed by the Federal Government of Iraq (FGI) based in Baghdad, and northern Iraq focused on the semi-autonomous Kurdistan Region of Iraq (KRI), governed by the Kurdistan Regional Government (KRG) centred in Erbil. Both sides have been locked in a mutually destructive relationship centred on the Kurdish region being granted full independence.

Oil Reserves Potentially Greater Than Saudi Arabia's

Even more so than Iran, Iraq remains the greatest relatively underdeveloped oil (and gas) frontier both in the Middle East and the world. Officially, it holds a very conservatively estimated 145 billion barrels of proven crude oil reserves (nearly 17% of the Middle East's total, around 8% of the globe's, and the fifth biggest on the planet), plus the 12th largest proven natural gas reserves, at almost 112 trillion cubic feet. Unofficially, as shown in detail below, it is extremely likely that it holds much more of both resources.

Three Huge Hydrocarbons Basins Running Through Iraq

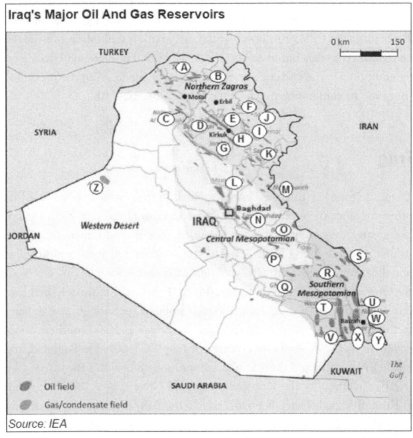

[Chart Key: A = Tawke, B = Shaikan, C (1) = Najma, C (2) = Al Qayyarah, D = Bai Hassan, E = Kirkuk, F = Taq, G = Jambur, H = Khormor, I = ChemChemal, J = Miran, K = Sarqala, L = Mansuriyah, M = Naft Khaneh, N = East Baghdad, O = Badra, P = Ahdab, Q = Gharaf, R = Halfaya, S = Missan Group, T = West Qurna, U = Majnoon, V = Rumaila, W = Nahr Umr, X = Zubair, Y = Siba, Z = Akkas]

Currently, it can relatively easily produce between 4.3-4.7 million bpd of crude (its highest output was 4.83 million bpd), although this is influenced by its OPEC quotas, and it does so at the same world-low lifting cost as

Saudi and Iran: around USD1-2 per barrel excluding capital expenditure or USD4-6 per barrel including capital expenditure.

However, there remain in the Oil Ministry plans which would yield crude oil output of at least 12 million bpd for many years to come on the provisos that it was the recipient of sustained investment by good international oil companies and that this funding actually ended up in oil sector development projects. Such output would easily trump that of any other country – including Russia and Saudi Arabia – except the US.

Amazingly to many, given the relatively advanced state of development across the global oil and gas sector, much of Iraq – north and south – remains comparatively unexplored. In basic geological terms, as delineated by the IEA, there are three main hydrocarbon basins of Iraq, each at a different stage of development, although none particularly advanced by international standards. The first is the 'The Zagros Foldbelt' in the north of Iraq that includes the supergiant Kirkuk reservoir and the other major fields in the KRG area. This foldbelt is close to the Iranian border on the eastern side and continues into Iran itself. The second is the 'Mesopotamian Foredeep Basin', the location for most of Iraq's supergiant fields, which, in turn, also extends into Iran and additionally into Kuwait and Saudi Arabia. The third is the 'Widyan Basin-Interior Platform' to the west and broadly overlapping with the Western Desert that extends into Saudi Arabia. This is also the least explored of these relatively minimally explored three main basins.

In October 2010, Iraq's Oil Ministry increased its figure for the country's proven reserves to 143 billion barrels, almost 25% more than the previous 115 billion barrels. This was then increased to 145 billion barrels. Both of these increases – unlike those notably seen in Saudi Arabia and the UAE in recent years (see above) – did reflect reality. In fact, the current reserves figure may well turn out to be a huge underestimate as, at the same time as producing the first upwards estimate in official reserves figures, the Oil Ministry stated that Iraq's undiscovered resources amounted to around 215 billion barrels. This was also a figure that had been arrived at in a 1997 detailed study by respected oil and gas firm Petrolog.

Even this, though, did not include the parts of northern Iraq in the semi-autonomous region of Kurdistan, administered by the KRG. Prior to the recent rise in exploration activity in the KRG area, more than half of the exploratory wells in Iraq had been drilled prior to 1962, a time when technical limits and a low oil price gave a much tighter definition of a commercially successful well than would be the case today, as highlighted by the IEA. Based on the previous limited exploration and development of oil fields in the KRG area, the proven oil reserves figure was first put at around 4 billion barrels. This was subsequently upgraded by the KRG to around 45 billion barrels but, again, this may well be a very conservative estimate of the oil resources there.

Even Conservative Estimates Show Huge Further Potential

Iraq Oil Resources By Region And Supergiant Field (in Billion Barrels)					
	Proven reserves, end-2017	Ultimately recoverable resources	Cumulative production, end-2017	Remaining recoverable resources	Remaining % of URR
Southern Mesopotamian	113	164	25	139	85%
West Qurna	47	55	3	53	95%
Rumaila	17	35	16	19	55%
Majnoon	13	15	1	15	96%
Zubair	7	11	3	8	70%
Central Mesopotamian	13	19	0	18	98%
East Baghdad	9	10	0	10	98%
Northern Zagros Fold Belt	23	62	19	42	69%
Kirkuk	7	25	16	8	34%
Western Desert	0	1	0	1	100%
Total Iraq	149	246	45	201	82%

Note: Proven reserves are approximately broken down by basin, based on information provided by the Iraqi Ministry of Oil, supplemented with company presentations. Figures include crude oil and natural gas liquids. URR = ultimately recoverable resources

Source: IEA

Even using the most conservative figures, Iraq had produced only around 15-20% of its ultimately recoverable oil resources back in 2017, compared with 23% for the Middle East as a whole, according to the IEA. This figure for Iraq has not significantly changed since then. Further exploration is highly likely to add substantially to the proven reserves figure over the coming decades, particularly given the high success rate of drilled prospects in Iraq. For example, less than half of the potential hydrocarbon-bearing geological prospects identified by geophysical means in Iraq have been drilled but, of these, oil has been found in 65% of them. In sum, the IEA puts the level of ultimately recoverable resources at around 246 billion barrels (crude and natural gas liquids).

Oil Production Could Rise Significantly

Given the severe underestimates of its oil and gas reserves and the relative lack of exploration and development in Iraq's oil and gas sectors, compared to its regional peers, it is reasonable to expect production of both resources to rise, and Iraq is focused currently on executing this, albeit with the principal focus on oil for the time being.

Iraq's crude oil production increased from 2.4 million bpd in 2010 to around 4.5+ million bpd on average (excluding the OPEC+ mandated quotas) in 2020/21. This made it the second largest crude oil producer in OPEC and brought back into view a trend that prompted many oil market players to believe that Baghdad's much-vaunted 'realistic' production target of 9 million bpd might again be attainable.

This occurred despite comments in 2018 and 2019 from the then-head of Iraq's State Oil Marketing Organisation (SOMO), Falah Alamri, that the country had temporarily slashed its oil output targets for the end of 2020, from 8.4-9.0 million bpd to 5.4-6.0 mbpd. Later in 2020, though, Iraq's then-new Oil Minister, Ihsan Ismaael, stated that the country was targeting oil production capacity of 7 million bpd by 2025 and, by the same year, targeting oil export capacity of up to 6 million bpd (from the 2020/21 level of around 3.8 million bpd). Through 2022, Iraq was again able to achieve a mean average crude oil output of around 4.5 million bpd.

All these figures fall within the parameters of the government-sponsored report – the Integrated National Energy Strategy (INES), launched in 2013 – which formulated the three forward oil production profiles that still form the basis of the Iraq government's energy plans today.

At the high end of the spectrum, the INES' best-case scenario is for crude oil production capacity to increase to 13 million bpd (at that point by 2017), peaking at around that level until 2023 and finally gradually declining to around 10 million bpd for a long-sustained period thereafter. The mid-range production scenario is for Iraq to reach 9 million bpd (at that point by 2020). The worst-case INES scenario is for production to reach 6 mbpd (at that point by 2020), which would still mean Iraq overtaking Canada as the world's fourth largest crude oil producer.

Still A Huge Scope For Increases In Crude Oil Production

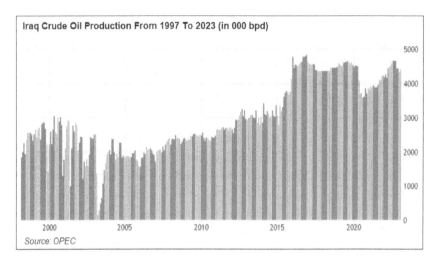

Iraq Crude Oil Production From 1997 To 2023 (in 000 bpd)

Source: OPEC

Achieving these targets, though, will depend on three key factors. One is the building out of the Common Seawater Supply Project (CSSP). Another is the improvement of political relations between the Federal Government of Iraq (FGI) in the south of Iraq and the KRG in the north. And the final one – which is more general in its terms but critical to address – is reducing the level of corruption at play in all Iraq's business sectors.

Endemic Corruption Constrains Oil And Gas Ambitions

It is impossible to explain the vast discrepancy between Iraq's massive oil and gas reserves and its permanently deleterious financial state without examining the endemic corruption that permeates the country but that is particularly focused on its most lucrative business sector – the oil and gas industry. There are too many corruption cases involving Iraqi and international oil and gas companies to go into in this book but, in broad terms, the central role that corruption (and most significantly, huge graft payments at every level of administration) plays in Iraq on a day-to-day basis have been characterised by the highly respected independent international non-governmental independent organisation, Transparency International (TI).

In various of its 'Corruption Perceptions Index' publications Iraq normally features in the worst 10 out of 180 countries for the scale and scope of corruption. 'Massive embezzlement, procurement scams, money laundering, oil smuggling and widespread bureaucratic bribery that have led the country to the bottom of international corruption rankings, fuelled political violence and hampered effective state building and service delivery,' TI states. Although acknowledging that the country's anti-corruption initiatives and framework have expanded since 2005, TI adds that they still fail to provide a strong and comprehensive integrity system. 'Political interference in anti-corruption bodies and politicisation of corruption issues, weak civil society, insecurity, lack of resources and incomplete legal provisions severely limit the government's capacity to efficiently curb soaring corruption,' it concludes.

What this means in practical terms is that many high-profile international oil companies (IOCs) are reluctant to get involved in Iraq for fear of the potential reputational damage that being involved in such a corrupt business environment may bring for either themselves or for their governments (if they are a neo-state corporate proxy). They are also concerned about the effect of the never-ending graft payments on their profit margins (or the lack of any progress on projects if they refuse to dish out these graft payments). The company-specific examples, as mentioned, are too numerous to go into here but they pale into insignificance when compared to the wholesale rape of Iraq's finances by its own government and related entities for many years.

Staggering from every perspective was a statement made in 2015 by then Oil Minister – and later Prime Minister of Iraq – Adil Abdul Mahdi that Iraq 'lost USD14,448,146,000' (that is 14 'billion') from the beginning of 2011 up to the end of 2014 as cash 'compensation' payments supposedly to international oil companies. 'Cash compensation' includes what to many people (oil and gas industry experts included) would be classed as bribery and corruption payments that ended up either in the hands of Iraqi officials, or brokers of various exploration and development deals, or others involved in these deals. To put this into some sort of understandable perspective: if this amount in dollar bills was laid end to end then it would stretch from the Earth to the Moon nearly six times over.

The following describes how it was done at this scale. From around 2002, the key clause of Iraq's standard long-term service contract (LTSC) that related to compensation payments – both when they should be paid and how much – was Article 12.5. This asserted that compensation related to reduced oil production levels was allowed for three reasons: first, to minimise associated gas wastage; second, for any failure of oil and gas transporters in receiving net production at the transfer point through no fault of the contractor or operator; and third, due to the government itself imposing such a reduction. In turn, according to Article 12.5, compensation payments could be made in three ways: a revised field production schedule; extension of the duration of the contract; and/or actual cash payments to IOCs.

However, on the basis of the standard LTSC contracts, there are two additional factors that need to be considered in assessing and estimating the USD14 billion-plus of lost income. First, the incremental production above the base-line production and second, the 'net' remuneration fee. In the case of the former, nine major oilfields were covered by the LTSCs awarded in the first round of bidding: Zubair, West Qurna 1, Rumaila, Missan, Majnoon, Halfaya, Garraf, Badra and Al-Ahdab. These had a combined base-line production in 2011 of around 1.6 million bpd. Therefore, the theoretical total baseline production for these fields from the end of 2011 to the end of 2014 (totalling three whole years) is just over 1.75 billion barrels. If one subtracts a natural rate of production decline of 5% for each year (totalling just under 263 million barrels) then the figure is around 1.5 billion barrels. On the second matter of compensation for these barrels: according to the concluded contracts, the remuneration fees would give a simple average of around USD2.5 per barrel for the nine major oilfields covered. However, the weighted average of the remuneration fees (by plateau production of related fields) was around USD1.90 per barrel.

From these gross remuneration fees contained in the contracts, the share of the State partner and income tax and would be deductible. And so, crucially, would be 'the accounting factor used in calculations'. This factor – which 'solely relates to expenses of various kinds' has never been disclosed by the Oil Ministry but it is key to the merging of public funds with private ones. It saw its true genesis in 2009 when IOCs in many cases were asked to make large upfront payments as part of their bid, which would supposedly be repaid at a later date.

These later dates were broadly understood by the IOCs to be at points after the initial production thresholds were reached but there were no regular payment schedules incorporated into many of these contracts by the Iraqi authorities, which instead viewed them as being payable on an *ad hoc* basis. Some of these sums related to 'infrastructure support payments' on a per barrel basis of output relating not just to general field maintenance but also incorporating the 'development costs and security of the fields'. All of these were billed separately from the remuneration per barrel fee, all of them were liable for payment by the Iraqi government and all of them were highly opaque in their terms of reference. In practical terms, the scale of these payments was often at least as great as the headline per barrel remuneration fee itself and, according to Iraqi sources, 'ended up – presumably unwittingly by the IOCs – as being just massive bribery payments.'

So bad, so pervasive, and so lacking in any idea of the 'greater good' is this corruption that it even brought to halt a cornerstone of Iraq's ability to defend itself, with the suspension in 2020 of the F-16 fighter plane programme – that was a key part of the US-led coalition's operations against ISIS – due to rampant corruption at the Balad Air Base. As brought to light by local news reports, an extremely sizeable portion of the hundreds of millions of dollars over the years that should have been spent on maintaining the F-16 fleet instead ended up in bank accounts of all layers of management involved in the programme locally. So large a portion was stolen that by the middle of 2020 only seven jets out of the fleet – just 20% of the total – were still able to fly without serious risk of crashing.

The Common Seawater Supply Project

Iraq has the resources to become the Middle East's top crude oil producer – easily overtaking Saudi Arabia in that regard – and even outstripping Russia. This, though, will require – in addition to dealing with corruption and settling the ongoing problem with Kurdistan – the roll-out of the Common Seawater Supply Project (CSSP).

This project involves taking and treating seawater from the Persian Gulf and then transporting it via pipelines to oil production facilities for the purposes of maintaining pressure in oil reservoirs to optimise the longevity and output of fields. The basic plan for the CSSP is that it will be used initially to supply around six million bpd of water to at least five southern Basra fields and one in Maysan Province, and then built out for use in further fields.

The Key To Further Significant Oil Production Increases Is The CSSP

Iraq's Common Seawater Supply Project

Source: CH2M Hill

Both the longstanding stalwart fields of Kirkuk and Rumaila – the former beginning production in the 1920s and the latter in the 1950s, with both having produced around 80% of Iraq's cumulative oil production – require major ongoing water injection. The reservoir pressure at the former dropped significantly after output of only around 5% of the oil in place (OIP). Rumaila, in the meantime, produced more than 25% of its OIP before water injection was required because its main reservoir formation (at least its southern part) connects to a very large natural aquifer that has helped to push the oil out of the reservoir. Although the water requirements for most of Iraq's oilfields fall between these two cases, the needs for oilfield injection are highest in southern Iraq, in which water resources are also the least available.

To reach and then sustain Iraq's future crude oil production targets over any meaningful period, the country will have total water injection needs equating to around 2% of the combined average flows of the Tigris and Euphrates rivers or 6% of their combined flow during the low season. While withdrawals at these levels might appear to be manageable, these water sources will also have to continue to satisfy other, much larger, end-use sectors, including agriculture.

Informative in terms of the potential timeline for the completion of the Common Seawater Supply Project is the case of Saudi Aramco's Qurayyah Seawater Plant Expansion. The 2 million bpd expansion of an existing facility took nearly four years from the awarding of the front-end engineering, procurement and design contract – in May 2005 – to the time that water first began to flow in early 2009.

ExxonMobil's Risk/Reward Analysis Led To Withdrawal

There were always only two companies with a realistic chance of taking on the giant CSSP work: US supermajor ExxonMobil and its nearest Chinese equivalent, the China National Petroleum Corporation (CNPC). However, it was understood by all involved that only the US company had all of the technology, equipment and expertise required to complete the entirety of the CSSP on its own, with CNPC being involved for various geopolitical reasons already mentioned and for funding. Early in 2018, though, negotiations between Iraq's Oil Ministry and ExxonMobil over the CSSP broke down, leaving the road to complete the project unclear.

ExxonMobil had originally been brought into the project in 2010 when it was first announced that it would take the lead in co-ordinating initial studies for the project. At that point, Baghdad was looking to raise its oil production capacity to 12 million bpd by 2018, to overtake Saudi Arabia. ILF Consulting Engineers, which carried out the front-end engineering and design for the project in 2014, estimated the cost at USD12 billion, based on treating 12.5 million bpd of seawater transported to six oilfields.

ExxonMobil was removed in 2012 when negotiations fell through – again owing to basic problems with the contract – and was replaced by the Iraqi state-run South Oil Co. (SOC). The US firm then resumed talks with the Oil Ministry in 2015 in partnership with CNPC. At that point, the CSSP had been folded into the broader 'South Iraq Integrated Project' (SIIP). The SIIP, in addition to building the infrastructure related to maintaining pressure at reservoirs, also included corollary projects to construct oil pipelines, storage facilities and pumping stations. Also, as part of luring ExxonMobil back into the negotiations, the US firm was assured that the new contract would not be of the straightforward, and deeply unpopular, Technical Service Contract (TSC) variety and was further given rights to develop at least two southern oilfields - Nahr Bin Umar, and Artawi.

Iraq Makes An Already Complicated Project Even Worse

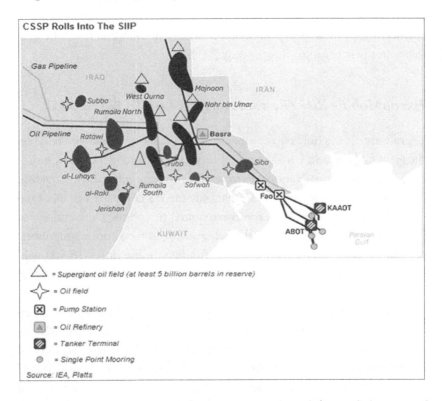

The central problem for ExxonMobil was that the risk/reward elements of the contract were profoundly unbalanced. In terms of the general risk/reward matrix that formed the basis of these negotiations, there were three key elements: 'cohesion', 'security' and 'streamlining'. Cohesion related to ensuring that building out the facilities connected to the CSSP were completed in full and in order. Security related not just to the on-the-ground security of personnel but also to the soundness of the basic business and legal practices involved in the agreement. Streamlining meant that any deal should continue as had been laid out in the agreement, regardless of any change in government in Iraq.

On the first point, hurdles had already arisen on several projects before in southern Iraq relating to the approval of contracts for service work, such as building new pipelines and drilling wells, as well as for obtaining visas for workers and customs clearance for vital technical equipment. Concerns surrounding such issues were shared by ExxonMobil, as a lot of what needed to happen in order make the project progress properly would be in the hands of people who were less concerned about it working than about what they could personally pocket in return for allowing it to occur.

The second part of the risk/reward matrix was also complicated by the systemic corruption pervading virtually all elements of Iraq's business environment, particularly in the oil and gas sector where 95% of all the country's revenues originate, as underlined earlier. This lack of a meaningful legal structure relating to the origination, monitoring and administration of business agreements would have opened ExxonMobil up to a plethora of problems in the future, especially when the third part of the risk/reward matrix was factored in.

This third major risk in the risk/reward matrix was that many leading politicians on the opposite side of whoever is prime minister at any given time in Iraq might not be inclined to stand by the decisions relating to the oil and gas industry made by the previous administration. Even more dangerous for ExxonMobil – and any other major Western IOC attempting to operate in Iraq – is that any realignment of Iraq with the US that had been seen from time to time could have been reversed at any point in the future. At such a point, any questionable practices that ExxonMobil might have been forced into to move the CSSP forward could well have been publicised across the world if Iraq's key sponsor, Iran decided it wanted to embarrass the US government, with ExxonMobil portrayed as a corporate proxy of Washington.

China Uses SIIP To Pursue Exploitative Contracts

The only way back for ExxonMobil was to have a contract designed by Western risk experts, drawn up by Western lawyers and administered by Western accountants, more along the lines of Iran's Integrated Petroleum

Contract (IPC), which better balanced the risks and rewards for participating companies. Given the practical costs involved in mitigating these risks for ExxonMobil, such an agreement would have to have been more front-loaded in terms of increasing payments, and therefore reducing the initial cost burden for the US company, than could have been provided under the existing TSC model. PetroChina, the listed arm of state-owned CNPC, came to a similar sort of arrangement on its Halfaya oilfield development with the Oil Ministry, which effectively lowered its upfront costs liabilities by increasing the level of investment capital repaid to it earlier. Given all of these factors, then, ExxonMobil had little choice but to withdraw from the CSSP.

CNPC, then, was the only player left in the flagship project. Despite the Iraqi Oil Ministry knowing perfectly well that it did not have the required technology, expertise or engineering capabilities required to complete the project to the top specifications necessary, it was assured by Beijing that CNPC was in the process of 'acquiring' all the additional elements that it was lacking to complete the CSSP to the required standard 'over time'. What the Chinese wanted to do – and what they achieved with ExxonMobil's withdrawal from the CSSP – was to gain first refusal on all other major oil and gas fields in Iraq, often at the expense of the US.

A case in point was highlighted in late 2020 when Chinese oil giants, CNPC and the China National Offshore Oil Corporation (CNOOC) were reportedly 'considering acquiring' ExxonMobil's 32.7% stake in Iraq's supergiant West Qurna 1 oil (and gas) field. These reports completely missed the point that China was already dominant at the site, not only through the 32.7% stake held by PetroChina but also through the gradual acquisition of a range of huge 'contract-only' awards made to Chinese companies for work on the field.

These included the USD121 million engineering contract to upgrade the facilities that were used to extract gas during crude oil production to the China Petroleum Engineering & Construction Corp (CPECC). These reports also missed the point that the second that ExxonMobil made it clear that it would not go ahead with the CSSP, the door was left open for China – in the shape of CNPC – to take over that project too, as well as any other major project that Beijing wanted, as part of the trade-off for taking on the thankless and expensive CSSP work agreed back in 2010.

However, given the delicate position of China-US relations at that point – especially with the Trade War still unresolved – it was thought wise by Beijing to not come out with big headline announcements of Chinese companies taking over major oil and gas field developments. Rather, it was thought apposite to just do this via a series of supposedly standalone individual contracts for specific work projects, such as engineering-only, maintenance-only, drilling-only and so on, which is exactly what has occurred, including at West Qurna 1.

Exactly the same 'contract-only' model was used in Iraq's massive Majnoon oil field. It was this field that was the focus of the extremely similar announcement that two major new drilling contracts had been signed: one with China's Hilong Oil Service & Engineering Company to drill 80 wells at a cost of USD54 million and the other with the Iraq Drilling Company to drill 43 wells at a cost of USD255 million. In reality, it was China that was in charge of both, having given the funds required to the Iraq Drilling Company as a 'fee' for its own participation.

Also located very close to Basra is the supergiant Majnoon oilfield, one of world's largest oil sites, holding an estimated 38 billion barrels of oil in place. At that point it was producing around 240,000 bpd but longer term the original production target figures for the then-Shell-led consortium still stood. The first target was for 175,000 bpd (which had already been reached), with plateau production of 1.8 million bpd scheduled for some point in the 2030s. West Qurna 1, in the meantime, was producing around 465,000 bpd, with an original plateau target of 2.825 million bpd having been re-negotiated down to 1.6 million bpd by some point in the 2030s.

The deal secured by China for Majnoon – and the same terms were to be applied to West Qurna 1 – involved a 25-year contract but, critically, one that would only officially start two years after the signing date. This would allow CNPC (or CNOOC, or any other Chinese entity involved) to recoup more profits on average per year and less upfront investment. The per barrel payments to China were the higher of either the mean average of the 18-month spot price for crude oil produced or the past six months' mean average price. The deal terms also included at least a 10% discount to China for at least five years on the value of the oil it recovered. Finally, it involved China receiving a 30% discount to the lowest mean one-year average market price at the key gas pricing hubs for the gas it captured, as this is the deal that had already been agreed for CPECC on West Qurna 1.

Oil Export Infrastructure Improvements In Sight

In the last week of 2020, Baghdad announced plans to boost southern crude oil export capacity by 72% within the following three years. In this vein it signed a USD2.625 billion deal with South Korea's Daewoo Engineering & Construction (Daewoo E&C) to build out the Al-Fao main export depot to the south of Basra.

In broad terms, the Oil Ministry intended to increase the storage capacity at Al-Fao to 24 storage tanks, each of 58 thousand cubic metres (around 365,000 barrels), for a total capacity of around 8.76 million barrels. This would add to the six storage tanks already in place at that point and was to all intents and purposes a reiteration – and expansion – of the original crude oil export infrastructure build-out plan that was about to be launched before ISIS began to run riot across Iraq from 2006. At that time, the Oil Ministry had realistic plans in place to construct at least a further 12 full-time operational storage tanks and blending facilities in and around Al-Fao by the end of 2016. The longer-term target remained the 24 storage tanks and 8 million bpd+ targets above.

Although Iraq's crude oil export routes to the north and into mainland Europe via the Turkish port of Ceyhan appear theoretically the better export options, the practical political considerations involved render the theory obsolete for the time being. The original Kirkuk to Ceyhan Pipeline, also called the Iraq-Turkey Pipeline (ITP), consisted of two pipes, which had a nameplate capacity of 1.6 million bpd combined (1.1 million bpd for the 46-inch diameter pipe and 0.5 million bpd for the 40 inch one).

Even before ISIS entered the picture, though, this pipeline was subject to repeated and ongoing attacks by various militant groups in the region. This led to the KRG overseeing the completion of a single side track, from the Taq field through Khurmala. This also runs into the Kirkuk-Ceyhan pipeline in the border town of Fishkhabur, with a nameplate capacity of 0.7 million bpd, which was then increased to 1 million bpd. Further complicated by the ongoing disagreement with the KRG over the budget-for-oil deal originally struck in 2014 (analysed in depth shortly), Baghdad instead planned to renovate and re-open the Federal Government-owned oil pipeline section that runs from Kirkuk to Ceyhan, bypassing any Kurd control, before its finances dried up. Such a build-out of export facilities in Al-Fao aligns with the fact that virtually all export efforts in the Federal

Government of Iraq running from Baghdad are focused on the Basra facility in the south.

Not Much Is Required To Make Iraq The Top Oil Superpower

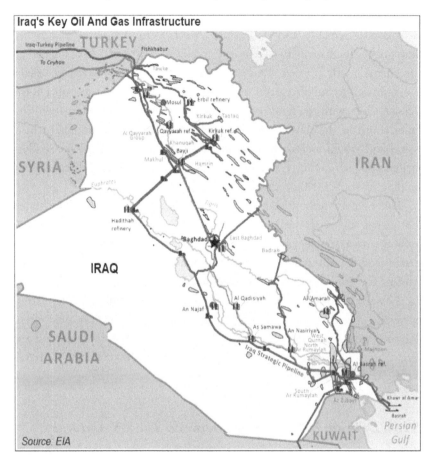

To get to Basra, oil is moved via internal pipelines, but these have previously been found to be unsound and in need of upgrading. From there, oil makes its way into the Al-Fao main export depot, where it is stored and blended. Here again, though, there has not been adequate investment and anything over current levels of oil coming in has not been sustainable, meaning that oil supplies have been backed up in the oil fields themselves, which has led to production bottlenecks. Previously, this also held up the roll-out of the Iraq's new oil grade – Basrah Medium – that was to have added to the revenue streams generated by the existing Basrah Heavy and Basrah Light.

Once past Al-Fao, the situation is slightly more efficient as Al-Fao pumps the oil to the single-point moorings (SPMs), and there has been some expansion in the capacity of the existing offshore terminals at Khor al-Amaya (KAAOT) and Al-Basrah (ABOT). In the same context of dramatically increasing its oil export capabilities, Iraq late in 2020 signed an agreement with Dutch marine construction firm, Royal Boskalis Westminster, to build an artificial island south of the ABOT terminal in the Persian Gulf, with the new artificial island project to be located 4 nautical miles south of the ABOT. An export terminal would be attached to the island and would include four jetties. These, in turn, would have loading facilities for up to four very large crude carriers at a time, each capable of holding up to 320,000 deadweight tonnage.

This contract announcement came shortly after the Oil Ministry stated that discussions were well advanced with BP and ENI to run a USD400 million project to replace two old seabed pipelines, including one that would feed the other main offshore terminal at the KAAOT terminal. The tenders for the broader plans to add another 1.8 million bpd of pipeline capacity from Al-Fao to the ABOT terminal were preliminarily planned to have taken place towards the end of 2020. They were, however, postponed due to the outbreak of COVID-19. On its own, when completed, the Sea Line 3 export pipeline project would add at least 700,000 bpd to Iraq's southern export capacity.

Iraq's Delicate Balancing Act Between The US And Iran

The influence of Iran over Iraq does not begin or end at shared oil and gas fields or co-operation over re-branding and moving Iranian hydrocarbons products as Iraqi ones. Iran also has a long history of wielding enormous influence in Iraq via financing projects across the country, through the presence of pro-Iranian political groups, and by dint of its militias.

Perhaps the most recent significant example of this influence was seen in the aftermath of the independence referendum in Iraq's semi-autonomous region of Kurdistan in the north of the country, which received well over 90% of votes for independence, as analysed briefly in the first section of this book and again in full shortly. It is also seen in the very touchy subject – as far as the US is involved – of the ongoing waivers granted for Iraq to import gas and electricity from Iran.

Former senior intelligence operative and later Iraq's Prime Minister Mustafa al-Kadhimi spent much of 2020 trying to maintain his exceptionally dangerous balancing act between Iran (and its sponsors, China and Russia) and the US. On the one hand, Iraq maintained its multi-layered relationship with Middle East powerhouse, Iran, enforced by Tehran through its ongoing on-the-ground presence of political, economic and military proxies. On the other hand, Iraq has a shorter but nonetheless highly eventful history with the US, which had for years demanded an increase in its own on-the-ground presence in the country, particularly relating to its oil and gas sectors, in return for not sanctioning Iraq and giving it financial support.

The immediate concern of al-Kadhimi during 2020 was to secure sufficient funding from the US to avert another round of extensive protests, violence, bloodshed and death. The disastrous 2020 Oil Price War instigated by the Saudis pushed Iraq's financing even more firmly into the red. Oil-related revenues fell by nearly 50%, with oil-related revenues still accounting for at least 90% of all of Iraq's government budget. Its finances were further hurt by the enduring effects of the COVID-19 pandemic and by ongoing arguments with the government of the semi-autonomous region of Kurdistan in the north over oil-for-budget disbursements. These factors forced Baghdad into proposing delaying foreign debt payments, introducing salary cuts of 60% for various state sector employees and reducing all non-essential spending.

It also pushed Iraq into temporarily producing much more oil than its OPEC+ production quota, meaning that it would have to make up for this overshoot by producing less in the future. This, in turn, meant a further reduction in its already-decimated state revenues. This cash crunch could not have come at a worse time as, towards the latter half of 2020, al-Kadhimi needed to come up with at least IQD12 trillion (USD10 billion) just to pay the salaries of more than four million employees, retirees, state beneficiaries and the food relief for low-income families. These groups together constitute the majority of households in Iraq, and it was believed in senior Iraq government circles that any failure to pay any of these obligations could have resulted in the sort of widespread protests and bloodshed that occurred at the end of 2019.

It was little wonder, then, that al-Kadhimi did the rounds in Washington in the middle of 2020 looking for money and willing to promise the US anything in return. Top of the list was to put more distance – economically, militarily, and politically – between Iraq and Iran. Matters in this regard had reached yet another crunch point for the US in 2020, with the flip-flopping of Iraq's dealings with Iran that brought Baghdad to the brink of being sanctioned by the US itself. Specifically, having looked on as Iran was able to sell its oil in vast quantities through Iraq's export channels, launch attacks against US military targets in Iraq and provide financing routes for money into and out of Iran, the US had finally had enough.

Instead of the rolling 90- or 120- day waivers granted by Washington for Iraq to continue to import Iranian electricity and natural gas in the past, the US granted a waiver of just 30 days in April 2020, its shortest ever. At the accompanying press conference, US State Department spokeswoman Morgan Ortagus also pointedly announced new sanctions against 20 Iran- and Iraq-based entities that were cited as funnelling money to Iran's Islamic Revolutionary Guards Corps' (IRGC) elite Quds Force. This Force functions in large part as Iran's chief foreign intelligence operation, as well as its most zealous military unit, having been built up and led by General Qassem Soleimani until his assassination by the US on 3 January 2020.

According to Ortagus, these 20 entities had been exploiting Iraq's dependence on Iran as an electricity and gas source by smuggling Iranian petroleum through the Iraqi port of Umm Qasr and money laundering through Iraqi front companies, among other sanctions-busting activities. Prior to this 30-day only waiver being granted, the US had originally granted an initial 45-day waiver to Iraq after the US re-imposed sanctions on Iranian energy exports in November 2018.

This was followed by another five waivers – two 90-day waivers in a row followed by two 120-day waivers in a row in June and October 2019 and then a 45-day waiver in February 2020 before the US specifically asked that Iraq show signs that it was reducing its imports of Iranian gas and power to meet its electricity demand. Clearly these were not forthcoming, hence the 30-day waiver in April 2020. At that point, the White House made it clear that it had been down the same road before with Pakistan.

The parallels between Iraq and Pakistan from the US perspective went beyond just money, as former US President Donald Trump himself highlighted. In Pakistan, the government had long pretended to help the US in the fight against Al-Qaeda but at the same time Pakistan's Inter-Services Intelligence agency (ISI) offered all the help it could to Osama bin Laden, including housing him in a very large compound in Abbottabad just a short journey away from the Pakistan Military Academy.

In a similar vein, at the beginning of January 2020, Iranian surface-to-surface missiles hit two Iraqi military bases housing US troops. Following this, Trump said that he would impose sanctions directly on Iraq if the US military was forced out of the country by further such incidents. Early in 2020, though, 30 107-mm Russian-made Katyusha rockets were fired at the US allied Camp Taji military base north of Baghdad, killing three service members, two of them Americans and one British, according to US and Iraq military officials. This attack was in the same style as the rocket attacks on 4 January on the US's Balad Air Base near Baghdad and on the Green Zone. All of them were reportedly Iran-sponsored retaliation for the assassination of IRGC and Al Quds Major General Qassem Soleimani.

Although these were the most high-profile attacks on US assets in Iraq to that point, and only the 4 January attack was cited as a direct act of retaliation for Soleimani's killing by Iran, there were at least 15 further attacks on US military and neo-military personnel (and those of its allies) in Iraq by Iran proxies in 2020 alone, according to US military sources.

To avoid wider sanctions at that point, al-Kadhimi promised the US that it would allow a raft of in-principle agreed contracts with US companies to finally go ahead, with a substantial presence of US 'security personnel' on the ground to safeguard these interests. This, the argument ran, would help to put distance between Iraq and Iran and this was a key reason why Iraq received a new 120-day waiver in May 2020 from the US for its continued importation of electricity and gas from Iran.

Just ahead of al-Kadhimi's arrival in Washington in August 2020, then, five US companies – Chevron, General Electric (GE), Honeywell International, Baker Hughes and Stellar Energy - signed agreements with the Iraqi government for deals aimed at boosting Iraq's energy independence from Iran, worth at least USD8 billion. Among the most noteworthy of these, according to the relevant statements, was that Chevron was to examine the potential for exploration work in the long-side-lined Nassiriya oilfield, estimated to hold about 4.4 billion barrels of crude. GE, meanwhile, said it had signed two new agreements with the Iraqi Ministry of Electricity valued at over USD1.2 billion to undertake maintenance programs across key power plants in the country and to bolster its transmission network. Honeywell also said that it was negotiating a deal that would involve the development of the Ratawi oil field, the construction of a gas processing hub and new electricity generation.

However, there was no reason to expect any of these new deals with US companies to come to fruition, any more than ExxonMobil's much-vaunted and much-delayed participation did in Iraq's crucial Common Seawater Supply Project analysed earlier in this section.

Iraq-Fronted Regional Power Network With Iran Central

It was no coincidence that just over a month after Israel and the United Arab Emirates declared that they would normalise relations and Israel, Bahrain and Morocco did the same, Iraq announced that it had signed new oil deals with Jordan and Lebanon, with extra elements to be attached to them later. A core strategy in Iran's effort to build out its influence across the Shia Crescent countries in the Middle East and beyond is to build out a pan-Middle Eastern power grid with Tehran at the centre. This is based around oil, gas and electricity supplies, which allows for not just the installation of permanent infrastructure linking one country to another but also for the on-site presence of permanent 'technical and security' personnel, many of which are already – or will be – Iranian and Chinese.

In just the same way that Russia's huge level of gas supplies to Europe gave it immense power across that continent up until changes to that arrangement were made after the invasion of Ukraine, so Iran's electricity and other power supplies will give it enduring power over the Middle East. 'Roping in' potential countries into this notion initially through a less overtly threatening proposition – Iran's 'front agent' Iraq offering oil supplies, for example – is a standard tactic for Tehran to achieve its aim, and deals announced between Iraq and Jordan and Iraq and Lebanon are illustrative in this context.

Jordan was always a natural contender to be drawn into the alternative Iraq-fronted Iran-led alliance, given its strong historical anti-Israeli bias.

Jordan's current king, Abdullah II, is the son of King Hussein, a key leader in the 1967 Six-Day War waged by Jordan, Syria, Egypt and Iraq against Israel. He also supported the 1973 Yom Kippur War, also again principally involving Egypt and Syria fighting Israel, although it additionally involved expeditionary forces from a wide range of Arab states, including Jordan and Iraq. Egypt, for its part, although flirting with the US over the years for monetary gain primarily and since 2014 for the US's assistance in shoring up the power of former field marshal and now President, Abdel Fattah el-Sisi, has long regarded itself as being a leader of the Arab world, along with Syria. Slightly shifting this pro-Arab ideology to a point where it coincides in large part with the ideas involved in the Shia crescent is seen as a not insurmountable objective in Tehran.

Securing Jordan in this alliance was the initial aim of the oil deal that was resuscitated by Iraq and although the deal might appear innocuous it is not. The formal announcement was the extension of a previous contract that had lapsed at the end of December 2020 for Jordan to import crude oil from Iraq. Jordan's Energy Minister, Hala Zawati, stated in July 2020 that the Kingdom would resume imports of at least 10,000 bpd of Iraq crude oil via tankers at a discount of USD16 to the Brent price, reflecting the transport costs and quality differential. These supplies came from Baiji in Iraq direct to the Jordan Petroleum Refinery Company (JPRC), constituting around 7% of Jordan's daily demand. The original deal that had been struck in 2006 mandated a discount to Brent of USD18 pb, on the basis that Jordan bore the transport costs between Kirkuk in northern Iraq and Zarqa in the Kingdom and presaged a broader build-out of energy ties between the two countries.

Underpinning this agreement, though, were broader discussions about the future relationship between Jordan and Iraq and these resulted in a contract being signed to connect the electric power grids of the two countries. By extension, this would provide a direct link between Jordan and Iran (which by that point had signed a two-year deal with Iraq to supply it with electricity, the longest such deal between the two countries). Iran's landmark two-year deal to continue to supply vital electricity to Iraq (both directly from the grid and indirectly via gas supplies that are used in power plants) was regarded by both countries as being important enough to their broader regional strategy to risk being further sanctioned by the US, which is precisely what happened. With Iranian energy accounting for 30-40% of the electricity consumed in Iraq, depending on the season, the US had been pushing Iraq towards committing to reducing these imports from its neighbour prior to the visit of Iraq's Prime Minister, Mustafa al-Kadhimi, to Washington in August 2020, as mentioned above, but Iraq's assurances to reduce its dependence on Iran came to nothing.

Prior to the meetings between al-Kadhimi and senior officials in Washington, there were various comments from White House officials along the lines of being pleased to see Iraq pushing for a regional energy network – including links across the GCC states (Bahrain, Kuwait, Oman, Qatar, Saudi Arabia and the United Arab Emirates) – as this might reduce Iraq's dependence on Iran and help bring Iraq into the US sphere of influence. But it subsequently appeared that the US had got it round the wrong way: it was Iran that was pushing Iraq into this to bring the same states, including Saudi, out of the US sphere of influence.

In this context, just a month or so before Iraq Prime Minister Mustafa al-Kadhimi's visit to Washington in 2020, Iran's Energy Minister Reza Ardakanian stated that Iran and Iraq's power grids had become fully synchronised to provide electricity to both countries by dint of the new Amarah-Karkheh 400-KV transmission line stretching over 73 kilometres. This also 'paves the way for increasing energy exports to Iraq in the near future, from the current 1,361 megawatts per day now', he said. He added that Iranian and Iraqi dispatching centres were fully connected in Baghdad, the power grids were seamlessly interlinked, and that Iran had signed a three-year co-operation agreement with Iraq 'to help the country's power industry in different aspects.'

At the same time, it was announced by the Iranian Electrical Power Equipment Manufacturing and Provision Company that Iran's electricity exports to other neighbouring countries in the previous Iranian calendar year (ended on 19 March 2020) reached over 8 billion kilowatt-hours (kWh), a mean average increase of 27.6% year on year. So far, the countries receiving power from Iran's grid are Armenia, Azerbaijan, Pakistan, Afghanistan and the Nakhchivan Autonomous Republic, plus, of course, Iraq. This network does not include the parallel network connections that Iran is consolidating in terms both of direct electricity and gas exchanges, which further includes Turkmenistan and Turkey.

In the meantime, Iraq's Electricity Minister, Majid Mahdi Hantoush, announced that not only is Iraq currently working on connecting its grid with Jordan's electricity networks through a 300-kilometre-line – a project that will be finished shortly – but also plans have been finalised for the completion of Iraq's electricity connection with Egypt within the next three years. This, in turn, he added, would be part of the overall project to establish a joint Arab electricity market.

Initial Plans Have Been Tilted To Put Iran At The Centre

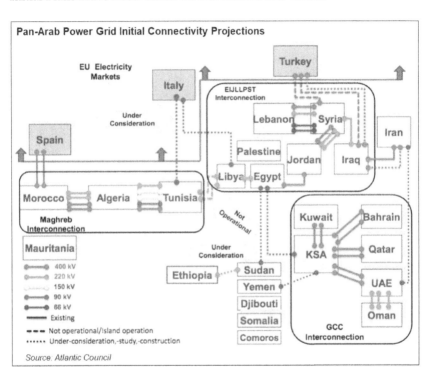

Specifically, under the electricity deal signed between Iraq and Jordan, the Kingdom will provide Iraq with 1,000 gigawatt (GW) hours per year in the first phase of the project, after the completion of the electricity linkage project. This will be followed by a second phase that allows for the two sides to further increase the power exchange capacity. Jordan's Zawati highlighted that the project will enhance the stability and reliability of electricity networks in both countries, as well as adding impetus to the creation of a joint power market in the Arab world. This, Hawati added, should include Saudi Arabia, with which Jordan had just signed a similar agreement to connect the two countries' electricity power grids.

Running in parallel with these pan-Arab plans are the ongoing pipeline initiatives that build out from the original idea for the Basra-Aqaba route spanning around 1,700 km and that do not include Israel's land or sea territory. December 2019 saw an announcement from Iraq's Oil Ministry that it had completed the prequalifying process for companies interested in participating in the pipeline project, with the first phase of the project including the installation of a 700-km pipeline with a capacity of 2.25 million barrels within the Iraqi territories. The second phase includes the installation of a 900-km pipeline in Jordan between Haditha and Aqaba, with a capacity of one million barrels.

For Iran, this allows another alternate Iran/Iraq oil export line to the historically vulnerable Strait of Hormuz route, to add to Goreh-Jask pipeline route and plans to roll out a pipeline to Syria as well. It will also provide another 'cover' route for Iranian oil disguised as Iraqi oil, which can then be shipped easily both West and East. In March 2021, Iraqi and Egyptian officials discussed the possibility of extending the Basra-Aqaba pipeline to Egypt, as this would be 'an important addition and a new outlet for Iraqi oil exports to North Africa' (according to representatives of the two negotiating teams). There are several options for this Iraq-Aqaba-Egypt pipeline route, even the favoured ones that avoid any Israeli land or sea threats, including a very short route following the same ground as one of the Arab Gas Pipeline flows: from Aqaba to Taba and then if required up north to Arish and then west to Port Said.

The Iraq-Lebanon deal also appeared to be a perfectly standard and straightforward agreement on the face of it: Baghdad agreed to sell Lebanon 1 million metric tons per year (just over 21,000 barrels per day or just under 7.8 million barrels per year) of heavy fuel oil in return for goods and services. This deal, the Iraq Oil Ministry added, will help Iraq to reduce its surplus of fuel oil while at the same time enabling the financially troubled Lebanon to obtain the fuel stock for its power plants required to avoid the widespread and frequent power outages from which it periodically suffers. According to official comments from Iraq's Oil Ministry, the fuel oil would be sold at international prices and will be paid in exchange for Lebanese goods and services.

A more careful look at the details underpinning the deal reveals that it is anything but standard and straightforward. A key point is that Iraq does not have any fuel oil at all that meets the specifications of any power plant anywhere in Lebanon. Indeed, Lebanon's own caretaker Energy Minister, Raymond Ghajar, openly stated in February 2021: 'Iraq's heavy fuel does not match Lebanon's specific needs.' Given this bewildering premise, the 'plan' is that because Iraq's fuel oil cannot be used in Lebanon – despite the country pledging to buy 1 million metric tons of it every year – Lebanon will resell the Iraqi fuel and use the proceeds to buy spot cargoes of a fuel that does meet its specifications and that it can actually use. At least as baffling, on the surface at least, is precisely what 'goods and services' Lebanon is going to use to pay for this useless Iraqi fuel oil.

Lebanon's two major exports categories – by a considerable margin, accounting for well over half of its GDP – are 'gems and precious metals' and 'arms and ammunition', a very handy combination in the Middle East as a whole and particularly for a country such as Iraq that is intimately tied up with Iran, politically, economically and militarily. Given these principal exports it is perhaps no surprise to find that the single country that accounts for by far the largest proportion of all of Lebanon's exports is the number one global centre for discrete trade and banking services and facilities – Switzerland. On the other side of the equation – the root in the square root of the equation, it might be said – Iran has been under considerable financial pressure itself ever since the end of 2018 when the US re-imposed sanctions on it after Washington's unilateral withdrawal from the JCPOA in May of that year. Despite promises from China for massive financing facilities to be extended to Iran under the wide-ranging 25-year deal between the two countries, the threat of retaliation from the US should it overstep the mark has kept Beijing wary of giving all the help it promised to Tehran.

This has meant that Iran has been finding it increasingly difficult to pay its military proxies in the Shia Crescent countries, including those in Lebanon, so this deal between Iraq and Lebanon could well be regarded simply as an effective way for Iran to pay its militias in Lebanon. In this scenario, the oil will supposedly come from Iraq – although it is impossible to tell whether it is from Iraq or Iran as there are so many shared fields, as mentioned earlier – then Lebanon sells it for US dollars. Lebanon then uses some of these dollars to buy fuel oil for its power stations and the rest to either pay Iran, via Iraq, US dollars that Iran needs to pay its militias in Lebanon and elsewhere or it pays the militias itself on Iran's behalf. This triangular deal structure is an extremely common way for states under sanctions to circumvent them.

Iraq's Gas Potential Is Huge And Largely Untapped

The same sort of hidden value is also to be found in Iraq's gas business as in its oil sector, both in the couth of the country, and in the northern semi-autonomous region of Kurdistan. Plans to develop these gas resources in the south of the country remain stymied by Western IOCs' concerns relating to the corrupt system in the region. In the north of the country these concerns are compounded by uncertainty over the region's governance going forward.

Certainly, the raw figures are compelling. Official estimates are that Iraq's proven reserves of conventional natural gas amount to 3.5 trillion cubic metres (tcm) or about 1.5% of the world total, placing Iraq 12th among global reserve-holders. This said, around three-quarters of these proven reserves consist of associated gas – a by-product of oilfield development.

However, Iraq did not revise its figure for proven gas reserves in 2010 at the time of the upwards revision of proven oil reserves. Logical figures for non-associated gas were not provided at the time – or since – from the Iraqi oil and gas authorities either. The IEA, though, estimates that ultimately recoverable resources will be much larger than the official estimates of 3.5 tcm – its estimate is 8.0 tcm, of which around 30% is thought to be non-associated gas. This means that almost 40% of the resources yet to be found are expected to be in non-associated gas fields.

In the northern part of Iraq, Kurdistan's Ministry of Natural Resources (MNR) estimates that there is 25 trillion cubic feet (tcf) of proven gas reserves and up to 198 tcf of unproven gas resources, around 3% of the world's total deposits. The figures look realistic, given that the US Geological Survey (USGS) believes that undiscovered resources in just the Zagros fold belt of Iraq, a large part of which falls in the KRG area, amounts to around 54 tcf of gas. Discovered reserves, though, total less than 10 tcf of proven plus probable reserves and less than 30 tcf of contingent resources. The bulk of these are non-associated gas deposit located in the Region's central and southern areas, especially those in the Bina Bawi, Khor Mor, Khurmala, Miran and Chemchemal fields.

Iraq's Gas Resources Are Also Hugely Underestimated

Iraq Gas Resources By Region And Supergiant Field (in Bcm)			
	Ultimately recoverable resources**	Remaining recoverable resources	Remaining % of ultimately recoverable resources
Southern Mesopotamian	4 298	3 947	92%
West Qurna	1 139	1 121	98%
Rumaila	838	550	66%
Majnoon	388	386	99%
Zubair	334	295	88%
Nahr Umr	379	375	99%
Central Mesopotamian	700	700	100%
East Baghdad	367	367	100%
Northern Zagros Foldbelt	2 027	1 869	92%
Kirkuk	256	102	40%
Western Desert	906	906	100%
Total Iraq	7 932	7 422	94%
Associated	*5 279*	*4 773*	*90%*
Non-associated	*2 653*	*2 649*	*100%*

** Ultimately recoverable resources (URR) for associated gas is derived from oil URR and known gas-oil-ratios. This gives higher associated gas URR than the USGS analysis. As the total URR is derived from the USGS data, this results in a lower non-associated gas URR, which may be underestimated by several hundred billion cubic metres (bcm).
Source: IEA

Additionally, judging from the 65% success rate of drilling activity in its oil operations, a high degree of prospectivity in gas operations is likely and this is set to push up gas to the near-1,300 mmcf/d analyst forecast by the end of 2025. This, combined with increasing attention on gas sector development due to increases in domestic demand – especially for power generation – has refocused the attention of the KRG on looking to develop these assets.

Given this relative lack of focus on its gas sector, Kurdistan still lacks a fully developed gas infrastructure. Aside from a gas pipeline that runs from Khor Mor via the relatively undeveloped Chemchemal field and the Bazian power plant to the Erbil power plant, and a short pipeline that links the

Summail field with the Dohuk power plant, facilities for processing plants and pipelines for domestic gas transmission to power plants – and exports to Turkey – still need to be fully completed. This lack of internal and external infrastructure has tended to deter investment in the past, leaving several fields – most notably Miran and Bina Bawi, which together hold 12 Tcf of recoverable gas – effectively stranded and offering operators little value for gas exposure in the market given the lack of export infrastructure.

Aside from the vast and relatively untapped potential of the gas fields, foreign operators do benefit from the more preferential production sharing contracts (PSCs) available from Kurdistan than the technical service contracts (TSCs) generally on offer from the Federal Government of Iraq in the south. As there have been no formal bid rounds for these contracts, each varies accordingly from field to field, but nonetheless conform to a fairly standard basic pattern. This is: a royalty (about 10% of gross revenues) to the government, cost recovery from a fixed share (around 40-50%) of oil and gas revenues, and profit sharing (approximately 30% initially, sliding down to about 15% over time) of the remaining revenues based on a ratio derived from cumulative revenues to cumulative costs.

Gas Flaring Reduction Initiatives May Push Output Increases

As a corollary of its new target for oil production of 7 million bpd by 2025, Iraq has also stated that it is to stop flaring gas by the same point. As with all statements by Iraq, this commitment should be regarded as highly fluid in its practical application, but any move towards this will allow the country to monetise this burnt off resource and to begin to develop a true gas export business. It will also allow it to use some of these resources in power generation, which would allow it to end its dependence on power and gas imports from neighbouring Iran, a situation which consistently brings pressure on it from the US, as highlighted earlier.

Currently, after Russia, Iraq flares the largest quantity of gas in the world, with some 17 billion cubic metres burnt in 2022, according to a World Bank study. It has little choice but to do something to properly address the issue of flaring its associated gas anyway, as it recently joined the United Nations and World Bank 'Zero Routine Flaring' initiative aimed at ending this type of routine flaring by 2030. In practical terms, this costs the economy billions of dollars in lost revenue from gas exports. It has also contributed to the frequent power outages in Iraq, particularly during the summer months, which is difficult to equate with Iraq's status as a leading global oil producer or having the world's 12th largest gas reserves.

Plans To Reduce Gas (And Export Cash) Burn

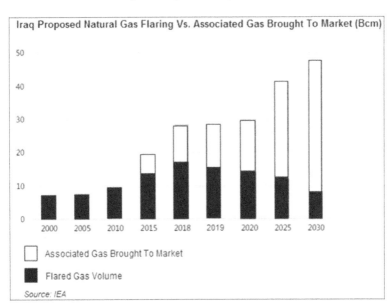

Iraq Proposed Natural Gas Flaring Vs. Associated Gas Brought To Market (Bcm)

Associated Gas Brought To Market

Flared Gas Volume

Source: IEA

Various announcements in recent years have provided some reason for vague optimism that this deleterious situation may change at some point. One notable example was the announcement in 2020 that Iraq's Oil Ministry had signed a natural gas capture deal with oil services provider Baker Hughes to harness 200 million cubic feet per day (mmcf/d) from the Gharraf oil field (and neighbouring ThiQar site, Nassiriya), plus other oil fields north of Basra.

According to the Oil Ministry, the first stage would involve the advanced modular gas processing solution being deployed at the Integrated Natural Gas Complex in Nassiriya to dehydrate and compress flare gas to generate over 100 mmcf/d of gas. The second stage would involve the Nassiriya plant being expanded to become a complete natural gas liquid (NGL) facility that would recover 200 million standard cubic feet per day of dry gas, liquefied gas and condensate. All of this output would go to the domestic power generation sector, with Baker Hughes stating that addressing the flared gas from these two fields would allow for the provision of 400 megawatts of power to the Iraqi grid.

According to an accompanying statement from then-Oil Minister, Jabbar Al-Luaibi, Iraq was also negotiating a similar gas capture deal for the state-run Nahr Bin Umar field with Houston-based Orion Gas Processors. Additionally, according to recent comments from Iraq's South Oil Company, gas-processing facilities are to be constructed in the Missan and Halfaya fields that will have a combined capacity of 600 mmcf/d of gas when completed, and the construction of gas-processing facilities in the West Qurna, Majnoon and Badra fields will also move ahead, with respective overall capacities 1,650 mmcf/d, 725 mmcf/d and 85 mmcf/d.

Even more recently, early 2023 saw a restatement by France's TotalEnergies of its commitment to move ahead with a four-pronged USD27 billion deal, one key project of which is to collect and refine associated natural gas that is currently burned off at the five southern Iraq oilfields of West Qurna 2, Majnoon, Tuba, Luhais, and Artawi. The USD27 billion deal is analysed in full in the first section of this book.

Build-Out Of A World-Class Petrochemicals Sector

Given the development of its natural gas resources – be they associated or non-associated – together with its already world-scale oil production, there would be no reason why Iraq could not become one of the leading producers of petrochemicals in the world. This is why Royal Dutch Shell signed the deal in January 2015 to build the USD11 billion Nebras petrochemicals plant in the southern oil hub of Basra, having signed the original memorandum of understanding back in 2012.

For Shell, the Nebras project offers a natural synergy for the gas feedstock that comes from its 44% stake in the USD17 billion 25-year Basra Gas Company (BGC) project. The BGC is designed to enable Iraq to increase its energy independence and to achieve economic diversification by capturing currently flared gas from the fields of Rumaila, West Qurna 1 and Zubair, in the first instance.

As of 2019/2020, the BGC reached a peak production rate of 1035 mmscf/d, the highest in Iraq's history and sufficient gas to generate approximately 3.5 GW of electricity – enough to power three million homes. The BGC is also responsible for currently supplying around 70% of Iraq's liquefied petroleum gas (LPG) and for enhancing Iraq's export capabilities, which helped the country to become a net exporter of LPG from 2017.

For Iraq, the creation of a value-added petrochemicals sector generating a sustainable stream of export revenues to add to its basic drill-and-sell crude oil operation would enable it to avoid the sort of cash-crunches that have become commonplace every year in the country, sparking violent protests and deaths. Such new revenue streams would also allow Iraq to avoid having to breach OPEC+ production caps in order to plug short-term financial holes and then have to suffer the consequences of having to make up the overproduction by cutting back on production in subsequent months.

The original design plans for the Nebras petrochemicals complex – formulated between Shell, the Iraq Oil Ministry, and the Ministry of Industry and Minerals – were for a project that could produce at least 1.8 million metric tonnes per year (mtpy) of various petrochemicals. This would make it Iraq's first major petrochemicals project since the early 1990s and one of only four major petrochemicals complexes across the entire country. The others – Khor al-Zubair in the south, Musayeb near Baghdad and the Baiji refinery complex in the north – are operated by Iraq's State Company for Petrochemical Industries.

In January 2015, Shell released the statement that Iraq's cabinet had authorised the Nebras project and that the company would work 'with the Ministries of Oil and Transport to develop a joint investment model for a world-scale petrochemical cracker and derivatives complex in the south of Iraq'. The then-Industry Minister, Nasser al-Esawi, told a news conference at the time that the Shell-run Nebras petrochemical complex would come online within five to six years and would make his country the largest petrochemicals producer in the Middle East.

From 2012, though, the development of Iraq's hydrocarbons chain stalled in the upstream sector, with little impetus on the next stage that is critical for both the petrochemical and refining sectors: a focus on the midstream to attract sufficient capital with the strategic objective of developing an integrated master gas system.

However, Shell's efforts on the BGC in the past three to four years have changed the basic landscape for the future development prospects for Nebras. Shell has done a good job with the BGC, especially in getting the gas volumes up to over a billion standard cubic feet per day. This means that the ethane can be extracted on a sustainable and reliable basis, and this allows for sufficient volume for a major petrochemicals plant to be viable. Ethane needs to be the initial feedstock for Iraq's first few plants in the same way that it was in the development of Saudi Arabia's master gas system that captured associated gas, which was then fractionated and supplied as primary feedstock to the flagship Jubail Industrial City.

The highest concentration of ethane (10%+) is usually found in associated gas streams, of which Iraq has a lot, and processing ethane produces ethylene with few by-products (mainly fuel gas) to process and manage. This reduces the capital required for construction and minimises the complexity of the logistics and distribution requirements, which will be important factors in Iraq's early-stage build-out of a viable petrochemicals industry. However, as the industry and corresponding infrastructure grows, heavier feed streams can be utilised, as happened with the use of propane, butane and naphtha in Jubail.

A world-scale facility for ethylene – one of the most in-demand petrochemicals products in the world, especially from China – is in the range of 1.0 to 1.5 million tons of ethylene production. A 1.0 million ton per year ethylene facility would require a supply of roughly 1.3 million tons per year of ethane. Additionally, this would need to be a sustainable and reliable supply for at least 20 to 25 years and, to build out all of the necessary parts for a functioning world-class petrochemicals sector in Iraq would require around USD40-50 billion.

Practically, though, as mentioned earlier, the endemic corruption across Iraq's various business sectors has also stymied progress in its petrochemicals sector development in the past. This has been a key factor in why Shell's progress on Nebras has been uneven at various points, according to a number of sources close to proceedings. According to these sources, the company would have been faced at times in the past with the prospect of paying out 'compensation' of around 30% of the total cost for Nebras on top of the USD11 billion headline figure, which is a major consideration both from an economic and reputational perspective.

Dealing With Kurdistan After The 2017 Referendum

As had been widely expected, the people of the semi-autonomous region of Kurdistan – who make up around one-fifth of Iraq's 38 million population – in September 2017 voted overwhelmingly for independence. As also expected, with around 30 million separatist-minded Kurds dispersed across the borders with Syria, Iran and Turkey, the reaction of Kurdistan's neighbours was as apoplectic as that of the Federal Government of Iraq in Baghdad.

On the KRG's part, then-President Massoud Barzani was quick to stress that despite the scale of the backing for independence – nearly 93% of the 3.3 million eligible ballots voted in favour of independence across the disputed regions of Kirkuk and Makhmour in the north, Sinjar in the northwest and Khanaqin in the east – the vote did not mean automatic independence from Iraq. Rather, he said, it could be seen as providing a mandate for negotiations with Baghdad and neighbouring countries over the peaceful secession of the Kurdish region from Iraq at some unspecified point in the future, and that he was ready for 'very long' talks with the FGI, possibly lasting years, on issues from borders to oil exports and water.

This was despite Kurdistan having been promised independence since at least the end of World War One, when colonial powers divided up the Middle East and left Kurdish-populated territory split between modern-day Turkey, Iran, Iraq and Syria. His reaction was all the more superficially mystifying, given that the Kurds had been quietly assured of full independence after the war against ISIS had concluded (or by 2023 at the latest) by the US and the other Western powers.

This assurance, specifically by the US, was in exchange for the Kurdish Peshmerga army providing the boots on the ground in the fight against ISIS. The widely held view amongst Kurds (and many non-partisan observers as well) was that Barzani was using the referendum to leverage Baghdad into honouring the deal originated in 2014 in which monies were dispersed from Baghdad to Erbil in exchange for the FGI's State Organization for Marketing of Oil (SOMO) handling crude supplies from KRG-controlled areas.

Kurdistan's neighbours were equally unsupportive. Almost immediately after the first wave of results had come in, Recep Tayyip Erdoğan, the President of Turkey – with around 18% of its population being Kurds, in the east of the country – threatened to invade the northern part of Iraq in which Kurdistan is situated. He then added that Turkey could also cut off the oil export pipeline from Iraq to the Turkish port of Ceyhan, which would affect around an average of 500,000-600,000 bpd of KRG oil exports, by far the mainstay of its economy but also around 15% of Iraq's total output. As a corollary of this, Turkey's then-Prime Minister, Binali Yildirim, stated that his country had agreed to deal exclusively with the FGI in Baghdad over exports of the crude oil sourced in the Kurdish region. This was in line with the long-running assertion from the FGI that SOMO had sole authority to export oil produced anywhere within Iraq's borders.

The reaction of Iran – with 9% of its population being Kurdish and located in its northwest – has been similarly strident, announcing a ban on direct flights to and from Kurdistan immediately after the result of the referendum became obvious. Shortly afterwards, Major General Yahya Rahim Safavi, a top military adviser to Iran's Supreme Leader Ali Khamenei, called on 'the four neighbouring countries to block land borders' with the Iraqi Kurdish region. Iran was – and remains – determined to safeguard its role as the key foreign player across all of Iraq, holding huge sway over the Shi'ite Muslim groups that have ruled or held security and government positions in Iraq since the US-led invasion that toppled Saddam Hussein in 2003.

In broader geopolitical terms, Iran regards the prospect of an independent Kurdistan with horror, as it jeopardises its strategy of rolling-out a Shia-dominated sphere of influence across the Middle East, led by Tehran, to overtake the US-backed Saudi power that had been the key force for the previous few decades. In this context, Iran's fears were not helped when Barzani stated at the end of 2017 that going forward Iraq should be divided into separate Shia, Sunni and Kurdish entities to prevent further sectarian bloodshed.

Iraq's then-Prime Minister, Haider al-Abadi, in the meantime, began by calling the vote 'unconstitutional'. He added that on this basis the FGI would take control of official border crossings linking the Kurdish region with neighbouring countries and restricting international flights to and from Erbil and Sulaymaniyah airports. Additionally, Iraq's parliament was given a mandate by al-Abadi to send troops to the disputed oil-rich region of Kirkuk – over which the FGI maintains it has sovereignty, despite it being recaptured by Kurdish Peshmerga troops in 2014 – and called on 'neighbouring countries and countries of the world' to stop buying crude oil directly from Kurdistan, only to deal with the FGI in Baghdad. This built on earlier statements by al-Abadi that he had ordered the Oil Ministry to mobilise all its legal resources to prevent all ships in the future from off-loading all crude oil exports by the KRG, to any destination, after a number of incidents in which KRG oil had been loaded onto tankers for export.

The US plan at that time was to destabilise Iran's influence in Iraq and Syria by sowing discontent and potential conflict between the indigenous Kurdish populations in those countries, together with the Kurds in Iran. As part of this US plan, Kurdistan would be allowed to gain its independence from Iraq within five years of the independence vote (that was, by 2023, as mentioned above).

After this, the plan went, the KRG would be allowed to accrete further territory through the Kurdish populations in the neighbouring countries, beginning with Iran, then Syria and finally Turkey. By sowing such conflict, the theory ran, Iran's economic and political advancement in Iraq and elsewhere in the region would be set back and its political vision would become more inward-looking.

The Budget Payments-For-Oil Deal

The dispute over how oil flows are handled in the Kurdistan region of Iraq – administered by the KRG in Erbil – and how the region is rewarded by the Federal Government of Iraq in Baghdad for its co-operation in this regard is not a transitory disagreement. It dates back to the very formation of the new system of governance in Iraq in 2003, immediately after the fall of Saddam Hussein.

At that time, it was broadly agreed that the KRG would export a certain volume of oil from its own fields and Kirkuk via Iraq's SOMO and would not independently sell oil from the fields on the international markets. In return, Baghdad would disburse a certain level of payments to the KRG from Iraq's central budget. From 2003 to November 2014, there was constant dispute from both sides that the other had not met the terms of that understanding.

In November 2014, however, a deal was struck between the FGI and the KRG in which the KRG agreed to export up to 550,000 bpd of oil from its own fields and Kirkuk via SOMO and, in return, Baghdad would send 17% of the federal budget after sovereign expenses (around USD500 million at that time) per month in budget payments to the Kurds. This agreement – which again functioned properly only sporadically – was then superseded by an understanding reached between the KRG and the new Iraqi federal government formed in October 2018 centred on the 2019 national budget bill.

This required the FGI to transfer sufficient funds from the budget to pay the salaries of KRG employees along with other financial compensation in exchange for the KRG handing over the export of at least 250,000 bpd of crude oil to SOMO. Since then, though, the FGI – nominally headed by various prime ministers but for a long time controlled behind the scenes by radical cleric Moqtada a-Sadr, whose 'Sairoon' ('Marching Forward') faction won the most seats in the last election – delivered the funding for the salaries of the KRG employees on a monthly basis less than reliably and the KRG delivered the agreed upon volume of oil to SOMO on the same *ad hoc* basis.

The key sticking point for the two sides at that stage was a fundamental disagreement over the amount of budget dispersals and oil transfers that should be involved in the deal – the same reason that the November 2014 deal did not survive intact for long. The situation was worsened by the 'yes' referendum vote for independence in Kurdistan in September 2017. Before this, Kurdistan had been hoping to raise oil exports above 1 million bpd, becoming one of the world's fastest growing oil regions and allowing for the full resumption of the November 2014 deal. After the 'yes' vote, the very basis of the deal became entirely null and void when FGI and Iranian forces took back control of the oilfields in Kurdistan, including the major oil sites around Kirkuk.

The FGI argued that the Kirkuk fields had been occupied illegally in the first place, having been under Kurdish control only since 2014 when the Iraqi army collapsed in the face of ISIS. From that point onwards, the starting point of any negotiations for the FGI in Baghdad over budget disbursements to the KRG was that they should accord with the percentage share of the Kurdistan population in the overall population of Iraq. This, according to the FGI, was 12.67% – a long way from the 17% of the federal budget after sovereign expenses that had been the cornerstone assumption of the November 2014 deal.

The legal position relating to the Iraqi oil industry and the distribution of its revenue sharing between the KRG area and the rest of the country has done little to clarify the ongoing impasse. Both sides have claimed – with some justification – a right to the revenues from the disputed oil flows. According to the KRG, it has authority under Articles 112 and 115 of the Iraq Constitution to manage oil and gas in the Kurdistan Region extracted from fields that were not in production in 2005 – the year that the Constitution was adopted by referendum. In addition, the KRG maintains that Article 115 states: 'All powers not stipulated in the exclusive powers of the federal government belong to the authorities of the regions and governorates that are not organised in a region.' As such, the KRG maintains that, as relevant powers are not otherwise stipulated in the Constitution, it has the authority to sell and receive revenue from its oil and gas exports.

The Federal Government of Iraq, and SOMO, however, has argued that under Article 111 of the Constitution oil and gas are under the ownership of all the people of Iraq in all the regions and governorates as administered through the central government in Baghdad.

Rosneft Took Control Of The Kurdistan Oil Sector In 2017

After the 'yes' vote on independence, the Kremlin's corporate oil proxy, Rosneft, effectively took over the ownership of Kurdistan's oil sector in 2017 through three principal means. First, Russia provided the government of the semi-autonomous region (KRG) with USD1.5 billion in financing through forward oil sales payable in the next three to five years. Second, it took an 80% working interest in five potentially major oil blocks in the region. And third, it established 60% ownership of the vital KRG pipeline by dint of a commitment to invest USD1.8 billion to increase its capacity to one million barrels per day.

Moscow considered itself well-placed at that point to leverage this presence into a similarly powerful position in the south of the country, in particular by striking new oil and gas field exploration and development deals with Baghdad as part of Russia's role in intermediating in the perennial dispute between Kurdistan and the Federal Government of Iraq in Baghdad on the budget disbursements-for-oil deal.

Given its presence in the Kurdistan area of Iraq, Russia has made its own demands of the FGI through the KRG. Having taken over control of the Kirkuk oil fields from Kurdish forces in October 2017, following rioting after Baghdad failed to recognise the 'yes' vote on independence earlier, the Federal Government found itself dependent on the KRG, as the KRG had control over the only operational export pipeline (to the Turkish port of Ceyhan). This affected some 300,000 bpd of crude oil previously pumped in the Kirkuk province.

Rosneft, though, also played a key role in this dispute. Moscow insisted through the KRG that oil flows would not restart until pipeline transit fees and pumping tariffs were paid to the Russian company, which by that point had its 60% stake in the Kirkuk-Ceyhan pipeline. Moscow also wanted the FGI to look again at its decision to deem 'invalid' the assignment to Rosneft by the KRG of the five exploration blocks in Kurdish territory in which it had secured an 80% stake. These are estimated to have aggregate 3P reserves of 670 million barrels.

Rosneft's involvement in the Kurdistan region of Iraq not only threatened Iraq's plans to meet its new in-house oil production targets but also its potential export routes for the new flows, given the Russian company's involvement in the northern pipelines leading into Turkey's Ceyhan port. The original Kirkuk to Ceyhan Pipeline – the ITP – consisted of two pipes, which had a nameplate capacity of 1.6 million bpd combined. The FGI-controlled pipeline's export capacity reached between 250,000 and 400,000 bpd when running normally, although it was subject to regular sabotage by militants of various types. The KRG, in response to the regular attacks on the FGI pipeline, completed its own single-side track Taq field-Khurmala-Kirkuk/Ceyhan pipeline in the border town of Fishkhabur. This was part of its drive to raise oil exports above 1 million bpd.

Under the previous FGI administration of Haider al-Abadi, the signs were that some accommodation of the demands of Rosneft and the KRG might be in the offing. There had been some movement on the percentage basis for the budget compensation, up from just under 13%. There had also been a ratification of the idea that Baghdad would return significant volumes of oil to Kurdistan for local refining, and it had even been acknowledged that a pumping tariff might be paid to Rosneft. At that time, then-Oil Minister Jabar al-Luaibi even said that he was willing to accommodate Rosneft in the Kirkuk oil hub itself, highlighting that

Baghdad did not want to close the doors in the face of anyone 'who wanted to help'. The only condition at that point was that Rosneft should work with BP which, as BP owned a 19.75% stake in Rosneft, did not appear to be an insurmountable requirement.

Russia And China Consolidate Their Presence Across Iraq

The oil-producing subsidiary of Russian state gas giant Gazprom, Gazprom Neft, announced in late 2020 that it planned to launch a fourth well at the Sarqala field in the Kurdistan region of Iraq in the first half of 2021. Not only was this aimed at consolidating its own foothold in the KRI, but it was also aimed at Russia's expansionist policy across the country as a whole, allowing for the exploitation of greater synergies for Russia in Iraq.

In this context, Gazprom Neft also planned to exploit associated gas from Sarqala to provide electricity to several regions in Iraqi Kurdistan through a 4.5-kilometre gas pipeline that would connect the field to various power generation facilities. Whether this still applies to the neighbouring Shakal block – in which Gazprom Neft has an 80% stake, with the remainder held by the KRG, and in which the company has drilled three wells so far – remains unclear.

With Russia's top oil producer, Rosneft, already holding all the cards in the KRI's oil industry it was Gazprom Neft – rather than the country's top gas producer, Gazprom – that was 'encouraged' by the Kremlin to also represent Russia in the KRI. Gazprom Neft is basically the advance party for Gazprom in difficult foreign projects and it can work as easily in oil and gas developments, which can then be connected into the bigger Gazprom development machine.

In Iraq's case as well, because it is seen less as the direct representative of the Russian state than either Rosneft or Gazprom, Gazprom Neft can work more under the geopolitical radar than those two companies. In this instance, it can work at oil fields in the KRI and in one of the south's bigger oil fields – with gas potential as well – Badra. This allows Russia to pursue a pan-Iraq strategy, which other countries have found difficult.

Such cross-country opportunities are why, despite recent obstacles, Gazprom Neft is to continue in Badra and to look for further opportunities in the north and south of Iraq. Initially, Gazprom Neft began to operate Badra under the profoundly unpopular Technical Service Contract model that was the norm for Baghdad for many years. The Russian company took 30% of the field, with the other consortium members being South Korea's KOGAS, Malaysia's Petronas, Turkey's TPAO and Iraq's Oil Exploration Company. The TSC contract runs for a period of 20 years, with possible extension for a further five. Gazprom Neft receives a fee of USD5.50 for each barrel of oil equivalent produced, although the rate declines once the payback point is reached.

Originally, the estimate for Badra was that it would produce up to 170,000 bpd, yielding good returns for Gazprom Neft, given lifting cost projections of around USD2.50 pb. The field, though, has a much more complex geological structure than originally thought – including very high sulphur content for the oil – so increasing the cost estimates. Indeed, the project costs have increased by around USD700 million from the original estimates and the output projection is for peak production of 85,000 bpd. Due to the geopolitical importance to Russia of Gazprom Neft's operations spanning Iraq, though, far from scaling down its interest in Badra after 2022 – when the payback point for the USD1.6 billion it invested had been reached – it is looking to expand its operations. This will involve drilling numerous horizontal wells to increase the oil recovery factor and extend the production plateau.

These plans were part of the wider discussion on further co-operation between Russia and Iraq when the president of Russian state oil proxy Lukoil, Vagit Alekperov, met one-to-one in 2020 with Iraq's Prime Minister Mustafa al-Kadhimi and Oil Minister Ihsan Abdul Jabbar Ismail. At the meeting, Russia pressed Iraq for definitive progress on the series of deals that had been agreed between the two countries in 2017.

Just prior to 2020's spate of attacks against US military sites in southern Iraq, Russia had made it clear to Iraq (and before that to Iran) that a number of its companies were ready to move on at least USD20 billion of oil and gas projects in Iraq in the very short term, including Zarubezhneft, Tatneft and Rosneft-related oil and gas entities. These companies and others had seen their already-agreed projects stalled by the effective seizure of power by the *de facto* leader of Iraq at that point, Moqtada al-Sadr and his ultra-nationalist 'Sairoon' power bloc. The targeted projects had remained slow-tracked as anti-American feeling in southern Iraq had gathered momentum thereafter, particularly in the aftermath of the 2019 assassination by the US of Iran's Qasem Soleimani.

At the beginning of 2021, China used the same strategy that Russia had been using in north and south Iraq to further expand its own influence across the two regions. The USD2 billion five–year prepayment oil supply deal between the Federal Government of Iraq (FGI) in Baghdad and China's Zhenhua Oil that was struck at that time, and its percussions, are analysed in depth in the first section of this book.

The US

Five Phases In The US Approach To The Global Oil Markets

In broad terms, the US's approach to the global oil markets from 1945 to 2023 can be demarcated into four fairly distinct phases.

Phase 1 from 1945 (when the foundation relationship agreement was signed with Saudi Arabia) to 1973 (the onset of the Oil Crisis, or the First Oil Price War) marked a settled period in which the US was easily able to control the global oil market through its big corporate proxies' deals with the big state oil producers of the Middle East.

Phase 2 from 1974 (the end of the Oil Crisis) to 2013 (before the beginning of the Second Oil Price War) marked a delicate balancing phase for the US in which it sought to exert control over the big state oil producers in the global oil market through the exercise of a divide-and-rule strategy whilst simultaneously looking to build its own independent energy resources through the development of its shale oil and gas sectors.

Phase 3 from 2014 (the beginning of the Second Oil Price War and the signing of the JCPOA) to 2018 (when the US unilaterally withdrew from the JCPOA) marked an alliance transition period for the US as it looked to substitute Saudi Arabian oil in its energy supply complex with other suppliers, including Iran and Iraq, before it gained complete energy independence through its own shale energy sector.

Phase 4 from 2019 (when it was clear to the US that a new version of the JCPOA would not occur quickly and COVID-19 emerged) to 2022 (before Russia invaded Ukraine) marked a major withdrawal of the US from the Middle East after its re-engagement policies with Iran and Iraq had failed and Saudi Arabia had moved closer to Russia and China through the OPEC+ grouping and similar cooperation initiatives. The US's disengagement from the Middle East and focus on its own economic and political needs was exacerbated by the onset of COVID-19 in late 2019/early 2020. There was a later attempt to build a counterbalance to the US's loss of influence in the Middle East to Russia initially and then China in the form of the 'relationship normalisation deals' programme but this foundered when President Trump left office.

Phase 5 from 2022 (after Russia had invaded Ukraine) to 2023 (one year after the invasion) marked a significant re-engagement of the US with its core political and military allies around the world to fight against Russian ambitions in Europe and Chinese ambitions in Asia-Pacific.

Because much of these early phases have been analysed in depth in the first section of this book and also touched on in some cases in other sections of this book, this section will analyse in more depth, or for the first time, elements of the US's actions in the global oil markets in the run-up to and the aftermath of its unilateral withdrawal from the JCPOA on 8 May 2018. This withdrawal was key to the shaping of the global oil markets from that point up to Russia invading Ukraine on 24 February 2022.

The Basic Rationale For The JCPOA Deal

Never has the adage from the ancient Chinese military strategist, Sun Tzu – 'Keep your friends close but your enemies closer' – been more apposite than in the JCPOA deal agreed in 2015 between the P5+1 group of countries (the US, UK, France, Russia, China plus Germany) and Iran and implemented from 16 January 2016. This rationale of wanting to keep Iran in a relationship agreement so that it could be closely monitored was exactly the point of the JCPOA as engineered by former President Barack Obama and his Secretary of State John Kerry.

The political timing of the deal was also right from the US's perspective. The Second Oil Price War, instigated by Saudi Arabia – just as the 1973 Oil Crisis had been – had reinforced the urgency with which the US needed substitute oil suppliers to Saudi Arabia from the Middle East. It was well known by the US that Iraq could ultimately produce much more oil than

Saudi Arabia and that Iran still retained enormous influence over it – both of these elements are analysed in full in the standalone sections on Iran and then Iraq in this book. The US's previous invasion of Iraq had officially ended in 2011 but it still had some degree of political influence there itself by dint both of its remaining military presence across the country and its ongoing financial disbursements to its governments. If Iran could be brought into some sort of agreement with the West then, it was thought, Iraq would also tangentially be brought into that agreement, as would several other countries in the Shia Crescent of Power.

The JCPOA Would Bring Shia Countries Into An Alliance With The West

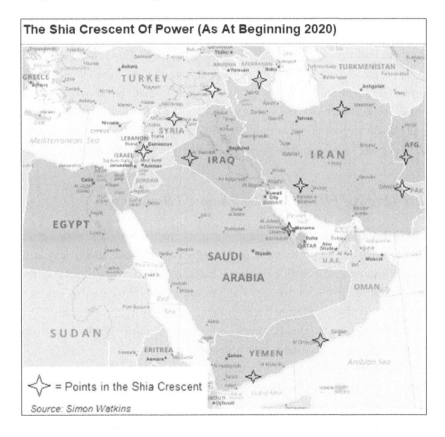

Not only would this strategy bring these Shia countries into a working relationship arrangement, but it would also take them away from the ongoing extension of China's and Russia's influence across the Middle

East. Such an alliance between the West and Iran (and the Shia countries) might also ultimately cause Saudi Arabia itself to seek to renew its own relationship with the West, for fear of what a politically- and financially-re--energised Iran might do.

Additionally, even back then, the US did not want Russia to increase its hold over Europe via its vital gas supplies to the continent with new pipelines (including Nord Stream 2) planned by Russia to pipe gas straight into the centre of Europe. The leading European powers were also keen to diversify their gas suppliers, and Iran had lots of gas and oil.

Iran's new President, Hassan Rouhani, was also the best political bet that the US had seen in Iran since the removal in 1953 of Iranian Prime Minister, Mohammad Mossadegh, by US and British intelligence services in 'Operation Ajax', and his replacement by General Fazlollah Zahedi. Rouhani had first become leader in August 2013, and had been re-elected in 2017, largely on the idea that re-engaging with the West would bring enormous economic benefits for Iran within a relatively short period of time. The majority of the Iranian people – which has a very youthful and well-educated demographic profile – also believed that a more prosperous future could be achieved by re-engagement with the West.

The Original Hardline Deal Proposed By Obama

It is highly apposite to note here that the original JCPOA deal that former US President Barack Obama's team had drafted – but which was later watered down into a softer version - was almost exactly the same as the 'hardball deal' proposed later by the Trump team as the basis for any new JCPOA deal after the US had withdrawn from the softer version in 2018.

All the key points in the proposed Trump/Pompeo deal were in the original Obama/Kerry deal and these are as follows.

The three 'core concepts' underpinning the whole deal were: 1. The safety and security of US troops from Iranian or Iranian-sponsored attacks in Iraq and elsewhere; 2. The safety and security of Israel; and 3. The inextricable link between Iran's nuclear enrichment programme and its ballistic missile programme.

The 12 'specific active' clauses were for Iran to: 1. Declare to the International Atomic Energy Agency (IAEA) a full account of the prior military dimensions of its nuclear programme and permanently and verifiably abandon such work in perpetuity; 2. Stop enrichment and never pursue plutonium reprocessing, including closing its heavy water reactor; 3. Provide the IAEA with unqualified access to all sites throughout the entire country; 4. End its proliferation of ballistic missiles and halt further launching or development of nuclear-capable missile systems; 5. Release all US citizens as well as citizens of US partners and allies; 6. End support to Middle East terrorist groups, including – but not limited to – Hezbollah, Hamas and Islamic Jihad; 7. Respect the sovereignty of the Iraqi government and permit the disarming, demobilisation and reintegration of Shia militias; 8. End its military support for the Houthi rebels and work towards a final peaceful, political settlement in Yemen; 9. Withdraw all forces under Iran's command throughout the entirety of Syria; 10. End support for the Taliban and other terrorist groups in Afghanistan and the region; 11. End the Islamic Revolutionary Guard Corps-linked Quds Force's support for terrorists and militant partners around the world; and, 12. End its threatening behaviour against its neighbours, including its threats to destroy Israel and its firing of missiles at Saudi Arabia and the UAE, and threats to international shipping and destructive cyber-attacks.

For its part, Tehran's negotiators began the discussions with the Obama team with the following conditions: 1. Compensation by the US for the damage done by sanctions to its economy; 2. Immediate access to all of Iran's frozen deposits in Europe, the Far East and everywhere else; and, 3. Guarantees that Israel does not continue to increase its intelligence and military presence in the region to threaten the security of Iran.

The US Wanted To Neuter The IRGC And They Knew It

As mentioned in the section on Iran, the notion of a clear division between 'moderates' and 'hardliners' in Iranian politics is erroneous. Institutionally, aside from any other reason of religion, culture, or education, it is not possible for someone who does not believe entirely in the spirit and execution of the 1979 Islamic Revolution in Iran to have a successful political career there. The only true difference in any of Iran's politicians from the West's perspective is the degree to which any of these politicians are prepared to engage with the West to advance Iran's own objectives.

Rouhani was prepared to engage with the West to a considerable degree but only within this context. He had managed to convince the Iranian people of the benefits of so doing as well. However, the degree to which he had been able to convince the IRGC to go along with this tilt to the West had been much more precarious.

As also highlighted at various points earlier in this book, but worth restating here at this point, is that the IRGC were the inheritors of the 1979 Islamic Revolution, not just in spirit but also in the manner in which it had been effected. In many cases, the senior IRGC ranks are the very same people who had taken to the streets of Tehran in 1979, and earlier, and overthrown an extremely entrenched, highly armed, and exceptionally hostile regime. They regarded themselves at the time of the JCPOA deal, and still do, as not just the inheritors of the spirit of that Revolution but also as its guardians. To do this, they need funding to spread the word of Iran's own particular brand of Islam around the world, which is why they agreed to the JCPOA with Rouhani.

However, when it became clear that the US wanted to disassemble the IRGC – by merging into Iran's regular army, taking away all its independent financial interests, and removing all its operational privileges, there was no chance that it would go along with Rouhani's engagement with the West any further. To do so, from the IRGC's perspective, would not only mean the death of it as an institution but it would also mean the death of the idea of the Islamic Republic of Iran and of the 1979 Islamic Revolution that had created it.

Aside from staging fresh military parades, ballistic missiles testing, and terrorist attacks to undermine the JCPOA, the IRGC made it very plain that it would personally target Rouhani if any further moves were made against its organisational financing, operational independence, or status. The key event designed to get this message across to Rouhani personally occurred with the IRGC's targeting of the President's key minister and supporter – the longstanding, highly respected, and well-reputed abroad Petroleum Minister, Bijan Zanganeh.

As the US pondered again in 2018/19 whether to officially designate the IRGC as a Foreign Terrorist Organisation, with all the negative implications that this would involve analysed in the first section of this book, the IRGC decided to censure Zanganeh to the degree that he was facing impeachment and subsequent removal from office. Nine charges formed the basis of the proceedings, with the key one being the huge rise in gasoline prices that had been a catalyst for protests across the country.

President Rouhani's Key Pro-West Ally Was Targeted By The IRGC

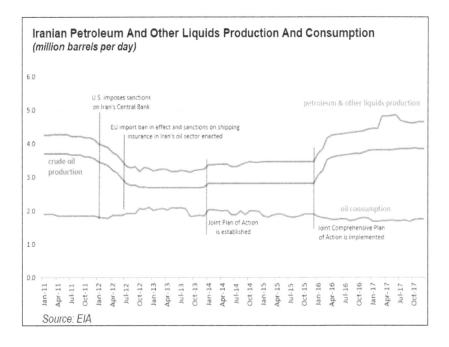

Iranian Petroleum And Other Liquids Production And Consumption
(million barrels per day)

Source: EIA

That the rise in gasoline prices should be the mechanism chosen by the IRGC to bring Zanganeh back into line was packed with irony. It was Zanganeh who was a key shaper of Iran's long-running 'resistance economy' model, the concept of generating value-added returns by leveraging intellectual capital into business development wherever possible whilst also ensuring self-sufficiency for key resources. Perhaps the most important of these was gasoline, as one of the most galling aspects of the pre-2015 international sanctions environment against Iran was that such a massive oil and gas power should have to beg other countries for sufficient gasoline to run its cars and other vehicles.

Zanganeh had made the build-out of Iran's gasoline capacity an absolute priority, personally intervening in the construction programme for the flagship gasoline-oriented Persian Gulf Star Refinery (PGSR) and other similar facilities to ensure their rapid completion. The original plan for the PGSR involved a three-phase development, each designed to produce 12 million litres per day (ml/d) of Euro 5 gasoline, plus 4.5 ml/d of Euro 4 standard diesel, 1 ml/d of kerosene and 300,000 litres per day of liquefied petroleum gas (LPG). To achieve these targets, the project's developers were given a EUR260 million additional loan from the National Development Fund of Iran – prompted by Zanganeh himself – as part of the estimated total cost for the three stages of approximately USD3.4 billion. Phase 1 was officially inaugurated in April 2017, with the first shipment of gasoline delivered for distribution just one month later in June, and Phase 2 began producing Euro 5 standard gasoline shortly after its own official launch in February 2018, running at full capacity by the end of June that year. Phase 3 saw its official inauguration just a few months later.

Given the indigenisation of foreign technology and products in its other gasoline-producing facilities as well – that Zanganeh ensured were part of the standard contracts signed by all participating foreign firms – Iran had been perfectly able to meet its own domestic demand for gasoline in the months leading up to his potential impeachment. The 10 refineries operational at that time across the country were supplying at least 110 ml/d of gasoline, up from an average of around 80 ml/d in the previous Iranian calendar year (running 21 March 2018 to 20 March 2019). On the other side of the supply/demand equation, domestic gasoline demand in the previous Iranian calendar year was around 80 ml/d, and for the 2020 Iranian calendar year that began in March it had been running at around 86 ml/d, leaving a surplus of at least 24 ml/d.

The problem came because the IRGC told Zanganeh that he needed to bring forward the plan to export gasoline to generate revenues in amounts much greater than had been agreed in the schedule and way before the timing that had been agreed. This post-US sanctions plan had been carefully worked out by Zanganeh and his close advisors and would have provided a consistent slight surplus for domestic demand over and above the 8% increase every year in demand that had been generously built into the Petroleum Ministry's demand/supply calculations profile curve.

The original target before the US re-imposed sanctions in 2018 was that within two and a half years from the final completion date of the PGSR, Iran would be meeting at least 10% of Southern Europe's gasoline and diesel needs, as it would be the top producer of gasoline in the Middle East by that point. Once the US had withdrawn from the JCPOA and put sanctions back in place, this timeline was changed to an empirical supply figure that took the lowest amount of gasoline being produced on average across all facilities together, added 10 million litres per day as an additional safety buffer, and designated that the remainder could be exported. The IRGC, though, told the Petroleum Ministry that they would ignore all of that and export everything they could, based on demand figures that were out of date, hence the discrepancy, hence the price hikes, hence the protests.

This was the real reason that led to the Iranian parliament's energy committee demanding answers over the government's decision to raise gasoline prices by at least 50%, prompting the protests, and the subsequent move to impeach Zanganeh. In the original impeachment document there were 72 signatures, with only 10 required under Iranian law to trigger a formal impeachment session. From that point, Zanganeh was due in front of the energy committee again on 8 December and, if it was not satisfied with what he had to say, then the committee was almost certain to advance the impeachment motion to the entire 290-member parliament.

From that point a simple majority vote of MPs present would be sufficient to remove him from office. The sting in the tail was that not only would he have to answer for the gasoline price hikes but also eight other charges, including the types of highly advantageous contracts that had been offered to foreign companies – Chinese and Russian companies, in fact – that he was not personally in favour of. The charges were quietly dropped, as the IRGC received assurances from Rouhani that the plans to fold the IRGC into the regular army and to force it to pull out of all of its business interests had been permanently shelved.

US Optimism Over A New JCPOA Dashed By The IRGC

The US's plans to expand its influence across Iran and Iraq as part of the roll-out of the JCPOA had faltered on the insistence of the Trump administration that unless Iran signed up to a 'new' tougher version of the deal (the one originally planned by Obama, as mentioned above) then the US would withdraw from the in-place version. As highlighted immediately above, the misjudgement – to not just remain in any version in order to keep monitoring Iran and Iraq anyway – was compounded by the failure to understand that the IRGC did not want any version of the JCPOA (that is, anything like the original tougher version) that would undermine its power. Therefore, rather than the JCPOA leading to a tighter alliance with the US at the centre that would have allowed for a closer monitoring of Iran, a huge increase in oil and gas flows from Iraq, and possibly even bringing Saudi Arabia back into the US's influence, the US had been left with the direct opposite result.

The US, therefore, in 2019 was much more open to flexibility in its approach to drawing up a new version of the JCPOA that Iran could sign, but by that time the IRGC was not at all interested in supporting Rouhani's vision for Iran, which included any JCPOA. This was evidenced for the US in any event occurred at the beginning of December 2019, which could have brought Iran and the US back to the table to negotiate an updated JCPOA: an exchange of prisoners between the US and Iran in Switzerland.

At that point, the US's willingness to meaningfully re-engage with Iran over a new version of the JCPOA that it thought Iran could sign was underlined by the US's lack of retaliation against Iran for two events that had occurred in just over the previous six months. First was Iran's downing of a US surveillance drone in June, and second were the Iranian-sponsored Houthi attacks on Saudi Arabia's Khurais oil field and the Abqaiq refinery in September.

In the former's case, military retaliation was halted at the last moment, and subsequently John Bolton – the most insistent proponent of military action against Iran over the years – was fired as National Security Adviser. In the case of the latter, various high-level officials from the US State Department repeatedly tried to persuade US allies in NATO and other supposedly sympathetic states in the Middle East to take part in a joint naval task force to patrol the Strait of Hormuz but to no avail. This was followed by the decision from the US to effectively disengage from the rolling conflicts in Syria, even if it involved leaving its former allies in the fight against ISIS, the Kurds, at the mercy of their longstanding mortal enemy, Turkey.

Given the twin realisation that the US was no longer willing to and/or could not meaningfully safeguard them and that Iran had everything to gain from further attacks on oil and gas targets in the region, Middle Eastern countries had been looking to row back on any hostility against Iran. Even the Saudi-led coalition that had been fighting the Iranian-backed Houthi rebels in Yemen since 2015 had begun releasing jailed Houthis in an attempt to bring some resolution to the conflict. Moreover, the US appeared to have realised that any change in regime in Iran would, far from getting rid of the IRGC – which was always the US endgame – in reality only strengthen its hold over Iran.

In addition, from the US side there was the realisation that, without the option to have an enduring (and costly in blood and money terms) military presence in multiple countries across the Middle East, it needed to have Iran on side to protect its political and energy interests there. The fact was that wherever the US was withdrawing, China was increasing its presence, with Russia close alongside, and the US was finding itself marginalised. This was happening not just in Syria but also in Iraq and further East in Afghanistan by China and/or Russia, as these places are central to China's 'One Belt, One Road' project and to Russia's attempts to isolate the US internationally.

The prisoner exchange between Iran and the US in December 2019, then, was seen as the US as a potential route back into negotiation with Iran over the JCPOA. The exchange included the release by Iran of Princeton PhD student Xiyue Wang (detained since 2016 on charges of spying), and the US dropping spying charges against Iranian scientist Massoud Soleimani (arrested in the US in 2018). Even more significant was the rhetoric (and absence of rhetoric in interesting places) involved.

At the time of the exchange, US President Donald Trump tweeted: 'Thank you to Iran on a very fair negotiation, … See, we can make a deal together!' Behind the scenes, US officials highlighted that Trump was willing to meet with Iran 'without preconditions' and added that the administration was 'hopeful [that the release of Wang] is a sign that the Iranians may be willing to come to the table to discuss all these issues.'

Rouhani's team, in the meantime, signalled that it was willing to engage in more prisoner swaps and, crucially, that it did not necessarily expect all sanctions to be removed before sitting down for negotiations with the Washington team. Central to this thawing on Rouhani's side was also the fact that during the then-recent protests across Iran the US did not unduly encourage the protesters or condemn the Iranian leadership, as might usually have been expected.

However, it was at this point that China reminded the IRGC of the benefits of the updated 25-year deal (analysed in full in the standalone Iran section). Beijing also reminded the IRGC that there may be no need for

Iran to enter into negotiations with the Trump team in which Iran might have to make serious concessions as Trump might well lose the Presidential election that was less than a year away. Critically as well, Iran's spiritual leader, Ayatollah Ali Khamenei took the IRGC's (and China's) view. Consequently, the prisoner exchange did not lead to the return to the JCPOA negotiating table that Trump had thought possible.

After this, the strong showing of the highly conservative anti-West elements in the 2020 parliamentary elections further laid down a marker by the IRGC that although some rapprochement with the West might be tolerated – provided that it was deal-specific and not part of a broader effort to moderate Iran – in reality it was more likely that Iran would continue to drift into the geopolitical orbit of China and Russia.

An Interim JCPOA Idea In Early 2022

In the early aftermath of Russia's invasion of Ukraine on 24 February 2022, the consequent spike in oil and gas prices looked like it would stay for some time and the longer it stayed the more likely the toxic mix of higher inflation and higher interest rates would cause economic damage to the West. All options to bring more oil and gas into the West's mix of supplies were on the table at that point – these are all examined in depth the first section of this book – but one of them that did not receive much public attention at the time was the idea of US entering into an interim new version of the JCPOA that left much of the issues surrounding the IRGC on the back burner. These could be revisited at some later time when a full new version of the JCPOA had been negotiated.

The key thing from the US's perspective at that point was to bring more oil and gas into the markets, especially into Europe, for two key reasons. First, new supplies would lower energy prices which, in turn, would lower inflation, which would reduce the need for interest rate hikes, which would reduce the likelihood of economic contractions in the West. Second, new supplies would reduce the clamour from key European Union (EU) countries – most notably, the EU's effective leader, Germany – to do some sort of a deal with Russia over Ukraine. This was what had happened when Russia had invaded Crimea in 2014. The US, and several of its major allies – including in Europe – did not want to do the same sort of agreement again with Russia, and instead wanted to draw a metaphorical line in the sand about how much more Russian advancement would be tolerated across Europe – which was none.

At that point it was thought that large volumes of Iranian crude oil and condensate production could bounce back very quickly. According to industry data at that stage, Iran could see an 80% recovery of full production within six months and a 100% recovery within 12 months. As at the beginning of Q4 2021 Iranian crude oil production capacity stood at 3.9 to 4.0 million bpd, according to the National Iranian Oil Company (NIOC). Output was holding near 2.4 million, of which 1.7-1.8 million bpd was consumed in domestic refineries.

An Interim JCPOA Could Have Led To A Quick 10% Drop In Oil Prices

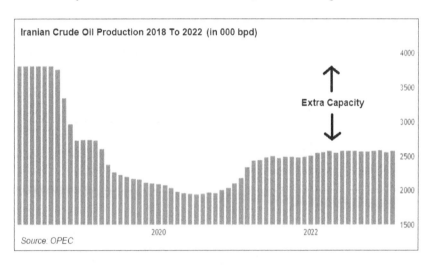

Close to 1 million bpd of condensate and natural gas liquids were also being produced at that point, primarily from the supergiant South Pars gas field. However, overall condensate and non-gas liquids production capacity stood at around 1.3 million bpd. Ultimately, it was believed that Iranian production could jump by 1.7 million bpd including 200,000 bpd of condensate and LPG/ethane, in a six- to nine-month period from when a new JCPOA was signed and US sanctions were lifted. This, it was predicted, would lead to an immediate 5-10 percent fall in the oil price, with more to come as new supplies emerged over the six-month to one-year time horizon. Given this, the US at that point was seriously considering removing the 'Foreign Terrorist Organisation' (FTO) designation of the IRGC caveat in negotiations, at least temporarily.

This move was likely to have been well-received by the IRGC as well. Since the IRGC's designation as an FTO in 2019, this inextricable link between the IRGC and Iran's economy has led to serious negative financial fallout for both. Only a few months before, due to the US's reimposed sanctions on Iran and the IRGC's ongoing designation as an FTO, Iran's foreign currency reserves had fallen to only US$10 billion. This compared to US$114 billion just before the US withdrew from the JCPOA in May 2018. Additionally, Iran's gold reserves had dwindled down to almost nothing during that period. This meant that the IRGC was close to a crunch point in its ability to fund its international network of proxies used to project Iranian influence, including those in Yemen, Lebanon, and Syria, as payment was usually made to them in US dollars or in gold.

Therefore, Iran since 2019 had needed an 'out' in the JCPOA negotiations. On the one hand it was not practically possible for the Iranian government to remove the IRGC from its business and financial networks, even if it wanted to. But on the other it could not commit to the Financial Action Task Force (FATF) – that the US had demanded as a pre-requisite for renegotiating the JCPOA - if the IRGC was still designated as an FTO with all the external monitoring ramifications that this brought with it. As it stood, Iran was one of just two countries – the other being North Korea – on the FATF's blacklist, with a particular failure on Iran's part noted by the FATF in its inability or unwillingness to address its deficiencies even after the Implementation Day of the first JCPOA on 16 January 2016.

Consequently, by removing the putting the issue of the FTO designation of the IRGC onto the back burner in the negotiations for an interim JCPOA, the US would have allowed Iran to pledge to join the FATF at some point, but in the meantime to bring a significant amount of new oil and gas into an under-supplied market.

At this crucial juncture in the preliminary talks between the US and Iran on formally restarting JCPOA talks – albeit, in reality only an interim version – a piece of diplomatic theatre was staged, with the creation of a false conflict narrative from the Iranian Parliament Speaker's Special Aide for the International Affairs, Hossein Amir-Abdollahian. He stated that US President Joe Biden 'should not include regional or missile issues in the JCPOA.' The key to this comment was that it conflated two separate issues

– missiles in general and regional missiles. The truth was that the Iranians had always been prepared to agree to curbs on their longer-range missiles (if not to rigidly stick by their promises on this issue) but had always wanted to retain their shorter-range ballistic missiles because of the country's major defence deficit in its conventional air defence capabilities.

The US, for its part, had long been pragmatically accepting of Iran having these shorter-range ballistic missiles, provided that they did not threaten Israel. More specifically, Washington believed that the threat of an Iran having very short-range missiles would keep the Saudis more dependent on the US for protection than it would otherwise have been and would also have necessitated it having to buy hundreds of billions of dollars more defence equipment from the US.

Therefore, this statement on regional and missile issues was designed by Iran to be able to claim to its people that the US had given in on Iran keeping its regional missile programme, although in reality the US had never cared about it, provided that there was no threat to Israel.

Ultimately, Iran – more specifically, the IRGC – pushed the US too far in terms of the pre-conditions for an interim JCPOA. In particular, the IRGC wanted the US to roll back sanctions on Iran immediately that a new interim JCPOA was agreed. The IRGC also wanted the time before the issue was raised again of Iran fully signing up to the FATF (and thus, its own designation as an FTO) to be extended much further.

The 'Relationship Normalisation Deals' Programme

Many senior foreign policy advisers in the Trump administration knew that the only lasting effect of the US's unilateral withdrawal from the JCPOA in 2018 was to have made the Middle East a much more dangerous place than it had been even before and to have expedited the shift in the geopolitical alliances of its major countries that had started to take place especially since the end of 2016. That was the point at which OPEC and its *de facto* leader Saudi Arabia had been reliant on Russia to help to move oil prices back up to levels that helped their economies recover after the disastrous 2014-2016 Second Oil Price War. Russia's ability to help them achieve this had marked a true new alliance between it and the OPEC countries – especially Saudi Arabia – that had been formalised into the ongoing 'OPEC+' structure. The Second Oil Price War had also seen the foundation set for a much greater relationship between Saudi Arabia and China as well, which gained even more momentum as Crown Prince Mohammed bin Salman's problems mounted over his much-vaunted promise of a landmark IPO for Saudi Aramco. In short, the US withdrawal from the JCPOA had come at precisely the time when key Middle Eastern states had already started to drift more into the orbit of influence of Russia and then China and the prospect of a newly energised and aggressive Iran, with the US apparently not interested in being too involved in the Middle East any more, only speeded up this drift in alliances. The same mixture of factors had also left Israel feeling exceptionally vulnerable to attack from all sides, but particularly from Iran, as analysed earlier in this book.

Against this backdrop, the 'relationship normalisation deals' programme attempted to redress some of this geopolitical shift, by building up an alliance of Middle Eastern states with the US at the centre again. This time, though, it was thought in Washington, the US would place more of an emphasis on pure diplomacy rather than the mix of financial and military factors that had gone before. This was a practical policy interpretation of Trump's 'Endless Wars' speech.

The problem with this approach was that between them Russia and China had all three of these angles – diplomatic, financial and military covered already. In Russia, there was the practical support for the Middle East's oil producers that came with its support in the OPEC+ alliance. Russia was also willing to become involved militarily very quickly when needed, as it did to prop up the longstanding regime of the al-Assad dynasty in Syria. Russia understood clearly that Middle Eastern autocracies are not interested at all in regime change towards Western democratic models and that they viewed with horror the fates of Muammar Gaddafi in Libya and Saddam Hussein in Iraq. Reassuringly as well to the Middle Eastern leaders was that Russia was also an autocracy, as effectively was China.

Complementing the decisive, tough, militaristic approach that Russia offered, China further smoothed the way for the two superpowers in the Middle East through massive financing connected to its 'One Belt, One Road' programme. Middle Eastern autocrats are no more interested in the fine details of loan agreements made by China for various projects in their countries than they are in the finer details of democracy and free speech, but some could see the benefits of keeping the US on side as well.

The details of the relationship normalisation deals done between Israel and the UAE and Bahrain, brokered by the US, are examined in the first section of this book, but broadly speaking they can be regarded as just part of a balancing act of those two countries between their interests with the US and their interests with China and Russia. Equally, without either the big Sunni player in the region, Saudi Arabia, or the big Shia player in the region, Iran, being closely tied into the US, there was little chance that a decisive shift in alliances towards the US would occur in any other Middle Eastern country either.

The US recognised this and hoped to garner the support for its new initiative from Saudi Arabia, despite the drift in its focus towards Russia first and then China since 2016 in particular. As mentioned earlier, Saudi Crown Prince Mohammed bin Salman was known to be more sympathetic to the relationship normalisation agreements than his father, King Salman. King Salman had told the Organization of the Islamic Conference (OIC) in 2019 that the Palestinian cause remained a core issue and that the kingdom, 'refuses any measures that touch the historical and legal position of East Jerusalem.' Saudi Arabia's clerical establishment retains a very powerful role in the Kingdom: each Saudi king is also the custodian of the two holy mosques, and Saudi Arabia founded the OIC.

However, more positively for the US's ambitions for Saudi Arabia to support the relationship normalisation deals programme, Saudi's Foreign Minister, Prince Faisal bin Farhan, had cautiously welcomed the Israel-UAE relationship normalisation agreement, saying: 'It could be viewed as positive.' Additionally positive was that back in 2002 it had been the Saudis who had launched the 'Crown Prince Abdullah Peace Plan' at the Beirut Arab summit, offering Israel full recognition in exchange for a return to its pre-1967 Six-Day War borders.

Nonetheless, by that time the OPEC+ relationship with Russia had become too entrenched for Saudi Arabia to risk jeopardising it. New large-scale deals were already being made with China – which remained the biggest buyer of oil in the world, and the biggest potential energy market for Saudi Arabia's oil and gas products going forward.

Additionally, the political outlook for a second term for President Trump looked uncertain and the Saudis already knew how poorly they were seen by the only alternative new US president, Joe Biden, as highlighted in the first section of this book.

The US's Crucial Shale Energy Outlook Became Mixed

The US shale oil and gas sectors had been key to the US's more energy independent approach to the Middle East since shale gas had been deemed a long-term viable resource back in around 2006 and shale oil had found to be the same in about 2010. From a modest start, US shale oil production had increased from an average of slightly less than 0.2 million bpd in 2011 to just over 0.8 million bpd in 2012, and then by nearly 1 million bpd in 2013, and then by another 1.2 million bpd in 2014, to 8.7 million bpd in total, according to EIA figures.

Prior to this, as analysed at length in the first section of this book, the US had been held as an energy hostage by Saudi Arabia and its fellow OPEC members in the 1973 Oil Crisis. From the resolution of that conflict in 1974 to the onset of the rise of US shale energy resources as above, the US had been forced to walk a diplomatic tightrope between its own interests and those of the energy producing countries upon which it had still been so dependent.

The key turning point for the US had come in the 2014-2016 Second Oil Price War (the 1973/74 Oil crisis being the first such conflict). Not only had the US shale energy sector survived intact – during the entire War, total oil production in the US had only dropped by around 0.7 million bpd – but it had also transformed itself into a leaner, meaner version of itself, able to stay in business with oil prices as allow as USD35 pb of Brent. This was slightly lower than Russia's longstanding budget breakeven oil price at that point and much lower than Saudi Arabia's, which remained above USD80 pb of Brent for years.

The outlook for the US's shale energy sector had also stayed bright for a long period, with the EIA having estimated back then that US crude production would surpass the 10 million bpd mark by late 2018. This it did, breaching the record high set in 1970, with the shale boom propelling non-OPEC output up by some 1.3 million bpd in 2018. The predictions from that point was that US shale oil would continue to go from strength to strength, surpassing 11 million bpd, then 12 million bpd, and then 13 million bpd and so on.

By the time that Biden took over from Trump, though, a high of 12.3 million bpd in US crude oil production in 2019 had been followed by a drop in 2020 to 11.3 million bpd. This was followed by annual totals of

11.3 million bpd and then 11.9 million bpd in 2021 and 2022 respectively. Much of the decline in 2020 and 2021 was attributable to the demand-destruction effects of the widespread onset of COVID-19 and the Third Oil Price War, both analysed in depth in the first section of this book.

US Shale Oil Growth Hs Stalled But Could Be Ramped Up Again

US Field Production Of Crude Oil (Thousand Barrels Per Day) - 1850s To Present

Decade	Year-0	Year-1	Year-2	Year-3	Year-4	Year-5	Year-6	Year-7	Year-8	Year-9
1850's										0
1860's	1	6	8	7	6	7	10	9	10	12
1870's	14	14	17	24	30	33	25	37	42	55
1880's	72	76	83	64	66	60	77	77	75	96
1890's	126	149	138	133	135	145	167	166	152	156
1900's	174	190	243	275	320	369	347	455	488	502
1910's	574	604	609	681	728	770	822	919	920	1,037
1920's	1,210	1,294	1,527	2,007	1,951	1,700	2,112	2,469	2,463	2,760
1930's	2,460	2,332	2,145	2,481	2,488	2,723	3,001	3,500	3,324	3,464
1940's	4,107	3,847	3,796	4,125	4,584	4,695	4,749	5,088	5,520	5,046
1950's	5,407	6,158	6,256	6,458	6,342	6,807	7,151	7,170	6,710	7,054
1960's	7,035	7,183	7,332	7,542	7,614	7,804	8,295	8,810	9,096	9,238
1970's	9,637	9,463	9,441	9,208	8,774	8,375	8,132	8,245	8,707	8,552
1980's	8,597	8,572	8,649	8,688	8,879	8,971	8,680	8,349	8,140	7,613
1990's	7,355	7,417	7,171	6,847	6,662	6,560	6,465	6,452	6,252	5,881
2000's	5,822	5,801	5,744	5,649	5,441	5,184	5,086	5,074	5,000	5,357
2010's	5,484	5,674	6,524	7,497	8,793	9,442	8,848	9,359	10,953	12,315
2020's	11,318	11,254	11,883							

Source: EIA

The US's crude oil production number for 2022 is more interesting, as it raises questions about the future direction of the US shale sector, both oil and gas. The key questions are firstly whether this number is about the best that the US can manage, and the second question is, if it is not, then how easy would it be for the US to increase production as and when required.

The answer to the first question is almost certainly 'no' – this is not the best the US can do. The difference between the absolute increases or decreases in total output figures now and those of the early days of the US shale energy sector is that back then the sector was in a business phase marked by the overriding requirement to go for growth.

At that point, for reasons analysed throughout this book, all other considerations bar none were put aside to achieve the key objective of making the US more independent from an energy perspective on any other country. Consequently, it did not matter if major investors in Wall Street made any money in the short term from their financing of the shale energy sector. In the US's pursuit of energy independence, what mattered was major increases in oil and gas output every year. It is estimated by several industry sources that the US shale industry registered net negative free cash flows of USD300 billion, impaired more than USD450 billion of invested capital, and saw more than 190 bankruptcies since 2010.

The US Shale Sector Has Been In A Different Part Of the Business Cycle

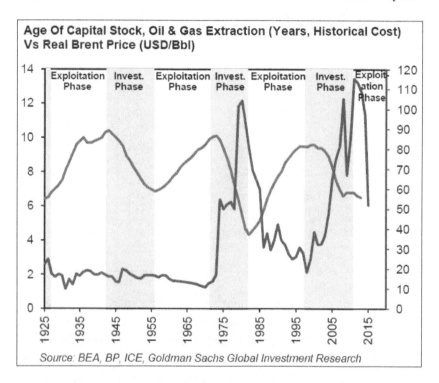

Age Of Capital Stock, Oil & Gas Extraction (Years, Historical Cost) Vs Real Brent Price (USD/Bbl)

Source: BEA, BP, ICE, Goldman Sachs Global Investment Research

This said, aside from the massive geopolitical importance of the US's increasing energy independence – which can barely be overstated – there were huge additional corollary domestic economic and political benefits to the growth in the shale energy sector as well. These cannot be so easily quantified as the headline figures for negative free cashflows or impairments, but they are likely to be much bigger.

A major corollary economic benefit for the US was that dramatic growth in the shale energy sector did reduce energy pricing in the US (which leads to increased consumer spending, which boosts economic growth). A major corollary political benefit is that the chances of re-election for a sitting US president (and for other major offices for the members of the party of the president) increases enormously in times of economic growth. The specific numbers involved in these statements are also laid out clearly in the first section of this book.

The key point here – and the answer to the second question posed just above - is that although the US shale energy sector could relax into a production level in which significant output keeps being generated whilst also allowing institutional investors to recoup their financing, it could – if required – dramatically ramp up production increases again. As also analysed earlier, the best US shale oil operations during the period of the 2014-2016 Oil Price War, and to this day, can bring their oil fields back online in as little as a week, from a standing start, although the refinery-related lead time is slightly longer.

In the context of the highly volatile geopolitical architecture of the previous few years, this ability to turn on the taps in the US's shale energy sector is extremely useful. It provides assurance to net energy consumers allied to the US that there are emergency energy supplies available in the very short term and it also allows the US very considerable ongoing leverage in the global oil and gas markets. This leverage, along with other levers that the US and its allies have available to them, can be utilised to make new energy alliances, which is what has been happening since Russia's invasion of Ukraine in 2022.

US Resumes Leadership Role Against Russia-China Alliance

Whatever anyone may have thought about President Biden and his administration before, the US's reaction to Russia's invasion of Ukraine has seen a broadly steely resolve, tempered with clever diplomacy when required. Galvanising the genuine support of most allies in Europe and Asia for Ukraine to continue to wage its resistance against Russia, whilst at the same time managing to avoid provoking the Kremlin into the use of nuclear weapons, has been done with greater expertise and finesse.

Over and above the situation in Ukraine itself, there have been military considerations relating to China's intentions towards Taiwan and others of its targets in Asia-Pacific. There have been political and security considerations relating to the Middle East and other emerging areas of the world. And most important in the early stages of the invasion of Ukraine were considerations of continued energy supplies into Europe to substitute for those that would be lost from Russia.

As analysed in full in the first section of this book, any failure to ensure the quick and effective substitution of Russian energy supplies with new energy supplies to Europe – particularly to its *de facto* economic leader, Germany – would have meant the collapse of collective will to signal to Russia that Europe and its allies would not tolerate this latest act of aggression or any others in the future. These efforts in the first instance were considerably helped in the early stages after the invasion, and beyond, by the US. Deals involving major US companies, directly and indirectly, were secured for new energy supplies from several sources in the Middle East and North Africa in particular.

These deals were mostly for gas in the early stages - in quick to buy and fast to ship LNG form – as this was where the largest and most immediate energy deficit from lost Russian energy supplies would come. As analysed in full in the first section of this book, the clamour for continued cheap and plentiful gas supplies from Russia was loud in Europe, especially from Germany. If the US had not been quick to help to secure new supplies, then there was a high chance that the response to Russian aggression in Ukraine from the US and its allies would have been as ineffectual as it was when Russia had annexed Crimea in 2014. This unified and strong response was also required to show China – which was watching how the Russian invasion of Ukraine proceeded – how any similar actions by it in Taiwan would be handled by the US and its allies in Europe and Asia

This necessary energy substitution strategy away from Russia has not only meant that Europe is no longer a weak link in NATO's collective defence programme but has also resulted in the foundations being laid for a build-out of relationships with countries whose energy supplies have filled the Russian deficit. These include in the past year Qatar, Egypt, Libya, and even the UAE, among others. Although these countries also continue to deal with China and Russia, there is every reason to see potential for a further building out of these relationships in the future. It may be that these will take up where the 'relationship normalisation deals' programme left off in the same way that Russian aggression in Ukraine beginning in 2022 resulted in a re-energisation of NATO and similar alliances in Asia.

Russia

The Key Oil Producer In The OPEC+ Alliance

From around the time that Vladimir Putin took over as acting president at the end of 1999, Russia has come to play a vital role in the world oil and gas business. This was made possible by the dramatic – and highly effective – reorganisation of the country's oil and gas sector following the fall of the USSR in 1991. During the Soviet Union period, both sectors had suffered from chronic under-investment and over-exploitation that had led in some cases to significant damage being done to the resource sites.

The detailed story of precisely how this reorganisation was achieved has been told in many other books so will not be gone into detail here, suffice it to say that it went along the following lines. During the break-up of the USSR, the KGB needed to hide Russia's key assets (including those of the strategically and financially vital oil and gas sectors) as they did not know what was coming next. It did this through various front companies, key parts of which were then sold off during former President Boris Yeltsin's 'voucher privatisation' scheme, which resulted in many highly valuable oil and gas assets being sold for a fraction of their true price to opportunistic businessmen, later termed the 'oligarchs.' These oligarchs then re-organised and rationalised these bureaucratic structures, making them much better operations. When Putin came to power, the Russian state took these assets back by whatever means were required.

As it now stands, Russia – in terms of oil and gas reserves (both conventional and non-conventional) – remains a global energy powerhouse. Although its official conventional oil reserves are not as much as those of some other major hydrocarbons powers, at around 80 billion barrels, its production punches well above this weight. For much of the past 20 or so years it has been in the top three largest oil producers in the world, together with the US and Saudi Arabia. Unlike Saudi Arabia, as highlighted elsewhere, Russia can easily produce 10-11 million barrels of crude oil per day. Additionally, as analysed shortly in this section, Russia is keenly and successfully exploring for, and developing wherever possible, new oil (and gas) reserves in the Arctic region (and has covert plans to do so in the Antarctic as well). These reserves, although not fully documented yet, are potentially enormous and are likely to significantly increase Russia's crude oil (and gas) reserves figures.

As large as Russia's conventional and unconventional oil reserves are, its gas reserves are unparalleled in the world. Russia still holds the official gas reserves of any country, of around 1,688 trillion cubic feet (Tcf), although again this figure does not make allowance for ongoing new finds, especially in the Arctic region, as many of these are still be quantified. These account for about one quarter of the world's total, with most of them located in large natural gas fields in West Siberia.

Russia Has Unparalleled Conventional Gas Reserves

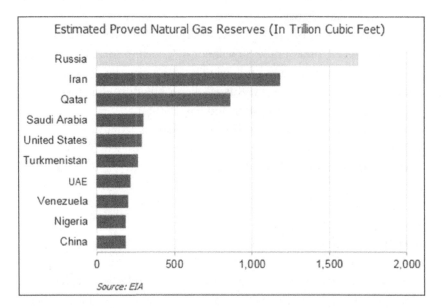

Rationales For Russia's OPEC+ Move

In petro-economic terms, up to the invasion of Ukraine in 2022, Russia occupied the middle ground between the US and Saudi Arabia, being less dependent than Saudi Arabia on crude oil exports for its state revenues (although the figure rose if the gas sector was also factored in) but more dependent than the US.

At the time of the 2014-2016 Oil Price War, for example, Russia's budget breakeven price per barrel of the benchmark Urals grade was around the USD60-65 pb level (compared to Saudi Arabia's Brent budget breakeven price of USD90-95 pb and US shale's USD37-42 pb level).

Also positive for Russia was that due largely to its flexible exchange rate to the US dollar it was better able to absorb oil price shocks than many of its OPEC+ allies whose currencies align closely to the US currency. For Russia when oil prices fall the rouble's value against the US dollar also tends to fall, which allows Russian oil producers – whose costs are mainly in roubles – to minimise the impact of low prices on their operations.

In late 2016, Saudi Arabia finally deduced that it could no longer take the economic pain of an enduring low oil price environment and moved to push prices back up by cutting oil production. However, the Kingdom found that it had damaged its own credibility, and that of OPEC, to such an extent with its failed 2014-2016 Oil Price War, that it needed the help of Russia to make the late 2016 production cut agreement work effectively. From that point, Russia has been instrumental in the effectiveness of all OPEC production deals – a relationship formalised in the 'OPEC+' (primarily, 'plus' Russia) alliance.

Russia Ahead Of Saudi In 2016 In Crude Oil Production...

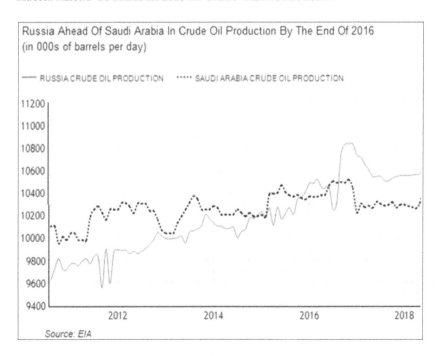

...And Ahead Of The US Too

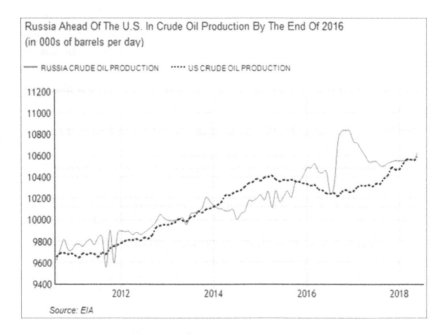

Russia Ahead Of The U.S. In Crude Oil Production By The End Of 2016
(in 000s of barrels per day)

—— RUSSIA CRUDE OIL PRODUCTION   ····· US CRUDE OIL PRODUCTION

Source: EIA

For Russia, though, its oil (and gas) resources have long held much more
significance than merely generating cash; their deployment around the
world has been the spearhead for the re-assertion of Russian power across
the globe. This idea was always central to President Vladimir Putin's core
vision for the Motherland, which harks back to the glory days of empire –
both the empire of the USSR and the one started by Peter the Great two
hundred years or so earlier. This view is highlighted in Putin's own words:
'The collapse of the Soviet Union was the biggest geopolitical catastrophe
of the century. For the Russian people, it became a real drama. Tens of
millions of our citizens and countrymen found themselves outside Russian
territory. The epidemic of disintegration also spread to Russia itself.'

For Putin, then, Russia's oil and gas resources were always seen a key
mechanism through which Russia could: firstly, keep the energy-needy
Former Soviet Union (FSU) states firmly in line; secondly, ensure that the
principal European Union (EU) states (especially Germany) did not seek
to interfere too much in any of Russia's dealings with the remaining non-
EU countries; thirdly, leverage whenever and wherever possible existing
disagreements between the EU and the US to critically undermine the core

NATO doctrine of 'collective defence' against attack; and fourthly, use the prospect of given or withheld energy supplies to project its power into 'chaotic states' (oftentimes Russia would create the chaos first and then project its own power into that destabilised and unfocused country to provide its own style of solution).

OPEC Deals Supported By Russia

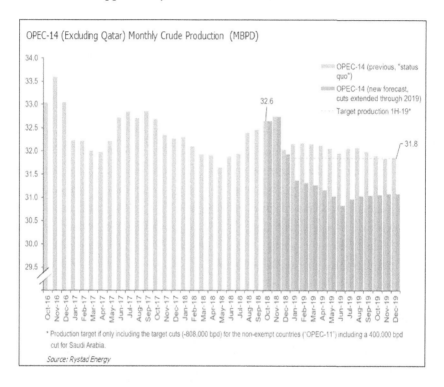

OPEC-14 (Excluding Qatar) Monthly Crude Production (MBPD)

* Production target if only including the target cuts (-808,000 bpd) for the non-exempt countries ('OPEC-11') including a 400,000 bpd cut for Saudi Arabia.

Source: Rystad Energy

In terms of the lead-up to the formation of the OPEC+ alliance, Russia's main focus had been Iran. Iran is not only a huge oil and gas power itself, but it also has enormous influence through its political, economic and military proxies over neighbouring Iraq – another massive and relatively underdeveloped oil and gas power. In addition, as the leading Shia Islam power in the Middle East, Iran also had a high level of influence over other Shai countries in the region, which collectively constituted the informal Shia Crescent of Power grouping.

Already in a controlling position in all key countries in the Shia Crescent in the Middle East – Iran, Iraq, Lebanon, Syria, and Yemen (via Iran) –

Russia continued to work on those countries on the edges of the Crescent in which it already directly or indirectly had a foothold. These included Azerbaijan (75% Shia and an FSU state) and Turkey (25% Shia and furious at not being accepted fully into the European Union). Others also remained longer-term targets, including Bahrain (75% Shia) and Pakistan (up to 25% Shia and a home to sworn-US enemies Al Qaeda and the Taliban).

The Russian influence in Saudi Arabia, Iran, and Iraq are analysed in depth in the first section of this book and in the standalone sections on those countries, and its influence in Syria is analysed in full very shortly in this section. In terms of the FSU states, all of them without exception are regarded by Russia as still essentially Russian, and moves have long been afoot to 'repatriate' them by whatever means necessary unless specifically threatened against doing so by the US and its NATO allies.

Even those FSU states with close relationships to the US – such as Azerbaijan – but that are not specifically seen as being on the US's 'off limits' list are regarded by Russia as being fair game and in play for various threats or bribes to bring them back on side (the division of the Caspian Sea's huge oil and gas reserves, analysed in full in the standalone Iran section above, is a case in point). All the previous FSU states that are now plainly part of Europe – and members of the European Union or seeking such membership - are also on this list.

Even before the full invasion of Ukraine in 2022, this view of Russia's had clearly been seen as early as the short-lived war in former USSR constituent state, Georgia, in 2008. This had followed the Russian-backed creation of two self-proclaimed republics in Georgia (of South Ossetia, and Abkhazia), which Russia had then supported militarily on the basis of unsubstantiated claims by Russia that the government of Georgia was persecuting the Russian-aligned inhabitants of the two breakaway republics as part of a wider 'genocide' being committed upon them. This was followed by the exercise of exactly the same idea in 2014 when Russia annexed the Ukrainian region of Crimea.

As most obviously seen as far back as the 2014 invasion of Ukraine and the subsequent annexation of Crimea, Russia's gas (and to a lesser extent, oil) supplies to Europe were being used as key weapons to achieve its objective with little in the way of negative consequences resulting from its actions. The other principal methods Russia has relied upon, often to great effect at relatively little cost, financial or otherwise, to assert control in various countries has been to create domestic political upheaval by leveraging anti-migration and more nationalistic sentiment in these countries through the funding of far-right and far-left political groups. In tandem with this, Russia has sought to manipulate elections in these countries (either directly or indirectly through conventional or social media) to sow chaos, an environment in which Russia thrives. The ultimate endgame of this strategy was always to break up the European Union and to end the NATO military alliance between Europe and the US.

This approach had been crystallised after Putin's early efforts – to whatever aim – to forge a closer relationship with the European Union and with the US had been rebuffed. In the case of Europe, Putin tried in his early years to make friendly overtures to the West, most apparently in his 25 September 2001 speech in Germany's Bundestag. In this, he outlined that Russia's destiny was in Europe and that the Cold War was definitively over, but he subsequently drew back from this conciliatory position. In large part this pulling back by Putin was a function of the European Union's continued invitations to former USSR states to join the economic and political bloc and EU censure over the Chechen Wars. It was also because of pressure on Putin from the stalwarts of the older-style political and security forces in Russia who were his sponsors at the time that to continue such efforts would be deleterious to his political future.

In the case of the US, Putin had believed early on that his attempts to reach an understanding with then-US President George W. Bush were being reciprocated. Bush had memorably stated that: 'I looked the man in the eye. I found him to be very straightforward and trustworthy [...] I was able to get a sense of his soul.' Putin was the first international leader to call Bush after the 9/11 attacks and express his condolences. As a practical adjunct to this, Putin also allowed the US military access to Russian military sites in Central Asia from which to launch air strikes and Special Forces ground attacks in Afghanistan.

The turning point for Putin of this 'betrayal' by the US - to add to the 'betrayal' by Europe of continuing to invite former USSR states to join the EU - came most notably in the US's unilateral withdrawal in June 2002 from the landmark Anti-Ballistic Missile Treaty. This was followed shortly afterwards by US statements that it was to build an extensive 'missile defence system' in former Warsaw Pact states in Eastern Europe. These aggressively anti-Russian moves – as Putin saw them – were compounded by NATO then inviting another seven Central and Eastern European countries to be part of the Western security bloc. As Putin saw it, all these moves added up to the West pushing into historical Russian territory and, more practically, into the land barrier that Russia had established after 1945 to ensure that aggressive forces from the West (in the previous two cases, Germany) could not so easily sweep into Russia in the future and threaten Moscow itself.

In sum, by the end of 2016, Putin had given up any hopes of any constructive future relationship with the US. He still had hopes of being able to forge more constructive relations with several European Union member countries, and with Germany especially, through leveraging its cheap and plentiful energy supplies to them.

He was also keen to exploit all divisions in the US sphere of influence and at the heart of this network was the oil and gas states in the Middle East. The key one of these for the US had been Saudi Arabia since the foundation-stone 1945 agreement. This is why Russia joined alongside OPEC in its efforts to cut production and push up oil prices: to take the Al Saud-ruled Saudi Arabia away from the US or to destroy the dynasty and then take what was left of the country.

Syria Was A Turning Point In Russia's Middle East Strategy

Whilst the West's approach to the conflict that began in Syria in 2011 was characterised by confusion – unwilling to support President Assad due to alleged chemicals weapons use against his own people, so instead supporting anti-Assad groups, many aligned with ISIS or Al-Qaeda – Russia took a pragmatic view on what was best for its own interests. This was to stick with the regime that had held Syria together for decades rather than to remove yet another regional strongman from power only to have civil war and then unending chaos follow (as with Saddam Hussein and Muammar Gaddafi shortly before). From before onset of serious civil disturbance in 2011, Russia had been supportive of the al-Assad dynasty and in late 2015 it added direct military intervention to its support.

As it was, and remains, Russia identified Syria under the Assad regime as being crucial to it for four key reasons. First, it is the biggest country on the western side of the Shia Crescent of Power that Russia has been meticulously developing for years as a counterpoint to the US's own sphere of influence centred on Saudi Arabia (for hydrocarbons supplies) and Israel (for military and intelligence assets). Second, it offers a long Mediterranean coastline from which Russia can send oil and gas products (either its own or those of its allies, notably Iran) for export either into major oil and gas hubs in Turkey, Greece and Italy or into north, west and east Africa. Third, it is a vital military hub, with one major naval port (Tartus), one major air force base (Latakia) and one major listening station (just outside Latakia). And fourth, it showed the rest of the Middle East that Russia could and would act decisively on the side of the autocratic dynasties across the region. By happy coincidence for Russia, Syria also has significant oil and gas resources that can be used by the Kremlin to offset part of the costs it incurs as part of its geopolitical manoeuvring.

Syria Presented A Huge Opportunity For Russia From Several Angles

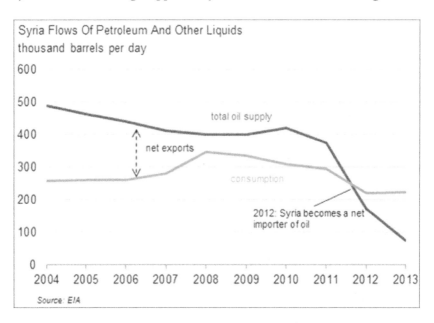

According to Russia's Deputy Prime Minister, Yuri Borisov, in the aftermath of Russia's direct military intervention in Syria in September 2015, Moscow was also working to restore at least 40 energy facilities in Syria, including offshore oil fields. This was part of a wider development programme aimed at bringing back the full oil and gas potential of the country as it was before July 2011 when, inspired by the Arab Spring revolutions, defectors from the Syrian army formed the Free Syrian Army and commenced armed conflict across the country. Prior to that point, it has been largely forgotten that Syria was an oil and gas producer of some significance in the global hydrocarbons markets.

As at the beginning of 2011, Syria was producing around 400,000 bpd of crude oil from proven reserves of 2.5 billion barrels. Before recovery began to drop off due to a lack of enhanced oil recovery techniques being employed at the major fields – mostly located in the east near the border with Iraq or in the centre of the country, east of the city of Homs – it had been producing nearly 600,000 bpd. For the period when the largest producing fields – including those in the Deir-ez-Zour region, such as the biggest field, Omar – were under the control of ISIS, crude oil and condensates production fell to about 25,000 bpd before recovering again.

It should also be remembered that a sizeable proportion of this crude oil output went to Europe, which was importing at least USD3 billion worth of oil per year from Syria up to the beginning of 2011, according to the European Commission, and much of the key infrastructure to handle oil from Syria remained operationally in place for a long time after the 2011 troubles began. Many European refineries, for example, were configured to process the heavy, sour 'Souedie' crude oil that makes up much of Syria's output, with the remainder being the sweet and lighter 'Syrian Light' grade. Most of this, some 150,000 bpd combined, went to Germany, Italy and France, from one of Syria's three Mediterranean export terminals - Banias, Tartus and Latakia. As an adjunct to this, a multitude of international oil companies were operating in Syria's energy sector, including Anglo-Dutch Shell, France's Total, the China National Petroleum Corporation (CNPC), India's Oil and Natural Gas Corp, Canada's Suncor Energy, Britain's Petrofac and Gulfsands Petroleum, along with Russian oil company Tatneft and engineering firm Stroytransgaz.

Syria's gas sector was at least as vibrant as its oil sector, and less of that was damaged in the first few years of the conflict. With proven reserves of 8.5 trillion cubic feet (tcf) of natural gas, the full year 2010 – the last under normal operating conditions – saw Syria produce just over 316 billion cubic feet per day (bcf/d) of dry natural gas. The build out of the South Central Gas Area – built by Stroytransgaz – had started up by the end of 2009 and had boosted Syria's natural gas production by about 40% by the beginning of 2011. This allowed Syria's combined oil and gas exports to generate a quarter of government revenues at that point, and to make it the eastern Mediterranean's leading oil and gas producer at the time. After the onset of the domestic armed uprising in July 2011 and then ISIS moving west from Iraq into Syria in September 2014, gas production fell off to less than 130 bcf/d before recovering again.

Russia Can Make Syria Pay For Its Own Occupation

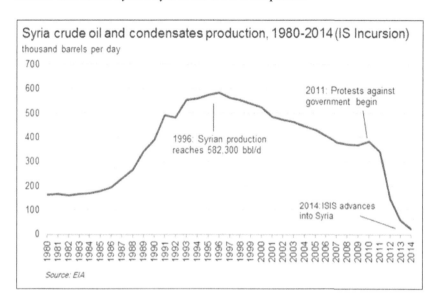

The energy plan to which Deputy Prime Minister Borisov referred was a re-working of the memorandum of understanding signed between Syria and Russia in the middle of November 2017, encompassing not just 40 energy projects but a lot more as well. For a start, focus would turn to expanding the power sector, following on from the original 2017 plan signed between Syria's then-Electricity Minister Mohammad Zuhair Kharboutli and Russia's Minister of Energy Alexander Novak. The deal covered the full reconstruction and rehabilitation of the Aleppo thermal plant, the installation of the Deir Ezzor power plant and the expansion of capacity of the Mharda and Tishreen plants, with a view to re-energising Syria's power grid and restoring the main control centre for the grid back to Damascus. This accorded with comments as early as the middle of December 2017 (by then-Russian Deputy Prime Minister Dmitry Rogozin after holding talks in Syria with President Bashar al-Assad) that: 'Russia will be the only country to take part in rebuilding Syrian energy facilities.'

Over and above the four power plant projects that were to be optimised as a priority, the key infrastructure project was the complete repair and capacity-boosting upgrading of the Homs oil refinery (Syria's other is in Banias). The practical project work was led by Iran's Mapna and Russia companies, with the initial target capacity being 140,000 bpd, Phase 2's being 240,000 bpd and Phase 3's being 360,000 bpd. The intention was that it could also be used to refine Iranian oil coming through Iraq if needed, before onward shipment into southern Europe.

Russia still has detailed plans for Syria to act as a natural conduit for oil and gas shipments into Europe once the conflict has been subdued further. In the post-conflict planning by the US, Europe and Russia, there were three options for Syria on the table. The US-led option involved moving gas from Qatar through Saudi Arabia and Jordan, then through Syria whereupon it would flow into Turkey and onwards to the rest of Europe, thereby reducing Europe's dependence on Russian gas supplies. The European-favoured option involved UN peace-keeping monitors on the ground in Syria, bringing in hydrocarbons industry experts from the UN Security Council member states, and letting both pipelines (Qatar-Syria-Turkey and Iran-Iraq-Syria-Turkey) develop organically over time. This was to allow the European Union to re-calibrate its energy sources gradually, in line with its strategy of reducing its dependence on Russia directly at that point.

The Russian option – the only one left on the table as the conflict continued – involves fully resuscitating the notion of the Iran-Iraq-Syria pipeline, moving Iranian, and later Iraqi, gas from South Pars to Syria and then into Europe. Such an option would also likely encourage closer co-operation in the Gas Exporting Countries Forum (GECF), but this option is opposed by the US and Europe, as the GECF comprises 11 of the world's leading natural gas producers (Algeria, Bolivia, Egypt, Equatorial Guinea, Iran, Libya, Nigeria, Qatar, Russia, Trinidad & Tobago, and Venezuela).

Aside from the fact that the core members of the organisation are Russia, Iran and Qatar, and that it also has some of the US's other designated previous or current rogue states on the list – notably Venezuela – GECF members together control over 71% of global gas reserves, 44%

of its marketed production, 53% of its gas pipelines, and 57% of its LNG exports. This makes it effectively a Gas OPEC+.

Consolidating Power Through Massive Arctic Finds

In the middle of 2019, Japan's Mitsui and Japan Oil, Gas and Metals National Corporation agreed to buy a 10% stake in Novatek's Arctic LNG (liquefied natural gas) 2 project for an officially undisclosed price, although Russia's President Vladimir Putin independently stated that the investment would be around USD3 billion. The fact that Putin himself commented on the deal underlines how important the exploration and development of the Arctic region is for Russia as a source of potentially vast new oil and gas resources and the accretion of further geopolitical influence, akin to the game-changing shale industry for the US.

Russia's current development of the Arctic region is centred around the Yamal Peninsula and led principally by Novatek, but further developments are in the offing from Gazprom and Gazprom Neft, even in the face of current and future US sanctions. Novatek's main Arctic project, the Yamal LNG (unofficially referred to as 'Arctic 1') announced at the time of the Japan LNG deal that it had produced 9.0 million tons of LNG and 0.6 million tons of stable gas condensate in the first half of that year, with all three (at that time) LNG trains running above the 5.5 million metric tons per annum (mtpa) nameplate capacity over that period.

This resulted in 126 LNG tanker shipments being dispatched in the six-month period via trans-shipment from the ice-class LNG carriers to conventional vessels in Norway and delivered onto the global markets, mostly to Russia's key target markets in Asia, including most notably China. Overall, the Yamal LNG project consists of a 17.4 mtpa natural gas liquefaction plant comprised of three LNG trains of 5.5 mtpa each and one LNG train of 900 thousand tons per annum, utilising the hydrocarbon resources of the South-Tambeyskoye field in the Russian Arctic.

Train 4, which had just begun to produce at the beginning of 2021 – following COVID-19-related delays (and non-COVID delays) – adds to the existing 16.5 million mtpa capacity available in the project's first three trains. Novatek has plans to build out an LNG export capacity of up to 70 million mtpa by 2030 as it adds new projects to its portfolio. Overall,

Novatek's then-chief executive officer, Mark Gyetvay, stated at the time that Novatek would be able to produce at least 100 million mtpa of LNG soon after 2030 if not before and would be able to do so at a very low relative cost of production. Specifically, he said that it would be possible to deliver LNG into northeast Asian markets on a sustained basis for 'a little over' USD3 per thousand (i.e. one million) British thermal units (MMBtu). This would be comprised of a USD0.07/MMBtu cost of feed gas, USD0.43/MMBtu of liquefaction costs, plus between USD2/MMBtu and USD2.50/MMBtu of shipping costs.

OPEC+'s Most Influential Player

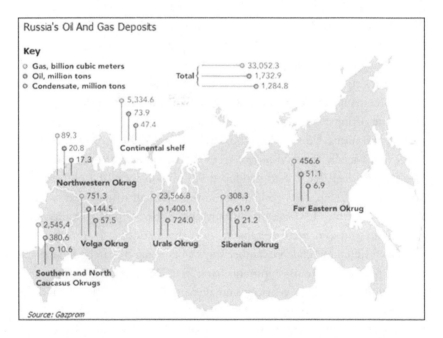

This dovetails into Russia's plans for LNG production of 80-140 million mtpa by 2035, which would exceed even the expanded output capacity of LNG powerhouses Qatar and Australia. The increase is aimed at bringing Russia's LNG standing in the world market into line with its status as a global gas superpower, as its LNG capability has always been way behind what its gas production power would warrant as far as Putin is concerned.

In this context, US sanctions imposed after Russia took over Crimea in 2014 only made Putin more determined that the Arctic LNG programme would not fail. Moscow not only initially bankrolled Yamal LNG from the beginning with money directly from the state budget but also supported it again later in 2014 by selling bonds in Yamal LNG (the programme began on 24 November 2015, with a RUB75 billion 15-year issue). It further provided RUB150 billion of additional backstop funding from the National Welfare Fund. After that, and months of wrangling, April 2016 saw two Chinese state banks agree to provide USD12 billion to the Yamal LNG project in euros and roubles. The project was helped by a tumble in the rouble in late 2014 that effectively cut the cost of Russia-sourced equipment and labour at a key moment in the construction.

Having insulated itself from US financial sanctions relating to its annexation of Crimea in 2014, Novatek stepped up its efforts to do the same for its technology requirements. Novatek indigenised as much of the technology and machinery involved with the Yamal LNG project as it could and in 2018 received a federal patent for its 'Arctic Cascade' natural gas liquefaction technology. This is based on a two-stage liquefaction process that capitalises on the colder ambient temperature in the Arctic climate to maximise energy efficiency during the liquefaction process. It was the first patented liquefaction technology using equipment produced only by Russian manufacturers. The overall goal of Novatek, as the company stated more than once, was to localise the fabrication and construction of LNG trains and modules. This would decrease the overall cost of liquefaction and develop a technological base within Russia, so that the Arctic LNG operations were not subject to the whims of other countries and future sanctions.

Given this backdrop, Novatek's second Yamal LNG project – officially 'Arctic LNG 2' – aims for three LNG trains of 6.6 mtpa each, based around the oil and gas resources of the Utrenneye field, which has at least 1,138 billion cubic metres of natural gas and 57 million tons of liquids in reserves. Novatek plans to commission the first train in 2023, the second train in 2024 and the third train in 2025, before reaching full capacity in 2026. To this end, it secured three other partners in the venture, aside from the Japanese. Two are from the key target market of China itself – the China National Petroleum Corporation subsidiary China National Oil and Gas Exploration and Development, and China National Offshore Oil Corporation, with a joint 10% stake – and France's supermajor,

TotalEnergies, also with 10%. Novatek has said that it plans to keep 60% for itself, with the remaining stake yet to be permanently assigned.

In the same vein, Russian gas giant, Gazprom, also announced in 2019 the full-scale development of the giant Kharasavey gas field in the Bovanenkovo production zone on the northern Yamal peninsula. This is part of the company's continuing shift in its production base northward, in line with Russia's other major tangential strategy of building out the gas capacity of Yamal to compensate for reserves depletion in West Siberia. Kharasavey is estimated to hold 2 trillion cubic metres of gas and is set to produce its first gas in 2023 with plateau output of 32 billion cubic metres per year. Gazprom's oil producing subsidiary Gazprom Neft is also looking at producing its own LNG from its Arctic operations.

Monetising its gas resources in the Arctic would be a relatively straightforward task for Gazprom Neft, allowing the company to recoup more of the RUB400 billion (USD6.4 billion) that it plans to spend on developing its Novoportovskoye field (estimated to have recoverable reserves of more than 320 bcm of gas) over the next three years, earlier than would otherwise be the case. Part of this development cost is planned to go on the construction of a key gas pipeline to run from Novy Port across the Gulf of Ob to Yamburg, which will carry at least 10 billion cubic metres of gas per year from the Novoportovskoye oil and gas field into Gazprom's main gas delivery system.

This infrastructure is also likely to be utilised by the third of Novatek's own Arctic projects – Ob LNG – which commenced development in June 2019. Based on the resources of the Verkhnetiuteyskoye and Zapadno-Seyakhinskoye fields, located in the central part of the Yamal Peninsula, the two fields hold a total of 157 billion cubic metres of natural gas and the projected new plant will produce up to 4.8 mtpa of LNG. The main plant, built exclusively with Russian-made technology in Sabetta, will cost USD5 billion and is set to come into operation in 2023. A key point in adding such production from the Arctic region is to dominate the Asian markets, particularly that of China,. This was tacitly acknowledged by Novatek's Mikhelson when he stated that he expected at least 80% of Novatek's future LNG production to go to the Asian market. This was further highlighted by the fact that Novatek is moving forward with the trans-shipment LNG facility on the Russian Far East coast in Kamchatka.

The Arctic Is Also Key To Russia's China Plans

The Russian Arctic sector comprises over 35,700 billion cubic metres of natural gas and over 2,300 million metric tons of oil and condensate, the majority of which are located in the Yamal and Gydan peninsulas, lying on the south side of the Kara Sea. According to comments from President Putin, the next 10 to 15 years will witness a dramatic expansion in the extraction of these Arctic resources, and a corollary build-out of the Northern Sea Route (NSR) as the primary transport route to monetise these resources in the global oil and gas markets, especially to China. It was revealed in late 2021 that a massive new gas field in the Kara Sea itself had been discovered by Russian oil giant, Rosneft.

The new gas was named after the Soviet military hero Marshall Georgy Zhukov, with natural gas reserves estimated at 800 billion cubic metres (Bcm). It is located in the Vikulovskaya structure, part of the East Prinovozemelsky-1 licence area, over which Rosneft has exploration and production rights running from 11 November 2020 to 10 November 2040. The large scale of the deposit was ascertained after Rosneft bored a well 1.6 kilometres deep close to the massive Pobeda oil and gas field, which – along with the newly found Zhukov field – are located in the East-Prinovozemelsky-1 area, in which exploration began in earnest in 2014.

In fact, it was US supermajor ExxonMobil that led the way in financing across an exploration area that included three huge and highly prospective licence areas in the Kara Sea after the signing of a broad exploration and development deal with Rosneft in 2011. The first well drilled in this development programme – by a Norwegian drilling rig in 2014 – led to the discovery of the massive Pobeda field, originally called the 'Universitetskaya-1' site, which was initially estimated to hold at least 125 million tons (about 916 million barrels) of oil and 422 Bcm of gas. Russia Energy Minister, Alexander Novikov, stated that new studies show the oil held at Pobeda could be as much as 500 million tons (nearly 3.7 billion barrels). ExxonMobil pulled out of its 2011 Arctic co-operation deal with Rosneft due to US sanctions on Russia over its annexation of the Crimea from Ukraine in 2014.

Given this, and the new discovery of the Zhukov field, Rosneft is extremely bullish about the prospects for the other fields under exploration and development in the Kara Sea. 'The results of drilling carried out by

Rosneft in the Kara Sea have shown the high oil and gas content of these structures, which confirms the discovery of a new Kara offshore oil province,' said Rosneft. 'In terms of resources, it may surpass such oil and gas provinces as the Gulf of Mexico, Brazil's offshore, the Alaskan and Canadian Arctic offshore, as well as the largest provinces in the Middle East,' it added. Moreover, it underlined that currently it has more than 30 'promising structures' in the aforementioned three Vostochno-Prinovozemelskiy areas of the Kara Sea.

Game-Changing 30-Year Alliance Between Russia And China

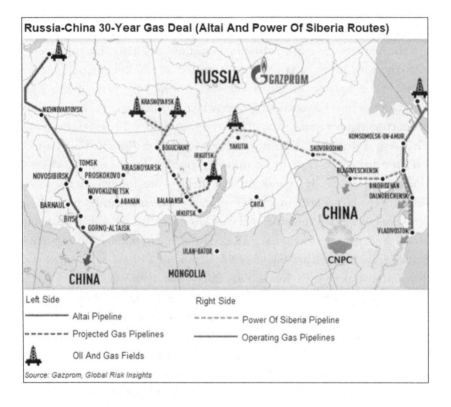

Russia's NSR Short Cut From West To East

Rosneft is also developing the Vostok Oil project in Russia's Far North that includes the Vankor cluster, Zapadno-Irkinsky block, the Payakhskaya group of fields and the East Taimyr cluster. Overall, it is estimated to hold proven liquid hydrocarbons reserves of at least 6 billion metric tons (about 51 billion barrels), all within the close proximity of the NSR that the company intends to exploit to deliver hydrocarbons to Europe and Asia. Rosneft chief executive officer Igor Sechin told President Putin that with exploration underway at the Vostok Oil project, and the design work for a 770-kilometre oil pipeline and port having been completed, the scheme would create a 'new oil and gas province' on Siberia's Taymyr peninsula. The complete project will cost RUB10 trillion (USD135 billion), including two airports and 15 'industry towns.' According to Sechin, Rosneft's Arctic developments would eventually produce 100 million tonnes of oil per year, with 30 million tonnes of oil being sent from the Arctic along the NSR between now and 2024 alone.

The NSR Allows Quicker Movement Of Energy From Russia To China

Russia's efforts in this area are being firmly bolstered by Gazprom Neft, the country's third biggest oil company by output and the oil arm of state gas giant Gazprom. July 2020 saw Gazprom Neft ship its first cargo of oil produced in the Arctic to China via the NSR, adding to its existing Western exports via the NSR to Europe. According to Gazprom Neft, it took 47 days to deliver a full cargo of 144,000 tonnes of sweet, light Novy Port oil

– that comes from the Yamal peninsula developments – to the Chinese port of Yantai on the Bohai Sea from Russia's north-western city of Murmansk. 'Successful experience in the sale of Arctic oil in the European market and in-depth insight of Asia-Pacific markets allow Gazprom Neft to offer Novy Port oil with a unique year-round logistics scheme to Asian partners,' said Gazprom Neft's deputy director general for logistics, processing and sales, Anatoly Cherner.

A month later, Gazprom Neft announced a new joint venture (JV) with Shell, focused on the exploration and development of oil and gas resources along the Gydan peninsula area, particularly at the Leskinsky and Pukhutsyayakhsky licence blocks. Both appear to be good prospects, with the Leskinsky block (located in the Taimyr district of Krasnoyarsk) estimated to contain at least 100 million metric tons (733 million barrels) of oil equivalent across its over 3,000 square km area. The Pukhutsyayakhsky block is estimated to hold at least 35 million metric tons (256.5 million barrels) of oil equivalent. Gazprom Neft-GEO will act as the operator on the exploration work at both blocks.

The development of the two blocks will neatly augment Gazprom Neft's increasingly Arctic-leaning business, with the area accounting for at least 30% of the company's oil production since 2019. The company started exporting oil produced in the Arctic sector from as early as 2013 and since then it has delivered at least 40 million tons of oil – including both the ARCO (Prirazlomnoye field) and Novy Port (Novoportovskoye field) blends – to various European countries.

The China side of these Arctic projects is fully in line with the USD400 billion or so 30-year deal signed in 2014 for Russia to export vast quantities of gas – through the 'Power of Siberia' pipeline project – to China over that period (managed on the Russian side by Gazprom and on the China side by China National Petroleum Corp). The agreement delivers some 38 billion cubic metres of natural gas a year to China (having formally started in 2018), totalling over 1 trillion cubic metres of gas being supplied during a whole contractual period. Although a relatively reasonable deal for Russia economically, the political benefit is huge, giving it a major second market for its gas in the event of further sanctions from the US. It also opened the way for massive Chinese investment in Russia's power and transportation infrastructure and for a much broader and deeper co-operation between the two countries (including militarily) over the 30-year period.

Russia To Leverage Arctic Expertise Into The Antarctic

Given the march that Russia has stolen on everyone else in the exploration and development of oil and gas resources in the Arctic region, it should come as little surprise that moves are afoot to do the same thing in Antarctica. According to an announcement in 2020, Russia's state-run geological survey firm, Rosgeologia, undertook a major new seismic survey that year in the Riiser-Larsen Sea, off the coast of Antarctica's Queen Maud Land. Moreover, Rosgeologia stated unequivocally that it did this 4,400-kilometre survey – the first seismic survey done in the area by Russia since the late 1990s – with the express purpose of 'assessing the offshore oil and gas potential of the area using the latest technology'.

There are those who cite all sorts of reasons why such plans cannot go ahead, at least for the next few years, principally citing the 1959 Antarctic Treaty, signed by 53 separate countries. This, unlike the treaties governing the Arctic (which allow for hydrocarbons exploration and development), supposedly protects the Antarctic's mineral resources in general, including potential oil and gas sites in particular. According to the Treaty, the seven countries with a specific claim in Antarctica – Argentina, Australia, Chile, France, New Zealand, Norway and the UK (not Russia, it should be noted) – are limited to just non-military scientific research in the region.

Despite this, Russia (and the US) has nonetheless constructed research facilities within the areas claimed by these other countries (Russia's is in Norway's claim). Theoretically, the ban on mineral activity in the Antarctic next comes up for possible renewal only in 2048. However, given what Rosgeologia has found so far, Russia may decide to unilaterally bring this date forward by around 28 years or whatever is most convenient for it.

According to Rosgeologia's seismic surveys and other related work since the 1970s, there are at least 513 billion barrels of oil and gas equivalent in Antarctica, although it is unclear as yet whether this relates to the entire region or just the area that it has specifically surveyed so far. There is a vast difference, of course, between the total resources in place and the recovery rate from such a challenging environment. This, though, has never stood in Russia's way before, especially when it factors in all the other mineable and extremely valuable minerals that may also be there, if results from the Arctic are anything to go by. These might well include gold, silver, diamonds, copper, titanium, uranium and rare earth elements.

Moreover, Russia has been at the forefront of these Arctic explorations – with huge success – ever since, including famously pitching its flag on the seabed under the Arctic in 2009. Since then, state-run behemoths Rosneft, Gazprom Neft and slick Western-style Novatek, have been at the forefront of all Arctic operations, with hundreds of billions of current and potential projects in view. The objective remains for offshore Arctic oil to account for 20-30% of all Russian production by 2050.

Given the close cooperation between the two countries, it is not surprising that China has a growing presence in the Arctic and Antarctica too, as well as Russia. This is a natural extension to China's unveiling in 2018 of its first official Arctic policy white paper in which it said that it would encourage enterprises to build infrastructure and conduct commercial trial voyages, paving the way for Arctic shipping routes that would form a 'Polar Silk Road'.

This followed China becoming an 'observer member' of the Arctic Council in 2013. Even before that, though, China had been building new 'scientific research stations' in the Antarctic since 1983 – the point at which it signed the aforementioned 1959 Antarctic Treaty. China commissioned the first of its new range of ice-breaker vessels at the beginning of 2016 – the Haibing 722 – which is capable of withstanding the Force 12 winds found in the Southern Ocean around Antarctica and beyond, has a range of 7,000 miles and has a landing pad suitable for big transport helicopters.

Sanctions In 2014, 2018 And 2022

Since Russia's annexation of Crimea in 2014, it has been under sanctions of one sort or another that have weighed on the country's GDP, interest rates, inflation, bonds and currency to varying degrees from that point. These have been dramatically increased in scale and scope since then, based on several further events, the most notable and far-reaching being Russia's invasion of Ukraine in February 2022.

Beginning with the 2014 annexation of Crimea-related sanctions, the negative effects of these on Russia were compounded by further sanctions related to the 2018 poisoning of Sergei Skripal. He had been a colonel in Russia's GRU military intelligence service and had once imprisoned for selling secrets to the UK, since which time he had settled in the UK following a spy swap. He and his daughter, Yulia, were both poisoned with the Soviet-developed chemical weapon Novichok in the small UK town of Salisbury in 2018.

The first and second tranches of the US and other sanctions related to this poisoning were in line with the 'Chemical and Biological Weapons Control and Warfare Elimination Act of 1991' (CBW), which requires the imposition of certain sanctions once it has been determined that either of this type of weapon has been deployed, in violation of international law.

The first wave of Skripal-related sanctions involved the US changing its licensing policy regarding the export to Russia of dual-use items that are controlled for 'National Security' reasons, including such items as certain high-performing electronics items, sensors, telecommunications equipment, other higher-tech products and software. These items were already subject to a licensing requirement for exports to Russia but, under these sanctions, the Commerce Department review licence applications with a presumption of denial, rather than on a case-by-case basis.

Russia Was Hit By Sanctions In 2014 And 2018 After Crimea And Skripal

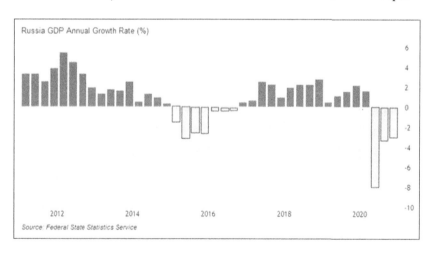

Even the first tranche caused Russia problems, as the US had the right to include in them equipment and technology that were vital for Russia's oil and gas field drilling and refinery efforts. It was true that some Russian companies could reproduce some of these even very complicated pieces of equipment, but they could not do so on the massive scale required by the country's oil and gas industry.

The second wave of sanctions posed an entirely different magnitude of seriousness for Russia's oil, gas and petrochemicals sectors. These ranged from sweeping financial and trade restrictions targeting Russia, including a near-complete embargo of trade. Included within the long list of further sanctions were US opposition to the extension of loans or financial assistance to Russia by international financial institutions, the prohibition of providing credit to the Russian government by US banks and the prohibition of most exports and imports involving that country.

The sanctions from the West that were introduced after Russia annexed Crimea notably reduced Western involvement in Russian energy and commodities projects, including large scale financing and exploration of hard-to-recover and deep-water resources. The second tranche of sanctions made the situation much worse and opened up the ability for the US to dramatically increase sanctions related to Western investment into Russia and Russia's use of the US dollar.

Western Investment Into Russia Hit After Crimea 2014 And Skripal 2018

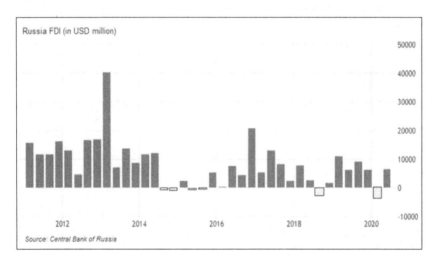

Source: Central Bank of Russia

Specifically, in mid-July 2018. the 'Secure America from Russian Interference Act of 2018' (SARI) bill was introduced, which directly restricted investment into energy projects with Russian state-run companies and US dollar transactions with several major Russian banks, among other measures. In practical terms, every company in the world that has any trade denominated in US dollars must have those dollars cleared in a bank domiciled in the US, so sanctions on the free use of US dollars in transactions related to Russia impacts all of its key business sectors, including oil, gas and sectors related to those. One negative effect of this US dollar-usage sanction at that point from the West's perspective was that Russia began to downsize its use of the US dollar wherever it could. The Central Bank of Russia had reduced the percentage of its overall FX reserves held in US dollars from over 40% in 2018 to around 15% by the beginning of 2022. Its sovereign wealth fund had also removed US dollar assets from its portfolio.

At around the same time as the post-2014 annexation of Crimea were being imposed on Russia, the chief executive officer of Russia's Novatek, Leonid Mikhelson, highlighted: 'This [switch away from using US dollars] has been discussed for a while with Russia's largest trading partners such as India and China, and even Arab countries are starting to think about it … If they [the US and its allies] do create difficulties for our Russian banks then all we have to do is replace dollars'. Mikhelson added at that point that future sales to China denominated in renminbi was under consideration and stated: 'The trade war between the US and China will only accelerate the process.' Such a strategy was minimally tested in 2014 when Gazprom Neft tried trading cargoes of crude oil in Chinese yuan and roubles with China and Europe.

As analysed in depth in the first section of this book, this view of the US dollar as a weapon was powerfully reinforced after Russia's invasion of Ukraine in 2022 and the accompanying US-led sanctions that followed. The most severe of those – as with sanctions on Iran from 2018 – related to exclusion from use of the US dollar. The idea to increasingly move away from use of the US dollar, including in oil and gas deals, has been reiterated many times by Russia's key ally, China. As recently as April 2022, the former executive vice-president of the Bank of China, Zhang Yanling, said in a speech that US dollar-related sanctions against Russia would: '[…] cause the US to lose its credibility and undermine the [US] dollar's hegemony in the long run.' She further suggested that China should help the world 'get rid of the dollar hegemony sooner rather than later.'

As also analysed in the first section of this book, there are many methods that Iran and Russia can use to get around nearly all of the US's and Europe's sanctions on it at any given time, but the US dollar-centric ones are much more difficult to circumvent, even now.

China

Economy-Driven Demand And Domestic Supply Disparity

China is included in this analysis of the world's most important oil and gas powers not for its supply capabilities but for its demand influence over the entire global hydrocarbons market. This huge demand arises from the vast disparity between, on the one hand, China's enormous economy-driven oil and gas needs and, on the other hand, its minimal level of domestic oil and gas reserves. As a result of this imbalance, China almost alone created the commodities 'supercycle' that has been seen over various extended periods from the early 1990s, characterised by consistently rising price trends for all commodities that are used in a booming manufacturing and infrastructure build-out environment.

China's Surging Economic Growth Drove The Commodities Supercycle

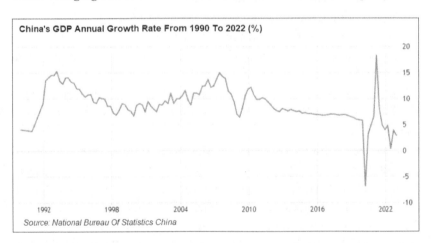

China's GDP Annual Growth Rate From 1990 To 2022 (%)

Source: National Bureau Of Statistics China

From 1992 to the middle 2010s, a large element of this growth was founded on energy-intensive economic drivers, particularly manufacturing and the corollary build out of infrastructure attached to the sector, such as factories, housing for workers, road, railways and so on. Even after some of China's growth began to switch into the less energy-intensive service sectors, the country's investment in energy-intensive infrastructure build-out remained very high. As late as 2017, China's high rate of economic growth allowed it to overtake the US as the largest annual gross crude oil importer in the world, having become the world's largest net importer of total petroleum and other liquid fuels in 2013.

This disparity is likely to continue in the coming years as China is set to overtake the US as the world's largest economy by nominal GDP by 2030 at the latest – despite already being the world's largest economy by purchasing power parity, the largest manufacturing economy and the largest trading nation – whilst the outlook for it to increase its domestic oil and gas reserves looks extremely limited.

It is true that in 2023 the near-automatic feed-through that the global markets have come to expect from rising economic growth in China into rising oil prices is unlikely to be as pronounced as in previous growth cycles. More specifically, although China officially removed the previous economy-damaging 'zero-COVID' draconian rules and regulations on 8 January 2023, President Xi in his New Year 2023 speech indicated that growth in the year would come from removing the previous COVID-19-related obstacles to it rather than implementing policies that would aggressively drive it.

Feed-Through From China Growth To Oil Prices May Be Limited In 2023

China's monthly crude oil imports, total and from Russia (2011–2022)
million barrels per day

Source: China General Administration of Customs, EIA

Several smart money investors and analysts predicted that this phase of growth recovery – to the Chinese government's target of 'at least 5.0%' –

would be a cyclical recovery, led by household consumption, mainly of services. As such, they predicted a 5-8% increase in net oil import volumes in China over 2023 but thought that this was unlikely to cause oil prices to surge during the year as they had during previous economic growth spurts, especially as China continued to buy oil at a discount from Russia.

Success In Boosting Domestic Supplies Remains Limited

On the other side of the oil price equation for China – its own domestic supplies – efforts are underway on several fronts to increase these, although the outlook remains uncertain that these will yield significant results.

It is not that China has no oil and gas reserves – up until the early 1990s, it was a net exporter of crude oil, based on its 24+ billion barrels of proven oil reserves, the highest in the Asia-Pacific region at that point. In 2021/2022, China was the fifth-largest petroleum and other liquids producer in the world, although most of this output did come from old fields that require expensive EOR techniques to sustain production.

Moreover, the period from the middle of 2021 to the middle of 2022 saw crude oil production in China rise by around 130,000 bpd to just under 5 million bpd. Nearly 80% of the total liquids production was from crude oil, and the remainder was from converting coal and methanol to liquids, biofuels, and refinery processing gains. China's problem is that even despite these resources and gains, its energy requirements to fuel its still-strong economic growth are much greater. Specifically, over the aforementioned period, as estimated 15.3 million bpd of petroleum and other liquids were consumed in China, up 840,000 bpd, or approximately 6%, from the previous 12-month period, according to the EIA.

For a long time, the China National Offshore Oil Corporation (CNOOC) – the country's largest producer of offshore crude oil and natural gas – was the key vehicle charged by the government with trying to boost China's crude oil reserves. As at the end of 2017, the company had a net reserve base of 2.613 billion barrels of oil equivalent, the highest level for the company since 2008. Since then, it announced that it would boost its capital spending to USD10.3-11.8 billion, of which 51% would be spent domestically and the rest on international projects. In 2018, the company also said it planned to expand oil production from 470-480 million barrels of oil equivalent (boe) in 2018 to 485 million boe in 2019 and then to 500 million boe in 2020. This said, the offshore sites operated by the company are generally located in very deep water, making them potentially very risky and very costly. Meanwhile, many of China's key onshore oil fields are old and others are reaching the end of their naturally productive cycle.

Huge Disparity Between Consumption And Production Still Exists

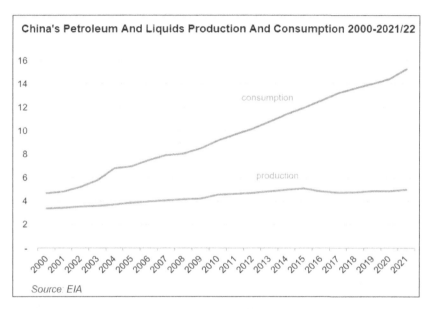

China's Petroleum And Liquids Production And Consumption 2000-2021/22

Source: EIA

Given this, Beijing also supplemented its exploration drive with various attempts to find and develop shale oil and gas resources, in the hope of replicating the US's success in this regard in recent years. Chinese oil majors – also including CNPC and Sinopec – invested heavily in an attempt to speed up drilling and exploration projects for shale oil and gas, especially in the country's western regions. However, China's known shale formations – be they oil or gas – are, again, all located in very difficult to exploit terrain.

For 2021, CNOOC was targeted to produce 545 million-555 million boe (or 1.49 million bpd), of oil and gas, up about 4.5% from its estimated production of 528 million boe in 2020 (its target was 505 million-515 million boe, set early in 2020) on the back of 19 new projects. These most notably included the Buzzard oil field Phase II in the UK's North Sea area, the commissioning of which was postponed from the second half of 2020, and the other major overseas project in Brazil's Mero oil field Phase I, in which CNOOC holds a 10% interest with 171,000 boepd of peak output. The other 17 projects are in China's offshore areas, given its focus to boost domestic oil production close to the areas in which it can be used by localised Chinese firms.

New Mandate For Exploration And Development In 2022

Following renewed government pressure in the first half of 2022, China's National Energy Agency set a domestic crude oil production target of approximately 1.5 billion barrels for 2022 - a 2% increase from 2021's target. In turn, the biggest of China's state oil companies - PetroChina and Sinopec – announced 4.6% increases in their capital expenditures for 2022 compared to the previous year. This meant that these two firms had the highest capex in 2022 of any national oil company except Saudi Aramco.

More specifically, according to the EIA, Sinopec's target for crude oil production moved up to 281.2 million barrels in 2022, an increase of almost 1.5 million barrels from the previous year. PetroChina's moved up to 898 million barrels, a 1.2% increase from 2021. In the meantime, CNOOC's kept its capex for the year largely where it was the previous year, at around USD14.1 billion.

According to local company and news reports, 2022 saw CNOOC tap a commercial flow of oil and gas from a shale exploration well in the Beibu Gulf Basin of the South China Sea, marking the first successfully drilled offshore shale oil well in the country. CNOOC stated that the Beibu Gulf Basin holds around 1.2 billion tons of prospective shale oil resources with broad prospects for future exploration. In the first quarter of 2023, CNOOC also announced the discovery of a major oilfield - Bozhong 26-6 - with light crude reserves of 100 million tons in the Bohai Sea, which stretches along the China's northern coastline. According to CNOOC, the Bozhong 26-6 oilfield is the third oilfield discovery with 100 million tons of reserves in the southern Bohai Sea, after Kenli 6-1 and Kenli 10-2.

The Bohai oilfield is now China's largest producing field, having surpassed the Daqing field in 2021. Bohai produced over 603,000 bpd in 2021/22, while Daqing produced 600,000 bpd in the same period.

Cultivating Stepping Stones In 'One Belt, One Road'

China's overriding goal since it began its drive for economic growth in the early 1990s has been to at least equal the leading superpower status of the US in the world, with everything that this entails.

One thing that it entails is to at least equal the US in terms of economic size according to nominal GDP, although its ultimate plan is to overtake the US in this regard by 2030 at the latest. China is already the world's largest economy by purchasing power parity, the world's largest manufacturing economy and the world's largest trading nation.

Another thing that it entails is to at least equal the US in terms of its ability to influence the future direction of other countries around the globe. Part of that comes through economic power and the trading relationships that it brings. Part comes through the usage of a country's currency in daily trading around the world and as a global reserve currency. And part comes through the military capabilities of a country in all its forms, both covert and overt.

To achieve any of these things, though, from a standing start, as effectively had before 1990, requires vast amounts of energy to feed the economic growth in the first place. In a country such as China with very limited energy resources, this, in turn, requires the building of relationships in energy rich countries around the world.

These relationships, initially based around energy, feed back into the other elements of China's overriding goal, as they necessitate massive investment by China into energy-rich countries, which in turn brings with it greater influence for China in them. This, in the case of investment-heavy energy projects, also allows for the presence of Chinese personnel of varying sorts on the ground in these countries to manage and safeguard these expensive assets.

Every single element of these requirements find their perfect resolution in China's 'One Belt, One Road' programme. The sole aim of this programme is to allow China to become one of the two leading global superpowers by 2030, along with the US – if not before then, and if not ahead of the US.

In structure, OBOR is an amalgamation of China's ancient land and maritime 'Silk Road' route. In concept, it is rooted in the admiration of President Xi Jinping and other top China leaders for the way that Great

Britain expanded its own great empire – the biggest the world has ever seen – into Asia around the peculiar alchemy of political and commercial objectives practiced by the East India Company (EIC). In brief, the EIC successfully used trade in the first instance to gain control over large parts of the Indian subcontinent, Southeast Asia and Hong Kong, which were then secured through the company's own armed forces, tacitly backed by the military might of Great Britain itself.

China's OBOR Economic And Political Takeover Plan

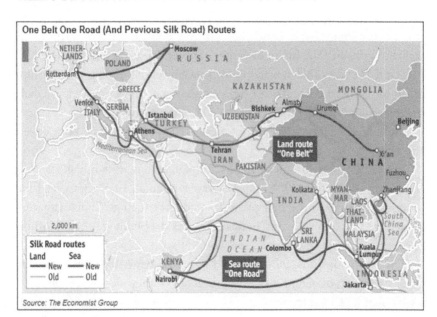

One Belt One Road (And Previous Silk Road) Routes

Source: The Economist Group

The details of how China is executing this plan across the Middle East in particular are analysed in depth in the first section of this book and in the standalone sections on Saudi Arabia, Iran and Iraq. To briefly recap here: in all cases the initial entry point for China was economic (massive deals promised in all countries), which was then leveraged into political influence of varying degrees in the countries for China.

The perfect model for China's OBOR strategy in the Middle East is the securing of extraordinary economic, political and military influence in Iran through the 'Iran-China 25-Year Comprehensive Cooperation Agreement' first revealed anywhere in the world in my 3 September 2019 article for Petroleum Economist. The full details of this are to be found in the '*Key*

Players In The Global Oil Market: Iran' section. China's resulting influence over Iran was then leveraged into Iraq through Iran's own longstanding hold over its neighbouring country.

China's Iran deal also gave it leverage into Oman, with which Iran has long enjoyed very close relations. This linkage is particularly useful for China in its strategy of taking control of the Middle East's only available shipping routes for oil into Europe and then into the rest of the West that avoid the more expensive and more nautically-challenging Cape of Good Hope route. Oman has long coastlines along the Gulf of Oman and the Arabian Sea offering unfettered access to the markets of the East and the West equally. As such, Oman and its key ports and storage facilities offer the only true alternative in the Middle East to the Strait of Hormuz - controlled by Iran, but also now by China - through which passes at least one third of the world's crude oil supplies.

The all-encompassing 25-year deal with Iran also gives China a hold over the Bab al-Mandab Strait, through which crude oil is shipped upwards through the Red Sea towards the Suez Canal before moving into the Mediterranean and then westwards. This has been achieved as it lies between Yemen (which has long featured Iran-backed Houthis) and Djibouti, over which China has also established a stranglehold. The 25-year deal between China and Iran also gave China leverage over the remainder of the Shia Crescent of Power countries in the Middle East especially, most notably comprising Iran, Iraq, Lebanon, Syria, and Yemen. This can be used when necessary to augment and benefit from the activities in these countries of Russia.

The breadth and depth of the China-Iran 25-year deal is similar to several others that China has used both in the Middle East and elsewhere, including in Asia and Africa. Broadly speaking, they can be categorised as 'Hotel California'-style deals ('You can check out any time you like/But you can never leave'), in which China first makes a huge investment in a target country. This investment is done through a contract, or several interlinked contracts, which feature penalty clauses for the target country if it does not meet its obligations under the contract. The penalties incurred for failure are extreme and, again, are based on the *modus operandi* of Great Britain's East India Company.

A prime case in point, although there are many more, was in China's self-proclaimed backyard of Asia-Pacific, in the island of Sri Lanka. China began its push into the country by extending unlimited loans to beleaguered former President, Mahinda Rajapaksa, for his Hambantota Port Development Project. This project – as the Chinese well knew – stood little chance of succeeding as a port and when it failed to generate any significant business and Rajapaksa was voted out of office, the new government was unable to meet the loan repayment demands.

At that point, the new Sri Lankan government had little choice but to pay the penalty, and the penalty was the obligation to hand over the entire Hambantota Port to China (plus 15,000 other acres of surrounding land) for a period of at least 99 years in restitution. Hambantota may have been useless as a standard port from the money-making perspective, but for China it is of enormous strategic significance, overlooking South Asia's major sea lanes and allowing it in the future to establish a dual use (commercial and military) facility for naval assets.

Exactly the same relationship template was used by China in the lead up to the creation in 2017 of its first overseas military base – to be precise, a huge naval base - located in Djibouti. The small African nation's only benefit to China is that it lies on the Horn of Africa, at one side of the entrance of the Bab al-Mandab Strait that leads upwards through the Red Sea towards the Suez Canal. On the other side is Yemen. China started to make major investments in Djibouti in the early 2000s until, by the time that the idea of the naval base emerged from China, it had spent around USD14 billion there, totalling over 70% of Djibouti's debt, and making it the country's biggest debtor.

Brokering The Saudi Arabia-Iran Deal

Although White House national security spokesperson, John Kirby, did his best to stress that the deal done on 10 March 2023 between Iran and Saudi Arabia to re-establish relations 'is not about China', it absolutely was about China. What it absolutely was not about was the US. The biggest diplomatic coup in the Middle East since at least the signing of the JCPOA between the P5+1 powers and Iran in 2015 had been brokered by China, without any involvement at all from the US, and every country in the world and in the Middle East knew it. The landmark deal between the two longstanding arch-regional enemies – Shia Iran and Sunni Saudi Arabia – was just the sort of far-reaching geopolitical coup that the US had wanted to achieve in its 'relationship normalisation deals' programme that had followed its unilateral withdrawal from the JCPOA in May 2018.

There are many solid reasons why the US pulled out of the JCPOA in 2018 and then reduced some or all of its presence from Syria (in 2019), Afghanistan (2021), and Iraq (2021) and these are analysed in full in the first section of this book and also in the *Key Players In The Global Oil Market: The US'* section. Specifically from Saudi Arabia's perspective, though, the withdrawal of the US from the JCPOA in 2018 meant that the Middle East had suddenly become an even more dangerous place than it was before.

Iran had been freed of all meaningful restraints to pursue its own style of Islam across the Middle East by whatever means it wanted and it was clear to the Saudis that this meant that the top Shia Islam country in the world, Iran, would go after the top Sunni Islam country in the world, Saudi Arabia, as soon as it could and as hard as it could.

This was precisely what happened in the September 2019 Iran-backed Houthi attacks on two of Saudi Arabia's key oil installations, as also analysed in full earlier in this book. Several similar attacks followed, all aerial missions, which also confirmed to the Saudis not only that the US was not going to defend it anymore in geopolitical terms but also that all of the military equipment that it had bought from the US over the years for hundreds of billions of dollars was effectively useless to prevent such attacks from Iran.

As bad as that was, much worse was in view, as an Iran unencumbered by the conditions of the JCPOA, as enforced by the US, was working flat out to finish its nuclear weapons programme. Within around a year of the US leaving the JCPOA, Iran had moved from a 'breakout time' - the time required to produce enough weapons-grade (90% of its fissile isotope U-235) uranium for one nuclear weapon – of about a year to around three weeks. China, through its very close relationship with nuclear powers Pakistan and with North Korea, had been instrumental in enabling Iran to make this progress, as analysed in depth in the *Key Players In The Global Oil Market: Iran'* section. It was at that point, after the US had unliterally withdrawn from the JCPOA and unleashed a re-energised and China-backed Iran, that Saudi Arabia understood that it had to make its own deals with whichever countries it could to ensure its own safety first, and then economic and political success thereafter.

China Had Brought Together The Two Great Middle Eastern Powers

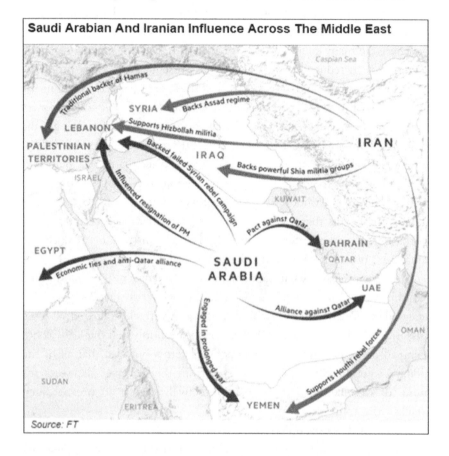

Given China's previous support to MbS personally in the matter of the flawed Saudi Aramco IPO and its subsequent investments into the Kingdom, the high-level relationship architecture between the two countries was already in place and ready to be expanded in scale and scope. At around the same time, as also analysed in depth in the first section of this book, moves were advanced for senior representatives of Saudi Arabia to meet with their counterparts from Iran. The first major public sign of a potential rapprochement between Saudi Arabia and Iran came from MbS in the first half of 2021 when he stated that he sought: '[…] a good and special relationship with Iran…We do not want Iran's situation to be difficult, on the contrary, we want Iran to grow… and to push the region and the world towards prosperity'.

Saudi Arabia Approves Advancement In China-Russia's SCO

Saudi Arabia's very public announcement at the end of March 2023 that its cabinet had approved a plan to join the Shanghai Cooperation Organisation (SCO) as a 'dialogue partner' was the surest sign to that point that any US efforts to keep it out of the China-Russia sphere of influence might prove futile. The Kingdom had already signed a memorandum of understanding on 16 September 2022 granting it the status of SCO dialogue partner. However, Saudi Arabia did nothing to encourage the release of the news at that point, unlike the March 2023 announcement, which came shortly after it had announced the resumption of relations with Iran, in the deal brokered by China.

The SCO is the world's biggest regional political, economic and defence organisation both in terms of geographic scope and population. It covers 60% of the Eurasian continent (by far the biggest single landmass on Earth), 40% of the world's population, and more than 20% of global GDP. It was formed in 2001 on the foundation of the 'Shanghai Five' that was set up in 1996 by China, Russia, and three states of the former USSR (Kazakhstan, Kyrgyzstan and Tajikistan). Aside from its vast scale and scope, the SCO believes in the idea and practice of the 'multi-polar world', which China anticipates will be dominated by it by 2030. In this context, the end of December 2021/beginning of January 2022 saw meetings in Beijing between senior officials from the Chinese government and foreign ministers from Saudi Arabia, Kuwait, Oman, Bahrain, plus the secretary-general of the Gulf Cooperation Council (GCC). At these meetings, the principal topics of conversation were to finally seal a China-GCC Free Trade Agreement and to forge 'a deeper strategic cooperation in a region where US dominance is showing signs of retreat'.

This idea of a multi-polar world not dominated by the US was the centrepiece of the declaration signed in 1997 between then-Russian President, Boris Yeltsin, and his then-China counterpart, Jiang Zemin. Veteran Russian Foreign Minister, Sergey Lavrov, has since stated that: 'The Shanghai Cooperation Organisation is working to establish a rational and just world order and [...] it provides us with a unique opportunity to take part in the process of forming a fundamentally new model of geopolitical integration'. Aside from these geopolitical redesigns, the SCO works to provide intra-organisation financing and banking networks, plus increased military cooperation, intelligence sharing and counterterrorism activities, among other things. The US itself applied for 'observer status' of the SCO in the early 2000s but was rejected in 2005.

This latest step by Saudi Arabia away from the US and towards the China-Russia axis should come as no surprise to anyone who has read this book to this point. As for where the SCO goes from here, a look through the list of its members of various types gives an excellent indication, comprising the most of the world's largest energy suppliers, together with strategically vital countries for China's OBOR programme, with China and Russia dominating from the geopolitical perspective.

As at the beginning of Q2 2023, the SCO's core Members are: China, India, Kazakhstan, Kyrgyzstan, Pakistan, Russia, Tajikistan, and Uzbekistan. Its Observer Members are Afghanistan, Belarus, Iran, and Mongolia. Its Dialogue Partners are Armenia, Azerbaijan, Cambodia, Egypt, Nepal, Qatar, Saudi Arabia, Sri Lanka, and Turkey.

The Ghosts In The China Machine

Concerns over the nature of China's growth model were fanned as long ago as March 2017 when then-Premier Li Keqiang made two major announcements at China's annual National People's Congress (NPC) in Beijing. The first was that the world's second-largest economy had cut its growth rate target to the lowest level in 27 years. The second was that: 'Developments both inside and outside China require that we are ready to face more complicated and graver situations.' Since then, China's real growth trajectory and, even more important perhaps, the fragility of its financial structures, has made it a major fear for smart money investors.

Even before this acknowledgement by Li, the markets were aware that China had for a while been demonstrating the three key symptoms that preceded all the major financial crises of the past three decades – the 1997 Asia Crisis, the 1998 Russia Crisis and even the Great Financial Crisis that began in 2007 – namely: a high degree of debt leverage, a rapid rise in asset prices and a decline in underlying growth potential. There is an analogue in China to every critical element that precipitated these other crises but, given the greater magnitude of each of them in China, when the crisis there unravels it will be at least on a par with the Great Financial Crisis.

Huge True Debt Leverage

The debt of any country can be divided basically into two components: domestic debt and foreign debt. China's foreign debt has risen from around USD52.55 billion in 1990 (about the start of the country's dramatic surge in economic growth) to about USD2.4 trillion in 2020 (around the time of the onset of COVID-19). China's government debt to GDP ratio was about 68% at that point.

Even with the increase in this government debt to GDP ratio after COVID-19 – to just over 80% at the beginning of 2023 - the other component, domestic debt, is where the serious problems lie. This domestic debt comprises among other things corporate and household debt. It is where the problems for China lie because it has long been an area beset by a lack of clarity and this persists to this day.

China's Spectre Of Hidden Debt

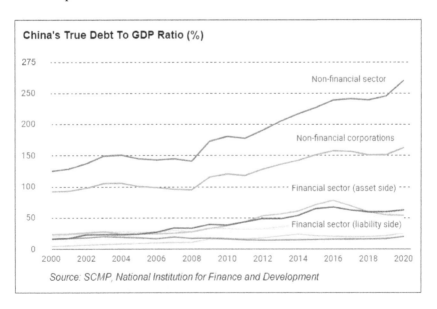

Source: SCMP, National Institution for Finance and Development

Unofficially, including this debt, China total debt to GDP ratio is anywhere between 270% and 300%, up from around 200% just five years or so ago. Even according to the People's Bank of China's own data, outstanding 'total social financing' (which measures overall credit supply to the economy and includes off-balance-sheet forms of financing that exist outside the conventional bank lending system, such as initial public offerings, loans from trust companies and bond sales) stood at CNY5.98 trillion (USD858 billion) in January 2023.

These figures look even worse when taking into account the potential debt hidden in lenders' off-balance-sheet portfolios of loans that have been re-packaged into 'wealth-management products' (WMPs). These products typically offer a high rate of return and were originally targeted for sale to the public until the sales' focus shifted to financial institutions. Up until very recently these products were effectively unregulated and their issuance continues to soar. Indeed, the stock of Chinese banks' off-balance-sheet WMPs has grown around 200% from 2014 to the end of 2022, compared to around 50% growth of on-balance-sheet assets during this time.

In practical terms, these products are layers and layers of liabilities built upon the same underlying assets, much as was seen with subprime asset-backed securities and collateralised debt obligations in the US in the lead up to the onset of the Great Financial Crisis. However, the range of assets used was even greater than in the US and the Western financial markets, and there is even less visibility or clarity on the types of assets bundled up in each of these WMPs than there was in the subprime sector.

These WMPs constitute a hidden second balance sheet, similar to the Special Investment Vehicles and conduits that the Western banks had in 2007/08, which nobody paid attention to until there started to be bankruptcies. When everything fell apart, these off-balance-sheet liabilities had to be incorporated on balance sheets, magnifying the banks' losses.

The scale of the WMPs has added to the overall risk in China's financial system that also arose from the rapid rise in asset prices during China's extremely rapid rate of growth from the early 1990s, most notably in the property and stock markets. These took off after the CNY4 trillion stimulus package unveiled in November 2008, aimed at mitigating the worst effects of the global recession that was gathering pace at that time. They were amplified again with the further stimulus packages in 2013 and 2016, making the bubble worse.

In theory, this money was to have made its way into government-mandated infrastructure projects via state-owned enterprises. In reality, however, much of it this huge amount of funding was 're-directed' by individuals into personal investments in the stock and property markets, which is why both of those rose very rapidly from 2008 onward.

Although the benchmark stock markets in Shanghai and Shenzhen have seen mixed fortunes more recently, as a result of the large proportion of 'hot money' retail investors in the country, property market values in China's major cities have continued to rise inexorably.

Stimulus Packages Inflated The Stock Market Bubble

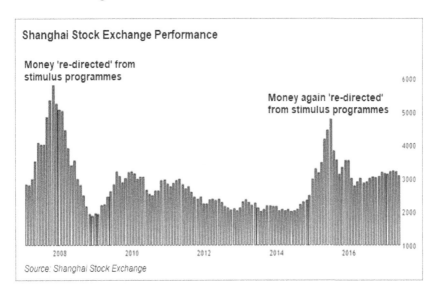

According to global data provider Numbeo, property prices in 2023 are just over 47 times the level of income in Shanghai, just over 42 times in Beijing, and just over 40 times in Shenzhen. These levels compare to 8 times in Tokyo during its 1980s credit bubble and to six times in the US at the time of its own housing bubble prior to the sub-prime catastrophe.

The Chinese Academy of Social Sciences in Beijing has estimated (based on electricity meter readings) that there are around 64.5 million empty apartments and houses in the urban areas of China, which is just over five times the level in the US at the height of the US sub-prime mortgage bubble. Despite various government initiatives (including buying properties itself and turning them into public housing), this figure has not meaningfully altered in the past five years and has simply moved debt from one set of balance sheets to another.

The concerns over China's mountainous debt position only increased with news in 2022 and 2023 of debt-related troubles at Evergrande.

Originally a real estate developer – therefore, at the centre of the Chinese government's previous initiatives to fuel economic growth by huge infrastructure building projects, including new towns and cities – Evergrande took on even more debt (including through extensive bond issues) expanding its business portfolio.

At minimum – and these are just the known figures – Evergrande's expansion in real estate (it owns more than 1,300 projects in more than 280 cities across China) and into wealth management, electric car production, and food and drink manufacturing, among others, cost it over USD300 billion in borrowing. Unsurprisingly, as the economic growth rate in China has slowed, the company has struggled to pay this debt and to service its international bond payments.

The Mathematical Impossibility Of China's Debt Strategy

Historically, China has taken the view that it could simply grow its way out of potentially devastating debt overhang. However, as signalled by its own official downgrading of growth projections in recent years, this strategy looks more flawed than ever. The amount of credit in China is increasing just over twice as fast as economic growth, so in purely mathematical terms the idea of growing its way out of trouble does not compute. Diminishing returns are setting in, as it is now taking even more credit to generate each unit of economic growth, which again is unsustainable.

A bailout would require trillions of dollars' worth of yuan being spent, which would create a massive capital shortage for much of the system overnight. For China, with a much weaker social safety net and a much poorer population than the West had at the onset of its Great Financial Crisis, social and political instability would be a serious concern.

Around 140 million people have migrated from China's rural areas to its cities over the past 20 years and another 300 million are predicted to follow suit in the next 20 years, according to UNICEF. Consequently, the Chinese government must provide these economic migrants with jobs, housing and food in order to avoid the sort of social unrest that we have seen in recent years in other countries. This means sustaining a sufficiently healthy economic growth rate, but most of that is being done through state-directed spending, which in turn adds to the debt mountain.

Part Three: The Essential Elements Of Trading

Technical Analysis

Why Technical Analysis Matters

In basic terms, Technical Analysis is a methodology by which past trading patterns originated around prices can be used to predict future trading patterns and, therefore, buy and sell signals. The basics of Technical Analysis – support and resistance levels – are absolutely essential to being able to maximise profits and to minimise risks, allowing as they do the clear identification of key price points at which other traders look to buy or sell a given asset. Without understanding the basics of Technical Analysis, any meaningful risk management cannot be achieved, and this is the fundamental reason why around 90% of retail traders lose all their invested funds within the first 90 days of starting to trade.

Many traders believe that in and of itself Technical Analysis reveals certain key truths about how the markets have worked in the past, how they work currently and how they will work in the future. Whether or not there is a genuine mathematical or otherwise logical basis for this belief is irrelevant for practical trading purposes; the fact that the vast majority of traders believe this makes it sufficient to make Technical Analysis a key driver – along with other factors that are examined elsewhere in this book - of trading patterns in the future. The belief that Technical Analysis predicts future trading patterns is, in fact, a self-fulfilling prophecy, and every trader – retail or otherwise – needs to know at least the basics of it.

This concept of the self-fulfilled prophecy is even truer now in the age of automated and algorithmic trading when the programs involved use key support and resistance levels – based on previous trading levels or other elements of Technical Analysis – to execute massive sell or buy orders, thus triggering other stop-loss orders centred on these levels.

Candlesticks

The key to Technical Analysis is the candlestick method of charting. This is particularly useful as it not only shows simply whether the market largely bought the asset involved (typically shown in green or white) or sold it (typically shown in red or black) but also how strong these buys or sells were (indicated by the length of the lines above each candle, 'wick', for buying or below, 'shadow', for selling). Exactly the same principles of Technical Analysis are applicable to every traded asset and to reinforce this idea of just looking at the charts and not thinking of the individual asset involved, the charts below cover a wide range of different assets, not just oil, and different time trading periods through the recent years.

Candlestick Structure

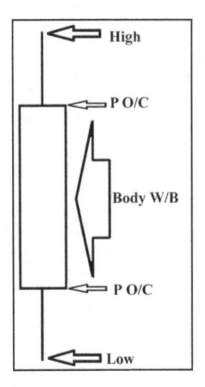

[Chart Key: High = Highest price during trading time period; P O/C = Trading time period open or close price; Body W/B = Real body is white (or green) if asset closed

higher over the trading period or black (or red) if it closed lower; P O/C = Trading time
period open or close price; Low = Lowest price during trading time period]

If a market is undecided as to where it views the direction of an asset then the candlestick will have no substantial body, wick or shadow ('doji'), reflecting that the price closed the day where it opened and that neither buyers ('bulls') nor sellers ('bears') prevailed in moving the asset their way over the course of the trading hours.

A similar inference can be taken from the 'Spinning Top' pattern, although not to quite the same degree, as some intra-day movement will have taken place. In either event, both can be viewed as marking possibly the end of the previous trend, as it has run out of steam. These patterns make ideal places to enter new trades or exit existing ones.

Dojis, Tops, Hammers And Shooting Stars

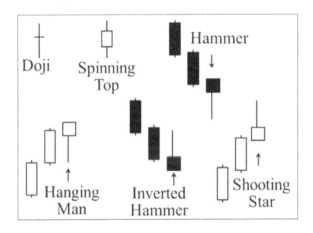

The 'Hammer' pattern appears after a previous move to the downside and indicates that a move to the upside is on the cards. The long shadow shows that, despite it trading substantially lower during the day, the weight of selling was not sufficient for it to stay at depressed trading levels. Consequently, the inference is that major buyers have stepped in at these levels and may well continue buying overnight or as the new Western trading period properly commences.

The same can be said for the 'Inverted Hammer', although to a lesser degree, as although buyers have stepped into the market, they have failed on this occasion to reverse the downtrend entirely.

Conversely, the 'Shooting Star' should be read as a sign that a move to the downside is on the cards, after a previous move to the upside, with bulls having failed to continue to push the pair higher and substantial bears having now entered the market.

The same can be said for the 'Hanging Man' although to a lesser degree, as although sellers have stepped into the market, they have failed on this occasion to reverse the uptrend entirely.

Bullish Engulfing, Bearish Engulfing And Haramis

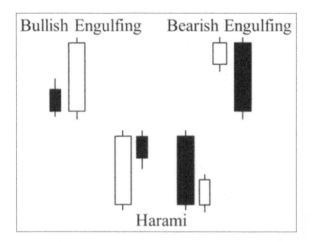

A 'Bullish Engulfing' pattern is a clear indication that the signs of reversal of a previous trend (either through a Shooting Star or Hanging Man) have gained momentum, and the reverse is true of the 'Bearish Engulfing' pattern (either through the Hammer or Inverted Hammer).

The 'Harami' pattern, though, which can occur after a move either up or down, can be taken again as a sign of uncertain price follow-through and may mark the beginning of a change of trend direction.

In all the above cases, the weight that should be attached to these patterns should be increased when additional confirmations are found.

These can be where they occur at major resistance and support levels, Fibonacci levels (key mathematical ratios of an original number, representing a move up or down: 23.6%, 38.2%, 50% and 61.8%) or Moving Average levels (simply, each day's price added together and then divided by a certain number of days: 20, 50 and 100 are the most used), including selected oscillators.

USD Vs CAD (Historical)

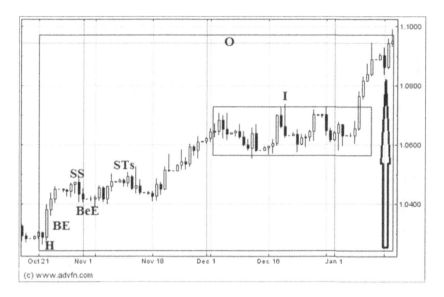

[Chart Key: H = Hammer; BE = Bullish engulfing; SS = Shooting star; BeE = Bearish engulfing; STs = Spinning tops; O = Overall uptrend; I = Indecision of the market]

In the above chart, for instance, aside from a few moves down (which fail to gather momentum, as indicated by the Spinning Top patterns) all the significant moves have been to the upside (as indicated by the rolling Hammer patterns).

Support And Resistance Levels

These two levels are also absolutely vital for all trading purposes and for risk management, as they determine at what levels entry, exit, stop-loss and take-profit orders should be placed. If nothing else is taken onboard about Technical Analysis, support and resistance levels should be, otherwise there is a very high risk that the retail trader – or any trader for that matter – will go broke in a very short time.

Support levels (where the market has overwhelmingly bought the asset in the past, once it has been in decline) will invariably be found below the current market price, whilst resistance levels (where the market has overwhelmingly sold the asset in the past, once it has been on the rise) will be found above the current market price.

In other words, in chart terms, support levels can be found where selling turns to buying (denoted on candlestick charts, see below, as a red bar turning to green or a black bar turning to white), whilst resistance levels can be found where buying turns to selling (denoted on candlestick charts as a green bar turning to red or a white bar turning to black). R1 is the first resistance level and so on, whilst S1 is the first support level, with the current market price indicated in the black box.

EUR Vs USD (Historical)

[Chart Key: S1 = First support level; S2 = Second support level; R1 = First resistance level; R2 = Second resistance level]

These levels should be the cornerstones of all serious trading activity, as they act as signals to buy or sell into a new position or to exit existing ones (together with other confirmations, discussed below).

To reiterate, though, it is essential to note that resistance and support levels do not always coincide with any/all of these additional confirmation signals. For example, if the asset is a currency, it may be that a particular level has been targeted by a country's central bank as being essential for the advancement of its economic or monetary policy and that it will act decisively to ensure either that its currency weakens at a certain level (to encourage exports and boost economic growth, for instance) or strengthens (to discourage demand-led inflation, for instance).

The chart below shows the extraordinary actions of the Swiss National Bank (SNB) over its implementation of a policy to ensure that the Swiss franc (CHF) did not appreciate to a degree that it hurt the country's economy. Originally, the floor was at 1.2000 against the euro but one day, out of the blue, the SNB stopped supporting the floor (i.e. buying euros and selling CHF). Consequently, the CHF shot up a rocket and a lot of traders and institutions went bankrupt in an instant. When the CHF appreciated beyond the parity (1 to 1) level with the euro – very damaging to Switzerland's economy – the SNB decided to intervene again.

EUR Vs CHF (Historical)

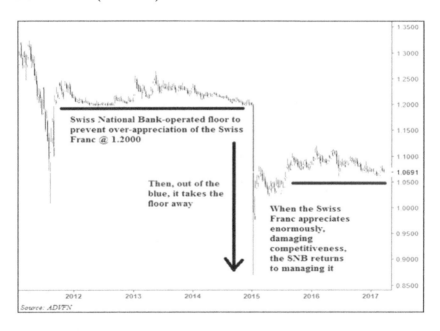

Similarly, it may be that there are enormous options contracts that would be triggered if an asset reached a certain level. In this case, whoever held the option would do everything cost-effective that they could to prevent it reaching the strike price for the option.

Often, one will see levels that apparently have little or no other obvious significance being resolutely defended up to a certain date (the expiration date for the option) and then dramatically going through that level once the option has lapsed.

Relative Strength Index

The Relative Strength Index (RSI) is in my view the best quick-glance indicator of them all, and the one that I always have underneath every basic price chart before I add in any other. In general terms, the RSI shows the momentum of a pair's trading – in effect, the degree of market participation in its current price movement – and can act as a valuable pre-emptive indicator showing a potential reversal of trend.

For example, even if a pair appears to be rising quickly, if the RSI is showing that negative momentum is occurring then it might be time to look at the other indicators that signalled a long position and look to either exit an existing long or establish a new short. Conversely, as shown in the chart below, there is a very notable shift upwards in RSI higher before the actual market price follows it.

EUR Vs USD (Historical)

= RSI confirms upward trend before actual price turns higher

[Chart Key: A = RSI rises sharply higher, in advance of the price movement; B = Actual market price catches up with bullish momentum on RSI]

More specifically, the RSI moves between a scale of 0 to 100, with 100 showing that every participant in the market is buying the base currency of a pair and 0 showing the opposite.

As a rule of thumb, any reading of 70 and above indicates that the pair is overbought, with a possible reversal on the cards, and any reading under 30 shows it is oversold and that the opposite is true. This, together with the formations of usual double top/bottom patterns, can show up even before they do in the actual price movement ('Divergence').

Similarly, areas of support and resistance show up very clearly on RSI patterns, as shown below.

EUR Vs USD (Historical)

= RSI confirms strong resistance before actual price turns lower

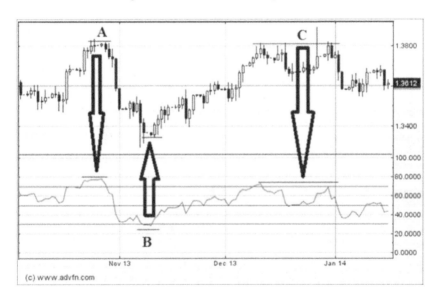

[Chart Key: A = RSI shows genuine resistance level in the price, in advance; B = RSI shows genuine support level in the price, in advance; C = RSI shows genuine rolling resistance level]

As is evident from the above, RSI's principal use is not in already trending markets, in which it can be used as a confirmation of direction or as an early warning indicator of a change of direction (if above 70 or below 30) but rather in range-bound markets looking for direction.

Here, as shown above, it can act as a proxy for volume interest in particular positions, so that, for example, a sharp spike up in RSI in a market trading around the mid-level could be taken as an early signal of a bullish move and vice-versa.

Fibonacci Levels

These are key mathematical ratios of an original number (price), representing a move up or down: 23.6%, 38.2%, 50% (not actually a Fibonacci ratio, but most Fibonacci users include it anyhow), 61.8% and 100%.

These can be overlaid on a chart, from the bottom of a trend to the top of it in a bullish market or from the top of a trend to the bottom of it in a bearish market.

As mentioned earlier, they can often mark resistance and support levels, as shown below.

DJIA (Historical)

[Chart Key: A = 23.6% Fib level acts as support; B = 38.2% Fib level acts as resistance; C = 50% Fib level acts first as support and then as resistance]

In the above chart, we clearly see the correlation between Fibonacci levels and those of support and resistance. Interestingly here we also see that at the 50% level, initially this starts out as a resistance but then, as the cycle progresses, it acts as a support.

Moving Averages

These are particularly useful in determining short-term indications as to whether a market is set to continue in its current trend, reverse that trend or trade in a range. As mentioned earlier, MAs are simply each day's price added together and then divided by a certain number of days: 20, 50 and 100 are the most used.

As an additional confirmation (to established support and resistance levels, for instance) they offer a good idea of whether an asset is likely to break to the topside or the downside, when different time-period MAs cross over each other, as illustrated below.

USD Vs JPY (Historical)

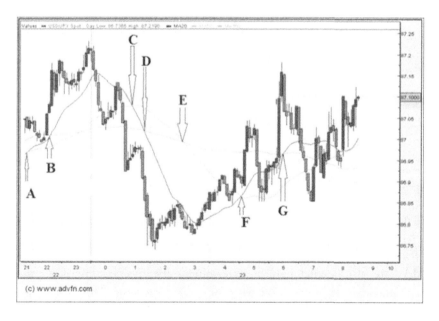

[Chart Key: A = MA20 up through MA50 = BUY; B = MA20 through MA100 = BUY; C = MA20 down through MA50 = SELL; D = MA20 down through

MA 100 = SELL; E = MA50 down through MA100 = OVERSOLD; F = MA20 up through MA100 = BUY; G = MA20 through MA50 = BUY]

Broadly speaking, as shown above, if the short-term MA20 breaks through a longer-term MA then one might expect the currency pair to trade in whichever direction that break has occurred. More helpfully still, MAs can be used for earlier trading indications, using the Moving Average Convergence-Divergence (MACD) indicator, as shown below.

USD Vs JPY (Historical)

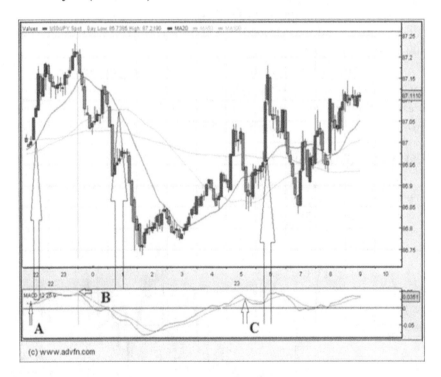

[Chart Key: A = Early signal for crossover = BUY; B = Early signal for crossover = SELL; C = Early warning for crossover = BUY]

MAs are also a vital part of determining the momentum of a price movement, in its application with the 3/10 Oscillator. This is a simple indicator constructed by subtracting the 10-day period Exponential Moving Average from the 3-day period Exponential Moving Average (virtually all charting packages allow one to replicate this with the MACD by setting the short-term parameter to 3, the long-term parameter to 10 and the smoothing parameter to 1.)

DJIA Price/Oscillator Convergence/Divergence Signals

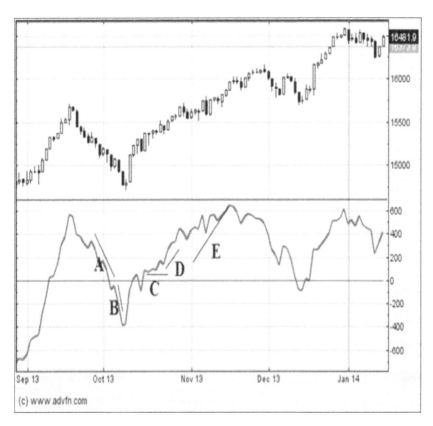

[Chart Key: A = Selling momentum gathers force; B = Selling momentum diverges = change of direction due; C = Range trading momentum; D = Buying momentum kicks in; E = Buying momentum gathers force]

Anyhow, the concept underlying this indicator (similar in theory to the RSI) is that if a price moves up or down and is expected to be sustained then one would anticipate that, along with a range of higher highs (for an upmove) or lower lows (for a downmove), the momentum (or force) behind each of these would also be sustained. If not, one would have to question whether the move can have the strength (more buyers than sellers or the other way around) to continue.

DJIA Bearish Regular Divergence Of Price/Oscillator

= Although the price is rising, momentum is falling = bearish divergence

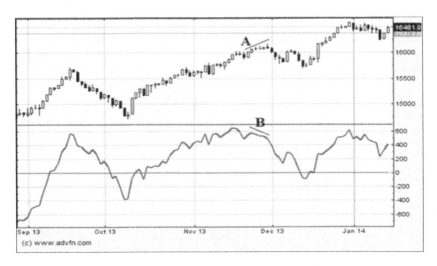

[Chart Key: A = Higher high; B= Lower high]

DJIA Bearish Hidden Divergence Of Price/Oscillator

= The price is still bid, but at a lower level, and momentum is gaining at lower prices

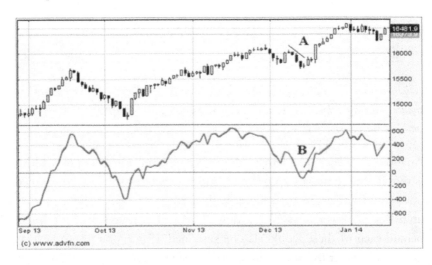

[Chart Key: A = Lower high; B = Higher high]

DJIA Bullish Regular Divergence Of Price/Oscillator

= Although the price is falling, there is less momentum pushing it down

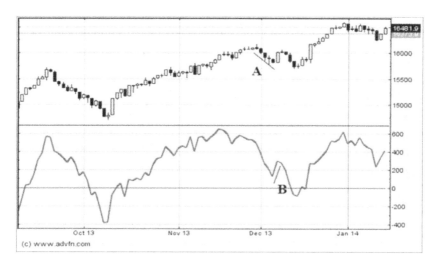

[Chart Key: A = Lower low; B = Higher low]

DJIA Bullish Hidden Divergence Of Price/Oscillator

= Although it is still offered, the momentum gains as the price rises

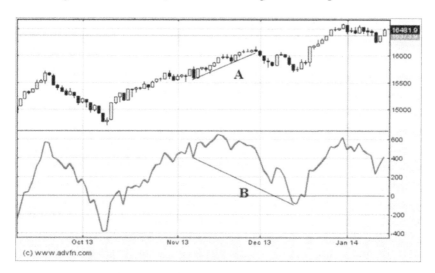

[Chart Key: A = Higher low; B = Lower low]

Bollinger Bands

Bollinger bands are plotted an equal distance either side of a simple moving average. The default settings on trading programmes use a 20-period simple moving average with the upper band (UB) plotted 2 standard deviations above the moving average and the lower band (LB) plotted 2 standard deviations below it.

In periods of low-price volatility, these standard deviations become smaller (this process is called a 'squeeze' in Bollinger parlance) than in periods of high volatility and vice-versa (a 'bubble').

Given this, there is money to be made from anticipating/participating in such a breakout/breakdown to the existing bands.

EUR Vs USD (Historical)

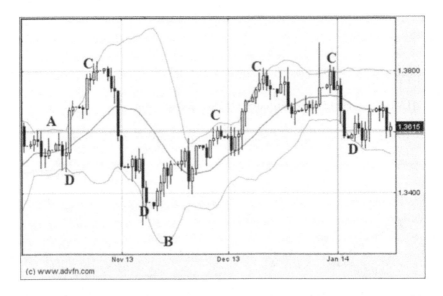

[Chart Key: A = Squeeze; B = Bubble; C = Upper band acts as resistance level; D = Lower band acts as support level]

More appositely, it is better to use Bollinger bands together with other firmer indicators such as support and resistance levels, Fibonacci levels and so forth, and to use them in such a way as to modify the results with what the Bollinger bands tell you about the probability of a move continuing/reversing.

If the price is moving towards the top of a band then beware longs, and if it is moving towards the bottom of a band then beware shorts.

Elliott Wave Theory

Elliot Wave Theory is particularly useful as it shows major moves and minor ones, with the major moves likely to be caused by institutional investors (and well worth following, if they are not spoofs) and the minor moves likely to be caused by retail investors playing catch-up (normally a good time to start thinking about exiting a trade).

In its most basic form, Elliott Waves show that the market does not move in a completely chaotic fashion but rather is a product of patterns that repeat themselves over time. These patterns ('waves') define a trend, which can be the basis for predictive trading.

The Phases Of The Waves

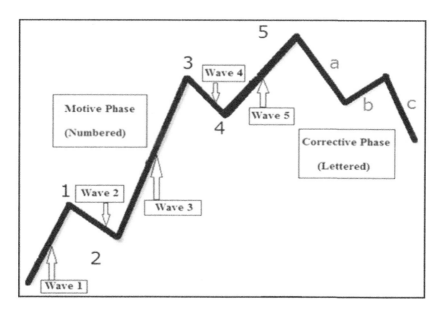

More specifically, according to Ralph Nelson Elliott, who posited his theory in around 1934, a trending market moves in a five-three wave pattern, where the first five waves ('motive waves') move in the direction of the larger trend. Following the completion of the five waves in one direction, a larger corrective move takes place in three consecutive waves ('corrective waves'), as illustrated in the above chart.

Interestingly, the patterns identified by Elliott occur across multiple time frames: that is, a completed five wave sequence on a lesser time frame (5 minutes, for instance) may well be just the first wave of a longer temporal sequence (in a daily chart, for example) and so on and so forth.

Elliott Waves On EUR Versus USD (Historical)

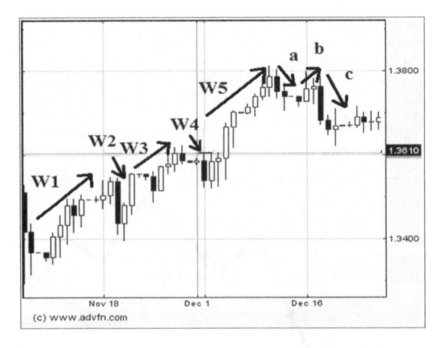

[Chart Key: W1 to W5 = Motive phase waves; a to c = Corrective phase waves]

The combination of Elliott Waves and Fibonacci ratios is particularly useful in trading into new positions or trading out of existing ones, as they are usually also important levels of support and resistance.

The motive and corrective levels are often measured by percentages of the previous wave length, with the most common levels being the Fibonacci ones of 38%, 50%, 61.8% and 100%; timings with a distance of 13, 21, 34, 55, 89 and 144 periods should be particularly monitored (e.g., if you find a crucial reversal or an unfolding of a pattern on a daily chart then expect another crucial unfolding at the above daily points thereafter); a corrective move that follows a motive move from a significant low or high usually retraces 50% to 61.8% of the preceding impulse; wave 4 usually corrects as far as 38.2% of wave 3; given that wave 2 generally does not overlap the start of wave 1 (i.e., the 100% of it), the start of wave 1 is an ideal level to place stops; and the target of wave 5 can be calculated by multiplying the length of wave 1 by 3.236 (2 X 1.618).

It is also interesting to note that long-term economic patterns (see later sub-section on this) can be seen in terms of Elliot Waves. That is, at the onset of a long-term economic cycle there is likely to be a lack of confidence and a fear of falling back into slump or depression, before inflation, interest rates and credit slowly start to rise as confidence in the new age increases (you might say, Elliot Wave 1).

Waves In Financial Markets

As the economy expands (indicated in this instance by inflation) and interest rates increase as an adjunct to this, then so business and consumer confidence grows further, and credit is extended more (Elliot Wave 3 correlation). As we enter the final up-phase of the move, confidence levels morph into over-exuberance and extraordinary loose 'bubble-like' credit conditions, with interest rates also declining (Elliot Wave 5 correlation).

Finally, rising concerns over loose credit, inflationary upward spiral and bad debt causes business and consumer reticence to embark on new projects (in business terms, expansion and in consumer terms, new purchases), default rates increase, credit is squeezed, the economic outlook turns negative, unemployment rises, disinflation turns into deflation, and we have a negative world view.

Triangles And Flags Continuation Patterns

These patterns allow the trader not only to understand from where the price action and momentum has come but also to anticipate where and to what degree it is headed.

As these patterns are also watched by many other traders around the globe, they also allow a retail trader to obtain an ongoing record of the sentiment surrounding an asset at any given time and consequently allow the trader to manage his order placing better as well.

EUR Vs GBP (Historical) Ascending Triangle

[Chart Key: A = Horizontal resistance level; B = Inclining support]

Triangles allow the trader to gauge which of the myriad support and resistance levels on a chart are the ones he should be watching most carefully in determining false or genuine breakouts. An ascending triangle, as above, is formed by a combination of diagonal support and horizontal resistance, implying that the bulls are gaining the upper hand in the ongoing trading dynamic of the pair and buying at higher and higher levels, while the bears are merely trying to defend an established level of resistance.

Clearly, in the above example, the trader has advance warning that the pair is more likely to break up through the resistance level than down through the support one. Also, of course, by anticipating the formation of the triangle the trader can gain/not lose further points, depending on his position, as currency pairs often trend, consolidate and then re-trend.

In the case of a descending triangle, as below, the bears are gaining strength and selling at lower and lower levels, while the bulls are merely trying to defend an established level of support.

AUD Vs USD (Historical) Descending Triangle

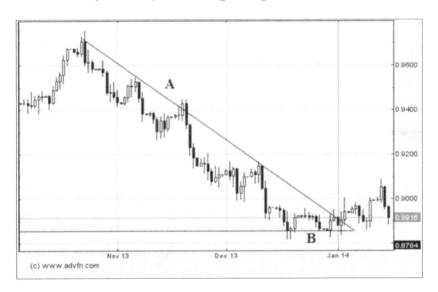

[Chart Key: A = Declining resistance; B = Horizontal support]

Given these two scenarios, it is easy to see that one can make money riding the principal wave up or down, respectively, and to see that triangles make the placement of stop-loss orders relatively simple as well; in the ascending

435

triangle example, they would be placed just under the inclining support line at a level that accorded with one's own risk/reward ratio for a rolling long position. Conversely, in the descending triangle example, they would be placed at a point above the declining resistance level that accorded with one's own risk/reward ratio for a rolling short.

In the cases of both ascending and descending triangles, any true break (more than one spoof break-out) of its direction (up for descending triangles, down for ascending ones) should be taken seriously by traders to consider exiting trades made on the trend until that point (taking profit) and reversing positions.

Flags

Flags generally represent a pause in trend and can be used either to take profits on a position going with that trend or to add to that trending position, if the trader is feeling particularly aggressive (and, preferably, has confidence bolstered by other factors meriting an increase in position size – for example, more favourable than expected fundamental or political developments).

USD Vs JPY (Historical) Continuation In A Downtrend

[Chart Key: A = Declining resistance; B = Horizontal support; F = Flag]

The example above is of a downward trending USDJPY, which pauses for consolidation in a flag pattern before resuming its downward trajectory. Often a trader can expect pretty much the same number of pips in the second part of the downtrend (labelled 'B' on the chart) as in the first part of the downtrend ('A' on the chart), but in the chart above, it seems on cursory glance that this is not the case.

However, as shown in the chart below, looking further into the distance and going on the basis of a longer-term trade, it becomes apparent that, in fact, the real second wave makes up the entire pips expected as a result of the first downtrend.

USD Vs JPY (Historical) Real Second Wave In A Downtrend

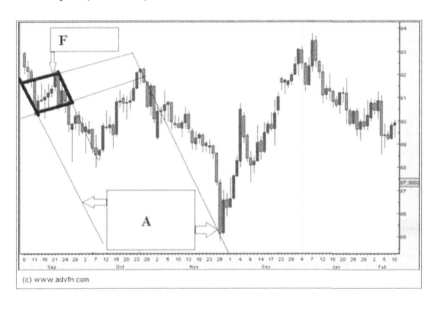

[Chart Key: F = Flag from previous chart; A = Logical conclusion of the original downtrend 1 = 700 pips had the trade been stuck with]

Trend Reversals

Given that the market has a way of generally correcting any untoward excessive movements one way or another in asset prices over time, spotting a real reversal in a trend from just a shimmering mirage is key to making money on a long-term basis.

In this respect, there are a couple of other, more basic, patterns that a trader should look out for.

Double Top And Double Bottom

A Double Top is when prices stop rising at the same point twice in a short sequence of time, as shown below. In order for a real reversal of trend to be indicated, the pair must break down through the key support level as indicated on the chart.

GBP Vs USD (Historical) Double Top

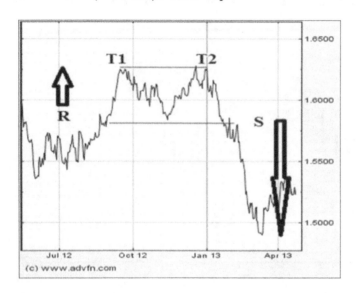

[Chart Key: R = Rising trend; T1 = First top; T2 = Second (double) top; S = Break below this double support level here implies downtrend]

A double bottom is the same principle, only reversed.

Head And Shoulders Pattern

A head and shoulders pattern, as illustrated below, develops with the asset price trending up and forming the left shoulder on a reversal. Then the market trends higher to form the head and falls back to the same support of the first shoulder to form the right shoulder. The neckline is thus the line connecting the troughs between the peaks. If it is broken, expect a downside move to occur.

AUD Vs USD (Historical) Head And Shoulders Pattern

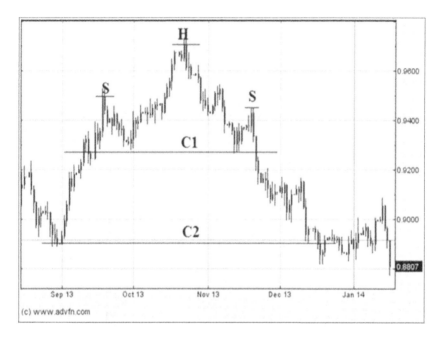

[Chart Key: S = Shoulder; H = Head; C1 = Confirmation of breakdown 1; C2 = Confirmation of further breakdown 2]

Ichimoku Kinko Hyo

Ichimoku Kinko Hyo ('Ichimoku' for short) is – like other Technical Analysis – extremely straightforward, providing that the trader focuses on the system's fundamentals: primarily support and resistance levels, and price momentum.

In Ichimoku all three of these key elements are combined in one chart pattern, which makes determining where and when to enter trades easy to see at a glance. In fact, this is what the name of this system implies: 'ichimoku' translates to 'a glance', 'kinko' means 'equilibrium' and 'hyo' is Japanese for 'chart'.

Ichimoku, created by Japanese journalist and trader Goichi Hosada, is also a trend trading system in and of itself in both rising and falling markets, across all time frames and for any liquid asset, with the caveat that it is not much use when no clear trend is present.

The Cloud

At its most basic level, the cloud ('Kumo') allows the trader to see at a glance what the current trend is and its momentum.

DJIA (Historical): 'Cloud' (shaded area) UNDER Price = UPTREND

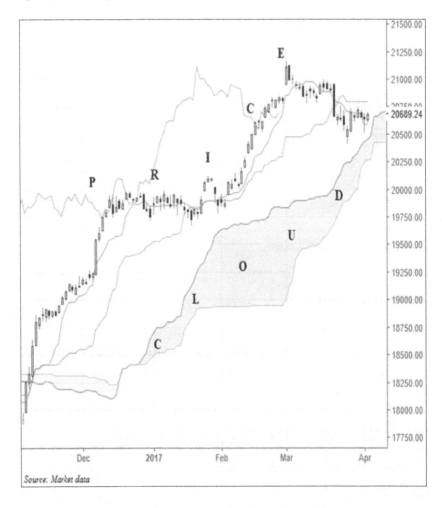

EUR Vs USD (Historical): 'Cloud' ABOVE Price = DOWNTREND

Source: Market data

The Basic Components Of Ichimoku

The 'Kijun Sen' (the blue line), also called the base line, is a calculation averaging the highest high and lowest low (see *Moving Averages* sub-section earlier) over the past 26 periods of a determined timeframe. The 'Tenkan Sen' (the red line), also called the turning line, is derived by averaging the highest high and the lowest low for the past nine periods.

There are three other key lines to monitor. The 'Chikou Span' (the green line), also called the lagging line, is the current closing price plotted 26 periods behind. Then there are two lines that comprise the 'Senkou Span' (the orange lines): the first Senkou line is calculated by averaging the Tenkan Sen and the Kijun Sen and plotted 26 periods ahead, whilst the second Senkou line is a calculation averaging the highest high and the lowest low for the past 52 periods and plotted 26 periods ahead.

Key Ichimoku Terms

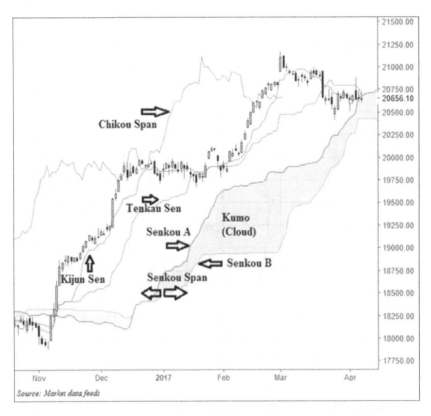

Source: Market data feeds

Traders do not need to know the ins and outs of how these lines are calculated, of course, they just need to know what signals they give off, which are as follows.

Key Trading Signals

'Tenkan-Sen': The key indicator of market trend. If this line is going up or down then a trend is in place but if it is horizontal then no trend is apparent.

'Kijun-Sen': The key indicator of future price movement direction. If the price is higher than the Kijun-Sen then the price will most likely rise but if the price is lower then the price will most likely fall. When the price intersects this line, changes in the trend are likely to occur.

'*Buy*' = Tenkan-Sen crosses the Kijun-sen from below ('strong' if above Kumo, 'normal' if within Kumo, 'weak' if below Kumo), known as the 'Bullish TK Cross'

'*Sell*' = Tenkan-Sen crosses the Kijun-sen from above (strong if below Kumo, normal if within Kumo, weak if above Kumo), known as the 'Bearish TK Cross'

'Chikou Span': It indicates the *strength of a buy or sell signal*. If the Chikou Span is below the current price then the momentum lies with the sellers, and when it is above the current price then the momentum is with the buyers.

'Kumo Support And Resistance Levels': If the price is trading up towards the Kumo from below, then the Kumo is acting as resistance levels (Senkou A and then Senkou B) but if the price is falling down towards the Kumo then the Kumo is acting as support levels (Senkou A and then Senkou B).

Additionally, if the *price is above the Kumo then the trend remains bullish* but if the price is below the Kumo then the trend remains bearish.

Finally, the volatility of the market for the asset being looked at is shown by the thickness of the Kumo: *the thicker the Kumo then the more volatile the market is* (and the greater the support or resistance encountered within the two lines of the Kumo).

Risk/Reward Management And Hedging

The Nature Of Risk

Ultimately, money goes to where it is best rewarded (in the most basic first instance determined by interest rates or dividends but later additionally from capital gains) for the concomitant risks involved (indicated broadly by credit ratings but also from more specific geopolitical, market and systemic risks). This, broadly speaking, is the definition of the 'risk curve'. Traders, to be successful over time, need to be constantly aware of this risk curve – as it constantly shifts – and to manage the risk/reward ratio of their own investment portfolio in a logical, sensible and emotionless fashion, otherwise they will go broke over time.

The key guiding principle here is never to run losses past a sensible stop-loss point, and it is always absolutely essential to put on the stop-loss order at the same time in the same deal ticket as the entry trade is put on. This is based on working out exactly how much one is prepared to lose on any given trade - the maximum should be 1% of total trading capital - and then subtracting that amount (as translated into pips) from the entry trade price. It is always useful to put on a take-profit order as well at the same time as putting on the entry trade (and the stop-loss order).

A risk/reward ratio of at least 4 to 1 should be used on all trades, in my view. That is, the potential loss in pips (based on a stop-loss order) for a trade should be one quarter or less of the potential profit in pips (based on the take-profit order). The stop-loss order should be set to a level under a major support level (if the trader is buying the asset) or over a major resistance level (if the trader is selling the asset) that means that the most a trader can lose on the trade is 1% of his total trading capital, as mentioned.

Orders Are The Foundation Stone Of Risk Management

Greed and fear are the two key emotions to which all traders at all levels of experience are innately prone and which are responsible for the vast bulk of all losses that they make throughout their careers. Greed manifests itself when the trader has positioned himself correctly in the market and finds that he has secured the profit he targeted at the outset of the trade. Instead of taking this profit, the trader decides to stay in the position, greedy for more profits. The logical outcome of this course of action is that the trader will continue to hold on to their position until such time as incremental profits are no longer being made. In financial markets trading, including the oil market, such a turnaround in direction can happen very fast indeed.

At this point, the prevailing emotion starts to shift from greed for further profits to fear of losing part or all of the profits already made. This fear increases if the market continues to go against the trader and the realisation grows that not only has the opportunity for further profits gone but also that the original profit that the trader had targeted, and achieved only moments before, has also gone. At this stage, the majority of traders are tempted to stay in the trade to see if they can get back to the target profit that they had.

This is the key reason why, as mentioned above, around 90% of retail traders lose all their invested funds within the first 90 days of starting to trade. It is crucial to long-term trading survival, and therefore to long-term profitability, to stick to target levels for potential profits and for potential losses based on risk/reward ratios determined by key support and resistance levels already identified at the outset of the trade. The optimal way to avoid the 'greed and fear' trading paradigm is by using orders properly. This practice makes it much more likely that a trader will be profitable overall and much more likely that the trader's stress levels will be dramatically reduced.

The Risk Curve

In its most basic terms, the risk curve is a function of the fact that the more risk involved in an asset, the more reward is required. The risks involved in any asset include all elements of the credit rating inherent in an asset, among others. These include the jurisdiction in which the asset is located (e.g. the US is less risky than Zimbabwe), and the nature of the asset (e.g. a government bond in a country is less risky than a stock in its stock market), among others. Risk also increases over time, given the likelihood that something negative happening to an asset rises the longer it is held.

The relative risk of an asset is reflected in the compensation that an investor is given for holding it. In terms of bonds, for example, this is in the form of an interest rate. Again, in basic terms, the more risk involved in holding an asset, the greater the reward (for example, interest rate) that an investor will require to keep the asset.

However, there is a major difference between probability and a risk/reward profile, in trading terms. The law of probability (more accurately, the *Law of Large Numbers*) is: 'If the probability of a given outcome to an event is P and the event is repeated N times then the larger N becomes, so the likelihood increases that the closer, in proportion, will be the occurrence of the given outcome to N*P.'

In practical terms, this means that if a two-sided coin is tossed a sufficient number of times, then the distribution of the results between heads coming up and tails coming up will be exactly the same. There is an evident problem here for the trader: there is a 50/50 chance on the first toss that heads will come up and, therefore, it would be perfectly reasonably to put half your money on heads. However, in reality, having put money on this outcome, it might come up tails instead. Nonetheless, according to the aforementioned rationale, the trader then puts everything on heads coming up as, given that tails came up first time and the probability of heads coming up was 50% (1 in 2), heads is bound to come up next time. In reality, though, it may not. The fact is that probability only goes a part of the way to explaining sequences of numbers.

There is also the random walk theory, in which market prices supposedly follow a completely random path, without any influence being exerted on them by past price action, making it impossible to predict with any accuracy which direction the market will move at any point or indeed to what degree. However, as has been proven repeatedly, this is also incorrect, as patterns of all sorts manifest themselves daily, indeed hourly, and all that is required is to know what to look for. And what the trader needs to know to navigate through this uncertainty is risk/reward ratios.

Straight Averaging Up

Given the premise that the aim of trading is to minimise any losses and to maximise any gains, averaging up – if done well – is a good way of achieving the latter. The basic averaging technique involves adding to a winning position as the trade continues into profitable territory. This is an antidote to the 'Greed' part of the 'Greed and Fear' paradigm, as it in effect creates new take profit and stop loss points as the overall trade develops.

So, for example, in the chart below, a position had been entered by buying EUR against the USD (selling USD) at 1.3000 (this is an historical example, but the point is the same for any time period and any asset class). After completing the technical analysis, it was clear that a break of this key resistance level would indicate a move higher, and it had been decided to add GBP1 per pip at every 50-pip upwards increment, with corresponding stop loss order added on each additional trade. Having done this three times, there was an average long position of GBP3 per pip at EURUSD1.3050.

On GBP1 per pip at 1.3000, a trader would have made GBP250 as the EURUSD hit 1.3250. Another GBP1 per pip at 1.3050 would have netted a further GBP200 and the final GBP1 per pip at 1.3100 a further GBP150. The total, therefore, would have been GBP600. Of course, had the trader put on GBP3 per pip in the first trade, the profit would have been GBP750. Additionally, the break-even on the trade has now moved up to 1.3050 rather than 1.3000.

EUR Vs USD (Historical)

(c) www.advfn.com

[Chart Key: A = Buy EURUSD at 1.3000, GBP1 per pip; B = Buy again at 1.3050, GBP 1 per pip; C = Buy again at 1.3100, GBP 1 per pip; D = Therefore, average long price at GBP 3 per pip is 1.3050]

If the trader had not sold at the top of that move and the pair had traded down to 1.3100 then he might have lost the third leg profit of GBP150, which would have resulted in a net profit of just GBP150. Also, if the pair had traded back down through the 1.3050 area then the trader would have incurred a loss on the third long, together with no profit on the second, which would have resulted in a net profit of nothing at all.

Layered Averaging Up

Another way of averaging up that tends against the above phenomenon of being averaged out of any profit is to add to a long position on pullbacks to the preferred entry level, or the other way around if a net seller. So, if a trader decided to go long as above then he would simply add GBP1 per pip on any move back towards the 1.3000 level, if he was expecting a sustained move upwards over time.

Such tactics are particularly useful if there is an ongoing struggle between two significant trading forces - a central bank and a big fund for example – on either side of a trade. For example in USDJPY, after the new Prime Minister Shinzo Abe came to power at the end of 2012, the Bank of Japan (BOJ) was buying USD and selling JPY very aggressively in order to support its export market (and thus aid broader economic recovery) from around the USD85.50 level, whilst certain funds – especially hedge funds – were selling USD and buying JPY anywhere above 87.00.

Once Abe was more firmly ensconced as PM, this battle moved up the values on USDJPY, as the BOJ was given a much broader policy mandate than before. This was in line with those given to the US Federal Reserve and the Bank of England at the time, which included looking at employment rates, interest rates and inflation. In this vein, the banks used quantitative easing where necessary, together with direct currency intervention and forward guidance as a means of manipulating their respective currencies. It was only when the BOJ was tasked with ensuring a broad-based policy strategy – engineering sustained nominal annual economic growth of 3% (there had been no average annual nominal GDP growth for 15 years) and at least a 2% annual inflation rate every year from 2015, as well as commencing a massive domestic bond-buying QE programme (Fed-style) – that the JPY managed sustained depreciation of the sort wanted by Abe and moved through the key USDJPY100 resistance level.

Alternatively, adding smaller amounts to the initial position is also a better way to take advantage of further moves (in the aforementioned case) whilst also limiting the potential – as shown above – for all profits to be eradicated (or even to start making a loss). The converse of this is averaging down, in which a trader adds to losing positions in the hopes of making money back quicker as the original position reverses.

Value Averaging

As a natural corollary of the above, value averaging is another way of efficiently managing positions, this time by constantly readjusting the risk/reward exposure to a pre-determined level. Therefore, in practical terms, a trader sets an amount that falls within his risk/reward parameters.

For example, he may decide that he wishes to have a total exposure per day of GBP100 in EURUSD, at GBP1 per pip. In this event, if the position makes GBP10 in one day then next day he takes the GBP10 out and still has GBP100 riding on the position (at the original price). Conversely, if the position loses GBP10 in one day then the following day he would add another GBP10 at whatever the new price is to compensate. Thus, he has now spent GBP110 on the long, albeit at a more favourable average, given a down-trading market.

Hedging

Hedging can either help to reduce overall net losses in a bad position (by making offsetting gains in other related areas) or help to add to overall net profits (whilst not actually proportionately increasing the risk involved). In this sense, then, hedging is a method of dynamically managing the risk/reward profile for the trader and knowing how to do it properly and quickly in any situation is vital.

Cross-Currency Hedging

As oil is priced in US dollars, it is necessary to manage the currency exposure involved. If a trader is long oil then effectively he is long the US dollar as well, and if he is short oil then he is effectively short the US dollar as well. Consequently, knowledge of cross-currency hedging is an essential tool in managing risk in oil trading.

In basic terms, all currency trades involve buying one currency and selling another and, because of this duality, hedging currency exposures is fairly straightforward.

For example, a trader is long (bought) the EUR, which means he is also short (sold) the USD: in market code '+EURUSD', as the sign related to the first currency (i.e. long – or bought – euros). The position is always marked in terms of the base currency first, then the amount (EUR1 million for bank dealers or, for spread traders, 1 per pip for example, be it GBP, USD or EUR, most commonly) and then the price (here, 1.5063). Therefore, in market terms, it should be written: +EURUSD1 @1.5063. In this example, EUR1 million is used but the points are the same for whatever amount the spread trader is using.

EUR Vs USD (Historical)

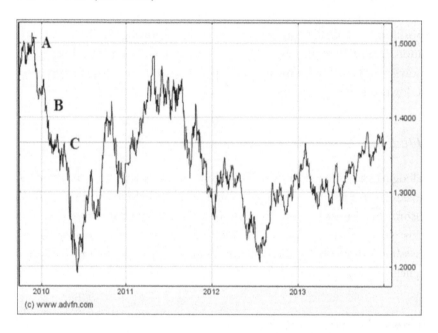

[Chart Key: *A= Trader buys euros, 1 million and sell US dollars at 1.5063; B = Getting nervous about the euro story, he buys US dollars, 1.5 million and sells Swiss francs at 1.0262; C = The trader now has options – he is long EURUSD, long USDCHF; making money on the latter going up as the former goes down. Additionally, he can re-weight positions, depending on how each pairing performs (he can, for example, add to his long USDCHF position or reduce his long EURUSD position) or simply sell EURCHF, as he is effectively net long of that, or he can do counter-balancing stock indices trades]*

The market is going against the trader, but he believes that the EUR will go up soon. However, he is not exactly sure when and how much the swing against him might be. He knows that, by definition, if the EUR element of this pair is going down then the USD element of it is going up. Therefore, he can go long the USD against something else to attempt to make money on the rising USD as the EUR goes down, so he goes long USDCHF1.5 million as EURUSD breaks through the 1.4750 level.

USD Vs CHF (Historical)

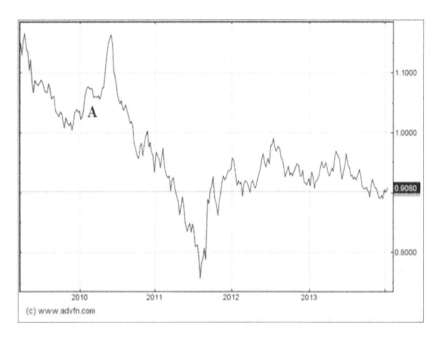

(c) www.advfn.com

[Chart Key: A = Buy USD/ sell CHF1.5 million at 1.0262]

Now things are looking up, as one trade is counterbalancing the other almost perfectly, as can be seen from the chart below, given that he is essentially long EURCHF.

As the EUR continues in its downward trend, the trader can use some of the averaging techniques described above to help loss turn into profit. This is simply a question of re-weighting each trade. As it stands, he has the same overall capital involved in each trade (EUR1 million or around USD1.5 million) but as the EURUSD continues to trade down, he can add to his long USDCHF position. Let us say that he doubles it, at 1.0400, to USD3 million for the entire duration of the downtrend in EURUSD.

Looking at these trades in profit and loss (P&L) terms then: +EURUSD1 million @ 1.5063, liquidate at 1.1800 = total loss of EUR326,300 (= USD at the new rate = USD385,034).

+USDCHF1 million @ 1.0262, liquidate at 1.1700 = USD143,800 and +USDCHF2 million @ 1.0400, liquidate at 1.1700 = USD260,000.

Therefore, the total profit for the venture (which did not start out well) was USD77,500.

EUR Vs CHF (Historical)

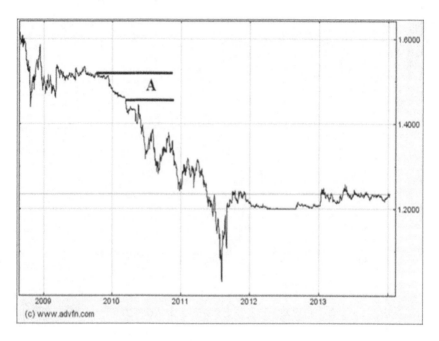

(c) www.advfn.com

[Chart Key: A = Overall, with just a flat long EURCHF position the trader is only down 250-300 pips but he can get rid of this entirely by re-weighting]

In the above example, he could also have sold EURCHF, which would have given him a flat position, as: 1. +EUR -USD; 2. +USD -CHF; 3. Therefore, net long EURCHF; 4. Therefore, sell EURCHF = flat.

However, there were many other options available whilst he was long EURUSD and long USDCHF. He could have increased the relative weighting of the long USDCHF position (as described above), or he could think more laterally still and buy the USD against something else as well.

This would have increased his net long USD position but also it would have allowed him to insulate himself against any CHF-specific good news that might cause it to rally and thus lose him money on his long USDCHF position – for example, if the central bank of Switzerland (SNB) raised interest rates unexpectedly.

Therefore, he would have looked around for other currencies where the outlook was grim and good news was not expected on the horizon. At the time, GBP looked especially ropey, so he could have sold GBP and bought USD. This again could be reweighted in terms of amount.

Cross-Asset Hedging

Sticking with the failing long EURUSD position example, another way the trader could have capitalised on the then-ongoing poor performance of the eurozone was to, for example, sell the major stock indices associated with the individual countries performing especially badly in the EUR region.

Greece Athens Stock Exchange (Historical)

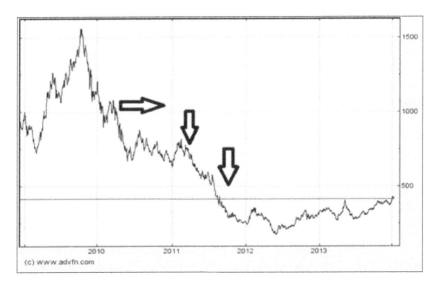

(c) www.advfn.com

Had he sold Greece's Athens Stock Exchange (ASE), say another USD1 million worth, his entry price at the time would have been around 2,250 and falling fast. He could also have sold the other major indices of troubled eurozone countries. Looking at it another way, he could have bought US stock indices instead/as well.

If he was, in the meantime, suddenly concerned about his net short CHF position then he could hedge out the CHF risk, by buying the major Swiss stock index.

Dow Jones Industrial Average (Historical)

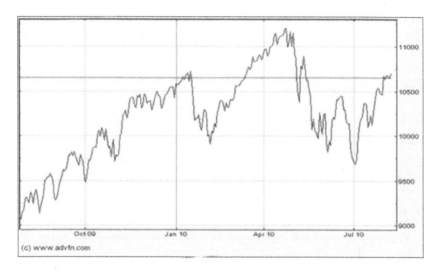

He could also have done a currency option to hedge risks either side (as analysed very shortly).

Cross-Sovereign/Credit-Rating Hedging

Given that the credit risk for the troubled eurozone members was increasing over the period when the EUR was falling out of bed, the trader could have bought credit default swaps (CDS) on those countries worst affected. CDS are basically insurance policies against entities going bankrupt. The more technical definition is: CDS pay the buyer face value in exchange for the underlying securities, or the cash equivalent should a government or company fail to adhere to its debt agreements; the higher the likelihood, the higher the price of the CDS.

Again, this would have hedged the EUR exposure as, broadly speaking, the more money that was lost on being long EUR, the more money was made on being long Greek CDS (that is, in essence, buying the likelihood of Greece defaulting on its debt).

Options

Options are best used as a form of hedging, in my view, although many traders deal in them as they would any other standalone asset class. In basic terms, an option is the right, but not the obligation, to buy or sell an asset at a particular price (the 'exercise price') on or before a specific future date (the 'exercise date'). The two most common types of option are 'American style' option (which can be exercised at any point up to the option expiration date) and 'European' style option (which can only be exercised on an exact exercise date). For the more 'exotic' Asian options the payoff is determined by the average underlying price over some pre-set period of time, conceptually different from both the American and European option types in which in both cases the payoff of the option contract depends on the price of the underlying instrument at exercise.

Barrier options, meanwhile, that often have a significant effect on market trading patterns, are a type of option whose payoff depends on whether the underlying asset has reached or exceeded a predetermined price. A barrier option can be a knock-out, meaning it can expire worthless if the underlying asset exceeds a certain price, limiting profits for the holder but limiting losses for the writer. It can also be a knock-in, meaning it has no value until the underlying reaches a certain price.

An option to buy an asset is called a 'call' option and an option to sell one is called a 'put' option. A trader can buy or sell either type of option (that is, he can buy the right to sell or buy, and he can sell the right to sell or buy). If he sells an option then he receives a premium from the buyer (a bit like an insurance premium), but he is obligated as the seller to pay out to the buyer if the option is exercised (and these pay-outs can be limitless, depending on how the option has moved). If he buys an option, then he receives these premiums.

In a currency option, then, if a trader bought a EURUSD call then he would be buying the right (but not the obligation) to buy EUR and sell USD, and if he bought a EURUSD put then he would be buying the right (but not the obligation) to sell EUR and buy USD. And vice-versa if he was selling a call or put; he has a liability then to meet the obligation implied in the option if the buyer decides to exercise it. The premium paid to buy an option is a reflection both of the exercise price of the option (and whether it is currently in profit or out of profit) and also the volatility of the market for the currency pair.

Buying A Call Option

This is used most simply by those who believe that an asset is going up in value (it is buying the option to buy a certain asset). If the asset price is higher than the strike price plus the premium paid, then the trader makes a profit. The only risk here, as with all options bought, is that the trader loses the premium paid if the underlying asset price moves the opposite way.

Long Call Option Structure

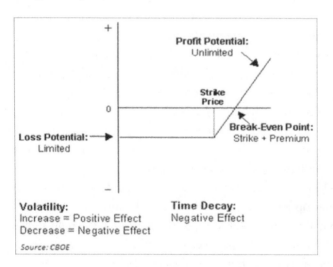

Buying A Put Option

This is used by those who believe that an asset is going down in value (it is buying the option to sell a certain asset). If the asset price is lower than the strike price plus the premium paid, then the trader makes a profit. The risk here, as with all options bought, is that the trader loses the premium paid.

Long Put Option Structure

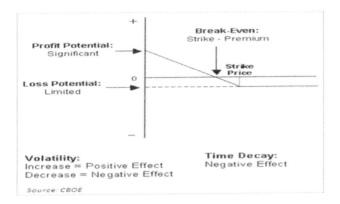

Long Straddle

This is used by investors who think an asset is going a long way in one direction but are unsure as to which direction that might be. Both a put and a call option are bought at the same strike price and the same expiration date. This offers unlimited potential upside but limited downside.

Long Straddle Structure

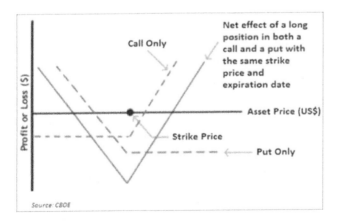

Long Strangle

Similar to the Long Straddle strategy but with the differences that both sides are usually some way out of the money and the call option and put option elements have different strike prices (but the same expiration date).

Risk-On/Risk-Off And Correlations

Risk-On/Risk-Off Trading Model

There are three key technical reasons – aside from attitudinal ones – why around 90% of retail traders lose all their trading money within 90 days of commencing dealing in financial markets. Two of these – lack of knowledge and experience in utilising technical analysis and inadequate use of risk management techniques – were examined earlier. The third – insufficient awareness of the interconnectedness of different assets and their trading patterns, 'correlations' – is the focus of this section.

To begin with, then, the degree to which the price action of all major financial assets is correlated positively or negatively has varied since this phenomenon fully manifested itself after the collapse of Lehman Brothers in 2008. Nonetheless, these correlations, which are a function of the risk of systemic failure across the global financial system, remain a significant common price component of all assets in all regions across the world.

When the risk of this failure rises there is a shift towards less risk-exposed assets ('Risk-Off') and when it falls there is a move towards more risk-exposed assets ('Risk-On'). These conditions together are acronymically termed 'RORO'. More specifically, RORO means that the price action of all major financial markets assets is correlated positively or negatively to a greater or lesser degree.

In the aftermath of the Lehman Brothers' failure and the blow-up of a full Global Financial Crisis thereafter, there were two diametrically opposed potential outcomes. One was that the dramatic actions undertaken by policymakers and governments around the world – which ranged from huge cuts in interest rates, currency devaluations and quantitative easing, or all three – would successfully result in a global economic recovery. The other was that these measures might not work quickly, in which case there would be at least a continuation of the global depression for a considerable period, if not a worsening of it.

Almost the same broad global scenario resulted from the peak 2020/21 COVID-19 pandemic. Therefore, the trading trajectory after the Great Financial Crisis that began in 2007/08 is highly instructive for the post-COVID-19 trading environment. However, a key difference to the post-

COVID-19 trading environment is that global policy makers were better prepared to deal with the ramifications of a global pandemic for the financial system, in part due to their experience during the Great Financial Crisis. Many of them very quickly announced a range of economy-supporting measures and measures aimed at shoring up the personal financial confidence of their citizens in order that the generalised panic associated with a pandemic and the economic malaise that went with it would not also create a crisis of confidence in the global economic and financial systems.

All Assets Are Related In One Way Or Another

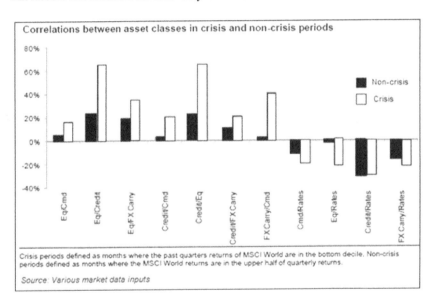

Correlations between asset classes in crisis and non-crisis periods

Crisis periods defined as months where the past quarters returns of MSCI World are in the bottom decile. Non-crisis periods defined as months where the MSCI World returns are in the upper half of quarterly returns.

Source: Various market data inputs

As far as the basic architecture of the RORO model goes, the two factors that determined the price of and relationship between different assets during the Great Financial Crisis also did so during the COVID-19 pandemic, and these are: firstly, precisely what policy measures would be taken to end the crisis and secondly, how quickly they might work. When confidence was running high that the measures would work in effecting at least an upturn in the world's economic fortunes (or in fighting back against COVID-19 via lockdowns or vaccination programmes, respectively), global investors moved towards more risk-exposed (risk-on) assets and when the opposite was the case they moved towards less risk-exposed assets (risk-off). This meant that there were very pronounced synchronised price moves – up or down – across varying asset classes, depending on whether they were regarded as more risky (risk-on) or less risky (risk-off).

In the aftermath of the Great Financial Crisis, there was a switch in the predominant market view from pessimism over the global economy to one that the US economy was ready to take off, boosting much of the rest of the world with it. This meant a shift towards risk-on assets. Because of the generally effective handling of the COVID-19 pandemic, largely as a result of the previous experience of the Great Financial Crisis, this switch in a more positive market sentiment overall – and towards a basic risk-on environment – occurred much earlier than it did after the onset of the Great Financial Crisis.

RORO Pattern From 2015

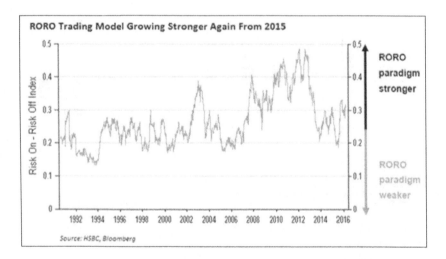

It is apposite to note, though, that in 2015/16 when the US Federal Reserve raised interest rates to attempt to offset the inflationary effects of QE – and signalled that it would continue to do so at a quicker pace and to a higher degree than many had previously thought – fear set in that these interest rate increases might choke off the tentative recovery. This meant a shift towards risk-off assets. From the first quarter of 2021 especially, these same fears bubbled up, with further concerns over a move from the US to embark on a sustained interest hiking trajectory resulting in a risk-off trading environment, most notably seen in fallbacks in equities valuations.

These fears after the Great Financial Crisis – and the corollary move into risk-off assets – were later augmented by additional heightened concerns over weakening oil prices, the near-zero real growth occurring in the eurozone, and the decreasing rate of economic growth in China. The first two of these factors (in addition to the fear over US interest rate rises) were also at play in the 2020/21 COVID-19 pandemic. Market concerns then shifted focus when surging energy prices following Russia's invasion of Ukraine in February 2022 stoked anxiety over the prospect of the high-for-longer interest rate environment that might be required to dampen down inflation. Correlations, therefore, not only remain a very significant common price component of all assets in all regions across the world in all market conditions now, but also they change with great frequency.

Looking back at the aftermath of the Great Financial Crisis as a guide to how the global investment landscape will pan out following the height of the COVID-19 pandemic in 2020/21 and Russia's invasion of Ukraine in 2022, the RORO trading model was a dominant theme again at the end of 2016, as shown below.

Assets In the RORO Mix

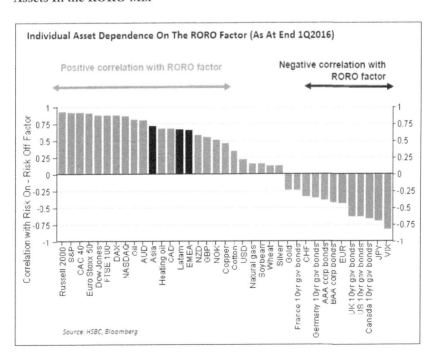

The fact that the prices of apparently disparate individual assets move in tandem (either positively correlated or inversely correlated) is even truer in periods when these correlations change quickly. There are, though, other much longer-term cycles of which the trader must be aware to optimise their trading strategies, and these are analysed later in this book *('The Business Cycle', 'The Kondratieff Wave* and *'The Minsky Cycle')*.

Correlations In the Lead Up To The Great Financial Crisis

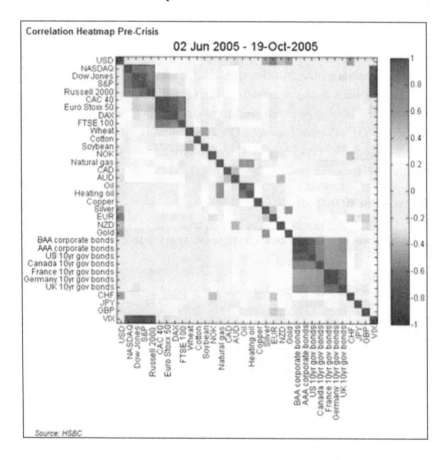

Consequently, in risk-on environments, a trader might prefer to have a higher allocation to selected commodities (including oil and gas) that are likely to respond well to increased appetite for risk. This would be instead of holding lower risk assets, such as straight cash (ultra risk-off) or government bonds (where the risk rises according to which country's bonds are held) or related developed market currencies. The trader could also build into this approach a more nuanced risk-weighted allocation to exposures such as equities, emerging market currencies and selected commodities as and when an element of higher risk/higher reward profile is required.

This might be considered a bar-bell approach to risk/return, with the former flight to quality exposures in government bonds being sized to zero in favour of more cash and an appropriately sized allocation to riskier exposures. This said, the idea of what may be classed as 'safe-haven' assets or 'risky' assets is subject to substantial changes, often in a very short time, and there is no reason to expect this to change. Above and below, we see these correlations 'heat maps' at various points before and after the Great Financial Crisis.

Correlations After The Great Financial Crisis

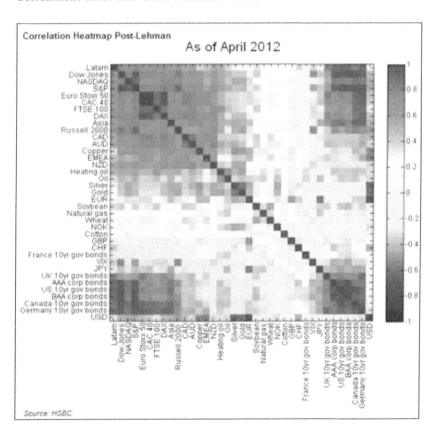

Correlations As The Fed Started To Raise Interest Rates

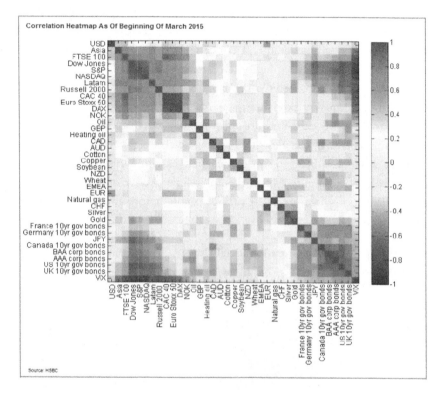

Correlation Heatmap As Of Beginning Of March 2015

Source: HSBC

This RORO factor has persisted as governments around the globe continued in their attempts to engineer sustainable economic recovery and real growth in their economies in the wake of the Great Financial Crisis and then in the wake of the 2020/21 COVID-19 crisis. It has also been sustained in the aftermath of Russia's invasion of Ukraine in 2022.

This means that a true understanding of RORO – that the prices of apparently disparate individual assets move in tandem (either positively correlated or negatively correlated) – is as vital to maximising profits and minimising risks for all traders now as it ever was. It also means, in broad terms, that classical methods of maximising returns whilst minimising risk will remain side-lined for the foreseeable future, calling for shrewder and nimbler trading approaches going forward. As shown below, this has also meant that an ability to switch to different trading techniques at different times for different assets – or a combination thereof – is also essential to successful trading over time.

Momentum Trading

This is a strategy in which traders buy and sell according to the strength of recent price trends. There are many technical indicators, as outlined in the earlier *'Technical Analysis'* section, which can be used to ascertain this strength or weakness, and therefore whether to buy or sell, respectively.

The most useful of these from my perspective is the RSI, followed moving averages (also the moving average convergence divergence indicator as an adjunct) and occasionally stochastics. As with all trading, though, any uncertainty over the strength of signal indicated should be corroborated with further technical and fundamental factors and these are all looked at earlier in this book.

There are two types of momentum trading: relative and absolute. Relative momentum is where the strength/weakness of a particular tradable commodity (say, WTI oil) is compared to the strength/weakness of another tradable commodity in the same asset class (say, Brent). In oil trading, disparities can arise if this strategy is applied, opening up tremendous profit opportunities. Absolute momentum is where the strength/weakness of one commodity is compared to its previous strength/weakness over different previous time periods.

In general terms, one principal driver of momentum in commodities trading, such as for oil, is inventories (effectively, supply) and demand profiles. These, in turn, can be anticipated through other macro factors that have been analysed in full in the earlier sections of this book.

Carry Trading

This is a strategy that is extremely well-known amongst FX dealers, involving the purchase of a currency of a country in which interest rates are higher than the currency of a country that has been sold. Doing this means that an FX trader will be holding a currency in a country in which he will receive a higher interest rate accrual for as long as he holds that currency than if he held the currency that he has sold to buy it. This positive interest rate accrual is made by the trader, regardless of whether a currency goes up or down relative to other currencies.

High interest-rate currencies tend to appreciate when domestic consumption is high and depreciate when domestic consumption growth is low, this latter phenomenon virtually necessitating a positive risk premium for buyers of the currency. In addition, an element of this 'compensation' risk is that with low domestic consumption (and growth), a country's assets, including its currency, have more potential to crash.

The long-running classic example of the 'funding' currency – the one that a trader effectively borrows to sell to buy another higher-yielding currency – was the Japanese yen, as the BOJ for years held interest rates very low in order to try to prompt some nominal GDP growth in the country. FX traders would effectively borrow yen (at virtually zero interest rates) and sell it to buy higher-yielding currencies (Australian and New Zealand dollars were popular for this, as the interest rates of the two countries were much higher than Japan's). In more recent years, the euro and the Swiss franc have also been used for this funding side of trading.

For oil and other commodities, the carry can be regarded as the slope of the asset price curve, which is closely linked to the fundamentals of supply and demand. Generally speaking, if there is a greater supply than demand in the short term than in the long term then the curve will rise from left to right; this is called a 'contango' market. This factors in expectations of how much supply and demand there will be in the future, which can be seen from the oil futures markets. Conversely, if there is greater demand than supply in the short term than the long term then the curve will fall from left to right; this is called a 'backwardated' market.

Value Trading

This is a strategy that tends to be mentioned in particular in connection with stock traders because there are all sorts of metrics that are readily available for them to try to find the 'fair value' of a stock, in the midst of swings either side away from that key point. These include 'Price to Earnings ratio', 'Debt to Equity' ratio, 'Price to Book' ratio and 'Price Earnings to Growth' ratio, to name the principal ratios involved, aside from other metrics such as long-term earnings growth and overall outright price.

However, FX dealers also use the notion of 'fair value' when trading, at least at the back of their minds, as 'real exchange rates' (nominal exchange rates adjusted for inflation) have a tendency to revert to 'fair value' over time, as defined by purchasing parity. In basic terms, this means that two currencies will find an equilibrium point at a level where the same product/service costs the same in each country, having taken into account the exchange rate. A commonly used example of this is the McDonalds' 'Big Mac' index. So, for example, if a Big Mac costs USD2 in the US and GBP1 in Great Britain then the exchange rate should be, according to the PPP measure, GBP1:USD2. The PPP, then, also reflects inflationary data, as if inflation went up in Great Britain to a degree that it cost GBP2 for a Big Mac then the exchange rate would be parity between the two currencies – that is, GBP1:USD1. Clearly the PPP, alongside other of these measures, are of longer-term use in discerning trading patterns.

For commodities trading, value trading is more nuanced. In its purest mathematical form, the nearest that traders can get to a 'fair value' for a particular commodity is to look at a period that most closely mirrors the period in which he is currently trading – as long a period as possible – and look at what the mean average price is for that period. Having said this, assessing the fair value of a commodity is a strategy that is best employed in conjunction with other trading strategies, to act as a central reference point around which the veracity of other moves can be judged.

Volatility Trading

This is a strategy in which the trader looks at the size and speed of changes in an asset rather than the asset itself. To trade volatility, traders can either take long or short positions on the VIX – the Chicago Board Options Exchange (CBOE) Volatility Index – or on the individual volatility of an asset. In particular on this latter point, the trader looks to take advantage from implied volatility being higher or lower than realised volatility, most often through options strategies.

Macro Trading

This strategy is focused on basing all trading tactics around big changes in the economic or political environment in a country or region or on a global basis. For oil trading, these factors are often the key driver of price and volatility in that they are integral to setting the underlying trading tone (bullish or bearish) and frequently find expression in hard supply and demand terms. Broadly, for oil trading, on a day-to-day basis the technical factors of the oil market in and of themselves matter less than they do in most notably the currency market (the equities market falls in between the two). It is extremely common that intraday or intraweek trading in currencies will revolve around the key technical levels described in detail above and that economic announcements from the countries whose currencies are a focus of trading at any point may play second fiddle to the technical factors. This is not true generally for the oil market.

The reasons for this difference are firstly that other markets are not in major part broadly subject to the simple laws of supply and demand (except, of course, when there is a QE operation underway), whereas the oil market is. Consequently, data releases relating to supply and demand or major statements by major oil producers on oil supply and demand outrank technical factors on the day in particular when they are due.

A second reason for this difference is that the forward guidance of major central banks – and countries' major independent financial bodies (like the OBR in the UK for example) – on expected major data numbers is generally far more transparent and accurate than the guidance that comes from big oil producing states. Saudi Arabia, for example, has often just increased or decreased its oil production with no advance warning whatsoever. Similarly, the US's Energy Information Administration's Weekly Petroleum Report will have no meaningful guidance in advance of its release, and even if there are rumours in the market about what the numbers will be (for oil inventory) then they are often way off the mark.

Consequently, the weight of data releases or statements by major producers can completely override any technical trading considerations, and shorter-term technicals in the oil market are optimally employed during periods when oil numbers have already come out or are not due. They are also very effective at determining longer-term trends.

Gap Trading

In a truly efficient market (one in which every participant knows the true price, what everyone else's position is, and which is open all the time), the ebb and flow of pricing would be seamless, up or down. In reality, of course, this is not the case, and in some conditions markets tend to 'gap' –

that is, they jump from one price to a much higher/lower level without trending up/down beforehand. This is seen particularly in the less liquid markets and, consequently, is often seen in the commodities markets in general (and in the oil market as well), which are less liquid than both FX and many equities markets. The most liquid market generally is when the London and New York markets are open at the same time and the least liquid is when only Asia and Australasia are in the game.

This gap phenomenon usually appears in markets that are not 24/5 (as the FX market is). For example, if trading the FTSE 100 then there is a timing gap between when the FTSE closes on Friday and when it reopens on Monday morning at 8am GMT, as illustrated in the chart below.

Taking Advantages Of The Gap

[Chart Key: Gap A = RSI shows no real buying momentum – the smart money is looking to sell on rallies, whilst the hot money is chasing the tail of the last move up; Gap B = Same pattern as in the previous example – hot money is still convinced it is going up but smart money is not – hence the small candlesticks; Gap C = With a new week, the smart money has made its profits on shorts and is now going long – with more commitment shown by longer candlesticks]

Above it can be seen from the RSI trends that there is only one real move up based on 'smart money': that punctuated by Gap 3. In the latter event, the 'hot money' (inexperienced retail trading money) is chasing the tail of the move or incorrectly anticipating the level at which the smart money may take profits on shorts. In smart money moves, the candlesticks themselves tend to be bigger than in hot money moves, which are shorter and often punctuated by small reversals (lack of confidence in fundamental positioning). With Gap Trading, though, good money can be made by correctly identifying the overall trend, both from the price action on the foremost graph and from the underlying momentum underpinning the trade trend (from RSI, Price Oscillator, MACD and so on).

In determining which way the smart money – or more particularly, the weight of smart money – is going, a good tool is to regard charts as combinations of 'impulse' moves and 'corrective' moves. In this context, in short, an impulsive move is one that covers more pips in less time than a corrective one. Additionally, impulsive moves are characterised by longer candlesticks than corrective ones. And finally, impulse moves comprise several of the same-coloured candlesticks in a row.

Tracking The Smart Money

Conversely, a corrective move is characterised by a more even distribution of bull and bear candlesticks and by the emergence of more wicks/tails on the candle's extreme points. Additionally, a corrective move will be made up of a more balanced mixture of winning candlesticks against losing ones, indicating persistent smart money in a trend.

As in the chart above, the corrective move down on AUDUSD clearly had heavy money behind it, consisting of 848 pips. Within that were three one-way (impulse pattern) moves that accounted for 646 pips. The impulsive moves were marked, as mentioned, by one-way trading (back-to-back black candles in this diagram, denoting selling) that are much longer than the bid candles showing fast price action.

Contrarian Trading

The key to this type of trading is to look at the markets in terms of the sentiment of those participating in it – particularly in terms of whether greed or fear is the dominant psychology at work at any particular time – to gauge when is the right time to buy and when the right time to sell and to use correct risk management techniques. Sentiment underpinning a trend can be gleaned from the 'Commitment of Traders Report' (COT), which is available from the Commodities Futures Trading Commission (CFTC) website.

Basically, the usefulness of the COT is that it shows the net long/short positions for every available futures contract for commercial traders (hedgers) and non-commercial traders (speculators, including currency traders, equities traders and commodities traders). As some of these futures contracts are simply hedges against real tangible positions (energy companies buying oil futures, for example) these contracts give excellent indications of powerful trends at one extreme end of the market.

As a rule of thumb, speculators tend to buy the market when it is still rising whereas hedgers tend to sell into any rises (and vice-versa for a falling market, of course). In a rising market, therefore, when hedgers bets are increasing substantially and/or those of speculators are diminishing in tandem, then the top of the market cannot be that far away. This is why it is important to use other technical indicators to assess exactly at what level one is going to exit a long position or enter a new short position.

Changing Correlations Between Oil And The US Dollar

The most obvious correlation to note is between the oil price and other assets is that to the US dollar, as oil is priced in the US currency. Around 30 years ago, it seemed that there was a fairly clear principle for investors to follow with regard to the link between the oil and USD prices: that is, the higher the crude oil price, the higher the USD. The rationale at that time was that as oil prices rose then the demand for dollars to buy it would increase and thus the USD would strengthen.

Inextricably Linked One Way Or The Other

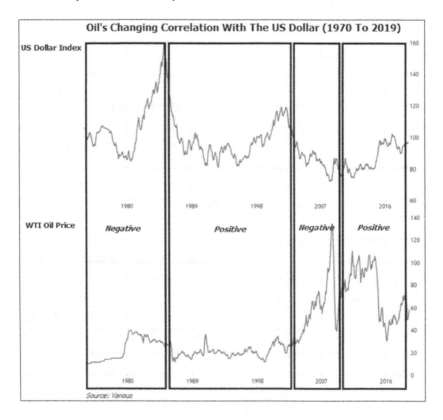

Around 20 years ago, this relationship completely reversed, as rising oil prices coincided with a broadly weaker dollar. This was explained at that time by the idea that rising oil prices lead to deterioration in the US trade deficit (oil and oil products historically represented around 50% of the entire US trade deficit) and thus a negative outlook for the USD and the corollary selling of it. The reverse, of course, was equally true at that point, which was that a downward trending oil price coincided with a rising USD.

Either Correlation Allows For Clear Profits To Be Made

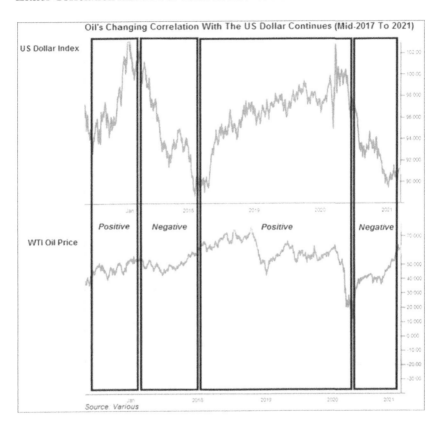

Part of this changing correlation was also due to the cessation of the vast number of dollars being released into the US economy as a result of the Great Financial Crisis (in the three QE programmes to that point by 2019, although a fourth then occurred from March 2020) and a consequent rebalancing of supply and demand rules in favour of the historical norm. Additionally, it was partly due to the fact that a lower oil price is a huge spur to growth in the US, as it both increases consumer spending and also lowers manufacturing costs (thus, in turn, making exports more competitive in the global market, as analysed in depth elsewhere in this book). During the height of the COVID-19 pandemic of 2020/21 and the

2020 Saudi oil price war, this correlation was again tested, with different trading periods veering between one and then the other.

Simply knowing this correlation during any of the prolonged periods of one distinct correlation or another between the oil price and the value of the US dollar would have netted a trader spectacular gains over the past nine years in particular (since the beginning of 2014 when Saudi began its US shale oil-destruction strategy and then reversed it and then started a new oil price war in 2020 and then reversed that as well). Had the trader been doing what he should have been doing on a daily basis (i.e. reading up on all markets from all major sources, watching the key business channels and looking at the trading charts from a technical analysis perspective), then his point of entry for the short USD and/or long oil trade, then for the long USD and/or long oil trade, and then the same again would have been very early on in these major trend changes and would have netted thousands of points in his favour with a relatively minimal level of risk.

These changing correlations between the oil price and the US dollar continue – with each different period of correlation easily lasting long enough for retail traders as well to make enormous profits. There are also likely to be further oil price wars, instigated by OPEC and OPEC+ aimed again at slowing down the next stage of growth in the US shale oil sector.

The direct positive or negative correlation between the oil price and the US dollar is clear but the relationship between oil and other currencies is slightly more nuanced. Part of it is a function of the macroeconomic profile of countries whose asset values are defined in significant part by the role that oil (or other commodities) plays in their balance of payments and part is a consequence of the US dollar's trading trend.

In respect of the latter to begin with, the end of the three rounds of QE by the US Federal Reserve up to 2019 after the Great Financial Crisis meant that the usual rules of supply and demand led to a natural strengthening of the US dollar across the board. This was seen in the USD Index charts above, with less dollars in the system and fairly constant demand putting a premium on the US currency. The end of QE and the corollary relative robustness of the US economy until the 2020/21 COVID-19 outbreak also led to market expectations of further rises in interest rates from the Fed at a faster pace than previously thought. Given that money goes to where it is best rewarded for the concomitant risks involved, the US dollar benefited from inflows looking for a relative safe haven offering some yield.

Part Four: Oil, Commodities And Economic Cycles

Oil Price Cycles

Financial markets are subject to the manifestation of a wide variety of patterns and the key to trading success is identifying what they are at any given time and how to extract the optimal value from them. The most favourable patterns – for retail traders especially – derive from broad-based long-term cycles and these are particularly evident in the oil market. The key fundamental elements that lead to them have been analysed throughout this book so far. This section looks at how these elements have variously combined to produce the range of long-term (and shorter-term) cycles in oil trading that we have seen to date and how they can be used for identifying and profiting from future cycles.

The Shale Oil Cycle

It is important to note at this point that previous cycles in the oil price were marked to a high degree by long time lags between when capital was spent and when production increased. However, the advent of widespread, well-funded shale technology in the US narrowed this time lag – and producers' ability to quickly throttle back production has also increased – which has provided the market with more levers for rebalancing in terms of credit, equity and cashflow.

In the initial few years of the US's shale oil industry, the short-cycle nature of shale and its ability to ramp up production quickly required that price pressure remained in place long enough to side-line the large amount of low-cost capital that was available until that rebalancing occurred. As the shale sector entered a different phase of development (as analysed in full in earlier sections), capital became less available for the purpose of output expansion and instead investors began to look for a return on earlier capital investment. This prompted the beginnings of the next phase of the business cycle that was characterised by a move to more mergers and acquisitions (M&A) activity, particularly by the acquisition of smaller shale operations by bigger firms.

Although this process was initially hastened by the onset of the 2020 Oil Price War, the extension of that low oil price environment paused the overall momentum of the M&A process, and this was then exacerbated by the continued effects of the COVID-19 pandemic throughout 2020 and beyond. The effects on the evolution of the shale oil sector in the US of the Russian invasion of Ukraine in 2022 to date of writing (April 2023) has been similar.

In the aftermath of the COVID-19 pandemic, though, and as the endgame of the Russian invasion of Ukraine becomes clearer, the move to the high-level of M&A in the shale oil sector that was evident up until 2020 will resume. It is also likely that a significant proportion of the new deals will feature the heavy equity-funded element of the major deals that took place before the widespread onset of COVID-19 in 2020, given that the stocks of the bigger oil firms have significantly rebounded whilst the valuations of the smaller firms still lag behind.

For many of the big oil firms, having a good-sized shale operation is still a very good fit in the overall business model. When prices are rising they can ramp up production quickly to take advantage of the quick turnaround capabilities of shale producers and when they are falling they can just cut capital expenditure quickly and trim back production. In the best shale oil operations the turnaround time to production from a standing start is very short, although the overall timing is lengthened by the ordering process for new shale oil supplies.

In this context, shale oil end-buyers (notably refineries) will buy the majority of their crude supplies 30-45 days out from when they actually want them delivered. So what happens in practice is that refineries will start to increase their run rates and will start buying. After that, crude oil buyers will begin to buy the oil from the shale producers to fill this demand, and then the producers will turn the supply back on. There are some risks for all oil operations from a shut-in (a temporary shutdown) – such as water encroachment in the reservoir, well bore or surface facility damage, plus other possible rusting, corrosion and deterioration – and these all have to be tested for. However, the vast majority of US shale wells can come back to full production capacity within a week of the order finally being given.

Current Cycle Vs. 1986, 1981/82 And 2009/10

The current pattern of oil price trading is caught between that of 1986 (which saw a predominantly supply-driven sharp decline in prices) and the 1981/82 and 2009/10 drop in prices (which were primarily demand-driven as the recessions led to a fall in global demand of more than 3 million bpd). Before the outbreak of COVID-19 across the globe, though, the oil price trading cycle was more akin to that of the 1986 cycle than the other two, even before the early 2020 Oil Price War (which only added to the over-supply price driver in the market).

In 1986, non-OPEC production was growing as well but the combined impact of both factors was offset by a sharp fall in OPEC volumes. As the world emerged from the recession at that time, global demand recovered gradually, adding around 1.5 million bpd in total over the period 1983-1985. However, this coincided with a period of strong non-OPEC growth, which in turn added 3 million bpd over the same period and put further pressure on OPEC's market share.

History Repeating

The 1986 price collapse: Supply, demand and price dynamics (mbpd)										
	1980	1981	1982	1983	1984	1985	1986	1987	1988	1989
Brent avg., USD/bbl	38	37	33	30	29	28	15	18	15	18
Global demand	61.2	59.4	57.8	57.6	58.9	59.2	61.0	62.3	64.2	65.6
Non-OPEC output	36.9	37.7	38.6	39.7	41.2	41.6	41.9	42.4	42.4	41.8
OPEC output (inc. NGLs)	26.0	21.9	18.8	16.9	16.5	15.9	18.5	18.4	20.7	22.2
OPEC share	42.5%	36.9%	32.4%	29.4%	28.1%	26.8%	30.4%	29.5%	32.2%	33.8%
change y/y										
Global demand		-1.8	-1.6	-0.2	1.3	0.4	1.7	1.3	2.0	1.3
Non-OPEC output		0.7	0.9	1.1	1.5	0.4	0.3	0.5	0.0	-0.6
OPEC output		-4.1	-3.1	-1.8	-0.4	-0.7	2.6	-0.2	2.3	1.5
change %										
Global demand		-3.0%	-2.7%	-0.4%	2.2%	0.7%	2.9%	2.1%	3.1%	2.1%
Non-OPEC output		2.0%	2.4%	2.9%	3.8%	1.0%	0.8%	1.1%	0.1%	-1.4%
OPEC output		-15.9%	-14.3%	-9.7%	-2.4%	-4.0%	16.7%	-0.9%	12.7%	7.3%
Source: BP Statistical Review Of World Energy										

Within OPEC, combined production from Iraq and Iran had fallen by more than 6 million bpd through 1979-1981, with the impact of the Iranian Revolution and the start of the Iran/Iraq war. However, it then recovered by nearly 1.5 million bpd from 1981-1985. The same dip occurred in Iran after the reimposition of sanctions by the US after its unilateral withdrawal from the JCPOA in 2018. It was similarly followed by a rebound as Iran sought – with considerable success – to secure an export channel to China for as much crude oil as it could produce and smuggle to Asia via the various mechanisms outlined in the standalone sections on Iran and Iraq earlier this book. The same sort of output pattern was also seen in Iraq in this current cycle, with a dip in production related to underinvestment in key oil assets caused principally by international oil companies exiting the country due to the endemic corruption in the country's oil sector. It was also a function of the OPEC-mandated production cut agreements variously in place since the end of 2016. This was then followed by a rebound in output as new money – mainly again from China and Russia – flowed in to plug some of the most easily fixable gaps in Iraq's oil production infrastructure.

The bulk of the sharp cutback in total OPEC output over this period was borne by Saudi Arabia, which cut its crude oil production from roughly 10 million bpd in 1980-1981 to average only some 3.6 million bpd in 1985. However, in 2H 1985, in the face of steady growth in non-OPEC supply, Saudi Arabia abandoned its role as swing producer and pushed instead to regain market share, increasing output dramatically in end-1985 and 1986.

For OPEC, output rose by some 2.6 million bpd in 1986. Again, the current cycle closely mirrors this pattern, with Saudi Arabia taking a lead in production cuts initially before then falling back into producing more to exploit the consequent price spikes through various overt and covert methods mentioned in the standalone section on Saudi Arabia in this book.

How 1986 Panned Out

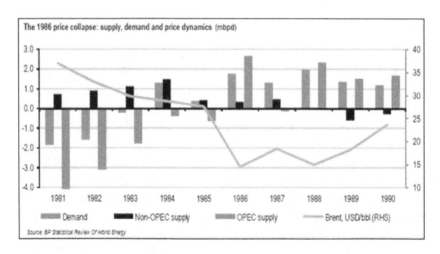

Overall, then, the result of this process was a collapse in Brent prices to a 1H86 average of sub-USD13 pb versus a FY1985 average of close to USD30 pb. However, this in turn spurred a prolonged period of demand strength, with global demand growing by an average of 2.4% over the period 1985-1990. In addition, the crash in prices had a dramatic effect on non-OPEC investment levels, with the result that non-OPEC showed minimal overall growth in the second half of the 1980s.

In the current cycle – even before the outbreak of the COVID-19 pandemic in earnest in 2020 – the trading risk was always skewed towards more supply coming into the markets against a backdrop of uncertain demand, so pushing prices down. As it stands, this pattern remains in place, all other factors remaining equal.

What Of The Commodities Supercycle?

The consensus view from statistically-driven oil industry watchers is that a commodities supercycle must meet three basic number-based benchmarks in order for it to be said that such a supercycle is truly in play. These three benchmarks are whether supply is rising, demand is rising, and prices are rising, all together. However, the oil market is a subtle thing, and it is much more likely in my view that the end of the overall multi-decade commodities supercycle that we have seen in one way or another since the very early 2000s is unlikely to have happened already. Rather, it has simply shifted into a different phase. This phase has been referred to by a range of notable market organisations as 'the age of the energy capital stock', which was evident as far back as the 1920s in the US According to this subtler idea, when the energy capital stock cycle is high it is old, and when it is low it is young.

Spotting where it is in the cycle allows the identification of periods of incremental investment, which, in turn, correlates to periods of high and rising commodity prices. These investment phases are then followed by an exploitation phase for a total cycle of around 30 years. The entire cycle can be summed up as: around 10 years and vast expense to develop a new supply source and the next 15 to 20 years of significantly less investment to keep production running smoothly. In these terms, the supercycle can be regarded as the supply cycle for commodities while the business cycle (see the next section) is the demand cycle for commodities. This is why it is important to note the earlier major oil price cycle analysed above and that the current cycle (and oil pricing) is largely supply-driven (similar to 1986, as highlighted above).

Looking at the chart below, it is clear that during the investment phase, currency and commodity markets reinforced higher commodity prices and stronger emerging market growth. During the later exploitation phase they were working in the other direction to support lower commodity and oil prices. As the shock factor of the Russian invasion of Ukraine continues to erode, then this later exploitation phase pattern is likely to resume.

Different Phases Of The Oil Investment And Exploitation Cycle

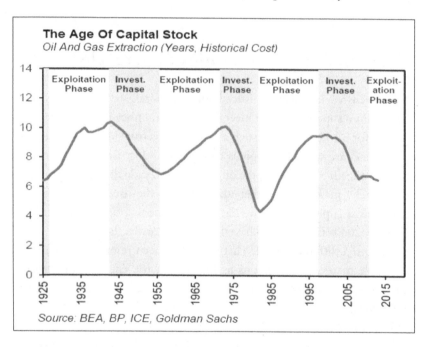

This is why identifying an equilibrium in one market is difficult without determining the equilibriums in the other commodity and currency markets. Nonetheless commodity prices tend to decline during the exploitation phase, which is why commodity industries do not earn their cost of capital when looking at it over extremely long periods of time. They invest during high and rising commodity price periods and produce during low and declining commodity price periods (see chart below).

Global Economic Cycles

The Kondratieff Wave

In broad trading cycle terms, the trader needs to be aware of the Kondratieff Wave ('K-Wave'), named after a Russian economist active in the 1920s named Nikolai Kondratieff. This seeks to show that there are long-term cycles in the entire global capitalist economy of between 45 and 60 years each, and even longer.

They are self-correcting and evolving and are defined by the emergence of new industries in ongoing technological revolutions. As an adjunct of this, each major cycle involves the destruction of much of the past cycle and the concomitant evolution of innovation.

Kondratieff's theory has been refined/distorted over time but the consensus of the major examples over the past few hundred years are: the 1770s – the Industrial Revolution; the 1820s – the Steam and Railways age beginning; the 1870s – the Steel and Heavy Engineering move; the 1900s – the era of Oil, Electricity, Automobiles and Mass Production; and, the 1970s – the shift to the age of Information and Telecommunications.

It is interesting to note at this point that one of the world's most successful stock investors, Warren Buffett, bases his investment strategy on such fundamental paradigmatic shifts, seeking to identify the onset of a new cycle (or 'wave'), buying shares in as many solid new cycle-related businesses as he can and just sitting on them.

It is also interesting to note, as seen in the Elliot Waves analysis earlier, that these cycles could be seen in terms of Elliot Waves. That is, that at the onset of a long-term economic cycle there is likely to be a lack of confidence and a fear of falling back into slump or depression, before inflation, interest rates and credit slowly start to rise as confidence in the new age increases (extremely akin to an Elliot Wave 1).

As the economy expands (indicated in this instance by inflation) and interest rates increase as an adjunct to this, so business and consumer confidence grows, and credit is extended more (Elliot Wave 3 correlation). As the final up-phase of the move is entered, confidence levels morph into over-exuberance and extraordinarily loose 'bubble-like' credit conditions, with interest rates also declining (Elliot Wave 5 correlation).

Finally, rising concerns over loose credit, inflationary upward spiral and bad debt causes business and consumer reticence to embark on new projects (in business terms, expansion and in consumer terms, new purchases), default rates increase, credit is squeezed, the economic outlook turns negative, unemployment rises, disinflation turns into deflation and there is a negative world view.

Kondratieff In Elliott Waves

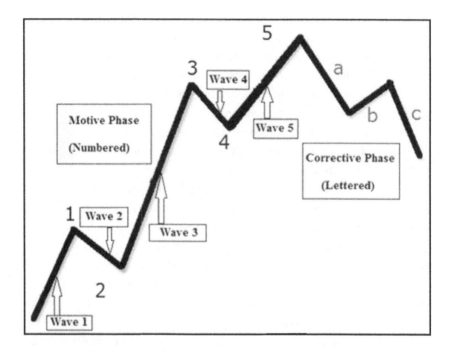

The Business Cycle

Within these longer cycles, there are other shorter-time patterns manifesting themselves, which is the recurring level of business activity that changes in an economy over a period of time. The four stages of a cycle (although some maintain that there are five) are: full scale recession, early recovery, late recovery, and early recession.

Since the Second World War, most business cycles have lasted between three to five years from peak to peak, with the average duration of an expansion being nearly four years and the average length of a recession being just under a year. However, as seen in the most recent major global economic contraction (and in the Great Depression era), recessions can last a lot longer.

According to the US's National Bureau of Economic Research (NBER), the US has experienced 12 recessions (including the most recent one) and 11 expansions since the end of the Second World War.

US Business Cycles Since 1857

Business Cycle Reference Dates		Duration In Months		
Peak month (Peak Quarter)	Trough month (Trough Quarter)	Contraction	Expansion	Cycle
Red indicates that the turning point quarter does not include the turning point month		*Duration, peak to trough*	*Duration, trough to peak*	*Duration, trough to trough* / *Duration, peak to peak*
	December 1854 (1854Q4)			
June 1857 (1857Q2)	December 1858 (1858Q4)	18	30	48
October 1860 (1860Q3)	June 1861 (1861Q3)	8	22	30 / 40
April 1865 (1865Q1)	December 1867 (1868Q1)	32	46	78 / 54
June 1869 (1869Q2)	December 1870 (1870Q4)	18	18	36 / 50
October 1873 (1873Q3)	March 1879 (1879Q1)	65	34	99 / 52
March 1882 (1882Q1)	May 1885 (1885Q2)	38	36	74 / 101
March 1887 (1887Q2)	April 1888 (1888Q1)	13	22	35 / 60
July 1890 (1890Q3)	May 1891 (1891Q2)	10	27	37 / 40
January 1893 (1893Q1)	June 1894 (1894Q2)	17	20	37 / 30
December 1895 (1895Q4)	June 1897 (1897Q2)	18	18	36 / 35
June 1899 (1899Q3)	December 1900 (1900Q4)	18	24	42 / 42
September 1902 (1902Q4)	August 1904 (1904Q3)	23	21	44 / 39
May 1907 (1907Q2)	June 1908 (1908Q2)	13	33	46 / 56
January 1910 (1910Q1)	January 1912 (1911Q4)	24	19	43 / 32
January 1913 (1913Q1)	December 1914 (1914Q4)	23	12	35 / 36
August 1918 (1918Q3)	March 1919 (1919Q1)	7	44	51 / 67
January 1920 (1920Q1)	July 1921 (1921Q3)	18	10	28 / 17
May 1923 (1923Q2)	July 1924 (1924Q3)	14	22	36 / 40
October 1926 (1926Q3)	November 1927 (1927Q4)	13	27	40 / 41
August 1929 (1929Q3)	March 1933 (1933Q1)	43	21	64 / 34
May 1937 (1937Q2)	June 1938 (1938Q2)	13	50	63 / 93
February 1945 (1945Q1)	October 1945 (1945Q4)	8	80	88 / 93
November 1948 (1948Q4)	October 1949 (1949Q4)	11	37	48 / 45
July 1953 (1953Q2)	May 1954 (1954Q2)	10	45	55 / 56
August 1957 (1957Q3)	April 1958 (1958Q2)	8	39	47 / 49
April 1960 (1960Q2)	February 1961 (1961Q1)	10	24	34 / 32
December 1969 (1969Q4)	November 1970 (1970Q4)	11	106	117 / 116
November 1973 (1973Q4)	March 1975 (1975Q1)	16	36	52 / 47
January 1980 (1980Q1)	July 1980 (1980Q3)	6	58	64 / 74
July 1981 (1981Q3)	November 1982 (1982Q4)	16	12	28 / 18
July 1990 (1990Q3)	March 1991 (1991Q1)	8	92	100 / 108
March 2001 (2001Q1)	November 2001 (2001Q4)	8	120	128 / 128
December 2007 (2007Q4)	June 2009 (2009Q2)	18	73	91 / 81
February 2020 (2019Q4)	April 2020 (2020Q2)	2	128	130 / 146
Average, all cycles				
1854-2020		17.0	41.4	58.4 / 59.2
1854-1919		21.6	26.6	48.2 / 48.9
1919-1945		18.2	35.0	53.2 / 53.0
1945-2020		10.3	64.2	74.5 / 75.0

Having said that, as mentioned earlier, different regions and countries within regions are obviously not all at the same point of their overall business cycle, despite their being part of the long-running K Waves that have to do with being part of the global economy.

The Minsky Cycle

The 'Minsky Cycle' is another important element in the understanding of where an economy is in the overall global investment mix (which equates to narrowing down the best trading options further) and is itself part of the broader Business Cycle, which is, in turn, part of the Kondratieff Wave.

The Minsky Cycle – coined around the time of the 1998 Russian financial crisis by an executive from the Pacific Investment Management Company – is a key part of the general psychology of trading. It seeks to chart the nature of the normal life cycle of an economy with particular reference to speculative investment bubbles.

The idea here is that in times of prosperity, when the cashflow of banks and corporations moves to excess levels (over and above that which is needed simply to pay off debt), a 'speculative euphoria' develops, which soon exceeds that which borrowers can pay off, which in turn leads to tighter credit conditions and so on. It is the slow pace at which the financial system moves to realise this and then to seek to accommodate it that produces a financial crisis, known as the 'Minsky Moment'.

Typical Minsky Cycle Characteristics

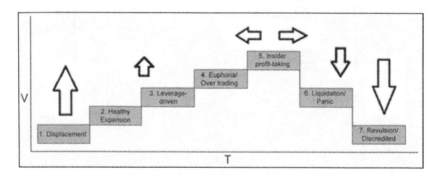

[Chart Key: V = Values, various assets; T = Time]

The above chart highlights that, in the immediate 'displacement' aftermath of the Great Financial Crisis in the middle or so of 2011, pockets of value might have been seen in Asian FX, for example, as several countries in the region continued to show exceptional performance.

As the cycle progressed, the major beneficiaries of leverage became particular high-yielding currencies (such as the AUD) and certain commodities (notably, gold). The parallels to the post-2020/21 waves of COVID-19 are evident in some of these decisions, but the specific RORO basis for individual investments accounted for the broadly sounder foundation of the global financial system going into the worldwide outbreak of the pandemic in the first part of 2020.

As credit became easier in the aftermath of the Great Financial Crisis, so investors became less discerning about the underlying fundamentals of the assets into which they invested and in the 'euphoria/over-trading' phase poured money into several of the already over-performing equities markets, such as China at that point.

At this stage, the smart money realised that a new indiscriminate phase of investment had manifested itself, so liquidated out of things like Japanese government bonds and toppish currency valuations.

Once this occurred, there was a much broader liquidation of assets (at that point it included things like selling USD and gold), which, given the need to make good on losses in margin calls, involved selling a much broader base of assets than would otherwise be merited.

Finally, the markets reached a point where investors were ultra-cautious in spending their money and regarded any asset that was not rated as absolutely solid (CHF is usually a beneficiary of this phase, for example) as being too great a risk.

Glossary Of Terms

AAOIFI = Accounting Auditing Organisation for Islamic Financial Institutions

ABOT = Al-Basrah Oil Terminal

ADNOC = Abu Dhabi National Oil Company

AEDPA = Anti-Terrorism and Effective Death Penalty Act

AIS = Automatic identification system

API = American Petroleum Institute

Aramco = Arabian American Oil Company (now Saudi Aramco)

AUD = Australian Dollar

AWACS = Airborne Warning and Control Systems

Bcf/d = Billion cubic feet per day

Bcm = Billion cubic metres

BOE = Barrels of oil equivalent

BOJ = Bank of Japan

BP = British Petroleum

Bp = Basis points

Bpd = Barrels per day

BOOT = Build-own-operate-transfer

BRIC = Brazil, Russia, India, China

C4ISR = Command, Control, Communications, Computers, Intelligence, Surveillance and Reconnaissance

CAD = Canadian Dollar

Capex = Capital expenditure

CBDC = Central Bank Digital Currencies

CBW = Chemical and Biological Weapons Control and Warfare Elimination Act

CCTV = Closed-circuit television

CDC = Centers for Disease Control and Prevention

CDS = Credit default swap

CHF = Swiss franc

CIA = Central Intelligence Agency

CIF = Cost, insurance and freight

CNOOC = China National Offshore Oil Corporation

CNPC = China National Petroleum Corporation

CNY = Chinese yuan

CPEC = China Pakistan Economic Corridor

CPECC = China Petroleum Engineering & Construction Corp

CSSP = Common Seawater Supply Project

DASKAA = 'Defending American Security from Kremlin Aggression Act of 2018'

DC/EP = Digital currency electronic payments system

DJIA = Dow Jones Industrial Average

DM = Developed market

DME = Dubai Mercantile Exchange

DUC = Drilled but uncompleted

EIA = *Energy Information Administration*

EM = Emerging market

EU = European Union

EW = Electronic Warfare

FCIC = Financial Crisis Inquiry Commission

Fed = US Federal Reserve Bank

FEED = Front End Engineering Design

FEER = Fundamental effective exchange rate

FGI = Federal Government of Iraq

FID = Final Investment Decision

FOB = Free on broad

FTO = Foreign Terrorist Organisation

FTOSR = Foreign Terrorist Organizations Sanctions Regulations

FTSE = Financial Times Stock Exchange

GBP = Great British Pound

GDP = Gross domestic product

GECF = Gas Exporting Countries Forum

GFC = Great Financial Crisis

GTSR = Global Terrorism Sanctions Regulations

GW = Gigawatts

IAEA = International Atomic Energy Agency

ICBM = Inter-continental ballistic missile

ICE = Intercontinental Exchange

IEA = International Energy Agency

IFAD = ICE Futures Abu Dhabi platform

INOC = Iraq National Oil Company

INSTEX = Instrument in Support of Trade Exchange

IOC = International oil company

IPC = Integrated Petroleum Contract

IPO = Initial public offering

IPP = Iran Pakistan Pipeline

IRBM = Intermediate range ballistic missile

IRGC = Islamic Revolutionary Guards Corp

IRR = Iranian rial

ISI = Inter-Services Intelligence

ISIS = Islamic State of Iraq and Syria

ITM = In the money

ITP = Iraq-Turkey Pipeline

JASTA = 'Justice Against Sponsors of Terrorism Act'

JCPOA = Joint Comprehensive Plan Of Action

JPY = Japanese Yen

JRPC = Jordan Petroleum Refinery Company

KAAOT = Khor al-Amaya Oil Terminal

KOGAS = Korea Gas Corporation

KRG = Kurdistan Regional Government

LNG = Liquefied natural gas

LOOP = Louisiana Offshore Oil Port

LPG = Liquefied petroleum gas

LSE = London Stock Exchange

LTSC = Long-term service contract

Mbpd = Million barrels per day

MbS = Mohammed bin Salman

Mcm/d = Million cubic metres per day

MIST = Mexico, Indonesia, South Korea, Turkey

Ml/d = Million litres per day

MmBtu = Million British thermal units

Mmcf/d = Million cubic feet per day

MNR = Ministry of Natural Resources

MOU = Memorandum of understanding

Mtpa = Million metric tonnes per annum

NATO = North Atlantic Treaty Organisation

Next-11 = Mexico, Indonesia, South Korea, Turkey, Bangladesh, Egypt, Nigeria, Pakistan, the Philippines, Vietnam and Iran

NIOC = National Iranian Oil Company
NMR = Net margin requirement
NOPEC = Non-OPEC oil producing and exporting countries
NPC = National Petrochemical Company
NTR = Net trading requirement
NYSE = New York Stock Exchange
OBOR = One Belt, One Road
OFAC = Office of Foreign Assets Control
OFZ = Obligatsyi Federal'novo Zaima
OIP = Oil in place
PEC = Organization of the Petroleum Exporting Countries
PMI = Purchasing managers index
Pip = Price in points
OECD = Organization for Economic Cooperation and Development
OPEC+ = OPEC plus NOPEC
OTM = Out of the money
P5+1 = Permanent 5 Members Of The UN (China, France, Russia, United Kingdom, United States) Plus Germany
Pb = Per barrel
PBOC = People's Bank of China
PGSR = Persian Gulf Star Refinery
PIF = Public Investment Fund
Pip = Price in points
PNZ = Partitioned Neutral Zone
PSA = Production sharing agreement
PSC = Production Sharing Contract
QE = Quantitative Easing
RDIF = Russian Direct Investment Fund
RDS = Royal Dutch Shell
REER = Real effective exchange rate
RMB = Chinese renminbi
RUB = Russian rouble
S&P = Standard & Poor's
SABIC = Saudi Basic Industries Corporation
SARI = Secure America from Russian Interference Act
SAC = Saudi Arabian Chevron
SCO = Shanghai Cooperation Organization

SDGT = Specially Designated Global Terrorist
SIIP = South Iraq Integrated Project
SIS = Secret Intelligence Service
SLV = Space Launch Vehicle
SNB = Swiss National Bank
SOC = South Oil Company
SOE = State owned enterprises
SOMO = State Oil Marketing Organization
SPC = Supreme Petroleum Council
SPM = Single point mooring
SPND = Organization of Defensive Innovation and Research (from Farsi)
STB = Stock tank barrels
TAPI = Turkmenistan-Afghanistan-Pakistan-India pipeline
TASI = Tadawul All Share Index
Tcf = Trillion cubic feet
Tcm = Trillion cubic metres
TPAO = Türkiye Petrolleri Anonim Ortaklığı
Train = LNG liquefaction and purification facility
TSC = Technical Service Contract
TSE = Toronto Stock Exchange
TSE = Tehran Stock Exchange
UAE = United Arab Emirates
UN = United Nations
UNSC = United Nations Security Council
USD = US Dollar
USGS = US Geological Survey
UST = US Treasuries
VLCC = Very large crude carriers
WEP = West Ethylene Pipeline
WMPs = Wealth management products
WTI = West Texas Intermediate

About The Author

After graduating from Oxford University with BA (Hons) and MA (Hons) degrees, Simon Watkins worked for many years as a senior Forex trader and salesman, including positions of Head of Forex Institutional Sales for Credit Lyonnais, and Director of Forex at Bank of Montreal. Having retired from the markets, he moved into financial journalism, including positions as Head of Weekly Publications, Managing Editor and Chief Writer of Business Monitor International, Head of Global Fuel Oil Products for Platts, Global Managing Editor of Research for Renaissance Capital, and Head of Developed Market Bond Analysis for Bond Radar.

He has written extensively on the oil market and other commodities markets, Forex, equities, bonds, economics and geopolitics for many publications, including: *The Financial Times*, *Euromoney*, *Financial Times Capital Insights*, *OilPrice*, *NewsBase*, *Risk.net*, *FTSE Global Markets*, *FX-MM*, *CFO Insight*, *The Edge Middle East Finance*, *Middle East Oil & Gas*, *FSU Oil & Gas*, *North American Oil & Gas*, *International Commerce Magazine*, *The Securities And Investment Review*, *Accountancy Magazine*, *The Emerging Markets Monitor*, *Asia Economic Alert*, *Latin America Economic Alert*, *Eastern Europe Economic Alert*, *Oil And Gas Middle East*, *European CEO*, *Global Finance Magazine*, *World Finance Magazine*, *The Emerging Markets Report*, *VM Group Energy Monthly*, *VM Group Metals Monthly*, *Islamic Investor Magazine*, *Finance Europe*, *Finance Emerging Europe* and *CIMA Financial Management*.

In addition, he has worked as an investment consultant for major hedge funds in London, New York, Moscow and the Middle East, and regularly appears as an oil- and financial-market expert on various international television networks, including the BBC, Al Jazeera, and CNBC. This is Simon's eighth book on the global financial markets and his fourth on the oil market, all of which are available from Amazon, Apple, Kobo, Barnes & Noble, and Blackwells, among others.

Made in the USA
Las Vegas, NV
22 August 2023

76422123R00282